Writing Peace

Studies in
Anabaptist and Mennonite History
No. 40

Studies in Anabaptist and Mennonite History

Series Editor Steven M. Nolt; with Editors Gerald Biesecker-Mast, Geoffrey L. Dipple, Rachel Waltner Goossen, Leonard Gross, Beulah Stauffer Hostetler, Thomas Meyers, John D. Roth, Theron F. Schlabach, and Astrid von Schlachta.

The series Studies in Anabaptist and Mennonite History is sponsored by the Mennonite Historical Society. Volumes have been published in cooperation with Herald Press, Scottdale, Pennsylvania and Waterloo, Ontario; Pandora Press Canada, Kitchener, Ontario; and Pandora Press U.S. (now being renamed Cascadia Publishing House), Telford, Pennsylvania.

1. Two Centuries of American Mennonite Literature, 1727-1928*
   By Harold S. Bender
2. The Hutterian Brethren, 1528-1931
   By John Horsch, 1931
3. Centennial History of the Mennonites in Illinois*
   By Harry F. Weber, 1931
4. For Conscience' Sake*
   By Sanford Calvin Yoder, 1940
5. Ohio Mennonite Sunday Schools*
   By John Umble, 1941
6. Conrad Grebel, Founder of the Swiss Brethren*
   By Harold S. Bender, 1950
7. Mennonite Piety Through the Centuries*
   By Robert Friedmann, 1949
8. Bernese Anabaptists and Their American Descendants*
   By Delbert L. Gratz, 1953
9. Anabaptism in Flanders, 1530-1650*
   By A. L. E. Verheyden, 1961
10. The Mennonites in Indiana and Michigan*
    By J. C. Wenger, 1961
11. Anabaptist Baptism: A Representative Study*
    By Rollin Stely Armour, 1966
12. Lost Fatherland: The Story of Mennonite Emigration from Soviet Russia, 1921-1927*
    By John B. Toews, 1967
13. Mennonites of the Ohio and Eastern Conference*
    By Grant M. Stoltzfus, 1969
14. The Mennonite Church in India, 1897-1962*
    By John A. Lapp, 1972
15. The Theology of Anabaptism: An Interpretation*
    By Robert Friedmann, 1973
16. Anabaptism and Asceticism*
    By Kenneth R. Davis, 1974
17. South Central Frontiers*
    By Paul Erb, 1974
18. The Great Trek of the Russian Mennonites to Central Asia, 1880-1884*
    By Fred R.Belk, 1976

19. Mysticism and the Early South German-Austrian Anabaptist Movement, 1525-1531*
    By Werner O. Packull, 1976
20. Conscience in Crisis: Mennonites and Other Peace Churches in America, 1739-1789*
    By Richard K. MacMaster with Samuel L. Horst and Rubert F. Ulle, 1979
21. Gospel Versus Gospel: Mission and the Mennonite Church, 1863-1944*
    By Theron F. Schlabach, 1979
22. Strangers Become Neighbors: Mennonites and Indigenous Relations in the Paraguayan Chaco; *available from Pandora Press Canada*
    By Calvin Redekop, 1980
23. The Golden Years of the Hutterites, 1565-1578
    By Leonard Gross, 1980; rev. ed. Pandora Press Canada, 1998
24. Mennonites in Illinois*
    By Willard H. Smith, 1983
25. Petr Chelcicky: A Radical Separatist in Hussite Bohemia
    By Murray L. Wagner, 1983
26. Maintaining the Right Fellowship: A Narrative Account of Life in the Oldest Mennonite Community in North America*
    By John L. Ruth, 1984
27. The Life and Thought of Michael Sattler; available from Pandora Press Canada
    By C. Arnold Snyder, 1984
28. American Mennonites and Protestant Movements: A Community Paradigm*
    By Beulah Stauffer Hostetler, 1987
29. Andreas Fischer and the Sabbatarian Anabaptists: An Early Reformation Episode in East Central Europe
    By Daniel Liechty, 1988
30. Apart and Together: Mennonites in Oregon and Neighboring States, 1876-1976
    By Hope Kauffman Lind, 1990
31. Tradition and Transition: Amish Mennonites and Old Order Amish, 1800-1900*
    By Paton Yoder, 1991
32. John Smyth's Congregation: English Separatism, Mennonite Influence, and the Elect Nation
    By James Robert Coggins, 1991
33. The Lord's Supper in Anabaptism: A Study in the Theology of Balthasar Hubmaier, Pilgram Marpeck, and Dirk Philips
    By John D. Rempel, 1993
34. American Mennonites and the Great War, 1914-1918
    By Gerlof D. Homan, 1994
35. Keeping Salvation Ethical: Mennonite and Amish Atonement Theology in the Late Nineteenth Century
    By J. Denny Weaver, 1997
36. Andreas Ehrenpreis and Hutterite Faith and Practice
    By Wes Harrison, 1997
37. Mennonite and Nazi? Attitudes among Mennonite Colonists in Latin America, 1933-1945
    By John D. Thiesen, 1999
38. Dancing with the Kobzar: Bluffton College and Mennonite Higher Education, 1899-1999
    By Perry Bush, 2000
39. The Earth Is the Lord's: A Narrative History of the Lancaster Mennonite Conference
    By John L. Ruth, 2001
40. Wripting Peace: The Unheard Voices of Great War Mennonite Objectors
    By Melanie Mock, 2002

A quick-print edition of the books marked with an asterisk is available by arrangement with Herald Press from Wipf and Stock Publishers in Eugene, Oregon; tel.: 541-485-5745; fax: 541-465-9694; email: WSPub@academicbooks.com.

Writing Peace

The Unheard Voices of Great War Mennonite Objectors

MELANIE SPRINGER MOCK

FOREWORD BY JAMES C. JUHNKE
AND SERIES PREFACE BY STEVE NOLT

Studies in Anabaptist and Mennonite History, Volume 40

Pandora Press U.S.
The original name of Cascadia Publishing House
Telford, Pennsylvania

copublished with
Herald Press
Scottdale, Pennsylvania

Pandora Press U.S. orders, information, reprint permissions
Use contact options for Cascadia Publishing House, the new name of Pandora Press U.S.:
contact@cascadiapublishinghouse.com
1-215-723-9125
126 Klingerman Road, Telford PA 18969
www.CascadiaPublishingHouse.com

Writing Peace
Copyright © 2003 by Pandora Press U.S., Telford, PA 18969
All rights reserved.
Library of Congress Catalog Number: 2002032182
ISBN: 1-931038-09-0
Printed in the United States
Book design by Pandora Press U.S.
Cover design by Merrill R. Miller

The paper used in this publication is recycled and meets the minimum requirements of American National Standard for Information Sciences—Permanence of Paper for Printed Library Materials, ANSI Z39.48-1984.

All Bible quotations are used by permission, all rights reserved and unless otherwise noted are All Bible quotations are used by permission, all rights reserved and unless otherwise noted are from *The New Revised Standard Version of the Bible*; quotes marked KJV are from the *King James Version of the Bible*.

Library of Congress Cataloguing-in-Publication Data
Mock, Melanie Springer, 1968-
  Writing peace : the unheard voices of the Great War Mennonite objectors / Melanie Springer Mock ; foreword by [ ] and series foreword by Steve Nolt
     p. cm. -- (Studies in Anabaptist and Mennonite history ; v. 40)
  Includes bibliographical references and index.
  ISBN 1-931038-09-0 (alk. paper)
  1. World War, 1914-1918--Conscientious objectors. 2. Mennonites--United States--Biography. I. Title. II. Studies in Anabaptist and Mennonite History ; no. 40

D639.M37 M63 2003
940.3'162-088282--dc21

2002032182

10 09 08 07 06   10 9 8 7 6 5

To my parents,
Ed and Esther Springer

Contents

Foreword by James C. Juhnke 11
Series Editor's Preface 13
Introduction 15

1 The Dragon War: Mennonite Conscientious
   Objectors' Experience and the Great War • 25
2 Against "The Old Lie":
   Mennonite Objectors and the War's Literary Legacy • 83
3 In the Tradition but Not of It:
   The Place for Objectors' Diaries • 106
4 What Service To Render:
   The Diary of Gustav Gaeddert • 139
5 Ura Hostetler's Lonely Witness • 177
6 Behind Prison Walls:
   The Diary of John Neufeld • 203
7 Jacob Conrad Meyer's Legacy:
   The Great War and Beyond • 223

Editorial Method 293
Notes 297
Bibliography 329
Index 335
Acknowledgments 344
The Author 347

Foreword

The "Great War" of 1914-1918 was a total war that engaged all the energies of citizens in the fighting nations. In the view of United States leaders, it was a holy war. President Woodrow Wilson said America was "an instrument in the hand of God to see that liberty is made secure for mankind."

Mennonites in 1917 were on the fringes of American society. But they were drawn into a close encounter with the nation's great democratic crusade. The encounter defined Mennonite identity for the coming century and beyond. Issues of war and peace would be central in determining who Mennonites were and what they must do.

Perhaps because the war was a time of confusion and embarrassment, Mennonite stories from the 1917-1918 war period remained long hidden. My personal experience is perhaps typical. I was born (in 1938) and reared in the Mennonite heartland of south-central Kansas. Although my family and community were committed to their religious heritage, and although I taught history in a Mennonite college, I did not learn until much later, in the 1970s, that my own great uncle, Otto Juhnke, in 1918 had been visited on his farm in McPherson County by an angry patriotic mob. Uncle Otto died before I had a chance to interview him about the event. It took many decades for Mennonite denominational historians to gather the stories and to craft a coherent narrative of their World War I experience and place it into a broader social and historical context.

Melanie Mock's *Writing Peace* continues the quest to recover and interpret the meaning of Mennonite stories from World War I. She focuses on the diaries of four men who were drafted into military camps. Remarkably, three of these men grew up in three different Mennonite congregations within ten miles of my uncle Otto's farm—all near the small town of Inman. Some readers may wish to turn immediately to the diaries themselves to get an immediate sense of the primary sources. Other readers, especially those who are not familiar with main outlines of national policies for conscientious objectors and of the response of Mennonites generally to the war crisis, will want to begin with chapter one.

A special feature of this volume is its treatment of the diary as literature. Why did these writers choose this particular form to record their experiences? How did the form determine the content? How did distinctive Mennonite cultural traits, such as habits of humility and self-effacement, influence the diarists' choices? How can these diaries be compared and contrasted with the more sophisticated published writing of British authors from the war, such as Wilfred Owen and Vera Brittain?

The war to make the world safe for democracy, contrary to its progressive goals, created the conditions for more war. Tragically, the "profiling" of German-speaking pacifists in World War I may now be compared with what is happening to Arabic-speaking Muslims in America, even as the nation may also again be giving heightened emphasis to a view of itself as "an instrument in the hand of God." *Writing Peace* represents a relevant resource for understanding the experience of outsiders in wartime in the twenty-first century.

—*James C. Juhnke, Professor of History (retired), Bethel College; and co-author (with Carol Hunter),* The Missing Peace: The Search for Nonviolent Alternatives in United States History

Series Editor's Preface

The cataclysmic events of the First World War—or, as it was then known, the Great War—still cast haunting shadows. Horrific images of battlefield trenches turned into mustard gas mass graves merge with historical analysis pointing to a conflict conjured by bumbling diplomats and short-sighted nationalists to leave one feeling, even nearly a century after the fact, numb in the face of human evil.

Making sense of such events demands, at least in part, attention to the experiences of ordinary participants in such extraordinary circumstances. How did people far from the capitals and the war rooms respond to choices that demanded their participation as soldiers or civilian supporters? In recent decades this desire to see human history from the "bottom up" has become a focus for scholars seeking to recover the voices of those who were central to history's events even while they were shut out of the decisions guiding those events.

Doubly muzzled are voices of conscripts in army training camps who, on grounds of Christian conscience, objected to the war by refusing arms and in some cases any cooperation with military orders. How can we understand American Mennonite Great War conscientious objectors (COs) in particular, whose peace stances rendered their already minor status as mere conscripts yet more marginal?

For literary scholar Melanie Springer Mock, a key to unlocking this hidden historical world is the private diary. In *Writing Peace: The Unheard Voices of Great War Mennonite Objectors,* she analyzes and contextualizes writings of Mennonite COs to see what these ordinary records of daily detail suggest about the larger issues that placed these men in army barracks and kept them from taking up arms.

As literary and communication theorists have contended, diaries represent a special sort of personal and historical record. In the leaves of a diary, one can retrospectively order the disorderly events of life, creating patterns on the page even when the elements of life seem maddeningly random. The often routine and even monotonous nature of diary entries actually belies a teeming world, the chaos of which is held in check by the regular entry of some small consistencies, some ability to point to the predictable. Perhaps no setting offers more chaos than a world at war, and the diaries of those caught in its global grip are especially telling sources.

Mock not only examines the diaries themselves, exploring how their owners inscribed reality on their blank pages; she also places the objectors' texts in a wider literary context. COs confined to army camps were hardly the only men whose Great War experience found literary outlet. Indeed, a generation of so-called trench poets and essayists emerged from the senseless carnage of World War I. For some, the brutal quest for manliness and patriotism gave way to cynicism; for others it birthed pacifism. For Mennonite objectors, Mock explains, the issues were both different and the same, caught as they were in a war that promised to remake the world and that used the language of future peace in its very call to arms.

Not content to give herself the last word, Mock allows four representative diaries to speak again through her edited transcriptions included here. The four writers—Gustav Gaeddert, Ura Hostetler, John Neufeld, and Jacob Meyer—brought Russian Mennonite, "old" Mennonite, and progressive Amish Mennonite convictions and sensibilities to their war-time CO stances and to the written records of their experiences, thoughts, and feelings.

The series Studies in Anabaptist and Mennonite History is pleased to present *Writing Peace* as a contribution to an ongoing and multidisciplinary conversation with the past. SAMH embraces reflection on the past from many sources and academic perspectives and Mock's contribution from literary studies is a welcome addition to Mennonite histories of the Great War that have focused on ecclesiastical concerns or theological developments.

As Mock notes in her opening pages, the personal response of these Great War objectors speaks to our contemporary concerns. The desire to run order through personal and global chaos, the ongoing celebration of war and violence in our society, and the claims of faith, family, and community remain keenly personal and pressing concerns in the twenty-first century even as they were for these diarists in the early twentieth. May their witness continue to find a hearing.

—Steven M. Nolt, Series Editor
 Studies in Anabaptist and Mennonite History
 Goshen College, Goshen, Indiana

Introduction

During a tour of Europe in May 2001, I took a group of students from my university to the Somme, an expanse of land in northern France upon which some of the Great War's bloodiest battles were fought. For many of the students, the Somme represented another day of a three- week study trip about the heritage of war and peace in Western Europe; for me, the journey to the Somme was the culmination of several years' exploration of the First World War, a pilgrimage of sorts to the land about which I had so often read.

The Somme today is little like I imagined it would be. There are few remnants of the war that destroyed a generation's men: the scorched landscape we see in Great War photography is now a verdant green; the demolished villages have been rebuilt; the trenches that once scarred the country are filled in and plowed over. Save for the wartime monuments and military cemeteries that scatter the hills, save for the occasional hint of a trench or a mortar hole, the Somme appears much like any other idyllic countryside: like the Ohio Valley, maybe, or like western Oregon, where I make my home.

Without the documents and other evidence left from the Great War, it would be easy to let that part of our world's history slide into the recesses of our collective past, to let nearly one hundred years' time blur our memory about the First World War and its nine million dead. The pastoral wheat fields of the Somme certainly make it easier to forget the wages of the conflict and its enduring effects on a century marred by total war. Even more broadly, the now-peaceful valleys of northern France do little to remind us not only what the great costs of violence were in 1914-18, but also what the costs of violence might be for us today.

Still, the monuments and military cemeteries dotting the French countryside disrupt the pastoral scene, providing one sort of reminder of the vast devastation caused by the Great War. The rows upon rows of grave markers document the tremendous loss of lives during the war, each marker itself representing the sorrow of parents, of siblings, of spouses, and of children. We have other artifacts from the Great War as well, pictures of the conflict, often grainy black and whites noting war's desolation: entire villages reduced to stony rubble, tangles of barbed wire masking water- and vermin-filled trenches, fields of mud littered with carnage. And we have the stories of war to remind us, too: literature written by ordinary soldiers who traced their own tragic rendezvous with death, and who attempted to make meaning of experiences that were, in fact, impossible to render in language.

The writing from the First World War initially compelled me to study that epoch at greater length. I was intrigued by the metaphors soldiers often used to figure their lives in the trenches, drawing on what they knew from their past selves to express what they could not understand about their present existences. That so many Great War participants chose to write about their wartime experiences interested me as well—more, that so many participants willingly published their writing, their memoirs, diaries, and letters, following the war's conclusion. And, as a pacifist, I was drawn to the Great War's literature because so much of it seemed inherently antiwar, a collective linguistic protest against meaningless slaughter, against aimless, dehumanizing violence.

This objection to war, constructed by soldiers who yet continued to fight in the trenches, often seemed to echo beliefs from my own Mennonite heritage, one firmly rooted in its peace tradition. Thus I turned to this heritage to discover what Mennonites had to say during the Great War, what they had written about their Great War experiences, and what kinds of observations Mennonites had produced during the war as a means of adding their own voices to the large body of literature emerging from that era.

For Mennonites, the tradition of peaceful resistance to violence reached far beyond the Great War, back to the church's very beginnings in sixteenth century Anabaptism. Nonresistance to violence, as well as believers baptism, nonconformity, and the separation of church and state, became a point upon which men like Conrad Grebel, Michael Sattler, and Felix Manz began their break from mainstream Protestant Reformers, and upon which the Dutch Anabaptist reformer Menno Simons would anchor his own extensive following in the mid-sixteenth century; these Anabaptist followers of Menno, soon known as Menists, became the forebears of the Mennonite church. Although the predominant Calvinist, Lutheran, and Catholic churches attempted to quell the Anabaptist movement, it nonetheless spread rapidly in Switzerland, Germany, and the Netherlands, and its adherents often faced persecution and death for their supposed religious heresy. Anabaptist leaders implored their followers to reject violence and the accouterments of warfare and urged them instead to embrace love and forgiveness as appropriate ways to deal with one's enemy.

For Anabaptists, Christ's message provided compelling evidence that they were to be, as Menno himself wrote, "children of peace." Christ had told his followers "Ye have heard that it hath been said, An eye for an eye, and a tooth for a tooth: But I say unto you, That ye resist not evil . . . Love your enemies, bless them that curse you, do good to them that hate you, and pray for them which despitefully use you, and persecute you" (Matt. 5:38-39,44). Spoken at the Sermon on the Mount, these words became the crux of Mennonite nonresistance, the very term *nonresistance* coming from Christ's edict to "Resist not evil." Mennonites carried this pacific belief with them through the church's early persecution; through their migration within the countries of Europe; and, finally, through their move across the Atlantic, to North America, where Mennonites began settling in 1683.

The United States provided a good home for most Mennonites, who found its rich soil agreeable to their livelihood as farmers and its vast tracts of available land open to the establishment of tightly knit Mennonite communities. Through the course of the eighteenth and nineteenth centuries, several waves of Mennonites emigrated to the new promised land from Switzerland, from southern Germany, from the Netherlands, and later from Russia. They settled in states from Pennsylvania to Kansas.

The American impulse to local liberty suited Mennonites well, for they could continue to embrace their religious faith without fear of reproach from those around them, including their government. In America, Mennonites could freely emphasize or privilege their nonconformity as well, affirming most assuredly the doctrine of two kingdoms: a kingdom of this world, not yet redeemed; and a kingdom of Christ, to which his followers belonged. Mennonites were in many ways separatists, and although they would interact with their American compatriots, theirs was often a life of quiet detachment from those around them who were not part of the Mennonite body of believers.

Nearly 80,000 Mennonites lived in the United States when the country entered the Great War in 1917. In varying ways, and to varying degrees, American Mennonites still held firmly to the convictions embraced by their Anabaptist forebears, and nonresistance remained at the core of those beliefs. Mennonites' nonconformity and their prevailing use of the German language, combined with their nonresistance and consequent refusal to support the war in any way, made them enemies of the United States—a country Mennonites had come to love and to claim as their own. Given the enthusiasm most Americans had when their country finally entered the war, the Great War was an especially trying, and especially pivotal, time in U.S. Mennonite history.

The American Mennonite church did not emerge unchanged by a war fought thousands of miles from home. Universal conscription, made law by President Woodrow Wilson in May 1917, further complicated Mennonites' place in America, as did the problem of conscientious objection to conscription. How were Mennonites to deal with a new governmental order that all able-bodied young men should report for military duty? And, in turn, how was the government to deal with able-bodied young men who refused to fight, to drill with arms, or even to wear a military uniform?

Historians like Gerlof Homan and James Juhnke have clearly documented this story of U.S. Mennonites in the First World War, tracing the challenges Mennonites faced in their opposition to a war much of America eventually wanted to fight. This history also includes the stories of at least 2,000 Mennonite conscientious objectors conscripted by the U.S. government, who were detained in military camps; who were often abused, both verbally and physically, for their nonresistant stance; and who were, in some cases, imprisoned for their refusal to participate in the military system.

Like combatant participants of the First World War, Mennonite objectors often used the written word as a way to make sense of their wartime lives. During their detainment, many conscientious objectors wrote letters home, describing their experiences; others kept diaries, recounting their daily existences in a military world that was undoubtedly foreign to them. Following the war, a good number wrote autobiographical sketches about their struggles. As with the Great War combatants, who relied on comprehensible metaphors to describe the incomprehensible, the Mennonite objectors likewise relied on language they understood to relay what they could not fully understand. And the writing of Mennonite objectors seemed to often echo the sentiments of Great War combatants, who themselves were objecting to a war in which they had become unwilling participants.

Although some of this writing was published in Mennonite periodicals, most remained unknown, tucked away in Mennonite archives or held in private collections. That few have read the writing of Mennonite objectors during the Great War is indeed unfortunate, for this writing is especially valuable in providing greater insight into the American Mennonite experience during the First World War. Further, the Mennonite objectors' writing challenges contemporary readers, especially those in the peace church tradition, to consider their own nonresistant testimony: to question the depths of their pacific convictions and the lengths each will go to sustain a peaceful witness. Finally, Mennonite objectors' writing provides a certain reminder about war: much like the pictures emerging from the Great War, much like the granite monuments that now dot northern France, much like the war literature produced by its combatants. The objectors' stories ask that we not forget their own sacrifices, their own witness against violence—a witness that too few people then, and too few people now, are willing to hear.

This volume brings to light several of the Mennonite objectors' stories, granting the men an audience for their testimonies about conscription, conscience, and an unwavering faith in God. The stories included here are told through the patterned device of the diary, an autobiographical genre that, more than any other, captures the nuances of daily life, the immediacy of experience as it is lived, and the range of thought and emotion, without the mediation of time and memory. Writers represented include Gustav Gaeddert, a teacher who assumed a leadership position among objectors in his camp; Ura Hostetler, a young farmer sent to military camp and so separated from his new wife; a Harvard-educated Amish Mennonite, Jacob Conrad Meyer, whose advanced degrees made him an anomaly among his people (though his nonresistant beliefs afforded him the same fate as his brethren); and John Neufeld, a Mennonite objector sent to the Fort Leavenworth Federal Penitentiary for his unwillingness to drill with arms.

These diary texts provide important historical insight into the American cultural climate during the Great War, exposing the country's rabid war hysteria, a hysteria that in turn bred intolerance and, in its extreme, mob violence. The conscientious objectors' experiences thus reflected the seeming deprivation of religious liberty in a country presumably founded on, among other things, the liberty of religious conviction. The diaries included here also highlight significant aspects of Mennonite life during the Great War, a life both at the cusp of transformation and at odds with American society. The importance of community and a faith in God, as well as the depth of nonresistant beliefs, became the subtext if not the text of each man's writing; their induction into a world they little understood and which little understood them informed the works they created. Finally, the diaries in this edition reveal the objectors' profound sense of isolation and alienation, from their ethnic communities and from the communities in which they were forced to live, communities that reviled them for not wholeheartedly embracing the country's militaristic fervor.

When read as history, these diaries provide a sense of what being a World War I objector was about for the four men who wrote each night in their journals and, by extension, for other men like them. When read as literature, the diaries reflect the centuries-old impulse of the wartime participant to make meaning of war: an event that, for its participants, often lacks meaning, confuses meaning, obfuscates meaning. That the objectors refused to use weapons, to fight at the front, or even to accept noncombatant responsibilities little undermined their role as wartime participants. After all, Mennonite resisters were in their own way casualties of a total war whose talons ripped deep into society's fabric.

This volume suggests that the diaries of Mennonite conscientious objectors should be read as both history and literature. Only in reading the diaries as literature can one fully understand the history of war; only in reading the diaries as history can one fully understand wartime literature.

To this end, this book's organizational structure endeavors to provide both historical and literary context to these diaries. Chapter 1 situates the diaries historically, as I describe there the different Mennonite groups represented by the diaries, then ground the diaries in the historical context of Great War America. Chapter 2 shifts focus, turning toward a study of the traditional Great War literary canon and arguing for the objectors' inclusion in that canon. I suggest that the Mennonite diaries provide a more complete understanding of the war and its literature. The third chapter applies literary interpretation to the diaries, examining the textual nuances Mennonites and other readers will find in the diaries, and providing comparison and contrast to other seminal Great War texts. The final chapters introduce readers to the Mennonite diarists themselves, and to the texts they wrote, beginning with Gustav Gaeddert, then Ura Hostetler, John Neufeld, and Jacob C. Meyer.

Editing a diary presents for the textual critic challenges both unique and specific. A diary is by its very nature a private document intended for a limited audience, usually for a readership of one—presumably the writer. Unless he is confident of his enduring fame, the diarist does not propose to write for some future publication; he is thus under no obligation to make his writing comprehensible to anyone but himself. And so the diarist may use abbreviations, symbols, and self-manufactured forms of punctuation he readily recognizes, even if these confound later readers (should his diary ever be read). In this sense, these diaries almost begged for standardization, for me to bear down with heavy black ink and revise punctuation, expand abbreviations, and interpret symbols.

Yet to read this edition's diaries as significant historical texts requires that they be reconstructed as closely as print allows to the original manuscripts, to how they were written in 1917-18, instead of conforming them to the sensibilities of readers some eighty years later. For the most part, then, I have resisted the urge to standardize in this edition. Misspellings, grammatical mistakes, abbreviations, and inconsistencies in capitalization and punctuation have been retained in the edited texts. No attempt has been made to emend a writer's flaws, for in many cases these idiosyncrasies reveal themselves to be patterns in the writer's work, part of his unique voice, his own imprint. I invite this voice to emerge rather than silencing it under the guise of standardization.

I realize, of course, that these voices of little-known Mennonite objectors from the First World War will not turn historiography on its head, nor will the diaries demand a complete revision of twentieth century literary scholarship. The Great War's narrative, both historical and literary, will remain fixed on the Western Front, on the nine million dead, and on a lost generation's sorrow—a sorrow symbolized so well by the large granite monuments of the Somme, monuments which often extol the virtues of sacrifice and of patriotic bravery on the battlefield.

During my European travels, though, I discovered a monument memorializing a different response to war. This one, a small boulder hidden in the corner of London's Tavistock Square, was placed there in memory of conscientious objectors from all wars. When I visited London in May 2001, the monument was strewn with carnations, each carrying a tag bearing the name of an objector and the war to which he or she protested, as well as the cost paid for that objection: in many cases imprisonment; in some cases, death. I thought then about the objectors whose stories I have studied at some length—about Gustav Gaeddert, Ura Hostetler, John Neufeld, and Jacob C. Meyer. Although the monument itself was a valuable reminder of the objectors' experience in all wars, I knew these Mennonite objectors' narratives reminded me more assuredly, more vividly, about the significance of a peaceful protest not only to the Great War, but also to any war. Yet these diaries, and the lives they represent, provide no lasting memorial if their texts remain hidden in library archives, if their stories remain untold. Only in being read can the diaries bear witness to the Mennonite experience during the Great War: to what the war meant for men drafted by their government, but who chose to serve their Christ and their conscience instead.

Writing Peace

CHAPTER ONE

The Dragon War: Mennonite Conscientious Objectors' Experience and the Great War

When the Virginia Mennonite Bishop George R. Brunk I penned his poem "War" in 1917, the First World War had already been raging for several years. Allied Forces had battled the Central Powers in theatres stretching from Europe to the Mediterranean and Northern Africa, the war's causes and its ends obscured by its means.

Brunk probably never saw the Western Front, never witnessed the blasted landscape, the millions dead, the twisting trenches, the rotting earth, the utter devastation from several years' battle between Allied and Central Powers. Up until 1917, his own country had ostensibly remained neutral toward the cataclysm, acting as peacemaker to a world at war. As Americans voiced support for their peace-minded president, Woodrow Wilson, Europe continued its destruction, carving trenches deep into the once-pastoral countryside. The trenches would themselves come to symbolize the war: both its methods and its stalemates, the inability to make any progress toward peace either militarily or diplomatically.

Lacking direct observation of this war's horrors seemingly mattered little to Brunk, who inscribed through visceral language the fear he and many others shared about the war's destructive potential and about a "dragon War" he had never seen. Published in the (Old) Mennonite periodical *Gospel Herald* two weeks after the United States declared war in 1917, Brunk's poem visualized war as a monster "Belched forth from the infernal world" and as a "terrible storm" which pummeled "millions . . .into the dust/By [its] leaden and iron hail." Although lacking the stark, gritty quality of poems written in the trenches, Brunk's work nonetheless proved a powerful portent for Mennonite readers. Because the "dragon War" had come to America, Brunk's poem proclaimed, the public would be blinded by "strange delusions," and would "dedicate their sons to the god of war,/And perpetuate the universal wrong."[1]

And so it came to pass, as Brunk and others had predicted. Having declared war with Germany on April 6, 1917, the United States quickly became engulfed in feverish support for the war. A little over one month later, when Wilson declared the need for universal military training, the country had indeed dedicated its sons to the war, to the terrible storm, to the belching dragon.

During the war's early years, Mennonites had by and large supported President Woodrow Wilson's neutral stance—as had many other Americans. Throughout the first years of war and into 1917, Wilson kept his country out of the conflict by arguing for "peace without victory," the establishment of a league of nations, and national self-determination. Appearing before the Senate on January 22, 1917, President Wilson made his stance clear: he would ask the warring countries to make peace and would continue to refrain from dragging his own country into war.

Most Mennonites were encouraged by this sustained neutrality, as a 1915 editorial in the *Gospel Herald* aptly noted: "Just now the President of the United States is setting a worthy example to the rulers of other countries by declaring himself for peace, although the United States has suffered greater provocation than some other nations that allowed themselves to become involved in war. We would be glad to see President Wilson go farther and declare himself against war under any circumstances, but we are grateful for his resolute stand for peace."[2] Even when America's intervention seemed inevitable, many Mennonites remained optimistic about President Wilson's power to maintain peace, believing that through a neutral stance, Americans had the "glorious privilege" to stop the "blood-red tide of war in Europe," as Levi Blauch wrote in the *Gospel Herald*.[3]

Two years after Blauch's editorial, however, the bloodshed in Europe was yet undammed. President Wilson's diplomatic efforts failed in early 1917: the warring parties would accept peace only at the price of total victory, having sacrificed too much to surrender with too few recognizable gains. Germany's increasing provocations on the high seas and its transmission of the infamous Zimmerman letter to Mexico led President Wilson to what seemed to him an inevitable conclusion: "I can't keep the country out of war," he reportedly told Secretary of the Navy Josephus Daniels.[4]

On April 2, 1917, Wilson spoke to a joint session of Congress, requesting a declaration of war against Germany. Wilson believed war was necessary "to bring the Government of the German Empire to terms and end the war," to fight "for the ultimate peace of the world," to champion "the rights of mankind," and to make the world "safe for democracy."[5]

In their publications, Mennonites voiced a certain sadness about their country's decision to make war. In its April 12, 1917 issue, the (Old) Mennonite *Gospel Herald* noted with a hint of resignation that "armed conflict . . . is apparently a matter of time." Yet the editorial also suggested hope that America's intervention would not be necessary: "We are still praying that, even though war has actually been declared, some thing may happen that will bring to an end the awful world conflict of the past few years before it can spread much farther, but that whatever happens God may continue to abide with His people and give them grace sufficient for every trial."

While refraining from discussing the "merits or demerits" of a military confrontation with Germany, the editorial expressed what Mennonites' "attitude" should be toward the war, the government, the battling countries, and God, reminding readers of the stance Mennonites had embraced—and should embrace even as America went to war. In the weeks and months following, Mennonite publications continued to reiterate their nonresistant stance and their hopes for a peaceful resolution without the need for "carnal warfare."[6] That peaceful resolution would not come, throwing America and its young men into the maelstrom of war—a maelstrom even the peaceful Mennonites could not avoid.

Defining the American Mennonites

As a people of peace, Mennonites remained consistent in their refusal to support the American war effort, even as most of their countrymen found space on the wartime bandwagon. There were, of course, members of the Mennonite church who chose to echo those American voices backing the war, or who advocated for the success of Germany; there were, too, men of Mennonite heritage who enlisted and fought on the Western Front. However, Mennonites who chose a less peaceful path during the Great War little reflected

Mennonites' widespread desire to uphold their nonresistant witness. After all, nonresistance had been woven into the fabric of Mennonite self-identity—a fabric not even a popular call to war could rend, strengthened, as it were, by biblical mandate, by Mennonite confessions of faith, and by a heritage deeply rooted in pacifism.

Although Mennonites as a whole remained steadfast in their objection to war, their differing ethnicities, geographical locations, and theologies influenced their understanding of what it meant to be a nonresistant Christian. Thus, it would be misleading to claim there was one monolithic U.S. Mennonite response to the Great War, just as it would be specious to claim there was one monolithic Mennonite church. Indeed, by the early twentieth century, at least sixteen clearly distinguishable Mennonite groups existed in the United States, each with its own ethnic, cultural, and/or theological identity. Members of all sixteen Mennonite groups faced difficulty during the Great War; the military itself made no distinction between Mennonite groups, and all varieties of Mennonite young men were conscripted and then forced to decide how best they could live their nonresistant witness within military cantonments. How they decided, and who helped them make their decisions, depended to a great degree on the Mennonite group that claimed them.

The diarists in this volume found home in several of the larger Mennonite denominations: Ura Hostetler was a member of the (Old) Mennonite Church; Gustav Gaeddert and John Neufeld were from the General Conference Mennonite Church; and Jacob C. Meyer was Amish Mennonite. To outside observers, the four men's denominational differences no doubt seemed minute, if the distinctions were noticeable at all; one Mennonite was as any Mennonite. Yet the singularities of these distinct Mennonite groups—forged through ethnic, cultural, and doctrinal differences—affected even what the conscientious objectors wrote in their diaries, whom they named in their diaries as family and friends, and whom they called upon for help while interned in the military cantonments.

Therefore, although the four diarists in this volume spoke in many ways for all Mennonite conscientious objectors, reflecting clearly the Great War experiences of those objectors, they also spoke from within their own distinct Mennonite vision and their group's particular understanding of what it meant to sustain a nonresistant witness.

Hostetler's (Old) Mennonite Church was the largest Mennonite group in 1917, claiming at the time nearly 35,000 members. Like most (Old) Mennonites, Hostetler had deep American roots. His ancestors had immigrated some 150 years earlier from Switzerland and the Palatinate. (Old) Mennonites shared this Swiss and south German ethnicity, an ethnicity that drew the group more tightly together and helped to more assuredly inform its cultural identity. Hostetler's family followed migration patterns similar to that of many (Old) Mennonites. The first of his forebears settled and began farming in eastern Pennsylvania. From there his family radiated westward to Indiana and Nebraska, his own parents continuing the westward push from Missouri to Kansas. By the early twentieth century, concentrations of (Old) Mennonites were also located in the Ohio Valley, the Midwest, and in the Northwest.

Typical of many (Old) Mennonites who had long lived in the United States, Hostetler's family was somewhat acculturated to American ways. His family spoke some German at home, but was comfortable speaking English, especially as the children started attending public school; his parents read English newspapers as well as denominational periodicals. When he was old enough, Hostetler drove a car as well as a motorcycle, and his family was open to using other modern technologies. Like other (Old) Mennonites, Hostetler's family embraced the convictions of nonresistance, nonconformity, and humility. The Hostetlers spoke and dressed simply, refused to take oaths, did not participate in public and political events, and so did not vote. They attended to their quiet, productive lives as farmers in a rural Kansas community.

Nevertheless, at the turn of the century, (Old) Mennonites experienced what Theron Schlabach has called a "quickening," as the group became more revivalist in its tendencies, forging new inroads into education, publication, and outreach.[7] As a denomination, the (Old) Mennonites were well organized, with leaders—then called bishops—overseeing a group of churches or district conferences. Such organization provided a useful stay against confusion in the First World War, as the (Old) Mennonite leadership in good time assembled a catalogue of expectations for its body, both about military service and about conscientious objection.

Gustav Gaeddert and John Neufeld were General Conference Mennonites; both men also shared traits distinct to that Mennonite group. General Conference Mennonites had around 15,500 members by 1917, many of whom lived in Kansas, Nebraska, and Oklahoma. The General Conference Mennonite Church began in 1860 by bringing together immigrants from south Germany with a group of progressive Mennonites from Pennsylvania who sought a more outward-looking Mennonite church, one that would concern itself with missions, Sunday schools, and higher education. After 1873, the General Conference was strengthened by the massive exodus of Mennonites from Russia to the American plains states, thousands of whom eventually joined the General Conference body. Because so many General Conference Mennonites immigrated to the United States in the nineteenth century, their roots in America were not so deep as those of the (Old) Mennonites. Consequently, many General Conference Mennonites retained familial and cultural ties to Germany and to Russia, and continued to use German dialects in speech and in writing.

The families of Gaeddert and Neufeld were typical of General Conference Mennonites who immigrated from Russia in the mid- to late-nineteenth century. Both Gaeddert and Neufeld claimed a long lineage of leadership in General Conference congregations: Gaeddert in the Hoffnungsfeld Church of Inman, Kansas, and Neufeld in Inman's Bethel Mennonite Church. Like most General Conference Mennonites, the families of Gaeddert and Neufeld did not privilege the doctrine of nonconformity to the degree that many (Old) Mennonites did; additionally, they were more progressive than most (Old) Mennonites. These characteristics stemmed in part from the ethos General Conference Mennonites carried with them from Russia, where they had enjoyed a good deal of autonomy and a positive relationship with the Russian government and with its people.

Although some General Conference Mennonites who immigrated from Russia struggled to acculturate once in America, Gaeddert's and Neufeld's families had less difficulty making their new country feel like home. Gaeddert reported that his own parents learned English quickly after arriving from Russia. They read English newspapers, they voted in American elections, and they were concerned with the education of their children—as with many of his siblings, Gaeddert attended Hoffnungsau preparatory school and Bethel Academy. Neufeld's life also mirrored General Conference Mennonite concerns for mission work. He spent his younger years on the mission fields of Oklahoma before the war and a good deal of his career following the war on the mission field of Chicago.

The struggle both Gaeddert and Neufeld had in deciding what kind of military duties they could conscientiously complete reflected the General Conference Mennonites' lack of centralized authority. Instead, General Conference Mennonites affirmed each congregation's autonomy and each person's conscience, and did not dictate rules of faith or praxis, as did the (Old) Mennonites. Lacking a definitive set of principles to follow during the Great War, conscientious objectors like Gaeddert and Neufeld were often compelled to decide for themselves what they could conscientiously do in military cantonments—and, sometimes, to question the decisions they had made.

Amish Mennonites, the group to which Jacob C. Meyer belonged, traced their own history through a complicated series of separations and schisms. The first occurred in 1690s Europe, when Jakob Ammann broke from the larger Mennonite body over issues of discipline and separation from the world. Like (Old) Mennonites, the Amish shared a Swiss ethnicity; like (Old) Mennonites, most Amish arrived earlier in the United States than did General Conference Mennonites, having settled as well in Mennonite epicenters like Pennsylvania, Ohio, and Indiana.

In nineteenth century America, however, a major division among the Amish created the Amish Mennonites. They were a group of believers who distinguished themselves from their more conservative Old Order Amish brethren because of the Amish Mennonites' progressive nature, which included a relative openness to congregational and cultural modernity. Indeed, in 1927, Meyer's Ohio Amish Mennonite Conference merged with the (Old) Mennonites, declaring that an affinity in thought and practice made such a union amenable.[8]

As Theron Schlabach has noted in *Peace, Faith, Nation*, Amish Mennonites at the turn of the century became involved in what he termed a "throbbing activism," an activism that distinguished them further from Old Order Amish and tied them more closely to (Old) Mennonites. Amish Mennonites began to establish Sunday schools, and took to publishing and bookselling. They became more concerned with advanced education and became more outward looking, turning to missions work as a means of spreading the gospel.[9] Meyer would himself voice the concerns of this denomination both during and after the war, urging his fellow Mennonites—Amish and otherwise—to work in the larger world, rather than remain separated from it, and so removed from the kingdom that needed Christ's redemption.

Like the Amish Mennonites, other smaller Mennonite groups emerged from schisms both in America and Europe, and remained both tied to and separated from their Mennonite brethren through similarities and differences in doctrine, culture, and ethnicity.[10] Yet the (Old) Mennonite Church and General Conference Mennonite Church remained the two largest Mennonite bodies in the United States, and accounted for over half of the country's Mennonite population.

During the war, of course, such differences little mattered to the outside world, nor to soldiers and officers dealing with Mennonite conscientious objectors. Mennonites became known for their nonresistant stance, their unwillingness to support the war effort, their seeming insularity, and their widespread use of the German language. These characteristics branded the Mennonites and made them all—whether (Old) Mennonite, Amish Mennonite, or a less visible Mennonite group—prey to the scorn of an American populace ready for war.

Mennonites Face the Great War

Following President Wilson's speech on April 2, 1917, the mood in the United States was festive. The country's patriotic flame would soon burn more fiercely, propelled by what historian John Higham termed "the most strenuous nationalism and the most pervasive nativism that the United States had ever known."[11]

The few in America who objected to wartime intervention found themselves in a precarious position. No longer sharing the ideals of their government, they became a diminishing minority amid the growing population of war supporters. The country, though seemingly swept up in an ever-widening vortex of war hysteria, stood firm on the principle of just war: the threat of German dominance was real, so intervention was necessary. Yet while many Americans were convinced their country's part in the war was a moral mission for democracy, some Americans, including Mennonites, rejected warfare on ethical grounds. For Mennonites and members of other peace churches especially, making war was clearly immoral.

Herein emerged a conflict. Those who embraced the war for what they believed were moral reasons could little accept those who rejected all war for moral reasons, and vice versa. This conflict of ideologies, coupled with a good dose of patriotic ardor, became a volatile mix, as the year and a half following President Wilson's address would show all too clearly.

In wartime America, Mennonites' belief in nonresistance, as well as their German ethnicity, precipitated problems in a country seeking "100 percent Americanism" and total support for the war effort. American citizens wholeheartedly embraced Wilson's program to make the world safe for democracy. To show their support for the president and the country, Americans participated in rallies, bellowed patriotic songs, displayed flags, bought war bonds, and celebrated their sons' induction into the army. These were the more innocuous manifestations of the country's wartime fervor, a fervor which at times bred violence. Those who opposed the war found their churches splashed with yellow paint and their homes emblazoned with graffiti, received threats from neighbors and the press, were tarred and feathered, and, in a few cases, were lynched by angry mobs.

In urging unfettered support for the war, both the government and the country's mainline churches appealed not only to America's patriotism but also to her Christian faith. The call to holy war was sounded not only from the pulpit but also in governmental campaigns, telling Americans that the war was ordained by God to rid the world of the antichrist Kaiser and vile Huns.[12] Politicians effectively employed Christian rhetoric to encourage constituents to buy war bonds and to advocate for conscription; mainline churches employed patriotic rhetoric to encourage parishioners to give their full backing to the war effort.[13]

The American populace bought this civic/religious message wholesale. Because so many were sure of the war's holy purpose, anyone who opposed the war met with immediate suspicion—and, too often, faced violent scorn. Mennonites across the United States fell victim to the destructive acts of ardent patriots; story after story has been told of the abuse done to Mennonites attempting to live their peaceful witness in wartime America.[14]

The country's embrace of a civic religion complicated the ability of Mennonites to sustain their nonresistant witness. Perhaps more significantly, few who conflated the intentions of church and state were fully able to understand the Mennonites' own ardent belief in a two-kingdoms ethic. Since their inception in sixteenth century Anabaptism, Mennonites had held firmly to this theology, founded on their understanding of Romans 13. Centuries of persecution by the state had only strengthened the Mennonites' interpretation, which is succinctly summarized by Perry Bush in his *Two Kingdoms, Two Loyalties*:

> Although sovereign over both, God endowed two orders, two kingdoms, for the ruling of human society. One sphere of activity was the world of secular activity and culture of all humans, to be ruled over by the state . . . The second kingdom was the church, the world of spiritual activity, mission, and discipline. In this kingdom, Christians carried out the divine mandates applicable only to themselves as citizens of this second, spiritual realm. Christians thus had a foot in both realms; they were to be "in the world, but not of it."[15]

The two-kingdoms ethic intensified the difficulties Mennonites experienced in Great War America, if only because it ran counter to the country's predominant civic religion. Additionally, though, a two-kingdoms theology influenced how Mennonites attempted to relate to governmental authorities in matters of conscription and conscientious objection.

Mennonites believed they were to follow the dictates of the state, but only when those dictates did not contradict the higher commands of God's kingdom. Fulfilling the military obligations demanded by the state, Mennonites believed, would certainly mean transgressing the mandates of God's kingdom. At the same time, as Bush has written, Mennonites believed God had established the state to maintain law and order; therefore, "nonresistant Christians must be the most law-abiding citizens of the state."[16] Great War conscription challenged these convictions. If Mennonite young men refused to be drafted, they would no longer be law-abiding citizens; if they accepted conscription, Mennonite men were in danger of compromising their allegiance to the greater kingdom of God.

At the war's beginning, Mennonite leaders worked tirelessly to secure exemption from the draft for their men. A two-kingdoms ethic confounded this process as well, as Mennonite leaders approached the government believing it could not ask Mennonites to violate their religious beliefs by joining the military. In turn, the government argued that Mennonites needed to fulfill their civic responsibilities along with all other citizens of the United States. Government and military officials felt that Mennonites could at least accept noncombatant duties in the military, and could little understand how such a role would compromise the Mennonites' allegiance to God.

As Mennonite men headed for military camps, the government continued to create policies that revealed an inability to comprehend or comply with Mennonite thought and belief. Mennonites, in turn, negotiated with government leaders in a way that exposed the Mennonites' own inability to comprehend or to comply with the demands of the country they claimed as their own.

The story of Mennonite conscientious objection in World War I is, to a great degree, driven by the complications of these conflicting ethical systems, as Mennonites attempted to live their nonresistant two-kingdoms convictions amid a country guided by an entirely different set of principles.

The Plight of Conscripted Objectors

When American men started their journeys to military camps and then were mobilized overseas, patriotism had reached a fevered pitch. Rallies celebrated the induction of American young men; monetary gifts to the government and the Red Cross became a way to support the boys at home and overseas; American flags became a symbol of the great sacrifice families were making, sending their men off to war. Mennonites refrained from such patriotic displays. They had no reason to celebrate, as they believed their young men were being forced to violate the will of God and their consciences. Attempts to secure complete exemption from the draft having failed, Mennonites packed their sons off to the military camps, believing that the men would face untold abuses for their unpopular stance, certain that the men would not fight but not always sure what the cost of such refusal would be.

This—the situation of conscientious objectors and their place in the military—became the most divisive issue alienating Mennonites from U.S. society. Others in America who were freely making the sacrifice of sons, fathers, and brothers resented the Mennonite pleas for exemption from equal sacrifice, and for good reason. Mennonites were asking for freedom from fighting when the very fighting itself was an apparent means of guaranteeing that freedom. Far from being loyal Americans, Mennonites seemed "parasitic," "selfish," and "legalistic," asking their country to release them from this grave responsibility but openly accepting all other rights offered them by the country.[17]

The conscientious objectors' plight really began in May 1917, when Congress passed the Selective Service Act. This act ensured the first mass conscription on American soil, "to be remembered as one of the most conspicuous moments in our history," according to President Woodrow Wilson.[18]

Although President Wilson had once believed conscription would undermine American principles of individual freedom and choice, the prolonged struggle on the Western Front, which had siphoned off many of Europe's most talented men, had convinced him otherwise. He now saw that American intervention necessitated a massive military force, much larger than the National Guardsmen and volunteer military recruits that then constituted the U.S. armed forces. Conscription was thus imperative if the United States wished to make the world safe for democracy.

Despite President Wilson's belief that a draft was essential, the Selective Service Act he proposed in early April 1917 met with reservations from many camps within Congress, from those who feared conscription cast a "great shadow of militarism" over the land to those who resisted any form of government coercion, of which they believed conscription was one.[19]

Echoing the concerns of varied Congressmen, members of other peace groups came to Washington to testify against conscription. Mennonites were not among them. Instead, several Mennonite groups convened their own meeting in North Newton, Kansas, on April 10-11, 1917, attempting to outline their policies regarding conscription. Although a draft appeared imminent, the statement they constructed remained decidedly vague: because of their nonresistant stance Mennonites should not participate in war, though the church also should support those wishing to serve in the Red Cross or in medical corps. The policy failed to outline exactly what "participation" in war constituted, and to what extent young men could live and work under military jurisdiction without violating their consciences.

Nonetheless, after the meeting a few of the delegates left for Washington, D.C., to speak with members of Congress about Mennonite concerns. There they found at least two other delegations of Mennonites acting in their own groups' interests. While one band of Mennonite representatives told legislators their men would accept any military duty save bearing arms, another presented congressmen with a more narrow policy, asserting their men would refuse any type of military duty, including noncombatant work.[20]

In any event, neither the Mennonites' uncoordinated arguments about the draft nor the concerns of others significantly impeded the institution of compulsory military service, which became law on May 18, 1917. The act required that all men ages twenty-one to thirty register for the draft, despite any infirmities or objections. Refusal to register was punishable as a crime; so too was aiding another in avoiding duty or failing to report for duty when called. Men were required to register at area polling stations on June 5 and were then to be deemed fit or unfit for induction into the army by local boards of citizens acting at the War Department's behest.

According to President Wilson, carrying out this law was critical. Because modern warfare had "changed the face of war," an entire nation, rather than an army, should be "trained for war," he said. "The nation needs all men," President Wilson told the country, and the day of registration was "nothing less than the day upon which the manhood of the country shall step forward in one solid rank in defense of the ideals to which this nation is consecrated." Therefore, Wilson argued, conscription was not a coercion of "the unwilling; it is, rather, selection from a nation which has volunteered in mass." Wilson called on Americans to participate in registering their men, believing it a patriotic "duty" for all citizens "to see to it that the name of every male person of the designated ages is written on these lists of honor."[21]

For Mennonites, President Wilson's proclamation dealt a stunning blow. They did not wish to "volunteer in mass," nor did they want their names on any "lists of honor." In many ways, they felt misled by their government; they had believed the government would grant them complete exemption from the military. Indeed, a few Mennonites argued that they had received such assurances even before immigrating to America and that the promise of military exemption should still hold.[22]

Instead of granting Mennonites exemption from conscription, however, the Selective Service Act required that all religious objectors join other male citizens in registering. Then, according to rule 14, section 79 of the act:

> Any registrant who is found by a Local Board to be a member of any well-recognized religious sect or organization organized and existing May 18, 1917, and whose then existing creed or principles forbid its members to participate in war in any form, and whose religious convictions are against war or participation therein in accordance with the creed or principles of said religious organization, shall be furnished by such Local Board with a certificate to the effect [that] . . . he can only be required to serve in a capacity declared by the President to be noncombatant.

While this provision received widespread criticism from peace societies because of its limited scope—only members of well-established religious organizations would be granted conscientious objector status—the Mennonites were more concerned about the vagueness of its wording.[23] They would be forced to serve in noncombatant roles, but those had yet to be determined by President Wilson. In fact, noncombatancy would not be defined for nearly another year.

June 5, 1917, arrived, and Mennonite men joined millions of Americans in registering for the draft. Despite other disagreements, Mennonite groups had all decided their young men should report for registration as well as for military camps. Doing so reflected the Mennonites' general desire to remain within the bounds of civil law, if possible. Yet it also meant, as historian James Juhnke notes, "that Mennonite conflict with legal authority on the draft question was removed from the local community and from the processes of civil law" and became an issue of military law, thus changing the relationship of Mennonites to the government, both local and national.[24]

Unlike other conscripts, most Mennonites who were drafted could little enjoy the festive atmosphere of the local registration sites, where bands played patriotic songs and young women handed out flags to America's newest heroes. Still, Mennonites had already prepared their men for this day, schooling them in appropriate responses to give to their local boards. A pamphlet published in mid-May 1917 used both German and English to instruct men in what to say. The pamphlet also cited Scripture supporting the men's religious objection to the war.[25]

At the local boards, citizens had two ways to register their objections to military service. On their registration cards, men could claim exemption from combat based on religious belief; they could also ask for noncombatant status by filling out governmental form 174. To substantiate that they were indeed members of a "well-recognized religious sect," and that they had been since before May 18, 1917, the Mennonites submitted church certificates of membership with their registrations.

In accordance with instructions from ministers and other church leaders, Mennonite men maneuvered through registration day. After this, their fates were in the hands of War Secretary Newton Baker and of local draft boards.

Baker initiated the draft process during a Washington celebration, drawing from a glass bowl slips of papers inscribed with registration numbers. Men who had been designated the first number drawn, 258, would report first to their draft boards. These boards, comprised predominantly of local community members, examined the registrants and declared them eligible or exempt. Few people could receive complete exemption: only those who were state and government officials, those with dependents, the physically or economically infirm, and armory employees.

Again, religious objectors could be exempt from combatant, but not noncombatant, service; their local draft boards issued them certificates endorsing their claim for conscientious objection to combatant duty. Ostensibly appointed by the president but in reality chosen by state and local officials, the draft boards were driven by both patriotic and political motivation and nearly always reflected the ideologies of the district's elected leaders. Therefore, men who received exemption in one district might not be exempted in another, depending on the partisan nature of their local boards.

In some places, too, local draft boards treated conscientious objectors more leniently than in other places. Homan reported that in parts of Pennsylvania, boards viewed applications "with exceptional sympathy. If such registrants had scruples against fighting, the boards apparently considered them to be more useful at home on the farm than in the military"; and so, on the farm they stayed.[26] Other boards looked upon conscientious objectors far less favorably, ignoring their claims for exemption from combat on religious grounds and granting neither economic nor dependency exemptions to those who seemed to qualify. Hence, the dependency exemption was applied liberally in some areas and conservatively in the next, so that some men left wives and children unprovided for, since their draft boards had decided the families were not "dependent" on their husbands' or fathers' incomes.

After appearing before the draft boards, men could only wonder and worry about their fates like every other draftee; throughout summer 1917, they awaited the call to report for duty. During this time, Mennonite leaders continued to work on the conscientious objectors' behalf, sending delegations to Washington and hoping for a miracle of sorts: that President Wilson would interpret "noncombatant" in the loosest sense, that their men could serve outside the military establishment or, miracle of all miracles, that Mennonites would still receive complete exemption.

As before, however, Mennonites did not present Washington with a unified voice. Representatives of the General Conference Mennonites, Mennonite Brethren, and Krimmer Mennonite Brethren told governmental leaders they would accept service in agricultural or the Red Cross and failing that, might even agree to do noncombatant work. Their offer of service contradicted the position of other groups. (Old) Mennonites took a firmer stance in their discussions with government authorities, rejecting any form of duty under military governance, combatant or noncombatant.[27]

At their own meeting on August 29, 1917, in Indiana, (Old) Mennonites constructed a statement representing the group's intentions for their conscientious objectors: they would under "no circumstance" accept duty within the military, though what constituted "duty" was ill defined. Delegates took that statement to Washington and to Baker, who agreed that conscientious objectors could be segregated in their own detention units, would not have to wear uniforms or drill, and would not be forced to "serve in any capacity that violated their creed and conscience," but "could be assigned to other tasks not under the military arm of the government."[28]

Baker was motivated by the goal of getting Mennonites into camps, then perhaps changing their minds about conscientious objection or at least about accepting noncombatant work. Therefore, according to Juhnke, Baker led "Mennonites of both conciliatory and uncompromising inclination to conclude that it was best to register in the draft, to report for duty, and to await an order from the War Department defining 'non-combatant service' in a way which would make it possible for them to work in good conscience."[29]

By early fall the United States government still had not issued any statement that clearly established the fate of conscientious objectors once they reached military camps. Baker informed Mennonite leaders that they had misinterpreted him, and that conscientious objectors who refused to serve could not work outside the military domain, but would be forced to stay in detention camps to await, Baker said, "such disposition as the government may decide upon."[30] President Wilson also had not defined what "noncombatant work" was, and so conscientious objectors were not sure what they would or would not be asked to do at the camps. But then again, neither had many Mennonite sects decided, with absolute certainty, what their men should and should not do once they were inducted.

Thus Mennonites had yet to answer questions soon facing their young men: Would wearing a military uniform violate their nonresistant stance? Would drilling? Would hauling trash for the camp constitute military service? Would cleaning one's barrack or cooking in the mess? The first Mennonite conscientious objectors reporting in late summer 1917 were placed in an unenviable position, uncertain of what the government would ask of them and uncertain too what the church expected of them.

Mennonite men began receiving their induction notices in late August, commanding them to report for military duty. Often men were required to report a scant few days after receiving notice, certainly saving them prolonged good-byes with loved ones (and probably saving them much chance to lose heart and flee).

Whether recognized by their local boards as conscientious objectors or not, Mennonite men faced induction procedures similar to every other conscript in the United States military, beginning with a train ride to one of the country's thirty cantonments, stretching from Camp Meade, Maryland, in the east, to Camp Travis, Texas, in the south, and Camp Lewis, Washington, in the northwest.

The train ride itself must have been a harrowing experience for some Mennonites. Placed in rail cars with regular inductees, Mennonite men often faced extended journeys alone, feeling already a longing for the communities they had left, feeling already a sense of alienation from those around them. For many the train ride was their introduction to the "carnal" world from which their ethnic upbringing had shielded them, a confrontation of sorts between two kingdoms in which the worldly kingdom proved overwhelming to those unfamiliar with it.

The Mennonite inductees aboard the trains were predominantly quiet, humble, simply dressed and, in some cases, spoke English with a German accent or not at all. There were newly inducted soldiers, on the other hand, who spent their journeys to military camps hollering, using profanity, smoking, playing cards, shooting craps, and drinking. E. E. Leisy, traveling from Harvey County, Kansas, to Camp Funston, wrote in his 1960 autobiographical sketch about the "Comanche yells" emitted from train windows, the "war-whoop of democracy" shouted by soldiers and received well by those who heard them, the "girls . . . greeted lustily" as the train passed by, soldiers hanging out its windows.[31] John Hege, from Hagerstown, Maryland, noted in his diary a man so drunk he was "stagering" and could "barley walk with satisfaction." Confronted with this inebriated man, Hege believed that if ever he needed the "company" of "Brethren . . . *it was now.*"[32]

Oftentimes Mennonite conscientious objectors had to make the journey to camp alone amid the soldiers. If fortunes proved good, they might meet other Mennonites with whom they could commune, a discovery providing them some comfort. In his 1963 autobiography, Clarence Shank of Hesston, Kansas, remembered well the "confusion" of a lonely train ride to Camp Lee, Virginia. Shank wrote that the presence of "at least five Mennonite boys on this train and also a few of other nonresistant faiths" was a comfort to him, and that the company of other nonresisters reassured him of "the promise my God had made to others, 'I will never leave thee nor forsake thee.'"[33]

Holdeman Mennonite Noah H. Leatherman recorded a similar experience during his journey from his hometown of Moundridge, Kansas, to Camp Funston, Kansas. Although he "had expected to be alone" on his sojourn to Camp Funston, he had discovered several General Conference Mennonites waiting at the McPherson, Kansas, train depot, and this meeting gave him "new courage."[34] Still, despite the solidarity afforded by this such company the train journeys became the first of many instances in which Mennonite conscientious objectors found themselves in the discomfiting position of being aliens in a strange land, unused to its customs and mores, separated by cultural differences and by differences in conscience as well.

After rides ranging from a few hours to a few days, trains filled with inductees arrived at the hastily built cantonments that housed and trained the new American army. Erected in only a few months, the military camps resembled small cities, some populated by 50,000 to 100,000 inhabitants. Rows upon rows of barracks sheltered the young men, and cots were crammed into each barrack so that a man had little personal space and even less privacy. Especially in southern climes, where shelter was not as essential, the camps supplied the men tents big enough to house eight or more soldiers; these tents were likewise used in places where barracks had yet to be built. Mess halls, latrines, canteens, office buildings, and YMCA and Red Cross clubs dotted the military camp landscape, as did vast fields intended for drill. For rural men accustomed to open spaces and the solitude of farm life, the crowded barracks and sustained activity would require some acclimation. So too would the guards patrolling the camps with guns, the loud booms of artillery fire echoing from practice ranges, and the continued profanity of military men. Hutterite Jacob Waldner of the Big Springs Colony in Montana wrote that the "miles" of "armed soldiers marching and shouting" had a chilling effect on him: "it went through bone and marrow. We had never in our life seen so much of this miserable world at one time."[35]

By the time men began arriving at military camps, antagonism toward conscientious objectors had already enveloped the country. This venom was fueled, one must imagine, not only by the general tenor of war hysteria, or by the conviction that everyone must do his part in the war for democracy, but also by the invective of military and governmental leaders, whose words against conscientious objectors found prominent display in national presses. Thus former president Roosevelt's indictment of conscientious objectors as "sexless creatures" and "half-hidden traitors," given voice in the nation's preeminent periodicals including the *New York Herald*, not only reflected the country's sentiment but also influenced it.[36] So too did Roosevelt's accusation that conscientious objectors "are actuated by lazy desire to avoid any duty that interferes with their ease and enjoyment, some by the evil desire to damage the United States and help Germany, some by sheer, simple, physical timidity."[37]

Within military camps, opinion was shaped by leaders like Commanding Officer Leonard Wood (Camp Funston), a career military man who believed conscientious objectors were "enemies of the Republic, fakers, and active agents of the enemy."[38] Whatever their opinion of objectors, other commanding officers and high-ranking military officials treated them with more respect than did Wood, whose camp was infamous for its abuses. Nonetheless, many soldiers, driven by the convictions of their country's leaders and by their own sense of patriotic duty, endeavored to make life for new conscientious objector inductees intolerable.

Hence, as Mennonite men followed other draftees through the process of induction, they faced difficulties at nearly every step. For some, their simple dress and quiet unwillingness to participate in train ride festivities probably branded them immediately. If not, they were quickly recognized as conscientious objectors by what they said to commanding officers, to whom they expressed objections about doing combatant work, wearing uniforms, and/or drilling. Those Mennonites who agreed to accept noncombatant duties, to wear a uniform, or to drill usually faced no more abuses, and were put to service in noncombatant roles (for example, in the medical corps, in sanitation, or as cooks in mess halls). Those who rejected one or all three faced further mistreatment.

High-ranking military officers usually had no role in the "initiation rites" that were inflicted on Mennonites during initial processing. According to historian Sarah Shields, some Mennonite objectors "encountered kicks, stabs with a pen, yellow paint, or attempted humiliation" from other soldiers; this abuse only subsided when an officer intervened.[39] However, officers were sometimes scarce—John Neufeld reported in his diary that one officer seemed always absent or sleeping—and Mennonites were left to defend themselves against mistreatment.

The objectors' general lack of knowledge about military hierarchy and procedure only made them more vulnerable: To whom could they safely report abuses? Who could rightfully give them orders? Therefore, while their own alienation was intensified by "attempted humiliation" which separated them further from other soldiers, the objectors also could little understand the military language or culture (what exactly was a muster?), which precipitated further humiliation, and so isolation. Such was the conscientious objectors' introduction to the military.

Along with their fellow inductees, Mennonite conscientious objectors relinquished their clothing and were compelled to bathe on arriving at camp. Sometimes, they were forcibly shaved and given a haircut; for Hutterites and Amish, such treatment was especially offensive, as wearing a beard was an expression of their church discipline. The Hutterite Waldner reported that "twelve brethren" were taken by soldiers and given "an ice cold shower under a water faucet. They used coarse brushes and soap on them and rubbed soap all over them including mouth and eyes to torture them."[40] The icy shower or some variation thereof (ice water then hot, or ice water coupled with stiff brushes) became one way to torment conscientious objectors, to compel them to do noncombatant work against their wills or to don uniforms and drill. Or at least Mennonite men reporting their experiences felt that this was so.

Others believed differently. George E. English, historian for the 89th division housed at Camp Funston, wrote that the "icy bath in the small hours of the cool nights of early fall was a splendid test of the qualities of the embryo soldier," and therefore was applied to Mennonite objectors and regular soldiers alike.[41] Sarah Shields, writing about the treatment of conscientious objectors at Camp Funston, agreed, arguing that when the "Mennonites frequently referred to icy showers as abuse," they were merely not used to the bohemian life of a military camp without water heaters and heating systems.[42]

Was this another clash of cultures? Did Mennonites merely misinterpret as abuse ice showers that were, in actuality, a hazing ritual for new soldiers or a lack of modern conveniences? Perhaps. However, considering that Mennonites in their simple rural lives were well used to foregoing the accouterments of modernity, and considering that Mennonites faced abuse via water (both ice cold and boiling hot) far after their induction as "embryo" soldiers, Shields's assertion seems questionable. Instead, this foray into military hygiene became but one method of provocation sometimes used by petty officers and soldiers to force conscientious objectors to comply with military orders, or as a form of torment if they refused.

After a shower and a shave, undergone willingly or not, newly inducted draftees were given uniforms. If the camp had not been issued uniforms, as was at first the case in some places, the men received blue overalls.

Uniforms presented Mennonites with another problem: would wearing military attire violate their consciences, make them soldiers, or represent an acquiescence to military authority? In some cases, objectors decided the answer was yes and refused to accept the uniforms; others wore the uniforms at first before changing their minds; still others still had no scruples against the uniform.

The uniform quandary was soon solved by Secretary of War Baker, who constructed a definitive policy for Mennonite conscientious objectors. In a letter to Mennonite leader Aaron Loucks in early fall of 1917, Baker's Adjutant General wrote, "all Commanding Generals of the national Army and National Guard Divisions" have been ordered "that selected Mennonites who report to camps for duty be not forced to wear the uniform, as the question of raiment is one of the tenets of their faith."[43]

Of course, as was often the case with conscientious objectors, officers and soldiers sometimes failed to yield to Baker's edict and forced Mennonite men to put on their uniforms. This was the experience of Adam H. Mumaw of Wooster, Ohio, who arrived at Camp Zachary Taylor in Kentucky nearly one year after Baker's ruling. In his 1970 autobiographical sketch Mumaw wrote:

> I was taken to the supply tent and offered a uniform or else . . . I refused to accept not wanting to be identified as a soldier. [The corporal] hollered to the group, take him. I was reminded of what the mob said of Jesus 'Crucify him.' Aside were a group of men [surrounding] a blanket holding on to the edge. The first grout threw me into the blanket and at the signal gave a sudden jerk which threw me into the air and caught me as I landed. The second attempt I got a grip on the edge and was tossed into the crowd.[44]

After this, when Mumaw still refused the uniform, the mob of men stripped him of his clothes, and were stopped only when a lieutenant appeared and ordered the melee to cease.

Ura Hostetler faced similar mistreatment at Camp Funston, Kansas, again long after Baker ruled that wearing a uniform was not compulsory for Mennonites. On the day of Hostetler's induction, he wrote in his diary, "it was almost impossible not to wear the uniform but thru Jesus our Lord I got thru, only after having the uniform forced onto me for several hrs. They put overalls into my sack and uniform on me but I changed when I got a chance, put overall and jumper on and uniform into sack." Several days later, the men in Hostetler's barrack "made sport" of him by taking his clothes and several personal letters after foisting a uniform on him. Hostetler found a sergeant. The officer told the soldiers that "if he had his way about it [he'd] go without clothes, but boys this man's clothes will come back tonight, I know he's h—- to live with but he'll be taken care of sooner or later."[45]

Hostetler's fate was shared by many conscientious objectors, who were put into units with regular soldiers on arrival at camp. In the first months of conscription, the government approved no plan for segregation of conscientious objectors, apparently believing that objectors placed in barracks with fighting men would discover the valor they lacked and would accept combatant or, at the least, noncombatant duty. However, military officials had failed to calculate the resiliency of many conscientious objectors and the depths of Mennonite faith in nonresistance.

Many conscientious objectors, including Mennonites, did choose to join the regular soldiers with whom they bunked, taking positions in the military that were inconsonant with a nonresistant stance. Of the 21,000 conscripted as conscientious objectors in the Great War, only 3,900 remained steadfast in their convictions and refused to accept even noncombatant duty. Yet military officials began to understand that housing conscientious objectors with other conscripts threatened soldier morale. Draftees who refused to drill or wear a uniform and who sometimes shared with bunkmates their testimony of nonresistance might infect other soldiers, who would themselves either embrace conscientious objection or, more likely, resent those who refused to work and who shirked their patriotic obligation.

By the beginning of October 1917, Baker had decided conscientious objectors should be segregated from other conscripts. Reports from various military camps had encouraged Baker that few problems had occurred between conscientious objectors, military officials, and soldiers. A personal visit to Camp Meade, Maryland, supported these reports, although conscientious objectors there had already been segregated and the camp had little problem with mistreatment. Conversations with the conscientious objectors convinced Baker they were "simple-minded" and "lazy and obstinate," and that only two were mentally normal.[46] Nonetheless, he wrote to President Wilson, "If it gets no worse than it is at Camp Meade, I am pretty sure that no harm will come in allowing these people to stay at the camps, separated from the life of the camp but close enough to gradually understand. The effect of that I think quite certainly would be that a substantial number of them would withdraw their objection and make fairly good soldiers."[47]

With this consideration, Baker constructed a new policy ordering camp commanders to create segregated units for conscientious objectors. The policy stated, in part, that objector units would be "under supervision of instructors who shall be specially selected with a view of insuring that these men will be handled with tact and consideration."[48] Government officials felt this order would prevent soldier morale from eroding, as conscientious objectors would be removed from the conscripts-in-training. Perhaps more significantly, officials hoped the "tact and consideration" of officers and kind handling might convince conscientious objectors to forego their nonresistant stance and accept the life of a soldier, either through combatant or noncombatant work.

Despite Baker's mandate, many conscientious objectors remained in regular units for various reasons and for varied periods of time. Sometimes, the conscientious objector barracks were placed under quarantine (as were regular barracks) to combat the spread of rampant diseases crippling army camps; conscientious objectors new to camp might be asked to stay in combat units until the quarantine lifted. More problematic, though, were the camps where officials never told conscientious objectors about the ruling, thereby forcing objectors to stay in units with other inductees and so face the wrath of their fellow soldiers. Especially in the early months of American intervention, Mennonite men did not always know about Baker's orders and so could not challenge their placement in combat units. Later, Mennonite leaders schooled their men in governmental rulings, making it more difficult for military officials to take advantage of or ignore the mandate to segregate conscientious objectors.

At the least, conscientious objectors would be forced into combat units for their first few days in camp, until they were granted an audience with military officials to announce their conscientious objection and to provide supporting documents, including church membership certificates and notices from local boards identifying their nonresistant stance. Finding such an audience could prove difficult and time-consuming; in the meantime, the men were compelled to stay in their assigned units, often without the company of their brethren.

Whether they were in combat units for several days or for several months, conscientious objectors found life among other conscripts especially isolating. Soldiers preparing for war fast became friends with their comrades in the barracks. Proving there is strength in numbers, they often ganged up on the lone conscientious objectors who shared their bunks. The pressure to fold, to renounce nonresistance, to drill, or to accept some kind of work within the camps was acute; objectors who did not succumb to the pressure faced even more ridicule and sometimes even greater abuse by fellow soldiers and by officers, from ice water treatments to being chased at gunpoint.

Conscientious objectors who still refused to drill or to work were often not allowed on their bunks while others trained. Instead, they had to sit on the floor or stand outside their barracks for hours, even in the most inclement weather. Waldner reported that some men in his camp stood in the cold yard all day, their clothes marked with a large *E* for *Enemy,* subjected to the taunts and jeers of soldiers. Verbal tirades also isolated conscientious objectors from their fellow conscripts. Accusations of being anti-American slackers stung Mennonites, who valued hard work and believed themselves loyal Americans. Norman Thomas, a socialist pacifist who worked tirelessly on the part of objectors during the Great War, said this of the objectors' time in combat units: "Any one with imagination enough to picture the isolation of the individual in a cantonment humming with soldiers will understand that to persist in objection took tremendous moral conviction" or "an abnormal indifference to environment."[49]

The writing of Mennonite objectors suggests they were not "indifferent" to the difficult environment of military camps, nor to the invectives and abuse they received. Still most Mennonites, impelled by "moral conviction" to endure the isolation, did not fold to soldier pressure, and instead waited anxiously for the day they could be transferred to a segregated unit, to be among their fellow resisters. And until that day came, they were fortified by visits from conscientious objectors living in nearby barracks who also sought the company of like-minded believers, even if they were strangers in every other sense.

Because of this isolation, the relief Mennonites finally felt when transferred to a conscientious objector unit must have been immense. After extended time with soldiers living a foreign ethos, it was nice to be among other pacifists, even if the only value they all shared was conscientious objection to war. Mennonites, after all, were not the only objectors placed in the segregated units. Indeed, any one barrack could house a full spectrum of theologies, ethnicities, and cultures. In addition to the sixteen different Mennonite groups, there might also be Quakers, Adventists, Russellites (the precursor to Jehovah's Witnesses), Dunkers, Christdelphians, and socialists, among others. Although conscientious objectors sometimes disagreed about the reasoning for their objection to war, that objection itself forged a brotherhood of sorts, placing those with opposing theologies in the same ranks. Despite such diversity, there was rarely any serious discord within conscientious objector units, as the men shared both a common misery and a common place as despised members of the military community.

Secretary of War Baker's edict that segregated objector units be commanded by officers with "tact and consideration" was not followed in all camps and caused difficulty many places. Abuse of conscientious objectors continued, carried out by angry officers and by the camp's soldiers. Military men were upset that "slackers" would not have to shoulder a weapon and face the trenches, would not do service for their country, would not make sacrifices of life and livelihood similar to those of fighting men. Passions became further inflamed when some conscientious objectors refused to perform any type of duty within camps, including seemingly benign chores like hauling trash or cutting grass. Military officials could not understand conscientious objectors who refused these noncombatant jobs. Their frustration would only intensify when a few Mennonites agreed to haul trash and others refused for conscience sake, or when a Mennonite initially acquiesced to officers' demands to work, then changed his mind.

This struggle to define noncombatant work, a struggle shared by military officials and by Mennonite groups alike, became a significant divisive factor in the Mennonites' military experience, causing the most internal strife (as men grappled with the decision of what work they could conscientiously do) and external strife (between Mennonite groups and between Mennonites and the military). The protracted battle continued far beyond the point at which President Wilson defined noncombatant duty, the definition itself inadequately addressing the objectors' concerns to do constructive work yet be outside the control of what they believed was a destructive institution. For this, for their unwillingness to accept any jobs under the government's military arm, the objectors faced derision and mistreatment from soldiers and officers, detainment in detention barracks, courts-martial, and in some cases prison terms in federal penitentiaries.

They received little sympathy from military and governmental officials, who like most Americans believed that able-bodied young men must do their part to serve the country—if only by performing the simplest tasks in military camps. Officials and ordinary citizens alike could not believe that washing dishes might violate one's conscience, nor that hauling garbage could be construed as participating in war. The objectors' actions (or inaction) made them appear even worse than slackers—as friends of the enemy. While other men were toiling on the Western Front, some conscientious objectors refused even to cut the grass at camp headquarters; the contrast was not lost on most observers.

Yet rather than develop policies that would allow objectors to work without compromising their ideals, the government dispatched orders reflecting its misunderstanding of the Mennonites' nonresistant and two-kingdoms ethic, if not the government's own unwillingness to compromise. Neither the Mennonites nor the government was willing to bend its principles or to recast them in ways acceptable to the "other" side. Although President Wilson may have believed his Selective Service Act looked kindly on religious objectors, his vague definition of noncombatant service made relationships between conscientious objectors and the military authorities more strained, as did prescribing noncombatant service as the domain of military, rather than civilian, institutions.

Until President Wilson finally defined noncombatant duty in March 1918, camp officials were left to decide for themselves what noncombatant duty was, and their own definitions varied from camp to camp, officer to officer. When conscientious objectors would not yield to the orders given them they violated military law: refusal to follow an officer's commands, a crime punishable according to military justice by imprisonment. Officials were left with the difficult task of either forcing conscientious objectors to work by whatever means possible or prosecuting them in military courts. Many officers, it seems, sincerely struggled with this difficulty, as Lieutenant Colonel C. E. Kilbourne at Camp Funston asserted in a letter to a Mennonite leader: "I have been so embarrassed by my inability so to govern events in this camp as to reconcile the claims of your people with my duty to the government."[50]

Mennonite conscientious objectors obviously had their own reasons for refusing any form of noncombatant duty. Homan has argued that some were compelled to resist military service by fear; they worried that accepting combatant, or even noncombatant, duty might meet with disfavor at home and church. Most Mennonites, however, were motivated to reject all military duty by their deeply internalized belief in biblical nonresistance, taught by their family and church communities. Biblical peacemaking was an integral part of the Mennonites' heritage and way of life, and rejecting military duty seemed the only appropriate response available a follower of Christ. Wearing a uniform, working in the camps, and drilling represented for them acquiescence to the military, an institution propagating violence and hatred for an enemy, rather than expressing Christ's love.

Furthermore, any form of duty under military authority, however small and seemingly innocuous, might compromise their principles, making it easier for military authorities to foist larger chores upon them. Mennonite conscientious objectors worried that if they cut grass, military officials might reason that objectors could also conscientiously cut and haul wood for the camp. If they did that, an officer might demand they haul ammunition, and so on. Better to avoid that slippery slope by refusing any work under the government's military arm. As one Mennonite conscientious objector said, the "further you went with the military officials the further they demanded one to go. The further I went the less reason I could give for stopping—so I concluded the best place to stop was at the beginning." Homan writes that although many who took menial jobs were not "drawn more deeply into the military net" as Mennonites had feared, their concern still seemed to have merit.[51] Baker's plan, after all, had been to use the kindness of officers as a ploy to convert conscientious objectors to the military's cause.

At its core, the confrontation between military officers and Mennonites over the issue of noncombatant duty again reflected differences in cultural expectations and an unwillingness for either side to forego their own ideologies. Government policy and objector reactions to policy forced a compromise of those principles on both sides. Officers had been trained to form their conscripted recruits into devoted fighting men, by whatever lawful means possible. Most officers longed to see combat duty, and resented being detailed to the boring duty of overseeing conscientious objectors; as Major Walter Kellogg suggested, "no more monotonous or exacting service was rendered than that of the red-blooded Army man whose duty it was to constantly care" for war objectors.[52] And soldiers, most of whom hoped to see action overseas, had been conscripted to become warriors, necessarily ready to answer their officers' every demand.

Additionally, insubordination had long been dealt with in the military not by "tact and consideration" but by brashness and brutality, in-your-face mockery and physical intimidation. Military officials resisted the demand for a kinder, gentler form of training. According to General Leonard Wood, the War Department's policy of "tact and consideration" was "not only a menace to good order and discipline" but it put "a premium on disloyalty."[53] Government policies asked that military officers compromise the military culture they had been taught for the good of conscientious objectors: in this light, we may more readily understand the difficulty military officials might have had in treating insubordinate conscientious objectors with kindness, especially when their nonresistance stance was so inconsonant with military ethos.

Yet the War Department's policy was difficult for Mennonites, too. At center, of course, was the issue of nonresistance: what constituted noncombatant duty, and what could men rightfully do without violating their consciences? Those who for conscience sake chose not to work were also being forced to compromise their culture's expectations: they were rejecting authority and refusing to be productive. A desire to work hard was part of a Mennonite upbringing, forged on farmlands throughout rural communities where young people toiled with their parents to sustain their families' livelihoods. Most Mennonites longed to be useful and felt they could find suitable roles during the war outside the military, by farming or working in civilian institutions. However, the government had decided conscientious objectors should work in camps rather than through civilian avenues. Hence if a Mennonite chose not to perform any military service, he was condemned to idleness in objector detachments, contrary to his nature.

Further, Mennonite youth had long been taught submission to authority—provided that authority did not contradict God's laws. In the military, Mennonites saw this contradiction and chose to disobey the military. Even such insubordination went against their upbringing, however. As the *Gospel Herald* argued in late November 1917, "let us notice that it is not natural for our brethren to act in this way. From their childhood they have been taught submission to constituted authority . . . they are, as a rule, hard working, self-denying, sympathetic, rendering obedience unto the higher powers."[54] Because a "principle is at stake," the article continued, Mennonites were being asked by the government to compromise tenets of their own ethnic upbringing—their desire to be useful and to obey authorities.

Like the military officials, Mennonites had to relinquish some of what they had been taught if they were to remain true to their convictions and stay within lawful bounds. In this light, too, we may more readily understand the difficulty Mennonites might have in being insubordinate, especially when their impulse was to work rather than to remain idle.

Amid this conflict, Mennonite men struggled to decide whether, or to what degree, they could accept noncombatant duty. Their belief in nonresistance, however deeply internalized, would not clearly point the way toward action. After all, Christ had said plenty about loving one's enemy, but he had commanded nothing about hauling military garbage. He had made it clear Christians should not wield a sword but did not mention whether they could wield a dish towel in military camps. The Mennonite history of nonresistance, also well known to Mennonite men, provided little certain illumination either. Mennonites in previous American wars did not have to make such choices, nor had the objectors' persecuted Anabaptist forebears, who urged believers to be "children of peace" but did not say what being a child of peace in the twentieth century required.

Especially in the early months of conscription, Mennonite groups had not constructed any definitive statements outlining what their young men should or should not do within military camps. The objectors were left to decide for themselves what jobs they could conscientiously accept. Most Mennonite men agreed at least to clean their own barracks and to cook their own food. Beyond that, each man made his own decisions, sometimes after agonizing consideration, about what work he could conscientiously do. Some, like Jacob C. Meyer, decided small chores done within the camps would not violate their principles. At Camp Sevier, South Carolina, Meyer forged favorable relationships with his officers, doing their clerical work and running errands. Meyer based his decision to perform these duties on 2 Thessalonians 3:10: "Anyone unwilling to work should not eat."

Others concluded they could accept no work whatsoever under military jurisdiction—not sanitation duty nor even positions in military hospitals. The goal of this service was not, they believed, humanitarian, since hospitals only sought to make men fit for fighting again. Echoing this sentiment, the *Gospel Herald* editorialized on October 4, 1917:

> Even the authorities recognize that a man in hospitals . . . is just as valuable in the work of overcoming the enemy as is the man who carries the rifle and actually shoots . . . Nonresistant people can not consistently have a part in this work, no matter whether their task be considered combatant or noncombatant. This principle must be recognized, or our claims for nonresistance are a farce.[55]

Wishing to stay true to one's pacific faith, therefore, meant refusing all tasks under military authority. This was the position chosen by many Mennonite objectors, who became known as "absolutists" for their unwavering stance.

Punishment was sometimes severe for those who felt they could render no service. Penalties were meted out by angry officers or by soldiers when officers were conveniently absent. At first, the mistreatment was often psychological; it included appeals to the objectors' loyalty and Christian goodwill, as well as taunts, ridicule, and humiliation. If this did not compel conscientious objectors to accept duty, physical abuse followed. Some camps became notorious for mistreatment, especially the smaller cantonments with sparse populations of objectors.

Yet even in a larger and well-established cantonment like Camp Funston, military men continually persecuted conscientious objectors with the acceptance if not blessing of their commanding officer,

Leonard Wood, who himself despised opponents of war. Waldner wrote that when fellow Hutterite Peter Tschetter of South Dakota refused to work at Camp Funston, soldiers said "Write down where we are to send your body for you are now going to be shot." They put a sack over his head and cocked their rifles then slapped two boards together, replicating gun shots. When Tschetter still refused, they threatened to scald him with boiling water. In this way, they forced Tschetter to wash dishes and peel potatoes.[56]

Emanuel Swartzendruber from Pigeon, Michigan, reported that a conscientious objector at Camp Greenleaf, Georgia, was thrown into a cesspool by soldiers, who shoveled sewage onto his head and said "we baptize you in the name of Jesus." The soldiers then choked the other objector and dunked him headfirst in the cesspool. They pulled him out, he recalled, only after asking "three times" if he would "do what they tell me to."[57]

Countless other forms of physical abuse, similar in severity if different in kind to Swartzendruber's, occurred in the country's military cantonments. At Camp Sherman, Ohio, John Witmer from Mahoning County, Ohio, and another Mennonite were forced to stand on boxes in the camp's public square and read their Bibles aloud for four days; masses of soldiers stood by and taunted them. According to Witmer, "this was the lighter of punishments he had received," for on a later occasion, several officers "dragged him down an alley and then charged with bayonets as if to kill him." The bayonets barely missed his head.[58]

Adam Mumaw refused kitchen duty at Camp Zachary Taylor, Kentucky, and was forced to run sprints with an armed soldier watching. When the soldier was dissatisfied with Mumaw's pace, he began chasing the conscientious objector who, despite exhaustion, outsprinted the guard; in this way, Mumaw gained the guard's respect, and they reached a compromise about the work he would do.

Yet compromise was rare. Like other objectors who refused orders to render service, Mennonites were subjected to mock executions, to beatings with fists and rifle butts, to water treatments, to prolonged stays in dank guard houses and a diet of water and bread. Some yielded to military pressure and accepted the work demanded of them. A good number, though, remained steadfast in their convictions, even after painful beatings or long days in the guardhouse.

At times men ceased working after several months in camp, infuriating their superiors further. The objector might decide he could abet the war machine no more, or that he had been duped by military authorities, or he sensed that his officers were attempting to draw him into the "military net." Such was the case of Noah Leatherman at Camp Funston. At first he agreed to haul garbage, told by military officials that "the work they wanted us to do was not at all military work but simply civilian service." According to Leatherman, he and his fellow objectors were informed that if they decided they "could not do the work," they could make complaints later. Yet when eight conscientious objectors refused to work on a Sunday several days later, they were taken to a nearby field and beaten with rifle butts. Another two weeks passed, and Leatherman realized "that the officers were endeavoring to gradually work us all into the Army and regular military service." Yet when he told his lieutenant he could no longer haul garbage, he was put in the guard house, fed a diet of bread and water, and forced to sleep on the cold cement floor. According to Leatherman, he was being punished so severely because "the lieutenant now claimed we had no right to say we were 'conscientious' about doing this work as we had been doing it so long." Nonetheless, Leatherman worked no more in the camp's sanitation department; he was later court-martialed and sent to Fort Leavenworth penitentiary for insubordination.[59]

Conscientious objectors came to conclusions about work, like Leatherman, only after continuous thought, prayer, and discussion with others, including Mennonite ministers. Gaeddert, who hauled trash with Leatherman at Camp Funston, reached a markedly different conclusion than his friend and continued to perform duties within the camp. He did so only after many "thots," discussions with former college professors and family, and correspondence with the Mennonite leader H. P. Krehbiel. Writing to Krehbiel on January 15, 1918, Gaeddert wished to know if the work he was doing in sanitation should be considered "evil." His query came, in part, because the (Old) Mennonites at Camp Funston had ceased working and were being readied for a move to detention barracks. Gaeddert wondered if "they" (presumably meaning General Conference Mennonites, of whom he was one) should join their Mennonite compatriots or persist in their present work.

Krehbiel's lengthy response, written several days letter, was significant:

> It is plain that the way of duty in the position which you have been placed is not always clear ... It again raises the old question in everyones mind, 'Am I doing military service when I do any work of any kind, inside of the camp?' And according as this question is answered so must consistently be the attitude of those who believe that Christ disapproves of war in any form. If

that question is answered finally and clearly, yes, work in the camp, any kind of work is military service, then no work can be done without violating conscience. However if the answer is—some lines of work are not military service, but only some work done of a useful nature inside of a military camp, but not thereby a military service, then very evidently work of that kind may be done in the military camp without doing violence to conscience.[60]

If, Krehbiel wrote to Gaeddert, one's conscience admits he can accept "purely utilitarian work about the camp," he should make it known that he will "do it gladly in the spirit of our Master Jesus Christ to serve and do good in such ways as are open to us." In the end, Krehbiel's message helped Gaeddert choose to continue with small chores, though Gaeddert had already admitted he did not believe his work was detrimental.

Krehbiel's advice provides insight not only about Gaeddert's case but about the General Conference Mennonite ethos Krehbiel voiced, and the ways that ethos differed from the (Old) Mennonites. The letter suggested that only Gaeddert and other men could conscientiously decide whether they could work in camps; their actions simply needed to remain consistent with those decisions. In this, Krehbiel reflected the General Conference conviction of individual autonomy—the understanding that the church could not dictate rules of faith and practice, but that each believer must interpret the Bible's message and live accordingly. In addition, Krehbiel's letter hinted at a disagreement many General Conference Mennonites had with other Mennonite groups regarding the roles men should play in military camps. While General Conference Mennonites predominantly believed conscientious objectors could accept some work, other Mennonites took a harder line.

At the center of this disagreement, it seems, were the two largest Mennonite bodies, the General Conference Mennonites and the (Old) Mennonite Church. Each group established its own committees to address the concerns of their brethren responding to the draft and reporting to military camps. The (Old) Mennonites constructed a War Problems Committee, and the General Conference Mennonites had an Exemption Committee representing the entire conference, as well as an Exemption Committee formed by Western District constituents. Representatives from these committees actively lobbied Washington in the months preceding conscription, and continued working on the conscientious objectors' behalf once they entered military camps. Committee members visited Washington officials as well as officers in military cantonments, wrote letters, and ultimately, suggested that their young men take some form of action, or inaction, as the case may be.

Yet often, the suggestions these committees made remained vague or were inconsistent with those made by other committees. This led to apparently incongruous action on the part of conscientious objectors who decided themselves, with the sometimes imprecise guidance of committee statements and church ministers, whether they could render any form of noncombatant service. In turn, this seeming inconsistency aggravated military officials, who believed disparity in action hinted at the conscientious objectors' general insincerity and poor moral character.

One of the first supposedly definitive statements of action made by a Mennonite group was that of the General Conference Mennonite Church, whose Exemption Committee advised its draftees in September 1917 to, as Gerlof Homan writes, "accept only service designed to support and to save life. They were not to participate in any work that would result in personal injury."[61] Some conscientious objectors must have been struck by the vagueness of this statement, as it still failed to prescribe action: Would accepting kitchen work "support life"? Would hauling trash? After all, these jobs sustained the well being of those in the camps. Once again, Mennonite men would be compelled to decide for themselves whether the duties ordered them fell within the realm of the committee's guidelines; once again, they would reach different conclusions.

However, the Western District Exemption Committee of the General Conference arrived at no clearer statement. This committee agreed that men could accept work which supported life outside military jurisdiction; that they should not perform any work that led to injury or loss of life; and that any work demanded of them that "virtually constituted military service" should be done "only under protest."[62] In this, the General Conference Mennonite Church seemingly suggested its men could render service in military camps if they made their objections known. The church still remained imprecise on what "constituted military service," thereby failing to provide any clear guidance to young men already in camps. Nor did the church outline how the men should voice their objections or how expressing objections assuaged the men's scruples against accepting military work.

Despite the vagueness of their statements, the General Conference Mennonite committees agreed that their men could perform some types of duty in camps. In this, they at first disagreed with the (Old)

Mennonite Church's Military Problems Committee, who believed the conscientious objectors should completely refuse to cooperate with military authorities and so incur placement in detention barracks. Many men did this upon entering military camps, facing the ire of military men and the idleness of detention. Though the (Old) Mennonite Church's position probably caused increased mistreatment for conscientious objectors, and though it contradicted the clearly more open stance taken by their General Conference brethren, the definitive statement nevertheless proved useful to conscientious objectors. Unlike General Conference Mennonites, who had to interpret vague position statements given them by their leaders, some (Old) Mennonite men knew what the church expected of them, and what they should do when ordered to perform chores.

Although these various Mennonite committees many times did not work in concord during the Great War, several events in the first months of 1918 compelled them more readily to see and even agree with each other's positions. First, in early January, delegates from eight Mennonite bodies convened in Goshen, Indiana, and drafted a statement to the effect that Mennonite conscientious objectors could not and so would not render either combatant or noncombatant service. The statement, sent to President Wilson, reflected the varying Mennonites' general agreement about the role their men should take in military camps, although once again the term "noncombatant" remained imprecise.

Several months later, Mennonites together reacted negatively to Wilson's final definition of "noncombatant duty," coming nearly one year after he signed the Selective Service Act into law. Mennonites had eagerly anticipated Wilson's statement, as they believed it might ease some of their young men's difficulties in camps. Yet the President's definition failed to alleviate much of anything.

In late March, conscientious objectors already in military cantonments were called together by their commanding officers and were read Wilson's order. Men were told they had three options if deemed exempt from combatant duty: they could work in the medical corps, in the quartermaster corps, or in the engineering corps. Those who refused these assignments, the order said, "shall be segregated as far as practicable and placed under the command of a specially qualified officer of tact and judgment, who will be instructed to impose no punitive hardship of any kind upon them." Wilson's decree also stipulated that, should they refuse all jobs, objectors could face a court-martial and imprisonment under Articles of War 64 and 65, "the willful disobedience of a lawful order or command."[63]

Not much had changed for Mennonite conscientious objectors. Though the government now offered a more precise interpretation of noncombatancy, the jobs provided by the executive order still fell under military rule, and still in the Mennonites' estimation required that they abet warfare. And, now more than ever military officers had the force of law in making conscientious objectors perform noncombatant duty, especially as the government gave the military license to court-martial objectors who seemed insincere or disloyal in their refusal to accept noncombatant service. Wilson's edict had not improved life for Mennonite conscientious objectors. If anything, they would now face more difficulty.

(Old) Mennonite leaders clearly understood this. According to historian Homan, the Military Problems Committee altered its stance, and now encouraged men to accept some chores within the camps. In addition to anticipating harsher trials for the men, committee members also were proceeding with more caution because of concern that their recommendations to objectors might violate the Espionage and Sedition Acts. Two members of the committee, Aaron Loucks and J. S. Hartzler, therefore told Mennonite men they should not openly refuse officers' demands, but should explain "mildly" why they found an order unacceptable.

According to Homan, Loucks and Hartzler reasoned that conscientious objectors could clean up around their barracks and cook, for in rejecting even these jobs men "were bringing trials upon themselves." Objectors might choose to wear a uniform if they wished. And, though Mennonites might still have to suffer in camps, "suffering for Christ would be an opportunity to glorify God more than they could possibly do at home or anywhere else."[64] In this, (Old) Mennonites came more into line with General Conference Mennonites who even after Wilson's edict predominantly believed their men could render some service and even wear the uniform, if their consciences allowed it.

Although Mennonite leaders now agreed to a greater extent about what their men should do in camps, little else changed for Mennonite objectors following President Wilson's order. Mennonite men continued to be drafted, continued to board trains bound for military camps, and continued to struggle with whether they should drill, wear a uniform, and accept noncombatant service. The imprecise language of church committee statements did not offer complete and clear guidance for Mennonite men in camps, who were still left to search their own consciences and to decide for themselves what action they could take within camps.

As before, Mennonite objectors reached differing conclusions about what military obligations they could meet; as before, military officials reacted differently to the conclusions they reached. Some Mennonites did accept duty under Wilson's plan, joining the medical, quartermaster, or engineering corps, and therefore experienced few problems with fellow soldiers and noncombatant workers. Many other objectors, however, would not sign up for noncombatant service under Wilson's plan, even if they continued to do small jobs around the camp. These men would in some cases receive abuse and/or courts-martial for their insubordination. Most would be placed in conscientious objector detachments, consigned to further idleness, still providing no service useful to their country, and wondering what would happen next.

The Military Camp Experience

Mistreatment, emotional turmoil, and conflict with military authorities: these things certainly colored Mennonite conscientious objectors' experiences during the Great War. Of course, one cannot really forget abuse, loneliness and isolation, a defining moment in a young life. Yet, though Mennonites' written texts mentioned the trials they received, rarely did such trials become a writer's sole focus. Instead, according to one Mennonite objector, "Somehow one does not care to remember the hardships and does not like to write about them. We would rather think of the goodness and mercy of God in carrying us through, and forget the unpleasant experiences."[65] Certainly this is not entirely true, since many conscientious objectors did remember—sometimes all too vividly—their painful time during the Great War, and did write about their "hardships." In addition to recounting their struggle during military confinement, though, the narratives of Mennonite conscientious objectors told another story as well: of life in conscientious objector detachments and of a brotherhood forged through shared experiences there.

Adam Mumaw's "Second Company Development Battalion" provided a detailed account of what a conscientious objector unit might look like. As in many places, the conscientious objector detachment was separated from the rest of the camp. Mumaw's unit at Camp Zachary Taylor, Kentucky, had its own tents for occupation in summer and its own barracks for winter, as well as a separate latrine. Most camps had their own mess halls where the conscientious objectors cooked their meals. Often, Mumaw wrote, their food rivaled any made by army regulars and received the accolades of officers who ate there. At a few camps, conscientious objectors shared mess halls with soldiers in training. At Camp Sevier, objectors were asked to serve meals in the same mess hall as stockade prisoners, something objectors did for a short while, but only under protest. Although not assigned to noncombatant duty, most conscientious objectors still cleaned their own living quarters, mess halls, and latrines daily. In addition to these light chores, some ran errands or did "office duty," including all-night stints by the company telephone.

In conscientious objector units, men did not always feel threatened by armed guards nor imprisoned by their detainment—though officers still commanded the units and soldiers bearing guns were posted as guards nearby. At some camps, objectors could leave barracks by receiving passes for varying lengths of time. Shorter passes were on rare occasions granted so men could visit camp canteens and sometimes nearby towns to buy goods, including candy and stamps. At Camps Sevier and Jackson, Jacob C. Meyer was given a "permanent pass" of this nature, and often spent his days wandering from canteen to his unit, purchasing goods he would then sell to his brethren.

Longer passes, usually of twenty-four to forty-eight hours, were issued less frequently. Those living close enough used one- or two-day passes to journey home for visits, traveling at night to be with their families by day. During their home stays, Mennonite objectors gave testimony in their churches about life in the military, received prayer and sometimes monetary gifts, and shared meals with church and extended family before once again bidding a sad farewell and returning to camp. Adam Mumaw wrote that these passes were sometimes withheld from conscientious objectors as a means of punishment or as an inducement to make men "take some kind of service with promise of freedom."[66] Still, as much as men cherished their visits with family, Mumaw was convinced that they did not compromise their principles to buy passes home.

Ministers often visited camps and gave sermons to the men. While a few camps, especially those close to Mennonite communities, received ministers often, other cantonments were rarely if ever visited by a Mennonite pastor and objectors there relied on the ministrations of leaders from other churches. Camp officials could also withhold the possibility of church services with the men's pastors, turning the civilians away at the camp entrance or demanding that they could preach to but not talk with the men. Speaking with their brethren was an important aspect of the ministerial visits, though, as doing so allowed men to voice their concerns, to ask questions, and to receive spiritual guidance. Perhaps military officials knew this, and knew that prohibiting Mennonite ministers in camp was another way to goad the conscientious objectors.

When Mennonite pastors were absent, officers might arrange for a YMCA minister to speak. From all indications, Mennonites did not always enjoy worshipping with these ministers, who often voiced the country's then-predominating theology of trench salvation and holy war. So much did Ura Hostetler dislike such preaching that on one occasion, he wrote in his diary that "some civilian Anti Christ was here and talked to us something awful. May God show him the light before it is to late . . . Claimed to be a minister of the gospel?"[67]

On nearly every day save Sunday, military officers recommended and sometimes compelled the conscientious objectors to take walks in the fields and hills surrounding the camps; the hikes could stretch as far as ten or twenty miles. Most men did not complain, as physical exercise staved off idleness and mental and spiritual dullness. Once in the countryside, the men sometimes sat together and studied their Bibles, using the peaceful space away from camp to worship their God. Physical exertion might continue when the men returned to camp, as they hauled and chopped wood for their kitchens or practiced baseball and football; they bought their own sports equipment and shared it with the detachment. Mumaw reported that in his camp the men had a healthy competition running during football games between married and single men. Hostetler suggested that at Camp Funston competition was more of a peaceful Mennonite brand; "base ball" was "played in good humor, but not as rival teams as world mostly plays."[68]

Other than the hikes, games, and small jobs around the camp, the conscientious objectors were mostly consigned to idleness, boredom, and feelings of uselessness, as most anyone would be when confined against his will. With hours upon hours yawning before them, men sought whatever means possible to remain active and useful. Some men took up woodworking and made simple furniture for their barracks and for their officers. At Camp Jackson, Meyer wrote, the Amish grumbled about the furniture they made, only because inferior tools compromised their handwork. Mumaw and his brethren at Camp Zachary Taylor learned the art of designing and sewing pillow tops. Mumaw believed one of his own creations, made with red, white, and blue threads, was stolen by his officer.[69] In the evenings the men would sometimes sing hymns together or would have a devotional period with one man acting as leader.

Whenever possible, objectors wrote letters and read books and denominational publications. At Camp Jackson, Jacob C. Meyer spent his time perusing books from the YMCA library stacks, and listed in his diary the works he read, including the classic epics of Homer and the contemporary novels of H. G. Wells. Several bunkmates, however, could not even read, and relied on Meyer's help to write letters home and to love interests. In time, Meyer's officers suggested that he and other educated conscientious objectors establish a school in their detachment. This they readily did, with course work covering the sciences, languages, and technical skills like typing.

The conscientious objector's life was not usually contented. Faced with the stifling monotony of their daily routine, objectors longed for a way to be useful, for a way to combat the idleness that made them sluggish and dull-headed. Small chores little quelled this drive, nor did games of baseball or hikes in the country. What they really wanted was to work—outside military jurisdiction of course—in a way that would prove themselves productive members of wartime society.

Idleness also increased their loneliness, as unoccupied time could readily be filled with thoughts of home and family. In both Ura Hostetler's and Gustav Gaeddert's diaries, the men's longing for home was closely related to their feelings of boredom. When they were busy, home was further from their minds. Hostetler admitted again and again that he was dreadfully homesick, so "blue" that he didn't "know where to go or what to do"; his only solace was ice cream, which he bought to cheer himself up.[70] Letters and visits to the camp from family and friends helped ease this loneliness temporarily, but ultimately intensified the men's homesickness. Hostetler wrote in his diary that he cried after reading letters from his wife; Gaeddert admitted he cried when he had to say good-bye to a brother visiting from Oklahoma.

Men profoundly felt their separation from loved ones, especially when someone at home had fallen ill or died, rather common occurrences in an influenza-plagued era. Wives and children died while men were in camp, as did parents and siblings. Although objectors were often granted passes to visit dying relatives or to attend funerals, they also had to return quickly to camp, where idleness encouraged them to dwell on their loss and only deepened their loneliness.

Some Relief: Furloughs and the Board of Inquiry

As 1918 progressed, conscientious objectors remained in military camps throughout the country. The war raged on, and thousands upon thousands of soldiers marched out of their cantonments, boarded trains bound for the east, then left for Europe. New men responded to the draft, journeyed to camp, and prepared for war, or else refused duty and accepted detainment in conscientious objector detachments. Meanwhile, additional registrations and extended age requirements (now from eighteen to forty-five) brought new replacements to the camps. Rumors about the possibility of a farm furlough began to spread through conscientious objector units, though no one—not officers or Mennonite leaders—could confirm the stories' accuracy. Until such meaningful work outside the military could be granted them, Mennonite men persisted in the same course, rendering service as their consciences saw fit, facing the monotony of another day spent idly and away from home.

Plans for enacting farm furloughs were indeed afoot, although not necessarily as a means of addressing the conscientious objector problem. Instead, the furlough law of March 16, 1918, was a response to the shortage of agricultural labor occasioned by the war. The law stipulated that soldiers who volunteered could be dispatched by Secretary of War Baker to render service on farms or in industry.

The legislation said nothing of the furlough's applicability for conscientious objectors, although some scholars have argued that the Farm Furlough Act was indeed intended for objectors. Historian Juhnke notes that President Wilson considered this legislation for conscientious objectors in February 1918.[71] However, Assistant Secretary of War Frederick Keppel, who oversaw the country's conscientious objector affairs, knew nothing of the act until May 15, 1918; likewise, in late April 1918, the Mennonite Gaeddert wrote in his diary with some disappointment that he had "learned that the furlough is not for us."[72] When the possibility of using the law for conscientious objectors did arise, governmental leaders argued that farm furloughs would solve nothing for military officials nor for objectors. Said the acting judge advocate general, "To use the Act of March 16, 1918, as a means of enabling so-called conscientious objectors to evade their statutory obligations would be to violate its spirit, and to furlough them as a mere subterfuge for exempting them from noncombatant military service would be plainly illegal."[73]

Nevertheless, Baker ultimately decided that conscientious objectors could be furloughed as well. Those who qualified would be sent to farms requesting assistance, where they would earn a private's wages of $30 a month. Any money made in excess would be sent to the Red Cross. Under the furlough legislation, a few men would also be granted relief work overseas with the American Friends Service

Committee, rebuilding the infrastructure of a war-torn continent. Mennonite conscientious objectors were by and large thrilled at the prospect of leaving the camps, even if they were not going home. They would finally be able to do something useful outside of the military's domain, and would be performing duties that many of them knew well and at which many excelled.

On June 1, 1918, Baker established the Board of Inquiry, composed of three men who visited military camps and met with conscientious objectors. After examining each man, the Board determined his sincerity as a war objector and recommended furloughing of those deemed sincere in their refusal to accept noncombatant or combatant duty. The Board was composed of two civilians: Harlan F. Stone, Dean of the Columbia University Law School, and Julian W. Mack, Judge of the United States Circuit Court of Appeals. The military had one representative, Major Richard C. Stoddard. When Stoddard was called overseas in August 1918, Major Walter G. Kellogg assumed his place. Kellogg would later write a book detailing his perceptions of conscientious objectors and of his time examining them.

In early June, the Board of Inquiry began its trek across the country, stopping at each cantonment to meet with the 2,100 conscientious objectors still detained in military camps.[74] Beyond the rigors of traveling, the Board of Inquiry faced an arduous chore: how could they certify the sincerity of men with only the men's pledge of sincerity to guide them? This "difficulty of determining the sincerity with which a conviction is held" was well recognized by Kellogg, who said doing so required that they "plumb the depths of a man's mind with the purpose of finding if truth is at the bottom."[75] The tools they had for plumbing minds were sparse, as was the time allotted the examination of each man and of each camp. Still, despite the potentially complex task of ascertaining the sincerity of a man's convictions, the examinations soon became "tedious" according to Stone, who said he hated facing the "long lines of stolid, bovine-faced Dunkards, Mennonites, Hutterites, and the like, each one supremely interested in the salvation of his own soul even though the world perish."[76]

For their part, the seemingly "bovine-faced" objectors anticipated meeting with the Board of Inquiry, seeing the examination as a chance to tell their own stories, to have their sincerity finally certified, and to receive their furloughs. Wrote Kellogg: "Occasionally the objectors were not informed that the Board of Inquiry was present and about to examine them; they nevertheless displayed a willingness to be questioned, whether or not they knew by whom or for what purposes the examination was to be conducted.... They appeared to welcome the visitation of 'The Board of Washington' and in all cases that I remember they evinced no reluctance whatever to answer questions of any sort that were put to them."[77]

If notified ahead of time, men prepared well for their examination; their officers asked them to shave, clean, and make themselves and their detachment presentable. Anticipation was often mixed with fear, as conscientious objectors did not completely know what to expect nor what questions would be asked of them: Would they be judged insincere? Would their troubles continue? For Adam Mumaw as for others the Bible provided the sustenance needed to face the Board. Directly before his examination, Mumaw related to an anxious friend the verses found in Luke 12:11-12 (KJV): "And when they bring you unto the synagogues and unto the magistrates and powers. Take no thought how or what thing ye shall answer or what ye shall say. For the Holy Ghost shall teach you in the same hour what ye shall say." The passage must have been useful for Mumaw, who was deemed sincere in his objection, and "marveled at the fairness" of the Board's "intelligence." His friend left the examination "Prais[ing] the Lord" because he could answer every question "with Scripture."[78]

At every camp the Board visited, men lined up to await their hearing. Sometimes they appeared singly before the three examiners; sometimes, especially when religious objectors like Mennonites, groups appeared before the Board, and little time was spent on individual objectors. During an examination the Board would first attempt to determine a Mennonite's religious convictions by his church membership certificate.[79] His sincerity could be ascertained if he was a member of a recognized peace church before April 6, 1917, the beginning of American's war intervention. If he had been baptized and joined the church after this date, his sincerity was considered suspicious, necessitating even more questions about the man's faith.

In most every case, after investigating an objector's church membership the Board generally asked a man several questions, as Jacob C. Meyer related: "Do you use liquor or tobacco? Do you use profane language? Have you lived a pure sex life? Are you a church member? Do you get angry? ... Are you afraid of death? Do you feel you can do more good by not taking a life?"[80] A conscientious objector might also be asked about his feelings regarding the war and about whether he wanted Germany or the Allies to win. Undoubtedly, most men knew the appropriate response to a query about Allied victories.

According to the historian David Kennedy, the Board—or at least Kellogg—was "hell-bent on shaming men out of their declared convictions," and sometimes provoked the objectors, asking on one occasion why a man belonged "to some nut society" and saying on another, "If I didn't know that you were a conscientious objector, I would take you for a good wholesome boy."[81] Meyer reported that after his own interview, Kellogg lamented that Meyer was far too intelligent to waste his talents on conscientious objection.

The Board also bombarded men with hypothetical questions, asking them how far they could be provoked before fighting back: What if they were face to face with a Hun? What if their houses were being robbed? What if their wives were being raped? Kellogg said that, "in all likelihood," a Mennonite would respond to such questions by testifying "that if some brute were to break into his mother's or sister's room and attempt to rape her, he would allow his mother or sister to be raped before he would shoot or otherwise injure her assailant."[82] Though consistent with the Mennonite doctrine of "resisting not evil," this response seemed unfathomable to Kellogg and perhaps to other members of the Board.

During most examinations, Mennonite men relied on Scripture that supported their nonresistant stance, including the Gospel of Matthew, Paul's letter to the Romans, and the witness of Christ's pacific life. Answering hypothetical questions no doubt proved more difficult, although the objectors still formed answers based on the biblical admonishment to love rather than strike their persecutors. For Mennonites as for other religious objectors, the ability to answer the questions "with Scripture" may have granted them furloughs but not necessarily the Board's respect. Indeed, the Mennonites' reliance on their biblical knowledge earned them the derision of Kellogg and Stone. Both men expressed dismay that some Mennonite conscientious objectors were not familiar with current events, could not identify what the *Lusitania* was, and did not recognize the names of Edith Cavell, General Foch, or General Pershing—all major players in the Great War.[83] How, the Board wondered, could these men be U.S. citizens and not know their own country's history and affairs, even as they knew every passage of the Bible?

Board of Inquiry members believed Mennonites mentally incompetent. As Stone commented in 1919, "all in all they presented a depressing example of dense ignorance of what was going on in the world, and stolid indifference to those moral and political questions which were so profoundly stirring the minds and hearts of their fellow countrymen."[84] Kellogg postulated that Mennonites were not only "ignorant" but also so "intellectually inferior" that they were "unworthy" of being American citizens. He wrote:

I doubt extremely if fifty per cent of the Mennonites examined, because of their ignorance and stupidity, ever should have been admitted into the Army at all; I am certain that ninety per cent of them need a far better preparation for citizenship than they have ever received . . . they are, doubtless, according to their lights, good Christians, but they are essentially a type of Americans of which America cannot be proud.[85]

Although Kellogg and Stone nearly always certified the Mennonite men as sincere and granted them furloughs, their indictment of Mennonites as "stupid" and "bovine-faced" idiots must have also reflected their general biases against Mennonites or their lack of appreciation for Mennonite culture. It is true that less than ten percent of Mennonite conscientious objectors received education beyond the eighth grade, but intelligence tests given to objectors during the Great War showed that the Mennonites scored higher than a normal company of draftees and above enlisted privates. Several studies published in 1920 reported, in fact, that more than 81 percent of conscientious objectors had "average" or "better than average" scores for intelligence, surpassed only by sergeants, commissioned officers, and candidates for officer's training.[86]

Of the more than 2,100 conscientious objectors examined by the Board of Inquiry, some 1,500 received furloughs, many Mennonites among them; 88 others were recommended for service with the American Friends Service Committee and began making arrangements for travel overseas. Another 390 were ordered to take noncombatant duty, and 120 were deemed insincere and assigned to combatant service.[87] Some of the men granted furloughs were assigned as well to mental hospitals. This was considered acceptable work by Mennonites because they would serve under civilian auspices, and because objectors affirmed that these hospitals were meant not to destroy human life, but to return patients to civilian life rather than to war.

Those receiving furloughs were, of course, eager to leave camp and begin to work. In some camps, however, officials continued to foment trouble for conscientious objectors, ignoring furloughs, detaining men in camp, and court-martialing those who refused to obey orders—even though the men were supposed to be on farms and working.[88]

Additionally, a few objectors met resentment once dispatched to the farms. An item in the *Oklahoma Leader* noted that conscientious objectors from Camp Dodge, Iowa, faced "threats of bodily harm" when furloughed to some Iowa farms, and the state's governor demanded that objectors be returned to camp.[89] Community members did not want objectors working in nearby fields when their own boys were dying in France.

Many other objectors were lucky enough to begin working on farms requesting their help, and faced no resistance from the surrounding communities. Mennonite farmers participated as well in the furloughing system, responding to notices placed in Mennonite publications that asked for farmers to apply for help. The furlough law dictated that a man be placed on farms at least fifty miles from his home community, but some worked closer than that; others, farther away from home but on Mennonite farms nonetheless, cherished the chance to attend Mennonite church services and to be in a Mennonite community again.

Though some objectors missed the brotherhood of camp, leaving the military environment was a relief, as was the opportunity to forego idleness, to take up the plow, and to feel again like useful and contributing citizens. Ura Hostetler, on a farm in Mason City, Iowa, detailed his first-day furlough chores: "polic[ing] up the horse stable," cutting weeds, and thrashing wheat. In this, the last words of his diary's final entry, Hostetler admitted that furloughing "Beats Army life all allow."[90] Gustav Gaeddert, shipped out to work at the Iowa State Hospital farm after nearly a year in camp, wrote that this "first nite of Freedom" felt so wonderful it was "not to be expressed in words."[91]

For many Mennonite objectors, receiving a furlough meant essentially that they were freed from military camps until the war's end. Following the declaration of Allied victory, conscientious objectors were called back to camp and discharged, as were those still in camp but deemed sincere by the Board of Inquiry. Before their discharge, men were required to sign the payroll. Many objectors had refused to do this during the war, believing that, as the *Gospel Herald* argued on November 1, 1917:

> If we accept the pay we consent to the idea that we have rendered military service. To accept it under such circumstances ... would show that they gave their consent to such service and would put a club into the hands of those who have been contending that Mennonites ought to be forced to do military service since they do not refuse to accept money or otherwise profit from the fortunes and misfortunes of war.[92]

However, to be lawfully discharged in November 1918, the men were compelled to accept pay; officers would not release discharge papers until this occurred. Thus most Mennonite men signed the payroll and received earnings for work in camp and on the farm. Most immediately sent the money directly back to the U.S. Treasury or forwarded their pay to relief agencies, asserting that as conscientious objectors they had no claim to it. A press release from the War Department News Bureau, issued on February 26, 1919, noted that the War Department received nearly $4,500 from conscientious objectors in the few months following the war; another $270 was given to the YMCA and $4,000 to the American Friends Service Committee. Thus nearly $9,000 of soldiers' pay was rejected by conscientious objectors, who were unwilling to accept what they felt was the Army's blood money.[93]

Prisoners of War

Still, Armistice Day and an Allied victory did not signal the end of wartime experience for all conscientious objectors. While their brethren received discharges and returned to home and family, other objectors remained imprisoned, a few manacled to their cells nine hours a day. Many of these prisoners, Mennonites among them, had been court-martialed and given lengthy prison terms of ten or twenty-five years, their sentences mandated by policies the government established in early 1918 and encouraged by public pressure to punish objectors. Regarded as common criminals, these objectors shared cell blocks with rapists and murderers and were compelled again to live in a world diametrically opposed to their own. Mistreatment continued in the prisons, and several objectors died as a result of abuses received there. For Mennonite conscientious objectors imprisonment would be the last chapter in their corporate narrative about the Great War; perhaps it was the most tragic chapter as well.

Before March 1918, only forty conscientious objectors in the country had been court-martialed, none of them Mennonites. After March, when the government imposed stricter guidelines for conscientious objectors, some 500 faced trials and prison; about 142 of these were Mennonites.[94] The March 1918 declaration of what constituted noncombatant service first endorsed the use of military courts to punish objectors "who fail or refuse to comply with lawful orders by reason of alleged religious or other conscientious scruples."[95] Shortly thereafter, Secretary Baker made military justice a more readily available tool for addressing conscientious objector problems, ordering that any objector engaging in propaganda, any appearing insincere in his beliefs, or any who was "sullen and defiant" should be "promptly brought to trial by court martial."[96] Military authorities now had a ready and legal device to punish objectors. Many officers made enthusiastic use of Baker's orders, charging objectors for "sullen and defiant" behavior and for refusing to obey orders, throwing them into camp guardhouses, and taking them to trial. Included in this number were men who had been seen by the Board of Inquiry and who had been granted furloughs, but whose officers kept them in camp—and then charged them with insubordination when they refused to obey orders.

Most objectors were charged with violating Articles of War 64 and 65, "the willful disobedience of a lawful order or command." Specifically, conscientious objectors who were commanded and refused to wear a uniform, to drill, or to perform duties ordered them could be tried if an officer chose to make such charges. Obviously, many military authorities refrained from interpreting the articles in this manner, given the large number of objectors who were not court-martialed for refusing to comply with military obligations. Those who escaped trial and prison, those who received furloughs and then discharges, were sometimes unlike their brethren only in one aspect: their officers remained truer to Baker's order to treat conscientious objectors with "tact and kindness" as well as "to impose no punitive hardship of any kind upon" those not rendering service, drilling, or wearing a uniform.

Most Mennonites brought to trial stood before five to fifteen men in a general court-martial, with a judge advocate or prosecutor presiding. Two Mennonites received a summary court-martial, arbitrated by only one officer who could sentence a man to not more than three months. Unlike a civilian court, a military court was not intended to "secure justice but to enforce and maintain military discipline," and those hearing the charges were not impartial; their opinions about conscientious objectors were shared by a majority of military men.[97] The panel hearing the case could not impose a sentence but could only recommend judgment to the commanding officer, who would then approve the court's decision.

A trial was in many ways perfunctory and pro forma. The abbreviated duration of the trials—some lasted a mere ten minutes or less—suggested as well that the trials were only a formality. Defendants had the right to civilian counsel, but only eleven Mennonites chose this avenue.[98] Further, though objectors were allowed counsel, during the Great War the counsel was not required to be a lawyer and did not spend much time with each defendant; some objectors reported that their counsel expressed open hostility to the man he was representing. Of his own court-martial John Neufeld wrote that the "counsil introduced himself about 15 min before our trial" and "told us that he would do the best he could for us, but that he really had no sympathy for us."[99] Often the counsel allowed defendants to testify in their own behalf, as detrimental as that testimony might prove.

The transcript of Neufeld's court-martial reflected the general tenor and procedure of conscientious objector trials during this time. Detained at Camp Cody, New Mexico, Neufeld was tried on July 17, 1918, for failing to obey a sergeant's order to drill with arms. Several officers testified at the trial that Neufeld had refused the demands, although none mentioned that, according to Neufeld's diary, the officers beat him for his insubordination. During Neufeld's examination the prosecution used a battery of questions similar to those applied at other courts-martial: What was his church membership? What did his church teach? To which church did his family belong? Why did he disobey orders? Did he wish for an Allied or a German victory? Did he believe Germany was being punished for its sins?

Like other conscientious objectors, Neufeld testified in his own defense, arguing that the order he disobeyed was not lawful, as it "contradicted the order of the War Department of May 30th" which said "that no person after he has made known his position as a conscientious objector shall be required to participate in any drill, in any form, that is contrary to his conscience." He articulated the biblical beliefs of his church and clarified his position on the war and his feelings toward Germany. In addition to the testimony of officers and of Neufeld, a psychologist who had examined the objector testified for the prosecution. Although, or perhaps because Neufeld had "a rather superior intelligence," the psychologist said, the objector's "conscientious scruples" were merely a means of escaping duty. Neufeld's cousin A. F. Neufeld was called by the defense to testify to the defendant's dedication to church principles. A. F. Neufeld's testimony little mattered, especially as he too was being court-martialed for disobeying orders. John Neufeld received a sentence of fifteen years and was soon transferred to Fort Leavenworth, Kansas. Though seemingly excessive, Neufeld's sentence was in actuality less severe than those of nearly half the Mennonite objectors tried during 1918, who received sentences of twenty-five or more years in jail.[100]

By November 1918, Fort Leavenworth had become what historian Stephen Kohn describes as a "concentration camp" for conscientious objectors, as most were housed in the Leavenworth penitentiary so that the government could localize and control any objector problems.[101] Once at the prison conscientious objectors were given a psychological exam, clothes emblazoned with their prison numbers, a book of rules, and a stark choice: accept work in the prison, or be placed in solitary confinement. A majority of Mennonite men chose to accept work, believing that since they were no longer under military rule they could work with a clear conscience. Noah Leatherman, sentenced to twenty-five years at Leavenworth, justified his decision to work by saying: "I certainly commend the ones who chose solitary and did not give up their faith because of hardship. I may have yielded somewhat here through weakness of the flesh for I thought I was here for punishment since they had stopped trying to make a soldier out of me. So I decided to try the work and if it conflicted with my faith, to refuse to do any more."[102]

If they chose employment and proved themselves trustworthy, the objectors were placed on "Star Parole," meaning they could work outside the prison grounds and under relaxed guard, since they were considered no threat to escape or to instigate violence. Star Parole jobs varied from working on farms to sewing civilian clothes for soon-to-be released prisoners. Leatherman spent his days digging stumps and pulling turnips, a "cold and disagreeable job" because the ground was frozen.[103] John Neufeld, working and living in a dairy barn near the prison, found the work "not hard . . . and as such I liked pretty good."[104]

Conscientious objectors who refused to render service once in prison did not find conditions "pretty good." Holding no distinction between being an objector in a military camp and a prisoner of the federal government, these men continued to believe that working in prison helped support the war; as Old German Baptist Brethren member Maurice A. Hess of McPherson, Kansas, told Leatherman, "without [the prison] they could not carry on this war."[105] For their convictions the objectors were placed in solitary confinement, manacled to the prison bars for nine hours daily, and fed a diet of bread and water. If the objectors relented and accepted work, they would be released to a normal cell; although Leatherman was "told that no man had ever been known to have stayed in solitary longer than four days," Hess remained confined for thirty-six days, and still refused to work.[106] Manacling could be particularly painful, as men were compelled to stand the entire time with their feet barely touching the floor. On December 6, 1918, the War Department finally issued a ruling against the practice of manacling, and some maltreatment of conscientious objectors ceased.

The ruling did not come soon enough for four Hutterite men, victims of gross mistreatment, whose experiences of persecution became well known in Mennonite circles and who became martyrs for the nonresistant cause. Drafted in May 1918, and sent to Camp Lewis, Washington, the four Hutterites—brothers David, Joseph, and Michael Hofer and brother-in-law Jacob Wipf, all married and with children—immediately faced ridicule and abuse from both soldiers and officers. After being beaten and put into the camp's guardhouse for refusing to follow orders, they were summarily tried and sentenced to twenty years in prison.

Sent to Alcatraz, in San Francisco, the Hutterite men were placed into a dungeon, or "hole," for their continued refusal to follow authorities. The dungeon's stone walls were thick and damp, as was the air. Handcuffed to prison bars, their feet barely touched the floor; their clothes were taken from them, although guards left in each cell a military uniform they could wear if they wished to combat the cold. All refused. This continued for thirty-six hours, during which the guards came periodically and beat them with clubs. For five days longer the men remained in the dungeon cells. While no longer "hung up," they were allowed no food and only one glass of water a day, had no toilet or washing facilities, and continued to be beaten by their guards. Finally, fearing reprimand for their abuses, Alcatraz authorities released the four men, who were then transferred to Leavenworth.

Mistreatment persisted after their transfer. Though conditions in solitary confinement were not as harsh as at Alcatraz, the men were still manacled to their bars, still placed on a severely limited diet of bread and water, and still forced to sleep on the floor. Joseph and Michael soon fell ill, were sent to the military hospital, and died. Joseph, who perished several days before his brother, was sent home in a coffin wearing the military uniform he had refused to accept—a stunning blow to parents already grieving the loss of one, then another, son.[107] David, at his brother Michael's bedside when he died, was immediately returned to solitary. He later said to a Mennonite leader, "All next day I stood and wept, but I could not wipe the tears from my eyes as my hands were chained."[108]

The men's deaths may have been caused by influenza as much as by their mistreatment, though Mennonites contended that the abuse weakened them, making them susceptible to disease. In any event, they quickly became exemplars to Mennonites of the horrific abuse meted out to objectors and of their patient suffering. The four Hutterites' fates were memorialized by a poem published in the

October 2, 1919, issue of the *Gospel Herald*. Written by Mennonite J. G. Evert of Hillsboro, Kansas, "The Martyrs of Alcatraz" related the punishments received by the Hutterite four, drawing parallels between their persecution and that of their Anabaptist ancestors. The poem indicted the "militaristic men" who "crush objectors with the heel." The final stanza connected the Hutterites to all objectors unwilling to compromise their stances:

> Thank God that these objectors four,
> So gentle and so meek, and odd,
> Are not alone; for many more
> Have love to man and love to God
> That prompts them to keep Jesus' laws:
> To love and bless, forgive and bear,
> But not help with warlike cause,
> Tho hatred threatens everywhere.

From all indications, the deaths of the Hofer brothers and Wipf represented the worst case of objector mistreatment in federal prisons. Other objectors found conditions in solitary confinement poor but livable, especially after President Wilson ordered that manacling of prisoners cease. And, although a few Mennonites were beaten upon arriving at Leavenworth, such abuse seemed the exception rather than the rule, particularly since Mennonites proved themselves model prisoners—conscientious, hard-working, and honest. Even without the obvious comforts of home, those not in solitary experienced few real troubles in the penitentiary beyond the hardness of fellow prisoners and the profanity and violence that sometimes exploded among regular prisoners.

Mennonite ministers were allowed to visit and to give church services. Kansas City pastor J. D. Mininger was the most notable of these, his work on behalf of imprisoned objectors well recognized by the Mennonite community. Mennonite services often took the place of, or were attended in addition to, those offered by the prison chaplains. As in the military camps, objectors forged a sort of brotherhood with others imprisoned for conscience sake, working together on Star Paroles, worshipping together, sustaining one another's spirits in a bleak prison setting and despite a bleak future; the men believed from their sentences that they potentially faced years of such confinement, however tolerable prison life seemed.

Fortunately for these men, the government that once ignored the objectors' severe prison sentences changed its mind in early 1919 and began releasing the men from penitentiaries. The transformation seemingly reflected the War Department's decision to return objectors to "civil life at the earliest practicable moment"—and so, perhaps, to be done with the conscientious objector problem.[109] In January, 113 incarcerated conscientious objectors were released from Leavenworth, and others soon followed. Over the next weeks and months others would be granted their liberty, as Secretary Baker reversed every sentence, freeing objectors from their confinement.

The public and the press were outraged that Baker would liberate objectors at all, let alone before soldiers fighting in France returned home; it seemed the war's objectors had not only evaded their military duty, but were now able to evade their punishment, even as other Americans remained stuck in France. An open letter to Baker in the *Kansas City Times* thundered, "By this act you have put a premium on cowardice. You have rewarded evasion of duty. You are permitting these men to return to their homes even in advance of the fighting men of the camps."[110] A resolution passed in the Nebraska legislature protested "the action of Secretary of War Baker in rewarding the slacker and the traitor which we stamp as a direct insult to the brave soldiers who so valiantly went forth to defend democracy and freedom against the awful blight of Kaiserism."[111] Kansas and Oklahoma passed similar resolutions. Even two years after the Armistice, when the last thirty-three conscientious objectors were finally released, the public had not forgiven those who shirked their military obligation. Baker's belated act of clemency was likewise met with outrage.

The American people did not soon forget the Mennonites' objection to war and apparent disloyalty to the nation's cause. Long after the Armistice, when the world had been made safe for democracy and soldiers began their journeys home to a hero's welcome, U.S. citizens still expressed indignation at Mennonites and other wartime dissenters. Great War patriotism continued even when battles "over there" ceased, the fervor driven now by the belief that American troops had secured victory and so had become the world's democratic salvation.

Like the victorious soldiers, Mennonite conscientious objectors returned to their communities and were joyfully reunited with families and church; unlike soldiers, objectors were reviled by neighbors who were not Mennonites and who could still not understand or sympathize with their stance. The fact that 50,000 American soldiers did not return home alive from the Western Front further fueled the citizens' anger. To the American public, it seemed that Mennonite objectors had been comfortably detained in military camps while other young men lost their lives to secure freedom for the good of all people, including the very objectors who would not help the democratic cause.[112]

"Never Such Innocence": Measuring the Cost

We in the early twenty-first century recognize the Great War as a period in which much was lost: a generation's men, a pastoral landscape, Europe's historic architecture, ancient notions of bravery and heroism, and innocence. The Great War also perpetuated far-reaching changes in worldwide culture, politics, and beliefs. Authors writing during the war and long after tried to express this loss of innocence and the upheaval that resulted from the conflict, as Philip Larkin did in "MCMXIV," in which he noted that "Never such innocence again" would touch our world.

Larkin was, of course, writing about the young recruits who in 1914 anxiously awaited their chance to fight Britain's battles, seeking their moment of military glory and a respite from cricket matches and peaceful afternoon teas. The phrase "Never such innocence again" reflected well the predominating view of the world held after the war, after so much loss, after the world was transformed completely. Certainly those who battled on the Western Front and those who experienced loss after loss on the home front knew what it meant to sacrifice innocence to the war god, and what if anything was to be gained by that sacrifice. It was about these people, Larkin wrote, those whose blissful parties on the dawn of war would never be the same as the somber soirees at its dusk.

Sensibility, moral codes, gentleman's warfare, optimism, civil liberties: these became victims of the Great War, irrevocably lost when German troops began their march through Belgium and the Allied forces responded, luxuries that vanished in America when President Wilson declared war. Yet are not other losses more significant, more unsettling? This is hard to say, since quantifying loss is difficult if not impossible. We can note that the Western Europe countryside was destroyed and may recount the number of villages shredded to rubble by artillery fire; but we cannot with accuracy measure the loss of those whose homes, farms, and livelihoods were demolished by warring armies.

We may also stagger at the massive human loss, the tremendous number of Great War dead: 3.5 million Central Powers soldiers and 5.1 million Allied soldiers killed, a toll of more than 5,600 every day during the war.[113] Yet statistics obfuscate, numbing us to the true loss incurred by millions more who mourned the deaths of fathers, sons, brothers, and lovers. Nor does the count of wartime dead include those who were maimed by gunfire, those whose lungs were burned by mustard gas, or those whose minds were addled by images of the Armageddon. The burden of such loss seems immense, even if we in the twenty-first century cannot wholly feel its weight.

In light of this destruction, addressing the wartime losses incurred by Mennonites and their young men becomes more difficult. Mennonite objectors did not have to face the searing fire of flame throwers, the blinding haze of poisonous gas, or the constant thud of artillery shells. Only a few noncombatant Mennonites witnessed battlefield horrors; objectors working in France with the American Friends Service Committee would see the devastation, but rarely what caused it. Some attempting to quantify the war's costs might rightly argue that, because of their nonresistance, Mennonites remained relatively untouched by the scourge of war, their losses nowhere near that experienced by so many others.

We must recognize that such arguments have merit, considering again the vast numbers of those who died on Europe's killing fields. Nonetheless, Mennonites in Great War America experienced losses, too. Many Mennonite men perished while in military camps from influenza, pleurisy, pneumonia, and other diseases. Their families mourned their deaths, just as millions mourned during that era. Other loses were less tangible. The Great War severed ties between Mennonites and their neighbors, and eroded some Mennonites' confidence in America, its government, and its citizenry. However insubstantial these losses may have seemed, they transformed the Mennonite church—an institution that, like much of the world, would never be so innocence again.

Mennonite young men returning to their homes following the Armistice entered communities that were often fractured. Some Mennonite men who had chosen combatant or even noncombatant work during the war did not return to their home communities: because they were not welcomed, or because they feared disapproval from their families and congregations. In this sense, church communities were broken, as were the larger communities in which the men lived. However much Mennonites were instructed by biblical principles to love their neighbors, doing so proved difficult when the wounds caused by wartime fervor were still fresh and deep. The mistreatment, the ethnic slurs, and the destruction of property made it difficult for Mennonites to trust those outside their flock. Intolerance for German-Americans in turn caused Mennonites to lose part of their ethnic identity, as many relinquished their use of the German language and so lost a portion of their rich heritage.

Additionally, the Mennonites' faith in the American government eroded during the war and after. Their frustrated attempts to secure exemption or safety for their young men challenged the notion that the government would help them, and showed the apparently illusory nature of Washington's promises. Even progressive Mennonites now refrained from involvement in government issues after the war, refusing to vote or to run for elections. Ultimately, the war forced Mennonites into what the historian Juhnke would call a "permanent crisis of identity": they discovered that to be good U.S. citizens in the twentieth century, they would have to compromise their citizenship in God's kingdom.[114] They could not retain full membership in both, not when the one demanded a weakened allegiance to the other. For this reason, many Mennonites embraced more fiercely the doctrine of two kingdoms, withdrawing even further from the world and insulating themselves further within their ethnic communities. The Mennonites' faith in American democracy had diminished, as had their trust in anyone beyond their presumed peaceable kingdom.

Yet just as the larger world experienced transformation from the destruction of World War I, so also did the Mennonite church. Through conscription, Mennonite young men made contact with the other kingdom; from the moment they left for military camps, their narrow-world innocence was lost in smoky railroad cars. Although seemingly inured to the soldiers' worldly ways, the men were also susceptible to the other influences of the larger culture. Many objectors returned to their Mennonite communities with a broader understanding of their world, and with the desire to enact change in that world rather than remain separated from it.

Forward-looking young Mennonites accused the church of myopia following the war, of attending only to preserving the Mennonite church rather than to healing an obviously wounded civilization. These Mennonites challenged the church to express the gospel outwardly rather than live the gospel in isolation. Some in the church responded to this challenge, volunteering for work in American Friends reconstruction and supporting other war relief agencies. Jacob C. Meyer was at the forefront of this progressive movement, organizing the Mennonite Young People's Movement to address what he believed was the church's need for transformation and a revitalized witness.

The greater Mennonite church was changed too by the shared loss of civil liberties during the war and by a shared persecution.

Military conscription affected all Mennonite bodies, forcing each group to recover and reaffirm the Anabaptist doctrine of nonresistance. After the relative tranquillity of so many years in America, World War I had caught Mennonites unawares, and so unable to clearly articulate a nonresistant stance so deeply embedded in their heritage. The war and the struggles of conscientious objectors forced Mennonite groups to turn again to their nonresistant testimony, to explore that testimony in light of modernity and global warfare, and to make it more than a closed way of life, only for Mennonites. This they did, affirming as a larger body that Christians must refuse to bear arms and must remain a nonresistant people. To revitalize their peace testimony following the war, Mennonite groups created official peace committees, generated literature outlining their peace stance, and joined together with other historic peace churches (the Friends and the Brethren) to propagate their message of nonresistance.

As a result, when World War II threatened in the late 1930s, Mennonites were much better prepared to witness to peace, their leaders better organized to share that witness with America and its government. Rather than remain stymied by the inaction, incertitude, and disagreement that sometimes characterized Mennonites in the Great War, varied Mennonite groups organized a Mennonite Central Peace Committee in 1939, believing that another draft was imminent. This committee developed a plan of action in case of war. Accepted also by other peace churches and then given to governmental leaders, the plan helped resolve conscientious objector problems in the Second World War.

As World War II approached, Mennonites were more effective than in the Great War at having their needs considered by the government. Unlike the Selective Service Act of 1917, the country's 1940 draft law included provisions for conscientious objectors which allowed them to work under civilian rather than military rule. When the new Selective Service Act was instituted, conscientious objectors had the opportunity to choose Civilian Public Service (CPS) as an alternative, and could work in church-supported CPS camps in forestry, park service, soil conservation, agriculture, dairy herd testing, public health, or land reclamation. The freedoms that conscientious objectors lost in the Great War therefore smoothed the road for later objectors, whose experiences during the Second World War were much more positive, and their roles much more useful, than those of their Great War brethren.

According to Juhnke, the trials of World War I also helped to forge a stronger Mennonite identity, as the varying Mennonite groups jointly affirmed their nonresistant faith, and so their separation from the predominating American culture.[115] With their identity strengthened, the differing sects began working in concord after the war, developing in 1920 an inter-Mennonite relief agency to respond to the needs of a war-torn world. At first the Mennonite Central Committee (MCC) concentrated its efforts on an impoverished Soviet Union, but it expanded its work with time. As Homan has argued, the Mennonite Central Committee successfully addressed many problems raised by the war and its aftermath. Through the MCC, Mennonites found they could cooperate among groups; they discovered a way to express their allegiance to America and therefore redress the wartime notion of slackerism and disloyalty; and they practiced the social gospel newly embraced by many of the church's youth.[116] The MCC rose, as it were, from the ashes of World War I: the immense loss experienced by so much of the world compelled Mennonites to create a relief agency which, almost a century later, still has great influence in the developing world, as well as in depressed North American communities.

The Great War marked a time when Western Civilization slid from innocent optimism into its modern malaise. It was a defining moment in our collective history when the barbarity of mankind reigned supreme and so destroyed a world. A new world emerged from the carnage, one which gave us Hitler, Bolshevism, and Fascism, but also fostered national sovereignty and provided the first real experiment in international cooperation. The gains made by civilization from the war were not, of course, worth its destruction, but they were gains nonetheless.

On a much smaller scale, the same might be said for the Mennonite church and its conscientious objectors. To many Mennonites the Great War was remembered as a difficult time in the church's history when the freedom to express one's beliefs and to live by those beliefs was threatened, both by governmental policy and by the American populace. The war was remembered as a time of grave persecution for Mennonite young men in military camps, whose steadfast faith in nonresistance and suffering love ironically instigated violence and intolerant hatred. And it was remembered as a time when much was lost: trust, liberty, even lives—those of the Hofer brothers, martyrs for the nonresistant cause, and of many others who died far from home.

Yet as with the greater "worldly" kingdom, a new Mennonitism emerged from the war, more vital in its nonresistant witness, more active in its outward manifestations of the gospel's message. The church's conscientious objectors were at the center of that transformation, their experiences in military camps and federal penitentiaries the catalyst for change. The American Mennonite church would not be the same following World War I, nor would its young men. True, for anyone the war touched there would never be such innocence again. But for Mennonites at least, what was lost in the war's firestorm refined not only those conscientious objectors who had walked through its flames, but the greater church body as well.

Chapter Two

Against "The Old Lie": Mennonite Objectors and the War's Literary Legacy

In October 1917, after nearly ten months fighting at the Western Front with Britain's Manchester Regiment, Wilfred Owen penned a poem that would become, over time, an exemplar of World War I literature. Owen's "Dulce et Decorum Est" starkly detailed the horrors he and millions of others experienced in the front's murky trenches. The poem's speaker recounts a nightmarish vision of watching a fellow soldier choked to his death by mustard gas, blood issuing from the soldier's "froth-corrupted lungs," as he is uselessly "flung" on a medic's wagon. The poem concludes with a seeming challenge to those who would venerate war without having witnessed its terrors. If the reader could experience the Western Front as soldiers did, the poem suggests,

> you would not tell with such high zest
>   To children ardent for some desperate glory,
>   The old Lie: Dulce et decorum est
>   Pro patria mori.[1]

A good deal of the literature produced about the First World War during the conflict and after its conclusion challenged this "old Lie," a famous Latin aphorism taken from Horace's *Odes*: "It is sweet and meet to die for one's country. Sweet! Decorous!"[2] Certainly at the beginning of the war many wrote romantically about battle, depicting the Western Front as a site upon which the old world mythologies could be daily replicated, as a playing field where godlike courage and strength could sustain the good in their triumph over evil.

Perhaps the most famous of the romantic war poets, Rupert Brooke, wrote sonnets praising the idyll of the battlefield, upon which brave young men sacrificed their blood, "the red Sweet wine of youth." In their sacrifice, Brooke inscribed in his poem "The Dead," soldiers restored "Holiness," "Honor," and "Nobleness" to a world that had "lacked so long" these principles.[3]

From the critical distance of a century marred by total war, Brooke's idealistic vision of battle seems naïve and simplistic, an old lie indeed. Many soldiers who spent endless days fighting in the trenches felt this lie, discovering over time that ideals like "honor" and "nobleness" had no place in modern war, where mechanized weaponry and the agony of trench warfare made battle inherently ignoble, dehumanizing, and unholy. Early in the Great War, however, such idealistic poetry had its moment, when antiquated notions of warfare swelled the patriots' hearts. Even Wilfred Owen, who would later be known for his indictment of the war, would write in 1914:

> O meet it is and passing sweet
> To live in peace with others,
> But sweeter still and far more meet,
> To die in war for brothers.[4]

These initial poetic conceptions of war, unable to imagine the possibilities of modern conflict, would likewise provide comfort and encouragement to civilian readers during wartime—readers with loved ones in battle who looked everywhere for signs of hope rather than of tragedy. The writer Vera Brittain, whose autobiographical *Testament of Youth* (1933) traced her time during the war, reported reading Brooke's 1914 book of sonnets and, "with my grief and anxiety then so new, I found the experience so moving that I should not have sought it had I realised how hard composure would be to maintain." Brittain, worried about her fiancé's fate at the front, found Brooke's poems at the time to be "courageous, and almost shattering in their passionate, relevant idealism."[5]

Only as the interminable war progressed and Brittain's grief became increasingly unbearable would she, and many others, question the idealism which Brooke and others had espoused during the dawning of war, and which they had then so readily embraced.

Over time, the poetry of Brooke and other wartime idealists came to symbolize not the Great War, but the innocence that preceded it; the sentiments expressed in romantic wartime poetry were not a true reflection of modern warfare or of the Western Front, but of the old world ideals destroyed by modern war. And so, in the years following the war and throughout the last century, attention to Great War literature has turned from the seemingly unrealistic poetry of Brooke, and has remained predominantly fixed on British authors such as Owen, an obviously talented artist who fought and wrote in the trenches, who deconstructed romantic sentiments of battle because he discovered how misguided such sentiments were, and whose creative life was cut short in November 1918 by a war he could not deem sweet or decorous.[6]

Across the Atlantic, thousands of miles from the Western Front, American Mennonite conscientious objectors were challenging the old lie as well. Of course, most Mennonite objectors had never seen gas attacks like that described in Owen's poem, nor could they fully imagine the kinds of demons that tormented soldiers on dark nights in the trenches. Yet these Mennonites too recognized that it was neither sweet nor decorous to die for one's country, and that the patriotic cant of bravery and heroism was a sham fed to the masses. Owen and others used their poetry and prose to realistically represent the war and in doing so, objected to its continuance; U.S. Mennonites, on the other hand, chose a less public but nonetheless viable means of protest by refusing to follow the military law of their land. The Mennonite objectors' writing, their diaries and later, their autobiographies, were a by-product of their opposition to military authority and, most assuredly, to war.

Yet like the war literature they probably never read, the writing of Mennonite objectors also questioned the predominating vision of war as a quixotic athletic arena upon which young men "ardent for some desperate glory" played.[7] The diaries included in this volume represent what was typical of most American Mennonite objectors' writing from the Great War epoch. Mennonite diarists questioned the idea that men should practice "killing devices,"[8] and articulated their certain belief that God's way was being obscured by the old lie America had told its young men. The Mennonites' objection to war was of course founded on their Christian faith and their biblical belief in nonresistance rather than the direct combat experienced by many wartime writers. Differences sometimes existed in the tone and tenor of the men's writing, in the technical complexity of their written work, and in their purpose for writing. Still, like many Great War combatant writers, Mennonite objectors produced wartime literature that was acutely antiwar in its sentiments.

In the nearly one hundred years since fire sounded across No Man's Land, however, only a few wartime authors have enjoyed any kind of reading audience, either critical or popular. Most texts written during the Great War remain unpublished and so unread, buried in archives or held in private collections. In this way as well, much of the writing produced while the war raged is like the Mennonite objectors' diaries: composed by ordinary citizens attempting to make meaning of war, composed for personal reasons, composed and then all but forgotten by nearly everyone. The Mennonites' writing has enjoyed only a small audience, as Mennonite historians have used the Mennonites' wartime autobiographical texts to construct the narrative of the Mennonite experience in World War I. Indeed, the Mennonite objectors' writing offers plenty of insight into what opposing the war meant in the years 1914-18.[9] Yet relatively few others have mined the rich terrain of Mennonites' wartime writing: even though the Mennonite objectors' texts compellingly resonate with much of the literature produced during the Great War.

That Mennonites' writing might be ignored by Great War literary enthusiasts is disappointing but not that unexpected. After all, Mennonites themselves have traditionally been suspicious of a literary culture which, according to John D. Roth and Ervin Beck, "suggested a culture of learnedness and leisure in tension with a tradition that valued simplicity and manual labor . . . [which] promoted flights of imaginative fancy over concrete deeds of human kindness and the transparency of letting your 'yea be yea.'"[10]

The hope of a place among the Great War literati certainly did not motivate Mennonite objectors to keep diaries during the war, nor to preserve their texts long after the war's conclusion. Why, then, should diaries by Mennonite objectors now be read as part of the Great War literary tradition, especially as the writers themselves did not intend for their texts to be appreciated by a wider audience? Why examine the sparse, seemingly unmetaphoric words of John Neufeld, a Mennonite sent to Fort Leavenworth for disobeying the military order to drill? Why read about the experiences of Gustav Gaeddert, a man remembered best only by those who knew him personally, although he organized conscientious objector activity in one Great War military camp? Why study the diary of Ura Hostetler, an obscure Kansas farm boy who, after the war, would return to a life of farming? When others wrote so eloquently about the Great War and their lives in the trenches, why read the reflections of men who sometimes could not even spell correctly, who struggled to render metaphorically what they were experiencing in actuality?

Literary scholars Felicity Nussbaum and Robert Sayre provide a convincing answer to these questions. Nussbaum writes that "the marginalized and unauthorized discourse in diary holds the power to disrupt authorized versions of experience, even, perhaps, to reveal what might be called randomness and arbitrariness of the authoritative and public constructs of reality."[11] Sayre's "The Proper Study—Autobiographies in American Studies" similarly argues that diaries we judge "merely boring or illiterate, repetitious and inconsequential" may in fact be "the unwanted messages of history."[12] Examining the diaries of Mennonite conscientious objectors affords the opportunity to expand our understanding of the Great War, and to hear the unwanted messages of wartime history, a history that has been chiefly informed by the battlefield rather than the home front, by the exploits of soldiers rather than the apprehension of civilians caught in the web of total war.

The daily musings of an obscure farm boy, trapped in military barracks; the reflections of a Harvard man, treated well for his scholastic honor if poorly for his religious values; the objector's serial narrative of months spent in a federal penitentiary—all voice an oft-unheard message: battlefield soldiers alone do not bear the tremendous cost of war, nor are they the sole participants of war. Because "combat is not the total sum of war," Margaret Higonnet notes, other perspectives of the war, other texts written about the war, also need to be read as part of the Great War's legacy. Otherwise, Higonnet argues, "the narrow focus of traditional history [literary and otherwise] tends to obscure from view the endemic, even epidemic, effects of war." This is especially true of the First World War (and of modern warfare in general), when the field upon which war was enacted extended far beyond the Western Front: to the oceans where civilian liners were destroyed; to the cities, over which zeppelins lurked; to many households, over which the pall of death hung.

In the preface to her anthology of women writers from World War I, Higonnet voiced a frustration shared by a growing population of readers dissatisfied with the traditional Great War literary canon. Historically, scholars have construed this canon quite narrowly, including only the artistic work of combatant writers, mostly British, who were at the front, who fought on French soil and drowned in its blood, who lived and died by the gun.[13] Such a canon reflects the bifurcated understanding of war many soldiers themselves had during their time in combat: they believed there was a class of people whose experiences with war were real, and so whose writings about war were legitimate; and they asserted that this legitimate vision separated combatants from all others, who had no claim to speak about the war or to challenge its necessity because they had not directly participated by fighting in the trenches.

Therefore, the exclusive nature of the Great War canon can be attributed, in some part, to the progenitors of the canon—the writers themselves—who asserted again and again that only those who were there could comprehend, define, and write about war. Samuel Hynes's translation of a French soldier's words underscore this belief: "How can they judge who have not seen?" So does Hynes's translation of a German soldier's remark: "Those who haven't lived through the experience may sympathize as they read, the way one sympathizes with the hero of a novel or play, but they certainly will never understand, as one cannot understand the unexplainable."[14]

Philip Gibbs, who lived in the trenches as a field correspondent for a London newspaper, wrote in his war memoir *Now It Can Be Told:* "as an onlooker of war I hated the people who had not seen, because they could not understand."[15] Similarly, Robert Graves, a British combatant and later an acclaimed writer, said in an interview, "The funny thing was you went home on leave for six weeks, or six days, but the idea of being and staying at home was awful because you were with people who didn't understand what this was all about." His interviewer asked, "Didn't you want to tell them?" Graves responded, "You couldn't: you can't communicate noise. Noise never stopped for one moment—ever."[16]

Soldiers in combat felt themselves drawn together by the experience and separated from everyone else; one need only read Siegfried Sassoon's *Counter-Attack and Other Poems* to feel how great this separation really was. Thus the chasm between those in combat and those who were not became a significant theme in the literature combatants produced; yet it also operated as a device separating what soldiers wrote (the true war literature) from what everyone else wrote (a manufactured, and therefore falsified, vision of war).

To a large degree, works by objectors, civilians, and by men and women who served in noncombatant roles have not been widely read because of this prevailing belief that only the soldiers' conception of war was—and is—legitimate. Therefore, interest in Great War literature has often centered on the literary work of only a few combatant writers, including Owen, Sassoon, Edmond Blunden, and Graves, as well as Edward Thomas, Isaac Rosenberg, and several other lesser known British writers who served in the war.[17] Although these writers willingly enlisted in the war, and although they on occasion bought into the patriotic ideal of war, their faith in fighting for the mother country was eroded by their experiences on the Western Front: by the seeming futility of trench warfare; by watching comrades and friends succumb to sniper fire, gas attacks, and shell shock;

and by the continually growing chasm between politicians, military officers, and civilians who unequivocally supported the war, and the soldiers who were fighting what they felt were someone else's battles.

These writers asserted, over and over, that this war was hell, and that they regretted having any part of it. And thus, literature written in the trenches relied on visceral imagery to convey a vision of war that was not, after all, possible to convey: how describe their journey to Hades to people who would never assume a similar quest? The trench poets tried, constructing nightmares for readers of stumbling over corpses still grasping blackened wounds, of "Strange Meetings" with enemy ghosts, of "Mental Cases" whose "minds the Dead have ravished." During the war, few people wished to read such poetry, which was often critical of civilians, the "Blighters" who continued to "shrill" patriotic songs while their countrymen burned.[18] Further, as noted earlier, readers sought solace in their literature, as in all things: what civilians would find comfort in knowing what really was happening to their lovers, their husbands, or their sons? Better to read the works of an earlier poet like Brooke, who never saw combat and so whose idealism about war could transform fields of rotting corpses into a vision of the contented dead, of dead who in dying, Brooke wrote, "have made us rarer gifts than gold."[19]

The works that constitute what scholars generally consider the Great War canon predominantly found their audiences after the war, when people were more receptive of, and more critical of, a four-year conflict that had destroyed a generation's men. Therefore, although the most heralded Great War writers have often been termed the "trench poets," their literary compositions rarely passed directly from trench to receptive audience. Indeed, many of the central texts in the Great War canon were published following the war, including Owen's poetry, collected in the posthumous 1920 *Poems of Wilfred Owen*; much of Owen's work was partly composed at the front, although many poems were also written and polished while Owen convalesced following shell shock. Sassoon had two volumes of poetry published during the war, yet he likewise achieved greater fame as a writer later, following the war.[20] Other writers critical of the war, both in Allied and in Central Power countries, would find little audience for their work during the conflict; such literature was published in small literary magazines, if at all.[21]

In the decade after Armistice, several established trench poets like Sassoon, Blunden, and Graves joined countless others in writing their memoirs about the war. These memoirs provide what might well be the best, the most complete, account of what being a combatant in the First World War was really about, enhancing the historians' chronicle of battles and the sometimes sterile counts of wartime dead. In their memoirs, the men describe more expansively their sojourns at the front, their anguished discomfort with a war they could not support, and the haunting shadow war cast over their post-Armistice lives. More than a decade's distance provided these writers an enhanced perspective of the war, allowing them to see more clearly the extreme naivety of their prewar patriotic innocence, as well as how their idealism in 1913 could never have prepared them for 1914 and beyond. Further, writing about the war in the late 1920s afforded these writers the opportunity to contemplate the capital they paid to buy their own lives' serenity—and how that purchase would affect their relationships with family and peers, relationships forever complicated by the experiences separating them.

As in their poetry, the memoirs of the trench writers turned to description to convey most clearly the horrors of war and its costs in terms of human life. Just as they had done ten years earlier, the writers used vivid imagery to write against the "old Lie." In the trench writers' memoirs this description again juxtaposed images of death and decay—the products of war—with images of a fecund natural world unfettered by war. In this juxtaposition, these memoirists reinforced their sense of war's nearly total annihilation of the world—but also its inability to destroy all life.

Turning to description of the natural world was, in many ways, but a return to the tradition of the pastoral, the evocation of a peaceful rural life found so often in British literature. By describing the beautiful power of nature amid war, trench poets were using what was familiar in their tradition to make sense of the completely unfamiliar, finding comfort, as it were, in that which reminded them of home and of their past innocence—"like rum," Paul Fussell wrote in *The Great War and Modern Memory*, or "a deep dugout, or a woolly vest." Moreover, Fussell argued, the extensive use of the pastoral was "a way of invoking a code to hint by antithesis at the indescribable."[22]

The antithesis to mortar thuds and the constant noise of artillery was the seeming innocence of the bird song, an incongruity noted by Sassoon, Blunden, and Guy Chapman, author of the autobiographical *A Passionate Prodigality*. Trees continued to sprout leaves in spring, and some farmlands still sprung forth with crops, revealing the stubborn life of the natural world despite humanity's compulsion to destroy every living thing. Gibbs observed the French farmers harvesting crops so close to the front line, and wondered at the sustaining of natural life so near the cessation of natural life. During a particularly brutal winter, he noted how the phenomena of weather drew life and death together:

> In its first glamour of white the snow gave a beauty even to No Man's Land, making a lace-work pattern of barbed wire, and lying very softly over the tumbled ground of mine-fields, so that all the ugliness of destruction and death was hidden under this canopy. The snowflakes fluttered upon the stark bodies there, and shrouded them tenderly. It was as though all the doves of peace were flying down to fold their wings about the obscene things of war.[23]

In his *Undertones of War*, Blunden likewise wrote of hiking through an abandoned area of the front line, and of being captivated by the natural world's permanency through war's turmoil: "Acres of self-sown wheat glistened and sighed as we wound our way between, where rough scattered pits recorded a hurried firing-line of long ago. Life, life abundant sang here and smiled; the lizard ran warless in warm dust; and the ditches were trembling quick with odd tiny fish, in worlds as remote as Saturn."[24] For Blunden as for others, nature provided continuity, outlasting man-made destruction. It was, after all, self-sown wheat that flourished, nature replenishing itself where man had destroyed himself.

By creating an opposition between two entities, between the intransigent natural world and the ephemeral world of war, writers discovered one way they could bring meaning to their incomprehensible combat experiences: in the opposition lay the Truth of good's (nature's) triumph over evil (a mechanized and destructive war). This impulse to dichotomize can be traced through the Great War literary canon, through Great War memoirs as well as fiction and poetry, as writers shaped their texts—and brought meaning to their wartime lives—through a series of oppositions: natural versus unnatural world, trench versus home, light versus dark, prewar innocence versus postwar knowledge, enemy versus friend, British versus German, Allied versus Central Powers, war versus peace, life versus death. At one pole stood, of course, all that was holy and good; at the other, all that was bad.

In *The Great War and Modern Memory*, Fussell argued that this "gross dichotomizing is a persisting imaginative habit of modern times, traceable, it would seem, to the actualities of the Great War. 'We' are all here on this side; 'the enemy' is over there. 'We' are individuals with names and personal identities; 'he' is a mere collective entity. We are visible; he is invisible. We are normal; he is grotesque."[25] This "versus habit," Fussell wrote, precipitated by and intensified by trench warfare, created a polarized worldview that offered no hope for mediation or reconciliation: one pole held "so wicked a deficiency or flaw or perversion that its total submission was called for."[26] In turn, this binary perspective, and the belief in an opposing evil in need of complete submission, became a central shaping device in the literature produced during the First World War.

A quick reading of one chapter in Blunden's memoir, *Undertones of War*, reveals the kind of polarization common among Great War writers. In "Steel Helmets and All," Blunden relates his experiences fighting on the front in summer 1916. At this point in the war, Blunden was able to note already a difference between the war of 1915 and that of 1916, creating an opposition between the "then" of war and the "now"; he explains that even though this was June 1916, the men were still fighting in "a kind of 1915 sector,"[27] and that 1915 trenches received closer scrutiny as something of a wartime antiquity. In the same chapter, Blunden intensifies the horror of the trenches by contrasting descriptions of his time at the front with the two or three days' rest he received when relieved from his trench duties. The constant thudding of artillery which made sleep impossible, the mud and vermin, and the observed death of a sixteen-year-old boy are juxtaposed, in the next paragraph, with descriptions of a French chateau, a mahogany bed, a "cool nook, earthly paradisal cupboard with leaf-green light to see poetry by," and a peaceful sleep.[28]

Next, Blunden turns to an opposition used extensively by Great War writers, that of dark and light, day and night: "Daytime was play in the Islands that summer; night was a perpetual tangle."[29] Patrol occurred at night, Blunden explains, and by cover of darkness, one was apt to stumble blindly into the German line, to see ominous figures, to mistake willow trees for the enemy, to become utterly confused and so an easy target. By day, though, Blunden and his men "sometimes got out of the trench into the dark grass behind, which the sun had dried, and enjoyed a warm indolence with a book."[30]

The leisure with which Blunden's regiment enjoyed daytime was a little unusual, though light commonly brought some relief to men along the front. Wartime activity took place mostly at night, when wiring and digging parties fortified or extended their lines, ammunition was moved forward, night patrols ventured into No Man's Land for recognizance's sake, and raiding parties attacked German trenches. For Blunden as for others, the opposition of light and dark, day and night, became a shaping influence in their wartime lives, measuring their days and, so it seemed, the extent to which their lives were in danger. Still, if in some ways the opposition of day and night reinforced the archetypal symbolism associated with light and dark, with good and evil, it also undermined that symbolism: for in the light of day, one could more vividly see the night's destruction and the accumulation of bodies left to rot in No Man's Land.

Relying on archetypal imagery and also literary allusion became yet another way Great War combatant writers could describe the indescribable, connecting what they knew and could understand with what they were experiencing. Many of the most prominent artists in the Great War canon were educated and well read in the classics, and continued their course of reading at the front, using poetry and philosophy as a welcome escape from the realities of the trenches. Fussell has gone so far as to term the Great War a "Literary War." The influence of literature on British troops was especially strong: the literature they read before the war, then during the war, had a profound influence on how they viewed that war.[31]

Thus a thread of literary allusion ran through much of the writing produced by combatants, from the literature of antiquity to Chaucer and Shakespeare, Keats and Tennyson.[32] For example, Brooke relied on a Tennysonian style and the ideal of the Romantics to forge his own understanding of the war; Blunden turned to Keats to describe the chateau he passed on his way to the front; Owen too relied on his affinity with Keats in constructing some of his wartime poems. Of perhaps equal significance, writers in the Great War canon began to quote their contemporaries, suggesting they continued to read deeply throughout the war, connecting or opposing their own experiences with that of others. In Owen's "Dulce et Decorum Est," the poet alluded not only to Horace's *Odes* but also to the poetry of Jessie Pope, a Great War writer whose anthems glorifying war were gathered in *Jessie Pope's War Poems* (1915) and were often read by British young. In response to Brooke's own romantic poem "The Dead," Sassoon wrote in "On Passing the New Menin Gate" about the "unheroic Dead" who will be all but forgotten by history, a counter to Brooke's own claim that "the years" would give the war dead "kindness."[33]

Although literary allusion was used as a way to connect the knowable with the unknowable, it was also used by many Great War writers to further their own public indictment against the war and its horrors, as the examples of Owen and Sassoon above make clear.

Literary allusion often served as ironic action, transforming the comforts of a familiar literary tradition into a horrific vision of war—Keats's symbolic Nightingale exploded by mortars, as it were. American combatant writers did not share this penchant for allusion nor, to a greater degree, the desire to protest the war, as we shall see. Instead, in many ways, the literature produced by a good number of British Great War combatants resonated more in theme if not in content with the writing of American conscientious objectors, whose literary work also protested the war. For, like Mennonite objectors, many British writers came to believe themselves conscientious objectors, if only to the war in which they participated.

Sassoon's own protest against the war became a significant piece of the Great War literary legacy. His objection may be seen to some degree in his poetry, in his vehement denunciation of civilians and officers who compelled him to kill without purpose. He described this conscientious objection more directly and extensively in *Memoirs of an Infantry Officer*, part of his six-volume series of fictionalized autobiographical works. Sassoon's *Memoirs* is now considered one of the more significant literary pieces to emerge from the Great War, an exemplar of wartime literature written by a combatant who had been at the front, and so could write with authority about its horrors.

Memoirs of an Infantry Officer follows officer George Sherston, the fictional counterpart to Sassoon, through his experiences leading men to combat in the war's bloodiest battles, and details his march as well toward a decision of conscientiously objecting to the war. As Second Lieutenant of Infantry in the Royal Welch Fusiliers, Sassoon was a patriotic and brave officer, earning the Military Cross for his heroic actions at the front; during the Battle of the Somme, Sassoon's successful evacuation of a German trench earned him recommendation for yet another military decoration.[34]

With time, however, Sassoon became increasingly disenchanted with war, with its apparent futility and its unfettered bloodshed. He continued to fight, however, lobbing bombs into German strongholds, leading his men on a recognizance mission. Then, when once raising himself above the parapet to look across No Man's Land in summer 1917, Sassoon suffered a sniper wound in his shoulder.

The wound would lead Sassoon home to Britain and to his declaration of objection to the war in which he had played his own heroic part. While convalescing in Britain, Sassoon was introduced to two of that country's leading pacifist intellectuals, John Middleton Murry and Bertrand Russell, named Markington and Tyrrell in *Memoirs of an Infantry Officer*. After discussions with Murry and Russell, and after

Against the "Old Lie" • 95

observing the seeming imprudence with which people at home talked about war, Sassoon felt compelled to write *A Soldier's Declaration*, which stated, in part:

> I am making this statement as an act of willful defiance of military authority, because I believe that the war is being deliberately prolonged by those who have the power to end it.
>
> I am a soldier, convinced that I am acting on behalf of soldiers. I believe this war, upon which I entered as a war of defence and liberation, has now become a war of aggression and conquest. I believe that the purposes for which I and my fellow-soldiers entered upon this war should have been so clearly stated as to have made it impossible to change them, and that, had this been done, the objects which actuated us would now be attainable by negotiation.
>
> I have seen and endured the sufferings of the troops, and I can no longer be a party to prolong these sufferings for ends which I believe are evil and unjust....
>
> On behalf of those who are suffering now I make this protest against the deception which is being practiced on them; also I believe that I may help to destroy the callous complacence with which the majority of those at home regard the continuance of agonies which they do not share, and which they have not sufficient imagination to realize.[35]

Sassoon expected a court-martial for his obstinate and vocal refusal to support the war. Instead, with the help of Robert Graves's intervention, military authorities deemed his objection a case of shell shock, and Sassoon was sent to Craiglockhart War Hospital to recover. His journey to Craiglockhart, called Slateford Hospital in *Memoirs of an Infantry Officer*, ended his second volume of autobiography.

Although he later became active in the church, Sassoon's public denouncement of war was not made on religious grounds. This sets his memoir apart from the writing of religious objectors, particularly Mennonites. Nowhere in Sassoon's *Memoirs of an Infantry Officer* will one find reference to the Sermon on the Mount or Christ's call to nonresistance.[36] Instead, Sassoon's protest was based on his experiences as a lieutenant who saw his men die uselessly while others continued to believe the war jolly good fun; he objected to a war lining the pockets of the British wealthy, "cackling" in London theatres about getting the Kaiser. Sassoon felt the sting of their seeming callousness, their unwillingness to stop the bloodshed of their young men.

Unlike religious objectors, who were often absolute in their denouncement of war, Sassoon's objection was to the particular war in which he was engaging, rather than to war in general. "I am not protesting against the conduct of war," he wrote in his declaration, "but against the political errors and insincerities for which the fighting men are being sacrificed."[37] And indeed, Sassoon returned to combat after several months' convalescence at Craiglockhart, feeling called to be with the men who were toiling at the front even as he objected to their need to fight. He was injured again in battle, thereby ending his meritorious military career in summer 1918.

Sassoon's activity as a combatant, and his unwillingness to protest war in general terms, separate him of course from Mennonite objectors, who protested the conduct of war in any form, at any time, by any means, because of the biblical mandate to do so. The views of Wilfred Owen, another pillar of the traditional Great War canon, may be more congenial. Although not considered a religious objector, Owen may be closer than Sassoon to objecting to the war on religious grounds similar to those of the Mennonites.

Faith did not prevent Owen from enlisting, but time at the front and disenchantment with the state and church led him to contemplate more deeply what Christ demanded of his followers. By 1918, Owen had decided the church played its part in propagating the old lie against which he was writing. On Easter Day, 1918, Owen wrote to his mother a bitter revision of John 3:16: "God so hated the world that He gave several millions of English-begotten sons, that whosoever believeth in Him should not perish, but have a comfortable life."[38]

In an earlier letter to his mother, Owen admitted the war had made him more a Christian. His strengthening of faith came not through some near-death experience or through a battlefield conversion, but because he so clearly saw "the unchristian ways of Christendom." He also understood that Christ's message remained inconsonant with the war and with the patriotic bromides preached from national church pulpits:

> I am more and more Christian as I walk the unchristian ways of Christiandom. Already I have comprehended a light which never will filter into a dogma of any national church: namely that one of Christ's essential commands was: Passivity at any price! Suffer dishonor and disgrace; but never resort to arms. Be bullied, be outraged, be killed; but do not kill. It may be chimerical and an ignominious principle, but there it is. It can only be ignored: and I think pulpit professionals are ignoring it very skillfully indeed. . . . The practice of selective ignorance is one cause of the war. Christians have deliberately cut some of the main teachings of their code.[39]

Compelled to live in accordance with Christ's message, Owen recognized he remained in conflict with "Brethren" who were "no nearer to the kingdom" for their religious posturing than Owen and his battlefield compatriots were for knowing "pure Christianity," a faith that "will not fit with pure patriotism." Because of his religious conviction, and because of his culpability in killing Germans, he declared himself "a conscientious objector with a very seared conscience."[40]

Mennonite objectors could no doubt resonate with Owen's claims, if not with his battlefield actions. Owen's writing in many ways echoed the Mennonites' own: Christ demanded nonresistance at all costs. Churches were misguided in their interpretation of the Gospels, and in their use of the Gospels to incite people to war. One could not serve two kingdoms by being both a pure patriot and pure Christian. Still, Owen believed that he was different from other conscientious objectors who had not been to the front, those who had not seen the atrocities, and so could only express their pacifism theoretically. Owen argued that anyone unfamiliar with the war could not effectively speak against the war, having no bases upon which to express his conscientious objection. Therefore the blood on Owen's own hands was ironically crucial to developing a sense of legitimacy as a conscientious objector, as a letter to his mother suggested: "I hate washy pacifists as temperamentally as I hate whiskied prussianists. Therefore I feel that I must first get some reputation of gallantry before I could successfully and usefully declare my principles."[41]

Owen's and Sassoon's conception of conscientious objection would no doubt seem foreign to American Mennonite objectors, who saw their antiwar stance as absolute and did not need combat experience to know the truth of their nonresistant stance nor to justify that stance to others. Still, writers like Owen and Sassoon seemingly came closer to sounding the theme of conscientious objection than did many American trench artists, and so appeared more similar in ideology (if not experience) to Mennonite objectors than to American combatants writing about their time at the front. As Samuel Hynes argues in *The Soldiers' Tale*, American combatant literature was distinctly different from its British counterpart, largely because Americans fought a different war: not one of lengthy stalemates in rotten trenches, but one of quick offense and certain victory. The grist for protest in a Sassoon poem was not observed by Americans who, Hynes writes, did not "seem to have lost their recruiting-office feeling that this war would be an American adventure, to be entered into for the goodwill of the thing, because Europe needed help."[42]

Thus, many American wartime writers were unlike their British counterparts in that U.S. combatants by and large refused to deconstruct the old lie, instead seeing the war as sweet and decorous, an arena in which to achieve honor and to find adventure. Their literary productions reflected the general mood of American soldiers embarking for the Western Front. They were certain of their holy mission to rid the world of a German scourge; they were seeking adventure in a foreign land; they were "ardent for some desperate glory"; and they were sure that combat at the front would provide the honor they sought.

For many American combatants, the realities of the front did little to quell this zest, as their writing made clear; this was no "Slough of Despond," but rather the site on which the Americans would save the world from evil. Instead of objecting to the war, then, many U.S. combatants celebrated their part in the great international fete. And this celebration—so repugnant to Mennonite objectors confined to military cantonments, so contradictory to the desolation described by British wartime writers—would find its voice in the literature American combatants produced.

Albert Ettinger's memoir, *Doughboy with the Fighting 69th*, well reflects this impulse to glorify the American participation in the Great War. A member of the famed Rainbow Division of the United States Armed Forces, Ettinger reached the Western Front late in 1917. In his memoir, Ettinger repeatedly affirms the gloriousness of the war, and of the U.S. role in it.

Ettinger was himself eager to be part of that glory. Enlisting at age seventeen, he longed for action in France; once in France, he hoped for quick advancement to the front. He admits to disobeying orders on several occasions so he could remain in the trenches, fighting with compatriots. Rather than reflect on the horrors of war, as Owen, Sassoon, and other British writers do, Ettinger focuses on his own heroism and his part in bringing a swift American, and by extension Allied, victory. There is likewise a difference in tone: the grave tenor of a Wilfred Owen poem suggests a different war than the one Ettinger saw. In Ettinger's war, men rollicked drunk in pubs, snuck off to brothels, had fist fights with compatriots, and battled the Boches in their spare time.

Ettinger's text might well be considered an anomaly, save that other American combatant writers embraced a similar approach in their wartime reflections. For example, at the height of war, in 1918, Scribners published the letters from the American Edmond Genet to his mother, a wartime memoir of sorts about Genet's adventures flying with the Foreign Legion. In her introduction to the *War Letters of Edmond Genet*, Grace Ellery Channing wrote that Genet "heard a call" to enter World War I, bravely answered that call, and at his death, was given the "singular honor [of being] the first American to give his life under the Stars and Stripes."[43] Genet, she argued, was predestined for glory, from the moment he donned a Navy's uniform as a child until his death in a French Nieuport cockpit. Of Genet's heroic mission in France, she wrote: "rarely is the cycle of life so swiftly, so surely, and so gloriously fulfilled—or so satisfyingly foreshadowed."[44]

Not your typical wartime memoir, Genet's letters yet traced his own narrative of war—a narrative that was, in many ways, figured differently than that of British writers. Although Genet often mentioned death, it was something he did not fear; rather, death in war represented honor for his family and country, a sweet and decorous end for sure. Genet believed his courage in death had special import, too, as America had not yet declared war when Genet wrote his letters. Thus Genet was battling not only for the freedom of Europe, but also for his own country—a country that would not stand and fight because it was yellow, and because its president and citizens sought peace:

> They crave for peace, those unthinking, uncaring voters, and what's the reason? Why, they're making money hand over fist because their country is at peace—peace at the price of its honor and respect in the whole civilized world—at peace while France and Belgium are being soaked in blood by barbarous invasion. . . . Peace—God forbid such happiness until the invaders have been victoriously driven back behind their own borders . . . and all the rest of their deeds of piracy and the blood of France and Belgium has dried up.[45]

Unlike the British writers Sassoon and Owen, who felt their countrymen should step away from the war, Genet believed his country should be a part of war. Like his compatriot Ettinger, Genet expressed the moral obligation to fight, to free Europe of the evil Germans, and to die an honorable, a decorous, death. Similarly, the American Alan Seeger, who also joined the Foreign Legion early in the war, expressed his own desire to find military glory at the Western Front. His most famous poem, "I Have a Rendezvous with Death," echoed sentiments found in his posthumously published *Letters and Diary*: that the war was just, and that he deserved to have some part in it, to—as his poem asserted—heroically "rendezvous with death" on "some scarred slope of battered hill" or "in some flaming town."[46]

Like Genet, Seeger felt that death in war was the most noble, most honorable sacrifice he could make for. As he wrote to his mother,

> We will go directly into action, magnificently, unexpectedly, and probably victoriously, in some dashing charge.... In that moment, trust, as I do, in the great god, Chance, that brings us in life, not only our misfortunes, but our greatest bits of happiness, too.... War is another kind of life insurance; whereas the ordinary kind assures a man that his death will mean money to someone, this assures him that it will mean honor to himself, which from a certain point of view is much more satisfactory.[47]

So ardent was Seeger's longing for battle that he envied those troops sent ahead without him to fight at Arras and Verdun. When word came that he would go into action, he wrote his mother from France in October 1914 that he would go forward "with the lightest of hearts."[48]

In September 1915, Seeger finally marched into battle. He noted in his diary then that "I have been waiting for this moment for more than a year. It will be the greatest moment in my life."[49] Seeger had his own rendezvous with death on the Fourth of July, 1916; it was the battlefield death for which he longed. Much earlier, Seeger had written his mother that, if he should die, she "must be proud, like a Spartan mother, and feel that it is your contribution to the triumph of the cause whose righteousness you feel so keenly ... If so large a part should fall to your share, you would be in so far superior to other women and should be correspondingly proud ... So do not be unhappy but no matter what happens walk with your head high and glory in your large share of whatever credit the world may give me."[50]

Such was the tenor of much American combatant writing from the war, putting these texts in opposition to ones written by U.S. objectors and by the British trench poets who are most often associated with Great War literature. Certainly there were British writers who supported the war wholeheartedly to its conclusion, just as there were American writers who expressed their discomfort with the war. Some American writers, like e. e. cummings and Ernest Hemingway, both volunteer ambulance drivers during the war, wrote critically about their wartime experiences and would later achieve distinction in American letters. Yet cummings, Hemingway, and a few other writers who would one day be associated with American literature were very often noncombatants, and so their stories of war lacked the stamp of legitimacy given the work of Owen, Sassoon, and other British trench poets. Because these American antiwar writers never "reached the front and actually fought there," Hynes suggests, their literary depictions of war are less significant than those texts written by combatants, whose works—Hynes implies—remain the only real literature of war.[51]

Similarly, many British civilian writers, including some who would find acclaim in English literary history, grappled with the war in their literature and soon after the war wrote compellingly about its effects on Britain and its people. Yet despite the large body of commendable work produced by these civilians about the Great War, Fussell believes "it was left to the lesser talents [Graves, Sassoon, Blunden]... to recall in literary form a war they had actually experienced." The "masters of the modern movement," including D. H. Lawrence, Virginia Woolf, and Ezra Pound, did not "recall in literary form" the Great War, Fussell asserts, because they were "not involved with the war."[52]

Hynes's and Fussell's convictions reflect well the century-long measuring rod used to determine what texts deserve canonization as Great War literature and what texts do not. In essence, literary scholars have believed and behaved much like the Great War's soldier-artists: because only those with battlefield experience could understand the war, only those with battlefield experience could legitimately write about it—so only their texts deserved to be studied. Throughout the last century, then, scholars gave the designation "First World War Literature" solely to literary works written by those who lived and died at the front. As James Campbell noted, what a critic of Great War literature "legitimates as war literature is produced exclusively by combat experience; the knowledge of combat is a prerequisite for the production of a literary text that adequately deals with war." Literary scholars, Campbell writes, are prone to the same belief embraced by war combatants—a "combat gnosticism" that separates the qualified few from the uncomprehending masses, the conviction that "combat represents a qualitatively separate order of experience that is difficult, if not impossible, to communicate to any who have not undergone an identical experience."[53]

Fussell's authoritative text on Great War literature, *The Great War and Modern Memory*, has propagated this restrictive view. As Michele Fry observes, Fussell has been "the critic most responsible for the construction of and popularisation of the dominant, mainstream crit-

102 • *Writing Peace*

ical tradition . . . ; for Fussell the experience of the First World War is synonymous with experience of the trenches."[54] Fussell's work remains one of the most comprehensive studies of Great War combatant literature; yet the influence of Fussell and other literary critics cannot be understated. Their focus has long shaped the study of Great War literature, informing what works from that era are studied in literature classes, what works are anthologized, and what works are privileged by scholars in their quest to understand war literature in its entirety.

Given this prevailing attitude, it is little wonder that the writing of American Mennonite conscientious objectors has received no critical or popular notice. Neither has the writing of women who worked as noncombatants at the front, nor of the civilians who waited anxiously at home for word about the war. According to Dominic Hibberd, "there were thousands, probably millions, of poems written in English during the First World War"; millions of people affected by the war kept diaries, wrote their memoirs, and sketched out stories about their experiences in letters home.[55] Yet like the autobiographical texts of Mennonite objectors, the literary productions of countless other writers remain buried and mostly unread, lacking the authenticating stamp of combat experience. Thus for more than eighty years, these extant texts, these varying perspectives on the First World War and its costs, have rarely been read.

In recent years, some literary scholars have challenged the exclusive focus on combatants, calling for a widening of the Great War canon. Most often of late, critical attention has turned to the wartime writing of women, whose suffering in war, and whose responses to war, have historically been ignored, something Frances Hallowes observed long ago, at the dawning of the Great War in 1914. Hallowes wrote: "The sufferings of women through war . . . are seldom dwelt upon. Books and treaties dealing with . . . war almost invariably omit to mention the damage done to one half of the human race."[56]

The conviction that women's wartime writing deserves space in the canon has spawned a number of anthologies and critical studies, all of which argue for an end to combat gnosticism. For example, Nosheen Khan, in her volume *Women's Poetry of the First World War*, argues that "war is a human event, not a happening which affects one age or sex rather than another . . . [therefore] anyone affected by war is entitled to comment upon it."[57] Because the literature of combatants has long informed modern concepts of war, Khan contends that only in broadening the wartime canon may we have a real understanding of the "'truth' of modern war."[58]

A decade after Khan's critical study was published, Higonnet anthologized not only the war poetry of women, but also their wartime fiction, autobiographical narratives, political treatises, and journalistic efforts. Higonnet suggested in her preface that she was also writing against the centuries-old combat gnosticism, endeavoring in her volume to give voice to women's concerns about, and reflections on, a war that forever transformed them. This voice, Higonnet wrote, was silenced by those who would deem only combatants' writing authentic:

> Whether nationalist or antimilitarist, women's vision of the war was thought to be tainted by the fact they did not do military service. That women volunteered as soldiers on the Eastern Front has been forgotten. That Rupert Brooke, usually thought to be a "war poet," died of disease before he ever saw combat was also forgotten. That women and children were used as human shields in Belgium and eastern France was forgotten or denied as mere propaganda. Inadequate concepts of "real" wartime experience and of its relationship to "realistic" or powerful writing have kept us from publishing or reading women's texts.[59]

Recent challenges to the Great War literary canon have not, of course, tried to diminish the very real, very powerful writing of the war's combatant authors. No one wishes to undermine the tremendous literature created by Sassoon, Owen, and others, or to suggest their wartime literature should be abandoned for something else. Rather, proponents of a newer, more inclusive Great War canon argue the study of texts produced by noncombatants can serve to broaden our understanding of war, providing a larger, more expansive portrait of what war meant in the years 1914 to 1918, and what it might mean to us now. Reading the work of noncombatants in conjunction with that of combatants can give us a fuller sense of the devastation caused by modern war, showing that while combatants bear the weapons of war they do not completely bear its costs, and that total war affects the total human race: soldiers, politicians, ambulance drivers, male and female civilians, children, and yes, conscientious objectors.

Richard Eberhart wrote in 1945 that in war, "The spectators, the contemplator, the opposer of war have their hours with the enemy no less than uniformed combatants"; the spectator, the contemplator, and the opposer thus have the right to explain their time with the enemy—be that enemy what it may—and to have their explanation be heard.[60] For Mennonite conscientious objectors in the Great War, that enemy was in some measure the war itself, but also their fellow citizens, Americans who viewed the objectors as slackers who bore no cost of the war. The public perception was, after all, that objectors would not fight in the trenches, and so would not pay the ultimate price of death, nor would they lose their friends, brothers, or comrades in battle. In large part, objectors became the scourge of military cantonments and of communities across the country because others believed they would sacrifice nothing for the war effort. In the years following the war, a certain combat gnosticism would tell Americans that the experience of a Great War slacker had no merit. The conscientious objector could say nothing, really, about a war in which he had not fought.

The diaries in this volume testify to a counter notion: that objectors did indeed incur heavy costs during the Great War, and that they definitely have something to say about the war in which they played their own part. John Neufeld's diary reflects the cost in terms of imprisonment in a federal penitentiary—of being treated as a criminal though he was not one. Ura Hostetler describes not only his long separation from a new wife, but also the humiliation and abuse that he and others faced as objectors. For Gustav Gaeddert, the cost of objection was a certain loss of innocence—about his country, but also about the church that had raised him. Jacob C. Meyer felt a similar loss of innocence about the Mennonite church and, like many, could also count the cost of war in terms of friends and family lost to influenza or to accidental deaths in military camps.

These objectors obviously did not themselves incur the cost of death, as Owen and millions of others did. Still, the fact that they survived the First World War should not invalidate their genuine sacrifices, nor should their writing be disregarded because of their distance from the front. Like the women wartime writers who are now receiving increased scholarly attention for their own responses to the Great War, Mennonite conscientious objectors were caught in modern war's web and were also changed irrevocably by the war. Like other wartime writing, Mennonite objectors' texts thus deserve consideration as part of a larger, more expansive Great War literary canon.

In the Great War's history, the Mennonite objectors' legacy of protest remains but a footnote; their literature seems almost an afterthought to that footnote. Indeed, although Mennonites continue to hold the witness of these conscientious objectors in high regard, the objectors' written artifacts about that witness remain, for the most part, unread. This is unfortunate. In hearing their voices—the voices of American objectors—we will no doubt hear again echoes of the old Lie, told even today to "youths ardent for some desperate glory": that it is sweet, and decorous, to fight and die for one's country.

CHAPTER THREE

In the Tradition but Not of It: The Place for Objectors' Diaries

For the first time in what must have felt like ages, Ura Hostetler found himself faced with the familiar. After several months of detainment in an American military cantonment, the Mennonite objector had been furloughed to an Iowa farm to help a man whose own son was fighting in France.

While detained at Camps Funston and Dodge, Hostetler had been bored and lonely, as had most of his objector brethren. Little seemed familiar there, not the officers who controlled his every move nor the artillery thuds he could hear in the distance nor the daily routine of inactivity. Now, with a furlough, Hostetler figured to make himself useful without having to worry about abetting the military. Although his new boss was not a Mennonite, Hostetler felt more at home back in the country, doing chores just as he had for years on his own family farm: cutting weeds, "thrashing," and, he wrote, "police[ing] up the horse stable."[1]

The phrase "police up the horse stable" appears somewhat dissonant, coming as it does from the pen of a Mennonite conscientious objector. After all, *police* was jargon meant to denote cleaning a military base or military barrack; it was being used in a diary by a Mennonite objector who had for months rejected any ties with the military, to the point of being verbally taunted for his refusal to comply with military orders. No slip of the pen, this use of a military word: Hostetler's diary employed other cantonment jargon as well, as did the diaries of many Mennonite conscientious objectors. They wrote about their "mess" and their "detail," about "double-timing" to their "bunks," about "HQ." The military language seems an uncomfortable fit in texts strong on biblical imagery and scriptural references to peacemaking—yet the terminology is used with apparent ease by the men who wrote each night about their strange experiences in a strange land.

It is clear that this use of military jargon did not mean Mennonite objectors began to embrace the values of a militaristic culture during the Great War, nor that increased exposure to the world of the military had weakened their stand against war. The Mennonite impulse toward nonresistance remained a strong one for these writers, and they were steadfast in their pacifistic convictions throughout their internment in American military cantonments. Still, what can be made of this seeming oddity, this military presence in Mennonite conscientious objectors' diaries?

In many ways, the appearance of military jargon in Mennonite objector diaries suggests an emblem for what these texts were in their time, and for what they can be for readers now. It would be easy to claim that these diaries belong solely to the Mennonite tradition of literature: that they were written by Mennonites and that only Mennonites of that time, and now, could understand and appreciate what has been written. Since the Great War, few people outside the Mennonite fold have studied these diaries, reinforcing the notion that the texts are best left to Mennonite readers, who can most readily interpret their significance. Certainly, Mennonites even today will find much in the diaries to commend, as the texts are replete with references most any member of the church might appreciate: Mennonite names, Mennonite towns, Mennonite doctrine.

Yet there is this other world that crept into the diaries, a world unfamiliar to Mennonite objectors then, and no doubt unfamiliar to many Mennonite readers now. Few Mennonites then, or now, would use *police* in everyday vernacular, nor would they speak about their *detail* or *mess,* unless they were talking about an unkempt kitchen or the detritus left behind by playing children. Such military language would be more characteristic in the writing of wartime combatants, fighting thousands of miles from where the objectors spent their own Great War. A closer analysis of the Mennonite objectors' diaries reveals some clear connections between what the Mennonites wrote and what was written by combatants: not only in the language both groups used, but more in the way each figured their wartime experiences through writing.

Thus in a way, the diaries of Mennonite objectors find home—if uncomfortably—in two literary traditions. The inherently Mennonite aspects situate the diaries in a Mennonite tradition; the unfamiliar world that seeps into the diaries places the texts within a larger Great War literary context. To some extent, the Mennonite objectors' diaries are a literary example of being "in the world, but not of it." In many ways, the texts mirror those written by other First World War authors; yet the diaries remain separated from those texts because of the Mennonite ideals expressed in the diaries' pages—and because of the ways the writers' faith affected their decisions during the war.

The Diary as Literature

The most pressing question may be, of course, whether the diary as a genre deserves to be part of either literary tradition, or of any literary tradition, at all. To compare the diary of a Mennonite conscientious objector with the well-wrought poem of the famed trench poet Siegfried Sassoon may appear as likening apples to oranges. The one is rough-hewn, unfinished, and privately inscribed; the other, thoroughly contemplated, polished, and created with publication in mind. The seemingly transitory nature of a diary, its hasty day-by-day chronicle, might also suggest comparison with the intentional work of fiction or of a memoir is tenuous at best. The memoir writer, after all, takes time to think carefully about his focus, about the words he uses, and the message of his life he hopes to impart; the diary writer, on the other hand, apparently writes what comes to mind, whatever that may be.

We might almost sense another bifurcation here, not only between the writing of the combatant and of the noncombatant in the canons of wartime literature, but of art and of the artless—of writing that is thoroughly reworked and intended for an audience, and of the diary, presumably private and hastily constructed. Yet Lawrence Rosenwald, in "Some Myths about Diaries," has aptly challenged this tendency to judge diaries as artless, questioning the conviction that because diaries are sometimes (but not always) casually produced, they are less worthy of our attention than other forms of literature. "The strongest argument against seeing the diary as a work of literature," Rosenwald writes, "is that diaries as wholes are the work of chance rather than design, and works of chance are not works of art." This view, Rosenwald suggests, is not necessarily true: diarists exert some control over their texts and in many cases have a sense of a design or pattern in the entries they create. Conversely, other works of literature are susceptible to the vagaries of fate or chance, and the author does not have complete authority over what is created or read by an audience.[2]

This dilemma over the diary's status as literature has existed for some time, with no easy resolution. Rosenwald may account for the central argument "against seeing the diary as a work of literature," but there are, of course, many others as well. Diaries have always stood at the periphery of literary studies, never at its center, where the triad of poetry, drama, and fiction has been held in highest esteem. Certainly some writers have developed acclaim in their own right as diarists: the fame of the British gentleman Samuel Pepys (1633-1703) rests solidly on his published diary, as does that of Anais Nin (1903-1977), whose prodigious diary writing—250,000 pages, spanning many decades—made her both famous and infamous.

Most often, however, literary scholars have viewed diaries only as an ancillary to a published writer's oeuvre; diaries have been used to gain special insight into a writer's cognitive or creative processes, for example. Diaries have also been used by historians (literary and otherwise) to trace one person's march through history, and often to discover in the account of one man or woman the material to understand the dealings of many. In this sense, diaries rarely have been read as literature for literature's sake, as a poem or novel might be. Rather, diaries have been viewed almost solely as utile texts that provide insight into the makings of an epoch or into the machinations of the diaries' creators.

Certainly diaries are that—a useful tool in historians' hands. In recent years, however, as interest in the literature of historically marginalized groups has increased, the diary has also received more attention as a literary genre in its own right, in part because the diary itself has often been seen as a marginalized form of expression, used by those who did not have other avenues for their creative energy. For example, in a literary culture that denied women entry—or forced them to assume male pseudonyms to be published—the diary became one way women could make art and could discover self expression, a means of allowing women to speak, as it were, without fear of reproach. The diary, produced in private and intended only for an audience of one, provided for women a forum in which to inscribe and develop their own world views; to construct and deconstruct versions of the self; and to weave together word, thought, and metaphor without the censure of others.

Contemporary arguments assert that denying the diary status as literature denies the creative voices of vast groups of people and privileges only the writing of those who have or had a predominating place in their culture—the literary work of mostly white, mostly male authors upon which much of Western literary history has been rightly or wrongly built. This line of reasoning is compelling, however uncomfortable some might be with the idea of a literary canon built not on merit but on gender and social status. At the least, the argument grants the diary status as literature in its own right, while also suggesting that the diary, like other forms of literature, is a reflection of and a response to the culture in which it was produced.

Although the Mennonite conscientious objectors whose diaries are included here were white and male, they were also marginalized—at least during the Great War, if not before and after. Indeed, American Mennonite conscientious objectors became for a time the exiles of their society, maligned because of their refusal to "do their part" for the country by taking up weapons and fighting. One might well argue that these objectors were ostracized at two levels. First, Mennonite objectors were maligned in their home communities by those outside their churches who could little understand their nonresistant stance. Once they were conscripted, Mennonite objectors were marginalized as well by the military establishment, which held control over the objectors' fates and futures. In their marginalization, Mennonite voices of protest were silenced. Objectors risked ridicule or worse should they speak against the war in their home communities; once in the military, their voices were silenced by officers who refused to listen and by censors who often controlled what they could write, and to whom.

We might conclude that the diary became for Mennonite objectors what it had been for other marginal people throughout history—an available means of expressing their thoughts and feelings when other modes of expression were not viable. This is not to say that Mennonite objectors who chose to keep diaries during their Great War detainment consciously did so solely as a means of self-expression. Assuredly, they did not say to themselves, "Because I feel I no longer have a voice in my society, because no one will listen to my protest against this war, I will begin to keep a diary." That some of the Mennonite objectors were prolific diarists before and after the war suggests as well that the pressures of Great War detainment alone did not compel them to begin chronicling their day-to-day lives. Still, the diary could have served for Mennonite objectors the function it has also served so well for many others, becoming a confessional of sorts, a place to voice one's feelings and thoughts without being censored, or censured, by others.

At the same time, for many objectors during the Great War, even the presumed privacy of a diary could not assure complete freedom of expression. In cantonments across the country, it was not uncommon for military personnel to search the effects of Mennonite objectors. On some occasions, officers confiscated reading material, especially if it was in German or was deemed inflammatory in some way. As Ura Hostetler noted in his diary July 7, 1918, "the officers went thru all our reading matter [and] took a lot of it to censor it. Took all German literature."[3] Those who kept diaries knew their texts could be seized and read at any time, and this influenced what they could, and could not, write.

Confiscation was a concern of Jacob C. Meyer, and probably of other diarists as well. When excerpts of Meyer's diary were published in the *Mennonite Quarterly Review* some fifty years after the war, Meyer explained that he had consciously written in "cryptic language." That way, if the diary was confiscated, "no one inside or outside the camp would be involved" and subject to prosecution under the Espionage and Sedition Acts.[4] Reading Meyer's diary, we can sense the restraint imposed on the writer, who often resorted to using abbreviations, code words, and sparse, undescriptive sentences. Meyer, a voluminous writer on many other occasions, clearly limited what he placed in his presumably "private" diary. Only after the Armistice, when detainment was wearing on Meyer and he apparently felt less threatened by military authority, did derogatory comments begin to appear in the diary. By December 1918, Meyer was criticizing his officers, their laziness, and the inefficiency of a military system that lost records, refused discharges, and kept conscientious objectors from doing meaningful work.

A similar kind of restraint can be detected in Gustav Gaeddert's Great War diary. As an objector based at Camp Funston, Kansas, Gaeddert—like Meyer in his own cantonment—clearly understood the dangers inherent in writing more than he should. Gaeddert noted on at least one occasion that "some boys were searched and their letters read."[5] Like Meyer, Gaeddert was a prolific writer in other circumstances; yet his diary entries were often sparse, and many times focused more on life at home than on life in the camp. This suggests again that he sensed the need to censor what he wrote in his diary, lest he get himself or others into trouble.

Hostetler, another diarist at Camp Funston, apparently did not share the compulsion for self-censorship, though he was aware his reading material could be confiscated, as he noted on July 7, 1918. In any event, Hostetler's diary entries were relatively longer than Gaeddert's and Meyer's, and they did not betray a sense of restraint; indeed, Hostetler wrote at some length about his officers, about abuses occurring in camp, and about his own objection to war. At one point, Hostetler addressed his concern about censorship directly, writing "we aren't allowed to write anything about military affairs (so here goes) in letters . . . the officers Don't want us to criticize them in our letters but here I can."[6]

For Hostetler, who was apparently unafraid of censorship, the diary truly became a means of expressing thoughts and feelings that might otherwise have gone unexpressed. For Gaeddert and Meyer, and no doubt for others as well, the diary could not serve one of its important functions: providing an avenue for unfettered expression, a space for an oft-silenced voice to be heard.

Despite varying degrees of concern about privacy and censorship, a good number of Mennonite conscientious objectors still chose to keep diaries during their Great War detainment. For some men, their Great War diaries would be the only ones they kept in their lifetimes; for others, like Hostetler, the Great War diary book was only one of many they used to chronicle their lives. While only four texts are included in this volume, other Mennonite objectors had Great War diaries; some of these have been donated to Mennonite archives and others remain in private collections.[7] Judging by Gaeddert's correspondence with H. P. Krehbiel, diary keeping was at least initially a popular endeavor for men at Camp Funston. On a postcard dated October 1, 1917, Gaeddert asked Krehbiel to send "a day book or Diary book a good book worth having" for himself and others in his detachment, as many men were requesting them.[8]

What accounts, then, for the decision so many Mennonite objectors made to keep a diary? As proposed above, likely these objectors, feeling their voices silenced in so many realms, turned to the diary as a means of relatively free expression. Diaries became one place they could inscribe thoughts about their officers, their detainment, and their objection, especially when they felt all other avenues of expression—letter writing, talks with Mennonite advisors and family—were restricted. Boredom may also have been a factor. Lack of activity provided time, space, and inclination to keep a diary, and this could have been cause enough for some men to begin writing down their thoughts. The stultifying monotony of days spent doing little or nothing probably compelled a few to take up journaling, an activity they might not otherwise have considered, given an alternative.

Still, a major motivating force for the diarists must surely have been the sense that this experience—this time in a military cantonment—had special import in the objectors' own lives, if not in the lives of their churches and communities. The gravity with which Mennonite objectors were sent to military camps; the special attention paid to objector concerns by home communities, by Mennonite periodicals, by church leaders, and by government officials; the varied troubles Mennonite objectors faced in camp: all implied to Mennonite objectors the uniqueness of their predicament. Theirs was an unrivaled time in the history of Mennonites in America, their nonresistant stance against the vast military machine a unique moment in the nation's history. The objectors were, as Hostetler wrote in his diary, "soldiers of the cross," fighting as it were for God's kingdom. In believing this, how could Hostetler not affirm the significance of his presumably historical mission?[9]

Keeping a diary provided objectors the opportunity to chronicle their own role as nonviolent soliders for Christ. Even the narrowly circumscribed focus of the objectors' diaries suggests that each writer sought, first and foremost, to describe this momentous occasion in his life: the personal history preceding the war and proceeding after it seemingly mattered little. Thus, most diaries written by objectors began with their first day in the military—the goodbyes to family and friends, and the long train ride to the cantonment—and ended when their detainment in military camps ended. For Gaeddert and Hostetler, the diaries concluded with their furloughs; Meyer's diary ended once he had finished reconstruction work in France; John Neufeld's diary finished with his release from Fort Leavenworth prison. In each case, the diary truly was a Great War diary, uncluttered by the events of life both before and after conscription.

In a similar way, many wartime combatants felt that their part in making the world safe for democracy would become a defining moment in their personal histories, if not in the history of their nation. This "need to report," as Samuel Hynes terms it, and to chronicle what happened in war, gave rise to numerous diaries.[10] The gravity of war, its frenetic activity, and the psychology of the conflict imbued its participants with a sense of the Great War's magnitude in human events. It became the war like no other, a war (it was said) to end all wars. As Hynes says,

> For most men who fight, war is their one contact with the world of great doings. Other men govern, sign treaties, invent machines, cure diseases, alter lives. But for ordinary men—the men who fight our wars—there will probably be only that one time

when their lives intersect with history, one opportunity to act in great events. Not to alter those events—no single soldier affects a war, or even a battle—but simply to be there, *in* history. So men feel a need to say, like the ubiquitous Kilroy, "I was there."[11]

By chronicling his wartime activities via the diary, the writer recorded his place in history's momentous event—as a combatant or, in the case of Mennonite diarists, as objectors to that event. As Hynes has argued, the diarists knew, perhaps implicitly, that their role in the Great War would be minor at best; no one soldier, or no one objector, believed he could change the entire course of humankind. In keeping a diary, however, a man could chronicle history as he stood in its midst, immersed in a moment that would transform his world. Like the soldier who documented his time in battle, leaving an artifact that said "I was there," the objectors too must have realized the significance of their diaries, marking their place in the history of the Mennonite church and of the country. At the least, the fact that several writers donated their Great War diaries to Mennonite archives after the war suggests the men were aware their diaries held some import, and that one man's day-to-day report about objecting to war could provide readers with a sense of what it was like to be a part of history.

The Offer of Immediacy

Hynes has argued that the "need to report" one's place in history differed from the "need to remember." Those who were compelled to report their role in history's making kept a diary; later, those who were compelled to remember wrote their memoirs.[12] Similarly, the writer May Sarton once opined, "Autobiography is 'what I remember,' whereas a journal [or diary] has to with what I am, in this instant."[13] The difference between reporting and remembering is sometimes stark, as can be seen in comparing memoirs of Mennonite objectors written half a century after the war with the diaries written by objectors during the war. By telling their stories years after the war's conclusion, many Mennonite men were afforded the luxury of time and distance. The intervening years allowed these men to view their roles as Great War objectors with some detachment, giving them ample opportunity to reflect on their conscientious objection and the influence of their First World War experiences on their postwar lives. The maturation of Mennonites' twentieth-century peace witness and its application to later U.S. conflicts may also have influenced these Great War narratives, as objectors from the First World War could see more clearly the ways their experiences were uniquely—even painfully—different from those of their World War II and Korean War brethren.

Some Great War objectors have noted that their part in America's history changed forever how the U.S. government dealt with, and how the Mennonite church provided for, conscientious objectors. In his "Experiences of a C.O. in World War I," Ernest H. Miller, who had been a Mennonite objector at Camp Funston, wrote: "I believe I can truthfully say that our M[ennonite] C[entral] C[ommittee], the C[ivilian] P[ublic] S[ervice] in World War II, our Voluntary Service Program . . . even some of the mission work in our church, and helpful reforms in our mental hospitals were an outgrowth of our experiences in World War I."[14] Miller penned his autobiography in 1972, allowing him to see more certainly the trajectory of his Great War hardships, and to envision more clearly the role he played in transforming the Mennonite church. His 1972 perspective changed his understanding of 1918 events, as is the case when any writer peers back at events lived long ago and writes what he sees.

In describing what they remembered, rather than reporting what they saw, Mennonite objectors who wrote their memoirs provided a different story of the war than the diarists; the memoirists' self-conscious awareness of how history had turned out affected, in many ways, the narrative they could or would write. Conversely, the diaries of Mennonite conscientious objectors provide a sense of immediacy not evident in the texts produced long after the war's conclusion. This immediacy is the special province of the diary, a characteristic which separates the genre from other forms of life-writing, and which gives us perspectives on history as it was lived day to day.

According to Hynes, "immediacy and directness" is a particular virtue in war diaries, which "tend to level war experience, reporting the ordinary days with the extraordinary ones, the boredom as well as the excitement, and [provide] close texture, the grain of life in war."[15] Though Hynes is writing about the diaries of combat soldiers, the same observations might apply to the conscientious objectors' texts. Rather than reporting only the graver moments of their Great War confinement, as their autobiographies tended to do, the objectors' diaries captured everything, the extraordinary moments and the mundane—nearly as such events occurred.

We recognize, of course, that this immediacy, this directness, is not complete. There cannot be a written representation of experience without the obvious mediation of language. What we read in autobiographic writing, including diaries, is but the metaphoric representation of actual experience and the recreation of the self likewise a symbolic identity. Scholars have long recognized this necessary use of metaphor in constructing meaning, in "grasp[ing]," as James Olney writes, "the unknown through the known" and in "connect[ing] the known of ourselves to the unknown of the world."[16] William Spengemann and L. R. Lundquist note that a writer sees his world through a prism of language, language itself being "the common possession of his culture . . . filled with the assumed values of his society."[17] The language of a diary therefore reflects not only the self in a certain place and time, but also the self constructed by that place and time. The diary's language reveals, as well, the writer's desire to use what he understands and knows as a means of representing what at the moment remains outside his realm of knowing. For Mennonite objectors, this meant using what was known and trusted, the Mennonite faith and community, to understand what was outside their experience, a life in the military.

Therefore, in many ways, these diaries provide an excellent means of understanding not only the writer's self but also the ways in which Mennonite culture influenced and shaped who he assumed himself to be. The language each writer employed, what he chose to include in his diary, what he chose to exclude: these all had significance, for they reflected the ways in which the author understood and viewed himself—a self constructed, in great part, by his culture, his Mennonite faith, and the church's historical past, but also by the military world into which the writer had entered. Although each diarist wrote about the day's events in his diary, he could do so only through his conceptualization of the self. As literary critic Felicity Nussbaum has noted: "[A diary] makes meaning inherent in the choice of words, the sequence of phrases, and the assignment of dialogue to self and other. The articulation of the event is itself an evaluative act—word itself a representation of reality complicated by self, culture, and history."[18]

The diarists, then, did not write mindlessly about the day's events without contemplating them, reflecting on what seemed significant to mention and what not. Neither did they write in a vacuum. Instead, the act of creating a diary became in its own way an evaluative act, demanding each writer's attention to the self and to the world he inhabited. What a writer believed significant enough to record in his diary depended, to be sure, on what he believed about himself and his place in the world. Because the diarists included here belonged to different Mennonite groups, because they had different upbringings in different families, and because they were their own discrete selves, each diary carries the imprint of one man's life and experiences during the war. At the same time, as members of the Mennonite church and as young men experiencing a comparable wartime fate, the diarists shared many similar beliefs about the self and about the world around them. And so the diarists also share characteristic ways of writing about that life and those experiences.

Perhaps the most notable shared characteristic among the diaries is the brevity of each day's entry. The four men included in this volume were prolific writers in other instances—in their letters home and later in Mennonite periodicals and in histories they wrote about their churches and their families.[19] Their diaries, however, are shorter than many other diaries written during the Great War, by combatants and by noncombatants alike. As mentioned earlier, some of the objectors could have been concerned about having their diaries confiscated, and about indictment under espionage and sedition laws; this fear may have affected how much they chose to write in their diaries. Yet given the broad possibility of topics they could safely write about, it is remarkable that the diarists still wrote so little, especially because they seemingly had ample time to write. Other diaries not included in this volume are even more brief in their day-to-day chronicle, listing at most the weather and the kind of work each writer did, or did not do, during the day. Of Mennonite objectors' diaries from the Great War, only Noah Leatherman's diary, published in 1951, sustained any extended exploration of a topic; because Leatherman's original diary has not been found, it is unclear whether Leatherman added information later, or if the long entries were part of the original text.

In the parlance of literary critic Lawrence Rosenwald, a diarist who focuses only on his daily actions in the world is an objective one, "seeking the self in daily manifestations." By contrast, Rosenwald says, a subjective diarist turns inward for extensive self-examination. The diary of such a writer does not ask "What have I done?" but "Who am I?"[20]

Mennonite objectors, in their brevity, emphasized their day-to-day actions rather than exploring at any length their inner selves—who they were and who they were becoming. A typical diary entry for an objector might describe the day's chores and to whom the man had spoken, or it might contain a few words, like Gustav Gaeddert's "hauled garbage." Compare an objector's diary entry with that of an American combatant, like Alan Seeger, or of a British civilian, like Cynthia Asquith, and the difference becomes stark. While Seeger and Asquith, among others, expended great space in their diaries, the objectors wrote little; while other wartime diarists found a place in the diaries to explore their selves and their place in the world, Mennonite objectors spent limited time in such self-examination.

We might do well to ask why such a difference exists and, moreover, what that difference in length and in focus might say about the objectors and about the Mennonite forces which had shaped them. The fact that Mennonite diarists wrote sparingly and tended to be more objective than subjective is, most assuredly, a reflection of the culture in which they were raised: a culture that privileged humility over selfish pride, a culture which also preferred, in Ervin Beck's terms, "doing over being; service over theologizing."[21]

Certainly, the Mennonite impulse toward humility and self-effacement was evident in Mennonite objectors' diaries. At the same time, the very nature of keeping a diary is to center on and be preoccupied with the self as it operates in the world. Therefore, the diary as a genre seemingly contradicts the Mennonite teaching of humility, of submission to God and of avoiding the sin of pride. Focusing too intently on the self, reflecting too deeply on one's thoughts and feelings, mentioning one's good deeds and heroics: such would suggest a love of self rather than of God, as well as a concern for selfhood rather than the vitality of one's religious community.

Robert Fothergill has noted that in most diaries, there is a "gesture of self-effacement" when writers refuse to use the first-person "'I' that would otherwise govern verb after verb, page after page."[22] It would seem that in Mennonite objectors' diaries this gesture was intensified, not only in the relative lack of the first-person pronoun, but in the tension created by the diary between writing at length about the self and effacing the self, between the virtue of humility and the vice of pride. By remaining focused on external action, on what they did rather than were, the Mennonite objectors could be relieved from self-promotion, from centering too exclusively on the self and its worth.

The entries' relative brevity and the focus on "what I did" likewise reflected the traditional Mennonite concern for labor as a foundation for self-conception. In "The Signifying Menno: Archetypes for Authors and Critics," Beck has outlined archetypes unique to Mennonite literature, all which are "embodied in more or less well known visual images from traditional culture." One of these images is that of the Anabaptist digger, whose icon served as the frontispiece for *Martyrs Mirror* editions published from 1685 to 1990.[23] Beck writes that the motto above the digger "interprets his significance:

'Work and Hope.' Those few words brilliantly epitomize Mennonites' traditional preference for doing over being; for service over theologizing."[24] Thus, the Anabaptist digger well represents what resided at the core of Mennonite self identity, where the ability to labor in many ways defined one's self worth.

The idea of "work and hope" certainly informed Mennonite objectors in the Great War, who predominantly grew up in agrarian communities where manual labor was an integral part of one's selfhood. The indolence created by detainment in military cantonments was especially difficult for many who could little tolerate idleness and the inability to make themselves useful. Thus, the impulse to write "what I have done" rather than "who I am" reflected, in a larger sense, the need to do something as a means of creating a self. Frustrations about not working and questions about conscientiously accepting work in the military were irrevocably tied to questions of one's self-worth. So, in the diaries, objectors focused almost solely on their desire to work, on their frustration because they could not conscientiously work, and on their hope that God would make clear the way to be useful while still maintaining a peaceful witness.

Both Gustav Gaeddert and Jacob C. Meyer especially relied on this idea in figuring their military experiences. Gaeddert's angst about working while in the cantonment was apparently acute, as he used his diary (as well as his correspondence with friends and family) to repeatedly grapple with the decision to work or not. For the first few months of his detainment, Gaeddert chose to do sanitation work. That he was usefully employed in the camp seemed to matter to Gaeddert, as he noted in his diary each day whether he worked or not; in some entries, his work hauling garbage was all he noted. Gaeddert's diary entries increasingly turned to the decision he had to make about whether he should work in the camp. When he made the choice to cease working, the diary's focus shifted as well—to the idleness Gaeddert hated, and to his unfulfilled desire to make himself useful. Throughout his diary, Gaeddert kept the idea of working at center, suggesting the power "work" had in his own conceptualization of a self. Years later, when Gaeddert was interviewed about his World War I experiences, he still focused on the concept of work—whether he had made the correct decision about not working, and whether God wanted Mennonites to do some form of work during the war after all.

The idea of "work and hope" also informed much of what Meyer wrote in his diary. Like Gaeddert, Meyer struggled with whether he could conscientiously work in his military cantonment; unlike

Gaeddert, Meyer ultimately chose to do some labor for his detachment. Reading over the first pages of Meyer's diary, one notices the repeated use of "work." The men "reported but worked nothing"; later, they "did not work at all." They were demanded to "work in barracks." The men in his detachment discussed the conscientious objectors' position among themselves, and wondered "why not work some kinds of work?"[25] Ultimately, Meyer held to the conviction found in 2 Thessalonians 3:10, that "anyone unwilling to work should not eat." He believed that he could remain steadfastly nonresistant but should, nonetheless, contribute to the army which held him.

Although Meyer chose to work, and let that choice influence what he wrote in the diary, he did not lose sight of hope, the other element of the archetypal Mennonite ideal. Meyer's hope can also be traced throughout the diary. He remained hopeful of his peaceful witness and its effect on those around him; hopeful that his role in camp would usefully serve both military officials and the objectors; and hopeful that a way would yet remain open for him to do reconstruction service in France, where Meyer could make himself useful through the work of his hands and of his mind.

Objectors and Combatants: On Common Ground

Given the specific imprint of Mennonite thought and culture in the diaries, it would be easy to claim that the texts belong solely to a Mennonite literary tradition. Yet remarkably, even the seemingly inherent "Mennonite" traits in the objectors' diaries—the reliance on Scripture, for example, or the privileging of a close community—appear as well in the texts of other Great War writers. These intersections, these similarities in the writing of objectors, combatants, and noncombatants alike, provide compelling evidence that the diaries, while part of a Mennonite literary tradition, find affinity with the larger body of literature emerging from the Great War. The objectors' diaries even have commonalities with the writing of combatants—with the literary work of those whose Great War was so unlike their own.

Because the Bible stood at the core of Mennonite faith and praxis, informing what Mennonites believed and how they lived, the objectors' understanding of their selves and their surroundings during their detainment was, perhaps obviously, influenced by Scripture. Most Mennonite objectors knew their Bibles front and back, and could quote Scripture from memory. Indeed, to the Board of Inquiry's Major Walter Kellogg, the Mennonites understood their Bibles to a fault. As he wrote,

> These men knew their Bibles. They had read in the Testaments daily, or almost daily, they testified, for a long period of years. They did not read so much for the story of it as they read it for a guide which, in all things, was to govern their conduct. They knew it narrowly, unintelligently, but they knew it. And they knew nothing else.[26]

Kellogg's vitriol colored his assessment of Mennonite objectors, yet there was truth in his observation. Mennonite objectors steadfastly studied their Bibles, finding in Scripture not only a comfort but also a guide, helping them discern how they should live.

In turn, the objectors' extensive knowledge of the Bible helped them to understand, and to convey in their diaries, what they were experiencing in their detainment. For Hostetler especially, the language of Scripture became an important feature in the text he created. In many diary entries, Hostetler placed himself and his objector brethren into Scripture, so that they became just as the characters in Christ's parables. On June 27, 1918, for example, Hostetler figured himself as one of the wise virgins, "gathering up oil for future use. When the bridegroom cometh may we have our vessels ready and lamp all filled."[27]

In an earlier diary entry, Hostetler felt no need to contextualize the parable of the two debtors or the objectors' place in it, writing only that in seeing Charles Hollcroft, a fellow Mennonite, he thought of Luke 7:41-49. And, in detailing his own homesickness and his desire to leave the military camp, Hostetler became one of the "laborers" described in Matthew 9:37-38. Although he wanted to go home, his place was in the camp where "God has a work for me to do": "behold the fields they are ready for harvest and the laborers are few. Fit we few, ready creatures to do thy bidding here and may we be able to carry thy message of love to a few hungry souls before it is too late."[28] Similar biblical allusions appeared throughout Hostetler's diary as the writer, so steeped in the Bible, found in its language an easy familiarity that he could use to detail what was, for him, unfamiliar territory.

Scripture surfaced less prominently in the other diaries printed here, although biblical allusion still served as a significant means through which the writers could understand and write about their military lives. For instance, Neufeld believed Scripture could most suitably convey his experience as an objector and then prisoner. Rather than reflect on his Great War life at any length, Neufeld ended his diary by encapsulating his thoughts "best expressed in the word of 1 Samuel 12:24: 'Only fear the Lord, and serve him in truth with all your heart: for consider how great things he hath done for you.'"[29]

This passage alone, Neufeld must have assumed, would make his state of mind clear. On the other hand, in Meyer's diary, the Bible appeared often in the text even though biblical allusion did not. Ever the scholar, Meyer often noted what text his objector group was studying, and provided a brief synopsis of the discussion about the Scripture. Even here, the use of Scripture was a significant shaping force in Meyer's wartime life: significant enough so that Meyer mentioned each time he spent time with the Bible and regularly explained his reaction to that day's study.

Mennonites were hardly alone in using Scripture when writing about wartime experiences. Many Great War writers used the Bible to justify war, informed as they were by the civil religion that was at the time prominent in both Allied and Central Power countries. As Dominic Hibberd and John Onions point out in their *Poetry of the Great War*, a good number of wartime artists (both literary and visual) used biblical imagery to equate the soldiers' suffering and sacrifice with that of Christ. Hibberd and Onions write that

> Christ's saying before the crucifixion, "Greater love hath no man than this, that a man lay down his life for his friends" (John 15:13), was frequently quoted and used as a title or epigraph for poems.... The soldier waiting behind the lines was like Christ in Gethsemane. As he carried burdens up the communication trenches, he was Christ carrying the cross.... Laying down his life for his friends (either the nation or his comrades), he saved humanity and earned eternal life.[30]

For numerous Great War writers, the image of Christ as soldier helped to justify the horrors of war. The soldiers' sacrifice of death was necessary in saving the world from evil, for they were only answering the call of Christ, as the writer William Evans noted. In hearing that call, Evans wrote,

> England's manhood stood by Christ the King,
> Who comes with love and healing in His wing,
> And gives His all.[31]

Evans concluded that by fighting for Christ, and against evil, the soldiers were themselves "transfigured by the conflict," thus echoing Christ's own resurrection from the dead.[32]

We find in many Great War literary texts, then, the same sense of trench salvation that American pulpits were espousing during the war. For some writers, scriptural allusion reinforced and intensified the righteousness of the soldiers' cause, and imbued soldiers with Christ-like status. Mennonites would no doubt have found this application of Scripture alarming, as it seemed to contradict all the Mennonites believed to be true about Christ's pacific teachings. Still, there were some Great War writers who saw in Scripture the same doctrine of peace embraced by Mennonites, and who wove that understanding into the wartime texts they created.

The poet Wilfred Owen would find in Scripture a different interpretation, and many of his poems used Scripture not to promote the ideology of trench salvation, or of the soldier as savior, but to suggest that a peaceful Christ would find no place as a combatant on the Western Front. In "Mental Cases," for example, Owen rejected the notion of salvific suffering, finding war's combatants not adorned in splendor as the resurrected Christ; instead, they were mired in hell, slobbering, baring teeth, and picking at themselves, "These men whose minds the Dead have ravished." The poem offered an ironic turn to Revelation 7:13-17:

> What are these which are arrayed in white robes? . . . . These are they which came out of a great tribulation, and have washed their robes, and made them white in the blood of the Lamb . . . . They shall hunger no more, neither thirst any more; neither shall the sun light on them, nor any heat. For the Lamb which is amid the throne shall feed them, and shall lead them unto living fountains of waters; and God shall wipe away all tears from their eyes. (KJV)

The soldiers had emerged from a "great tribulation" indeed, but rather than seeing in that tribulation their salvation, Owen believed the "Mental Cases" were damned to their own personal hell, tormented by the war's memories. In turn, the subjects of Owen's poem tormented those "who smote them" and "who dealt them war and madness." No glorified vision of the soldier becoming as Christ, Owen's reliance on biblical imagery instead became an indictment of war and of the unholy destruction it had wrought. Mennonite objectors, although perhaps unaccustomed to using the Bible ironically, would yet find in Owen's poem a kernel of truth. For Mennonites, too, war was a hell in which Christ would find no place.

Something about the passion of Christ and his suffering on the cross resonated with both Mennonite conscientious objectors and trench poets alike, for many writers continued to find in that suffering a parallel to their own Great War existences. Without question, soldiers on the Western Front suffered immensely, as anyone reading their wartime writing will recognize. The agonies of modern warfare were numerous: mud-filled trenches and vermin infestations seemed but lesser irritations to soldiers who had to beware of mustard gas, a sniper's bullet, or an unexpected mortar attack. Hynes writes that the soldiers' suffering was a "passive" one, in which the "men in the trenches were not agents in their soldiering but merely victims," victims of modern weaponry that made suffering and death accidental, anonymous.[33]

It was in this passive suffering, however, that soldiers felt themselves tied more assuredly to the Christ who suffered, who likewise was a victim of elements beyond his control, and whose violent death also proved a savior of men. As Hibberd and Onions note, the image of Christ's passion and martyrdom became invaluable for civilians and soldiers, as "it made sense of passive suffering and drew attention away from the fact that fighting involved killing as well as being killed. If death in this war was a martyrdom, its hideousness could be accepted."[34]

Combatant writers no doubt found succor in the martyr image. Confronted at every turn with death—their own death, the death of their comrades—the way of Christ and the martyr ideal proved comforting; the soldiers would, after all, bear pain and death for a greater cause, however immense their suffering might be. John Oxenham's "The Vision Splendid" suggested how encouraging the martyr image could be for combatants. The poet wrote that, in death, the soldiers would look back on life without "regret" and would see in their suffering and death the echoing of Christ's own sacrificial power. The dead soldiers, Oxenham said, were "God's holy martyrs" who "died that Life might live":

> You, like the Saints, have freely given your all,
> And your high deaths, God's purpose revealing,
> Sound through the earth His mighty Clarion Call.[35]

Obviously, Oxenham's poem was written not so much to the dead as to people grieving their loss—those who needed, in their suffering, an image of sacrificial death that gave meaning to the seeming futility of war.

Other trench writers echoed Oxenham's martyr ideal in their own poetry as well as in their letters home. Even those waiting on the home front embraced the image of the martyr, feeling more assured that wartime suffering and death was not in vain. Countess Anna de Noailles, writing from her home in Paris, implored the wartime dead, made divine by their faithful fighting, to "Help us, whose agony is but begun." Their deaths were given as a "gift" at Verdun, but provided no comfort to those left mourning.[36] Vera Brittain, struggling in England to comprehend the death of her fiancée Roland, sought comfort in his sacrificial death. On an Easter Sunday several months after he was killed at the front, Brittain sat in St. Paul's Cathedral and studied a picture of Hagar in the Desert:

> Her Gethsemane, I thought, had been even darker than that of the Man of Sorrows, who after all knew—or believed—that He was God; she was merely a human being without omnipotence, and a woman too, at the mercy, as were all women to-day, of an agonising, ruthless fate which it seemed she could do nothing to restrain. 'Watchman, will the night soon pass?' ran the inscription under the painting, and I wondered how many women in the Cathedral that morning, numbed and bewildered by blow after blow, were asking the self-same question.[37]

Later, after the service, Brittain concluded that she would live more heroically, as Roland had done, accepting like Roland and Hagar her own Gethsemane. In her diary she wrote,

> Perhaps now I shall one day rise, and be worthy of him who in his life both in peace and in war and in his death on the fields of France has shown me "the way more plain." At any rate, if ever I do face danger and suffering with some measure of his heroism, it will be because I have learnt through him that love is supreme, that love is stronger than death and the fear of death.[38]

For Brittain, as for Noailles and for the combatants, wartime suffering was not in vain. In suffering and in dying, the soldiers were, in Eva Dobell's words, "Slain for the world's salvation."[39] Few would not find a modicum of comfort in such a conviction.

American Mennonite objectors likewise suffered during the Great War, although theirs was a suffering different than that of many others. They did not suffer the agonies of trench warfare, as the combatants did, and many if not most Mennonites were spared the fate of civilians like Brittain, who lost a fiancée, a brother, and several other close friends on the Western Front. Still, Mennonite objectors faced their own kind of suffering in military cantonments. They were abused verbally and physically, tortured, and imprisoned; they were detained against their wills, separated from home communities, and compelled to act in ways that violated their religious and moral convictions. In some cases, they died in military cantonments, either because of the rampant diseases there, or because of the abuse they received. Thus, the image of a suffering, salvific Christ encouraged them as well. As with other combatant and civilian writers, Mennonite objectors, including the diarists in this volume, turned to the ideal of Christ-like suffering and sacrifice in figuring their own experiences.

Additionally for Mennonites, however, the idea of suffering and sacrifice had been woven into their church's history. A foundational text among Mennonites was, after all, the *Martyrs Mirror*, a hagiography of sorts that detailed the lives and deaths of the Anabaptist martyrs. Ervin Beck has noted that the martyr was another significant archetype used by Mennonite writers throughout the ages. It was symbolized—Beck argues in his own study—by the etching of the Anabaptist Anneken Hendriks, burned at the stake for her faith. The martyr archetype did not necessarily suggest that one had to be killed for one's principles, for one's faith. Merely accepting suffering in one's life was enough, especially if that suffering could be accompanied by forbearance and love for those who had inflicted pain, and if that suffering could be used to witness to God's Truth.

During the Great War, Mennonites returned to this idea of martyrdom. Just as combatants and civilians alike were extolling the "martyr spirit" of those at the front, so too were Mennonite denominational periodicals praising the objectors' "martyr spirit." Mennonite periodicals thus provided for objectors a constant reminder of their church's martyred history, and of the objectors' own need to have a persistent but peaceful witness to those who persecuted them. The *Gospel Herald*, for example, implored wartime readers to remain firm in their pacific convictions by remembering their past: "[The Mennonites'] early history has been written in blood, because of their abhorrence of strife and bloodshed. Their steadfastness and their very single-mindedness has produced among them thousands of martyrs, heroes, infinitely more heroic than the greatest soldiers of history."[40]

In the same periodical, an unsigned editorial evoked the objectors' "Martyr Spirit," writing,

> Now and then there comes to our ears a story of real persecution and real heroism on the part of our brethren in camp. . . . They have the martyr spirit. They believe they ought not in any way to aid or abet war, even if it is keeping up the noncombatant end of the military machine, and rather than have any part in the work

of destroying men's lives they will suffer persecution, even death, before they will give their consent to do any military service. This is a good time to read the story of how many of our fathers went to the stake rather than compromise their faith.[41]

Probably the most memorable use of the martyr archetype in Great War Mennonite literature was that which appeared in J. G. Evert's poem, "The Martyrs of Alcatraz." Evert relied heavily on the martyr image in memorializing the four Hutterite men who were persecuted as conscientious objectors at Alcatraz and Leavenworth penitentiaries. The poem drew parallels between their persecution and that of their Anabaptist ancestors, connecting the plight of the "objectors four" to the martyred spirit felt among all Mennonite objectors.[42] Although published in 1919, after the war's conclusion, Evert's poem reflected well the Mennonites' wartime reliance on the martyr, an ideal which was intended to uplift readers and to provide them with an image they could use to understand the significance of their peaceful witness—just as, in other ways, the martyr image was used to uplift soldiers and those for whom the soldiers fought.

Martyr imagery appeared in each of the four diaries included in this volume. Hostetler, however, relied on this ideal more than did the other diarists, figuring himself as a martyr of sorts who quietly accepted his lot and who was assured of the witness made possible through suffering. The military camp became his own trial by fire, a trial he willingly embraced, as had his own Mennonite ancestors. At Camp Funston, Hostetler was not treated as badly as many objectors; he could not claim to be persecuted to the extent others were. Yet in his diary, he repeatedly noted cases where fellow objectors, facing verbal and physical abuse from their officers, were still "firm" in their convictions or were "stickers" for the Mennonite cause.[43]

Hostetler's quiet acceptance of his own suffering characterized his diary entries as well. He suffered because he could not be with his wife, whom he missed so acutely; he suffered because of other soldiers who tormented him. Almost always filled with the martyr spirit, however, Hostetler embraced his own suffering as a way of strengthening his witness and drawing "closer to God."[44] Though he at times wished he could die "to get away from this cruel old world," Hostetler recognized as well that by staying in the world, and by accepting the suffering meted out to him, he could continue God's work in the military camp.[45] Still, Hostetler readily welcomed a martyr's death, and was willing to "die for our cause" if necessary.[46]

To somewhat a lesser extent, the other diarists in this volume also turned to the martyr ideal in figuring their wartime experiences.

Reading the diaries, one senses each man's acceptance of his own lot; however painful being in a military camp might be, the men enacted a "martyr's spirit," willingly embracing their suffering rather than backing away from their nonresistant stance. Neufeld, for example, described in his diary the physical abuse he received, an unfair court-martial, and a protracted prison sentence. Yet he remained hopeful, believing that in his persecution, he had served God "in truth" and with "all my heart."[47] Meyer, whose opportunity to go overseas with the American Friends Service Committee was repeatedly delayed by governmental red tape, accepted his fate, and worked hard in the military camp until the way to France would open up for him. Meyer believed God had a place for him in his cantonment, even if this meant suffering the verbal taunts of other men. In each case, the diarist suggested—through what he wrote, but also through what he did not write—that any suffering one felt while conscripted was not too heavy a burden. Rather, persecution became one more way of witnessing to Christ's message of peace and of suffering love.

Furthermore, Mennonite objectors were knit together as a community through their own particular kind of suffering. Lonely, confined, aliens together in a strange land, the conscientious objectors turned to each other for comfort and companionship, forging a brotherhood of sorts to combat their shared misery. For Mennonite conscientious objectors, the community they developed within their detachments became a vital part of their Great War experiences and a balm to their suffering; their diaries reflected again and again the centrality of this brotherhood in their wartime detainment. In a way, the diaries of Mennonite men became not so much about the authors but about the units in which they lived, as the writers mentioned those providing aid for the infirm among them; those encouraging others to remain steadfast in their nonresistant stance; those writing letters home for the illiterate in their ranks; those giving comfort to the lonely, who were longing for wife and children; and those facilitating evening Bible studies and hymn sings. Some men even inscribed in their diaries a list of every objector in camp, chronicling on paper the people that comprised a particular community.

Royden Loewen has noted a similar pattern in his study of those Mennonite diarists living in frontier Canada; in their diaries, also, Mennonite men and women often "recorded the social outline of household, kin group, community, and wider society." Thus, Loewen argues, Mennonites writers relied on diaries as a means of "mapping, defining, and articulating crucial social relationships." Similarly, by recording the names of the men in his camp, a Mennonite objector was (like the Mennonites of the Canadian frontier) "mentally designing, even celebrating, an envisioned community."[48]

And, indeed, objectors often used their detachments as a means of constructing communities to replace the ones they left, complete with church, Bible study, singing, and Sunday school. Even the practice of visitation between conscientious objector units replicated the social custom of visiting in their home communities, as men moved from one barrack to the other to meet friends and discuss the day's events. These visits were duly recorded in their diaries, an indication of their importance in the men's daily lives.

Disruptions in the community were noted with a sense of sadness, suggesting again how strong the communal bonds had become in the objector detachments. Hostetler, having been at Camp Funston only two months, wrote with great sorrow about the men who were "taken from us," using imagery that suggested an external force was severing his objector community. Why the men were removed from Funston Hostetler did not say. He wrote,

> Last eve. 9:30 14 of our No. were taken from us. Had a meeting before they left. The Lord really blessed me seemed like his spirit was there. Sure gave us inward pain to part with the brethern, not because we are afraid of them falling but because we love them. Tears started to come to my eyes as I bid some good by and Gods blessings. . . . Holcroft & I put arms around each other walked around the yard, sang some songs kinda to ourselves and talked about some blessed experiences, while the boys were being lined up to leave. Our whole bunch seemed to be out watching.[49]

Likewise Meyer, at his own cantonment, noted that when several men were furloughed, "some tears [were] shed in the 'parting' . . . since the 21 fellows left we felt a little lonesome but in pretty good spirits."[50]

In Meyer's camp, at least, the disruption of the community would not be permanent; his detachment made plans for a reunion once the war concluded, and Meyer was appointed to his company's conscientious objector reunion committee.

Although the idea of "community" was a significant shaping factor in Mennonite objectors' lives, and in the diaries they kept, the same might be said as well for the writing of Great War combatants. We need only read a doughboy's autobiography to see how community was forged in the hardship of the trenches and the rollicking good times at French pubs, a unity sealed by blood and wine, adversity and celebration, the creation of an "us" to stand against an enemy "them." The British soldier Guy Chapman wrote in his autobiography that his life during the Great War was "involved with the lives of other men, a few living, some dead." Chapman said that his memoir of war was more about his battalion than about himself, and he was right.[51]

Indeed, many Great War memoirs were as much about the writer's battalion as about the writer, so inextricably drawn together were the men in battle. It was through war that a bond was established, the American Alan Seeger wrote, a bond of "common dangers shared, common sufferings borne, common glories achieved." These things, Seeger continued, "knit men together in real comradeship."[52] Rather than using an autobiographical "I" to guide their Great War memoirs, authors such as Edmund Blunden relied on a corporate "we":

> We are still in the Somme battle . . . We marched to Martinsart Wood . . . We crawl or scamper along the wood edge as the plainest route, and are at once made the target for a devil's present of shells; they must get us; they do not.[53]

For Blunden, the "we" of his battalion seemingly mattered more than the "I" that would otherwise govern an autobiography. Blunden's community of fellow fighters helped define who he was in war, as well as what the war meant to him.

Rather than high-minded ideals like heroism and courage, it was often the wartime community of suffering soldiers that compelled men to continue fighting. Hibberd and Onions note that by 1917-18, "The comradeship which developed at the front became so strong . . . it was for many the principal motive for staying in the line."[54]

Siegfried Sassoon was among those who returned to the front to fight with his brethren. Sassoon declared his conscientious objection to the war in great part because of his concern for fellow soldiers who were uselessly dying. He was sent to Craiglockhart Hospital as a case of shell shock, where he comfortably convalesced. Yet as he rested, he was haunted by images of fellow soldiers continuing to fight the miserable war. While he protested the war from far behind the lines, his community—the men for whom he was protesting—fought and died at the front.

Although he could easily have remained at Craiglockhart, Sassoon applied for General Service and returned to the men he loved so much. Wrote Sassoon of his declaration and his decision to resume fighting:

> The darkness tells how vainly I have striven
> To free them from the pit where they must dwell
> In outcast gloom convulsed and jagged and riven
> By grappling guns. Love drove me to rebel.
> Love drives me back to grope with them through hell;
> And in their tortured eyes I stand forgiven.[55]

Sassoon's love for his fellow soldiers, his proverbial willingness to ride with them to hell and back, reflected clearly the significance of a soldierly community during the Great War. When all other motives for fighting failed, there was this: a brotherhood that bound the suffering soldiers together and compelled them to remain steadfast, if only for the sustenance of their community.

Most Great War combatant literature and the diaries of Mennonite objectors thus shared a common concern for and focus on the idea of community: of like-minded men standing together and suffering together for a cause, whether that cause was a fight for victory on the Western Front or a stand for peace in U.S. military camps. Perhaps more significantly, for both objectors and combatants the community was forged through opposition to some other entity. The significance of this opposition also found a place in the literature objectors and combatants created.

As noted in chapter two, Great War combatant writers often brought meaning to their wartime lives through a series of oppositions, including light and dark, life and death, good and evil. To a great extent, the same might likewise be said for Great War objector diarists. In *The Great War and Modern Memory*, Paul Fussell argues that this "versus habit," this need to dichotomize, was heavily influenced by trench warfare and by the fraternity of soldiers who were compelled to stand against, to oppose, an Other. For Mennonite objectors, of course, the realities of trench warfare could hardly infect them with the "versus habit." Although the penchant to dichotomize likewise appeared in objectors' diaries, objectors were themselves a community of wartime sufferers, opposing those who would send them to war.

Yet in their opposition to military leaders and their government, the objectors were not altogether unlike the war's combatants. The brotherhood of combatants was formed not only in opposition to the enemy, the often faceless entity against whom they were fighting; as countless historians have argued, many Great War combatants also believed themselves separated from, and in some senses opposed to, the civilians and officers who sent them to war. Troops were tied together by the horrors of their experience—horrors that even officers, strategizing far behind the lines, would not understand. Civilians could comprehend war even less than officers: their naive patriotism galled most soldiers, as did the civilians' inability to believe the unbelievable about war's realities. Fussell has written that soldiers had a "deep hatred" for civilians, and often imagined "the visiting of violent and if possible painful death upon the complacent, patriotic, uncomprehending, fatuous civilians at home."[56] Sassoon's poem "Blighters" dramatized the soldiers' fantasy, as he sent a tank through a London music hall full of patriotic civilians.

No, the only ones who could fully understand the soldier's experiences were his brothers in arms, and it was the "we" of this brotherhood that stood in opposition to "them": to the enemy soldiers, but also to the enemy at home. Communities of Mennonite objectors also established oppositions between "we" and "them," between those who accepted a biblical stance and those who did not. For Mennonites, the creation of such opposition no doubt found roots in the doctrine of two kingdoms, as Mennonites had long sought distinction between the kingdom of God and the kingdom of this world. Yet somewhat like the combatants, Mennonite objectors felt separated from and in opposition to those who had not shared their suffering. Although the objectors certainly did not witness horrors like those seen on the battlefield, their experiences, convictions, and absolute rejection of war could not be fully comprehended by persons who were not part of the Mennonite objector communities.

A penchant to create opposition appeared in the objectors' diaries, especially in the underlying current of tension between officers and objectors repeatedly hinted at in the diaries' pages. Even for Meyer, who developed close working relationships with his officers, the chasm remained. Though because of his education and intellect he was like his officers in many ways, Meyer was yet separated from them. Because of his objection to war, he was aligned more closely with his community of brethren—many of whom could not read and did not have any formal education.

Opposition existed as well between the objectors and other soldiers training in the military cantonments. When Mennonite objectors first arrived at camps, and were placed among other conscripts, they felt this opposition most acutely. Without the support and encouragement of brethren, objectors were left to face the conscripts alone. Conscripts could not understand the Mennonites' stance, why Mennonites could seemingly avoid the tedium of drilling or of working around camp, and more broadly, why Mennonites would not have to make similar sacrifices overseas. In his diary, Hostetler wrote at some length about his own confrontations with soldiers in his barrack, who "made sport" of him, stole his clothes, then shoved a military uniform on him. In a clear establishment of an opposition between himself and the soldiers, Hostetler wrote, "If they knew what the general orders were they would be afraid to touch me."[57] Though still "lonesome and blue" when he moved into an objector detachment, Hostetler felt the comforts of community, found joy in being with "the boys," and hoped that as brethren, they could convince the military world opposing them to "accept salvation."

Most Mennonite objectors held to this hope, that although they were separated from the military world, they still might witness to and change the minds of those who opposed them. Of combatant Great War literature, Fussell has written that in the "modern versus habit" there was a sense of "one thing opposed to another, not with some Hegelian hope of synthesis involving a dissolution of both extremes (that would suggest "a negotiated peace," which is anathema), but with a sense that one of the poles embodies so wicked a deficiency or flaw or perversion that its total submission is called for."[58] Fussell's ideation here might well apply to Mennonite objectors as well. In constructing an opposition between nonresistant believers and those who supported the war, Mennonites suggested war-making was a "wicked" and "flawed" position. There could be no "dissolution of both extremes" for Mennonites—they would not, for example, compromise with the military by taking combatant, or even noncombatant, roles. Instead, Mennonites sought through their peaceful witness to overwhelm the position of militarists, and of anyone who supported the war, bringing about some sort of conversion to the Mennonites' pacific stance.

In a study of the rhetorical techniques employed by men in their war diaries and memoirs, Robert Sayre has examined the published texts of predominantly political objectors, and found there a similar attention to conversion. According to Sayre,

> where works in the Augustinian tradition recount the author's conversion to a new faith and where most prison and captivity narratives recount a trial of faith, the most powerful of these CO autobiographies describe CO conversion of other COs to a more radical faith and then these men's power to move other soldiers and guards, other prisoners [at federal penitentiaries], and so the very people who have opposed them, their enemies, and, by the extension, their readers and the public.[59]

That the diaries of Mennonite conscientious objectors were not meant to be public documents matters little, for the diaries—like the memoirs published by other objectors to the Great War—expressed the significance of such conversion moments: moments when they were able to convince fellow objectors to remain strong; moments when they shared their nonresistant witness with soldiers and officers; moments when a soldier asked more questions about their pacifistic stance; moments when they found seemingly subversive ways to take a peaceful stand.

The diaries in this edition are rich with examples of attempts at conversion and stories of converts. For instance, Gaeddert mentioned "A certain Quacker" who "laid down all work" after being a "military police for six months"; he was welcomed into the nonresistant fold when the police "started using guns."[60] And for Gaeddert, the "interesting Epoch making event" in his camp was this: "Rev. Mr. Krehbiel spoke in our mess room preaching the Doctrine of Nonresistance to us boys in the presence of Colonel Kilborne, Captain Cole, Lieut. Jones, and other officers of rank."[61] Why would this be such a significant occasion? Likely due to the opportunity given Krehbiel and his Mennonite brethren to preach to "officers of rank" the message of nonresistance, to reveal to officers a Truth they have yet to understand. In his diary, Meyer celebrated the appearance of a regular conscript in objector barracks. Having stumbled unknowingly onto a Mennonite worship service, the soldier decided to stay and fellowship with the objectors, to Meyer's apparent joy.

Hostetler had a far more subversive method for spreading his nonresistant message. Faced with an order to have all letters turned over to a censor before they were mailed, Hostetler wrote that "I think we should write just such things that will do them [the censors] good."[62] Indeed, Hostetler's diary suggested he believed God called him to camp to do conversion work for the kingdom. After being forced to attend the hanging of three African-American soldiers, Hostetler mused: "Wish I could impress everyone to take the stand today as we don't know what a day may bring forth."[63] Following a Sunday service with the brigade chaplain, Hostetler wrote: "God has a work here for me to do. behold the fields they are ready for harvest and the laborers are few. Fit we few, ready creatures to do thy bidding here and may we be able to carry thy message of love to a few hungry souls before it is to late."[64] If he had to remain in the camp, if he must remain separated from his "dear Della," then surely God had another plan for him. In his mind, this was it—doing the conversion work necessary to show the soldiers God's peaceful kingdom.

It is hard to imagine that many soldiers fighting on the Western Front would have similarly tried to convert others to their cause—especially in the later years of the war, when that cause became dubious at best, and when combatants held widely varying opinions about the conflict. (Some were still assured of its justice; others were assured of its futility.) Rather than working in the language of conversion, many Great War writers chose instead to report the truth of what they saw—saving the conversion for the readers' minds and hearts. They described their experiences vividly, realistically, as a reporter of war might.

Stripped clean of romantic wartime ideals like bravery and courage, much of the writing from the latter part of the First World War endeavored to tell to those at home what war really was. Writers detailed what it felt like to fight in the trenches and to witness the horrors at the front for, again, most combatants believed civilians had no idea about war. Osbert Sitwell, in "Rhapsode," wrote of wartime poetry:

> You hope that we shall tell you that they found their happiness
> in fighting,
> Or that they died with a song on their lips,
> Or that we shall use the old familiar phrases
> With which your paid servants please you in the Press:
> But we are poets,
> And shall tell the truth.[65]

Samuel Hynes describes personal narratives from the war by saying that

> they subvert the expectations of romance. They work at a level below the big words and the brave sentiments, down on the surface of the earth where men fight. They don't glorify war, or aestheticize it, or make it literary or heroic; they speak in their own voices, in their own plain language. They are not antiwar—that is, they are not polemics against war; they simply tell us what it is like. They make war actual, without making it familiar. They bear witness.[66]

Although combatant writers did not necessarily produce "polemics against war," their use of raw, gruesome imagery in describing war reflected, to a great extent, the war's wastefulness, its futility, and its terrible human toll. In telling the truth about the war, combatant writers exploded the myth of the conflict, showing that it was to be abhorred rather than glorified.

136 • *Writing Peace*

To bear witness meant, of course, that the wartime writers were witnesses. Only by remaining at the front, and fighting with their community/battalion, could combatants describe most accurately the horrors of war. Owen, writing to his mother, asserted, "I feel that I must first get some reputation of gallantry before I could successfully and usefully declare my principles" against the war.[67] As discussed in chapter two, the traditional understanding of Great War literature is rooted in a belief similar to Owen's, a sense that those who could legitimately speak about war were those who had seen it. If Mennonite objectors likewise sought to tell the truth about war, they differed from Great War combatant writers in this: Mennonites believed they need not become soldiers of war to know its horrors. Mennonite objectors felt sure that in any war evil was used to resist evil, and that complying with an institution such as the military meant that they too were complicit in killing.

And so, Mennonite objectors remained in U.S. military cantonments, protesting the war taking place an ocean away. Their diaries traced this protest, articulating the objectors' nonresistant stance and their sense that their pacific conviction was the "ideal of Christ," as Meyer wrote, for which they hoped to remain "faithful." In publicly professing their objection to war, they felt they were likewise telling the truth about war and were, they hoped, converting others to that truth. Mennonite objectors were certain they did not need to be witnesses to bear witness.

No doubt the objectors' absolutist nonresistance, more than anything else, separated their diaries from those texts written by Great War combatants that most often make up the traditional World War I literary canon. Although objectors and combatants voiced similar concerns about the war, although they shared a similar brotherhood and sought comfort in the similar image of Christ's suffering salvation, objectors and combatant writers still had a chasm between them. Mennonite objectors felt they knew the truth about war, which is why they would not abet the military in any way. Conversely, many combatant writers believed they needed to see the truth of war to be able to oppose (or to support) it. There would remain this vast opposition between them—another wartime dichotomy—between the objectors and the combatants, writing about similar issues but from entirely different perspectives.

The Mennonites' ardent objection to war likewise separated their diaries from other texts now making their way into that canon: texts written by men and women who served in noncombatant roles during the war (for most Mennonite objectors would not even accept noncombatancy); texts written by men and women whose friends and family members were lost in the war (for Mennonite objectors rarely had close relatives or friends who fought overseas); and texts written by men and women who supported a war they had not seen (for, of course, Mennonite objectors did not support the war, even as they did not see it). If Mennonite objectors' diaries fit into any Great War literary canon, they do so uncomfortably—like other texts and yet unlike them in so many ways.

Perhaps this is how it should be, how the Mennonite objectors would have wanted it to be. After all, they believed their Mennonite faith and its attending objection to violence separated them from the world of those who would fight. We see in the diaries the special imprint of Mennonite doctrine and of Mennonite nonresistance. We see it in the language the objectors used and also in the diaries' focus on faith. We see it in the ways a Mennonite self influenced the writers' wartime lives.

In a large sense, then, the objectors' diaries remain firmly rooted in the tradition of Mennonite writing: among other texts that likewise defined and sustained the Mennonite faith, among other texts that were similarly formed by the writers' conceptions of a Mennonite self. Yet like other Great War writers, Mennonite objectors too were telling their own truth about war. It is this truth-telling that ties them inextricably to all others who were also affected by the Great War and who chose to write about their experiences—whether they picked up a gun and fought on the Western Front or waited anxiously at home for a telegram they did not want. Or whether, like the Mennonite objector Hostetler, they sought peace in the unfamiliar world of the military and found it, finally, in the familiar world of a farm.

Gustav R. Gaeddert, c.1921
Credit: Mennonite Library and Archives,
Bethel College, North Newton, Kansas.

CHAPTER FOUR

What Service To Render: The Diary of Gustav Gaeddert

The Good Samaritan's story is well known. It is an oft-repeated parable used in sermons and in Sunday school, Christ's lesson of unconditional love and compassion for all humanity. The narrative has become part of our common discourse, its protagonist emblazoned on corporate logos for hospitals and tourist companies. The original Good Samaritan, described in Luke's Gospel, saved from death a certain man slumped by the Jericho roadside, who had been beaten and stripped by robbers. Left to rot in a ditch, the weakened man saw pass both a priest and a Levite, supposed leaders of God who ignored the man's wounds and his pleas for assistance. A Samaritan, considered the scourge of the Israeli people, discovered the man, bound his wounds, and delivered him to an inn, where he paid for the stricken man's care. "Which of these three," Jesus' parable concluded, "was a neighbor to the man who fell into the hands of the robbers?" (Luke 10:30-37).

Fifty years after the Great War ended, Gustav Gaeddert found this narrative of the Good Samaritan especially compelling. During the half century separating him from his First World War experiences as a conscientious objector, Gaeddert had discovered within the parable a truth he and other Mennonites had not clearly seen during their Great War trials. Or so he suggested in a 1967 interview. Then, Gaeddert recalled the Good Samaritan parable, and noted that the Samaritan did not ask the bleeding man whether he was a believer, nor whether he embraced nonresistance; the Samaritan merely bound the man's wounds out of compassion and charity. In the same way, Gaeddert argued, Jesus Christ never interrogated people about what kind of noncombatant or combatant service they did before healing them. "That question never arose," Gaeddert said.

Why then, he asked, did Mennonite men refuse to serve in the medical corps, refuse to help heal men's wounds, refuse to play the Good Samaritan to the soldiers strewn by the roadside merely because, in so doing, they would be working under military authority? If Mennonite objectors were to be as Christ, they should have sought to aid all people. Finally, Gaeddert reasoned, if his brother were to become a combat soldier and be mowed down by gunfire, Gaeddert could not very well plead conscientious objector status and refuse to assist him; since all people were considered brothers and sisters in Christ, they all deserved aid, whether combatant soldiers or peaceful resisters. In 1967, as another war raged in Asia and the conscientious objector question again confronted the Mennonite church, Gaeddert affirmed that Christ would believe "the idea is to help," no matter the ethos of those needing medical or economic relief. In so helping, Mennonites could much more readily influence others to make peace.

What service to render? After fifty years, such a query still troubled Gaeddert, who believed that Mennonites in 1917-1918 had probably reached the wrong conclusion. During the Great War, Gaeddert had followed the path of most resistance taken by many Mennonites. As a conscientious objector at Camp Funston, Kansas, he had rendered virtually no military service. Gaeddert's diary and letters written while he was detained as a Great War objector suggest that the Mennonites' refusal to accept any noncombatant duty sat uncomfortably with him even then. The diary, kept from September 1917 until the end of August 1918, clearly reflects both the writer's struggle to decide how best to act while detained and the difficulties Mennonites had during the First World War in trying to arrive at conclusions about what constituted noncombatant duty, about how best to perfect their nonresistant witness, and about what kind of service objectors could conscientiously render while obeying Christ's precept to love their enemies.

Gaeddert was one of the first Mennonites conscripted. He must have considered himself unfortunate when, in mid-September 1917, he was called to report. Gaeddert, who celebrated his 22nd birthday shortly before his military induction, had just returned home from a trip to Reedley, California, where he and several friends had attended a Mennonite conference. A primary school teacher at Hill

Country School near Inman, Kansas, Gaeddert was just a week into the school year when the conscription notice arrived. Commanded to report on September 19, he had less than a day to bid farewell to his students and his family before traveling to the train depot at McPherson, a short journey from Inman. His brother remembered well the evening before his departure, when relatives poured into the Gaeddert household. It was, Albert Gaeddert wrote seventy-five years later, a time of "great anxiety and mourning, almost like a funeral, for no one knew what would be the fate of those first C.O. draftees."[1]

In McPherson, Gaeddert said good-bye to his parents and sister Marie, then boarded the train, which carried conscripts to Camp Funston, a massive cantonment located near Manhattan, Kansas, west of Kansas City. Two childhood companions of Gaeddert's, Paul Heidebrecht and David Goertz, had also been conscripted and joined him on his journey. The friends remained together throughout their internment and their furlough to an Iowa state mental institution.

Upon arriving at Camp Funston, the men were barracked with regular combatant soldiers and received some verbal harassment from officers who were, according to Gaeddert, "a little rough." Called before a company colonel shortly after his arrival at camp, Gaeddert was forced to explain his reasons for objecting to military service, the first of many times he would do so. As nearly every other Mennonite objector after him would do, Gaeddert detailed the Mennonite church's history and the biblical reasons for assuming a nonresistant stance. In his 1967 interview, Gaeddert related the gist of this initial conversation with the military hierarchy. The colonel asked Gaeddert, "If everyone took this position, what would happen?" Gaeddert's response, he later recalled, did not endear him to the colonel: "then there would be no war."[2]

Soon Gaeddert and other conscientious objectors took work hauling garbage in Camp Funston's sanitation department. Often the men toiled alongside regular conscripts, who drove the garbage truck and mobilized the sanitation crews. With a population of a small city, Camp Funston produced enough garbage to keep those on sanitation detail busy. Gaeddert wrote to General Conference Mennonite Church leader H. P. Krehbiel that the days were long, the job hard and dirty.[3]

Although the men worked readily at first, conflict arose between objectors and military authorities when, one month into their detainment, Gaeddert and others protested the demand to work on Sundays. When they did not report for duty on Sunday, October 14,

1917, the objectors were dragged to their captain's quarters and read the riot act. The men were ordered onto the garbage trucks, and all but eight followed the officers' demands. Those who refused to board the trucks were marched to a field outside of camp and beaten with rifles; they returned to the barracks with faces cut and bleeding. Gaeddert, who had conceded to the officers, was not among the abused. The protest was not completely effective, and the men still had to work on Sundays. However, Gaeddert's detachment did achieve modest gains through their defiance and the resultant mistreatment. They were transferred to another barrack, and were out from under the rough hands of their former captain.

Gaeddert's diary attested to the long days spent hauling garbage that first fall in camp—and apparently, doing little else. By mid-November 1917, Gaeddert admitted in his diary that he "felt uneasy about the work," especially as other Mennonite men had refused to haul garbage, arguing that sanitation detail abetted the military machine and was therefore against the moral imperative to remain nonresistant Christians.[4] Around the same time, Gaeddert wrote in a letter to Krehbiel that "the work in itself is harmless, really, and truely constructive, and is work that must be done; but the system or the Establishment under, or to which it belongs, is destructive."[5] Unsure now whether he should continue hauling garbage, Gaeddert wondered if Krehbiel and the Exemption Committee, of which Krehbiel was a part, could provide clear guidance. No matter the punishment he might receive if he stopped working, no matter if he was confined to the idleness of a detention barrack, Gaeddert wanted to do the right thing. He wanted to be told by his Mennonite leaders what service he could conscientiously render.

Gaeddert persisted in performing sanitation duty until the beginning of 1918, when he was stricken with the mumps and then with diphtheria. He spent a good deal of January convalescing in the base hospital. While ill, Gaeddert was informed by fellow conscientious objectors who visited him that the Mennonites in his detachment had decided to refuse all military jobs, including sanitation detail. If Gaeddert wanted to remain in solidarity with his brethren, he was informed, he would need to put his garbage hauling days behind him. In 1967 Gaeddert said this about the Mennonites' decision to lay down all work:

> I was not too enthusiastic.... [W]e really couldn't object to it conscientiously because no matter what we were doing we would be helping the cause somehow anyway, but, when I came to the barracks then [after being in the hospital] I was told that when

one breaks away from the group, why, then they'll try all the harder to carry that on. So we agreed to stay together.[6]

It is difficult to ascertain, of course, whether Gaeddert could say this only after fifty years' time, or whether he sincerely felt in 1918 that Mennonite men should continue to render some forms of service in military camps—at least until President Woodrow Wilson defined what being a noncombatant might mean for objectors. However, a letter to Krehbiel dated January 15, 1918, provides one clue to Gaeddert's feelings at the time. Gaeddert wrote: "We shall resist the evil. Now than finally the question is, is our work evil. I could not say that it is. There we are."[7] In his diary, too, Gaeddert suggested he felt unsettled about the Mennonites' decision. On a trip home, on February 5, 1918, Gaeddert discussed the matter with J. W. Kliewer, his former instructor at Bethel College. Gaeddert also talked with his father and brother-in-law about "whether it would be best to lay down everything."[8] In his diary, he admitted his hearers were also unsure whether quitting would be the best option. If his letter to Krehbiel accurately described his thoughts on the subject, and if his diary represented his sincere feelings at the time, we may assume he was indeed none too enthusiastic when told that, to sustain a united front, he needed to forever let go of the military garbage can and render no more service.

The belief that some forms of work done within military camps might be acceptable reflected the ethos of General Conference Mennonites, the church body to which Gaeddert belonged. On the whole, General Conference Mennonites approached objector concerns in ways different from their (Old) Mennonite brethren.

Gaeddert's views were fostered by his own upbringing and education within a rich tradition of General Conference Mennonitism. His grandfather, Diedriech Gaeddert, had led settlers to central Kansas in 1874 as part of the massive Mennonite tide flowing from Russia. Members of Diedriech Gaeddert's group later established the Hoffnungsfeld Church, a vital General Conference congregation, and in 1907 the Hoffnungsau Bible school. Gustav Gaeddert's father, Jacob, immigrated from Russia at age fourteen but assimilated quickly once in America. By the time of the Great War, he had learned passable English, was subscribing to English newspapers, and voted in American elections. Jacob and his wife, Katharina, apparently encouraged their children to attend school beyond what was then common for Mennonites. Gaeddert graduated from Hoffnungsau preparatory school and Bethel Academy before being conscripted.

After the war, he would earn a Ph.D. in history from the University of Kansas.

As a high school graduate, Gaeddert in 1917 had more education than most Mennonite conscientious objectors. Further, as a primary school teacher, he had different occupational interests than many other Mennonite objectors, although he continued to help on his family's farm before and after conscription. Nonetheless, it was probably Gaeddert's General Conference Mennonite heritage, more than his relatively advanced education, that guided his Great War thinking about what kind of service Mennonite men could, and should, perform while detained.

In a broader sense, Gaeddert's General Conference Mennonite roots informed his belief that he alone could conscientiously decide what constituted abetting the military machine. After all, General Conference Mennonites as a group affirmed each congregation's autonomy in deciding rules of faith and praxis; further, General Conference Mennonites privileged each congregation member's voice in making decisions that affected the congregation as a whole. General Conference Mennonites carried this belief in autonomy into the Great War, as evidenced not only in Gaeddert's moral dilemma about working or not working, but also in a letter the General Conference leader Krehbiel wrote to Gaeddert on January 21, 1918. In it, Krehbiel urged Gaeddert and his Mennonite brethren to make decisions at Camp Funston based solidly on their own individual consciences. Krehbiel affirmed that only one's conscience could decide, ultimately, whether a particular action was abetting war.[9]

Yet during this time, Gaeddert was pressured by other objectors in his camp, many of them (Old) Mennonites whose church polity privileged corporate decision making. From their group-oriented perspective, they told Gaeddert that any work in the military camp abetted evil, and that "if one breaks from the group, the group will be weaker." Thus, oscillating between whether to work or not meant oscillating as well between the General Conference Mennonite ethos and that of the (Old) Mennonites, between listening to one's own conscience or accepting the group's decision.

Five months into his Great War detainment, Gaeddert seemingly followed the Mennonite crowd rather than the urgings of his own conscience. Although others accepted noncombatant work and so broke from the ranks of absolutist objectors, Gaeddert opted for solidarity—a choice he seemingly regretted in the years following the war. And so, after his release from the base hospital in late January 1918, Gaeddert returned to the conscientious objector barracks and to a relatively idle life. During his detainment in the early months of 1918, Gaeddert helped clean at the YMCA on some occasions and worked in the detachment mess hall, but he performed no other in-camp duties. Rather, every day he participated with his fellow objectors in devotionals, hymn sings, and evening programs: one of the many "good tenors" in his crowd, Gaeddert joined a quartet and performed for his brethren.[10]

Like other objectors, Gaeddert took hikes and played baseball, wrote home and read. Gaeddert was apparently an inveterate letter writer, judging by the heft of his correspondence with Krehbiel. His diary suggested other family and friends, most notably John Thiessen and Sarah Lohrentz, were likewise the beneficiaries of his prolific letter writing. Because Camp Funston was within relatively accessible traveling distance from home, Gaeddert took advantage of twenty-four-hour passes when possible and visited his family and church community. In his diary, Gaeddert often wrote more about his journeys home than about his time in camp, so valuable were those visits to him. Yet, without the daily activity of sanitation detail while in camp, Gaeddert was left with hours upon hours to contemplate home—a place, he told Krehbiel, that "never before . . . meant so much to us boys" as during that time of idle loneliness.[11]

In late March 1918, Gaeddert's conscientious objector detachment was moved into tents at a detention camp located one mile from Camp Funston on the banks of the Kaw River. The scenery there was "beautiful," Gaeddert wrote Krehbiel. The camp was surrounded by the river, "steep mountains" (more likely large hills, given the Kansas terrain), and the slowly emerging "green grass which God calls forth to grow even in a military camp." Still, Gaeddert argued, it was "tragic to think of, that an attractive, beautiful, valley should be dedicated and used as a place to fill the mind with a hatred and developing in him an aim which is destructive."[12] No matter how pastoral the setting, Gaeddert and others were preoccupied with President Wilson's March 1918 ruling defining noncombatant services, and that ruling's failure to alleviate the objectors' plights, to turn back their idleness, or to provide them useful roles outside the military. After being read Wilson's executive order in late March, and after declining to accept medical, quartermaster, or engineering corps duty, Gaeddert wrote that only the "future will decide as to the hardships connected" with his decision, "besides those already received."[13]

By April 1918, rumors about the possibly of furloughs for objectors started circulating through Gaeddert's camp. Seeing the furlough bill as "a wise and clear cut law," Gaeddert wrote home and asked his father to help him obtain a placement.[14] Gaeddert also posted a letter to Krehbiel hoping to verify the rumor's accuracy. Before Krehbiel could respond, however, Gaeddert sent another letter explaining that "the Furlough Law doesn't seem to apply to us"; this information he likewise recorded in his diary on April 25.[15] Only later, when Secretary of War Newton Baker declared objectors eligible for furloughs, did Gaeddert begin the application process for doing reconstruction work. On June 18, 1918, he wrote to the American Friends Service Committee in Philadelphia, declaring his intention to join that group and asking for an application.

The next day, Gaeddert told Krehbiel he hoped to join the Friends in their ministry because "I think it offers a great opportunity for service, and besides, the kind of service which interests me; further, it offers at the same time chance for development and experience in this kind of service; also I think that than my sacrifice if carried out will come up, rather, almost measure up to the sacrifice of the average soldier, and also will the work be more appreciated probably, because of the indifferent feeling or spirit that seems to prevail here."[16]

But relief work in France was not to be for Gaeddert, no matter how much he wanted to provide such assistance. Fifty years after the war, Gaeddert still did not know why he had been refused the opportunity to do reconstruction in France, especially since he was as well-educated, and as physically fit, as some who worked with the Friends overseas. Gaeddert hypothesized that perhaps his application had been lost in the mail. However, military records reveal that the Board of Inquiry did not recommend Gaeddert for reconstruction work, and instead classified him as worthy for a farm furlough stateside.[17]

In early July 1918, Gaeddert joined his objector brethren in a forced sojourn to Camp Dodge, Iowa. There, conscientious objectors met with the Board of Inquiry. Gaeddert had his hearing before the Board on Independence Day, and maneuvered the examination with ease; later, he recalled the examiners were "three very fine men."[18] The Board of Inquiry classified Gaeddert as 1-A, finding him a sincere religious objector and recommending him for a farm furlough. Still, he remained at Camp Dodge for over a month more, suffering the vagaries of an Iowa summer in a dusty, windy, and oppressively hot detainment camp. Just as he had done at Camp Funston, Gaeddert hiked and exercised, worshipped and sang in a quartet, read his Bible and listened to the impassioned reasoning of military officers and civilians hoping to convert him. Especially at Camp Dodge, Gaeddert remembered, "they would bring ministers from various congregations and try to influence us but of course they wouldn't affect us."[19] His diary writing habit, however, suffered while at Camp Dodge. After July 8, 1918, Gaeddert ceased making regular entries in his diary, inscribing only two entries between that time and his furlough: one covering July 8 through August 27 and another detailing the day of his furlough, August 28.

When his furlough was finally granted, Gaeddert traveled with several other objectors to Independence, Iowa, to work at the state hospital there. The hospital covered an expanse of 1,300 acres and housed 1,300 inmates. Gaeddert wrote in a letter to Krehbiel; the grounds included a 700-acre farm, meadows and pastures, a beautifully landscaped lawn, and a compound of well-maintained brick buildings.[20] After a year idled away in cramped and dull military cantonments, Gaeddert and his companions "enjoy[ed] very much" their life in Independence. They received good meals, including "real butter and milk" from the 175 Holsteins milked by the hospital's patients; their supervisor was kind and understood their "condition"; they had plenty of work threshing crops, filling silos, tending to animals, and cultivating the gardens. At last, Gaeddert was proving himself useful, rendering service that would help others, being a Good Samaritan of a kind. "It seems to me this is a very fine place," Gaeddert told Krehbiel, "and very appropriate work."[21]

Gaeddert's furlough was to last until November 15, 1918. On that day the state hospital's superintendent phoned the judge advocate at Camp Dodge and requested a six-month extension for his furloughed workers; this extension was granted, although the superintendent told Gaeddert and other objectors they were free to leave the hospital once the government released them. As of November 17, 1918, Gaeddert still did not know when that date would be. In a letter to Krehbiel, Gaeddert expressed thanksgiving that the war was over, acknowledged that "the intense feelings of joy and laughter are again penetrating the air," and noted that November 11 would be the "second Fourth of July" to celebrate yearly. Still, he wondered about his fate—about whether objectors would be discharged with soldiers or would be the last released, as rumors then suggested. To Krehbiel he wrote: "We however are not urging any special favor from the Government in this respect of discharging us, for the greatest favor have we already enjoyed because of not having been forced to violate the dictates of our conscience, yet is it a very natural desire to be together with our dear 'home folks,' Father and Mother brothers and sisters and if possible spend a Christmas or thanksgiving together with them." [22]

Gaeddert was granted his wish, but not soon enough for the holidays. According to the orders established by Secretary of War Baker, Gaeddert returned to Camp Dodge with other objectors, received his discharge in early 1919, and journeyed home to Inman, Kansas, ending a sixteen month ordeal.

Following the war's end Gaeddert attended again to his education, and in 1921 earned a bachelor's degree from Bethel College in North Newton, Kansas. That same year in Moundridge, Kansas, he married Sarah Lohrentz, a friend from school who had, during the Great War, taken over Gaeddert's teaching duties at the Hill Country School. The couple settled in Kansas amid family and church community, but had no children during their fifty-year union. In 1926, Gaeddert earned a master's degree in history from the University of Kansas, then taught history and government for seven years at Bethel College. Following his release from Bethel, Gaeddert returned to the University of Kansas, earning his Ph.D. in history there in 1937; at the same time, he served as a curator at the Kansas State Historical Library in Topeka.

Gaeddert was too old to need worry about conscription or noncombatant service when World War II threatened. Nonetheless, while another war pulverized Europe, both Gaeddert and his wife chose to volunteer for the Red Cross and were sent by that organization to Fort Sill, Oklahoma. Perhaps the specter of Great War inaction haunted Gaeddert, and he wanted to provide the assistance he had not when an objector; perhaps he had realized, by that time, what the Good Samaritan parable meant to him. At any rate, Gaeddert believed he provided a useful, Christlike witness by helping during the Second World War, even though he worked with combatant soldiers and under the authority of the Red Cross—an institution suspected by Great War Mennonites as being pro-military. Said Gaeddert in 1967:

> When I was in Fort Sill I worked with the soldiers with their family problems and with their personal problems.... [W]hether that strengthened them in their determination to fight or not, that never entered my mind. What I did was try to help them.... I believe there are a lot of angles that could be helped that way. They [the soldiers] could be helped a lot of different ways."[23]

Both his experiences as an objector in the First World War and as a Red Cross volunteer in the Second compelled Gaeddert to believe that in any U.S. conflict, Mennonites should assume a more proactive witness, helping soldiers if necessary, doing relief work when possible. Otherwise, he said, the church could become "too narrow" in its assertion that nonresistant Christians should have no part of the military and that toiling in military hospitals meant supporting the war. Mennonites could work in war relief and could bind soldiers' wounds while holding fast to their nonresistant convictions if they could separate, in their own minds, the endeavor from the institution. Such, Gaeddert implied, was what Christ would have Mennonites do.

Some fifty years earlier, Krehbiel had voiced a similar belief in a letter to the young objector Gaeddert, concerned about what military service he could conscientiously render. Krehbiel wrote that working "in the military camp would be quite possible without doing violence to conscience. Only it must be understood to be no part of the military establishment."[24] Krehbiel challenged Gaeddert and other objectors to "shine as lights" in a "crooked and perverse nation," as Paul had said in Philippians 2:15, and implied that this was possible even if the objectors accepted some noncombatant chores. At Gaeddert's military cantonment, however, other Mennonites had already decided that their lights could not shine if they accepted any form of military duty; Gaeddert, in turn, followed the urging of his fellow believers.

Nonetheless, his thinking on the issue of what service to render clearly resonated with Krehbiel's, as reflected both in Gaeddert's Great War writing and in his actions and words following the war. In his postwar words and deeds, Gaeddert suggested some dissatisfaction with the ways he resolved the dilemma of service: by accepting no military duties, by ignoring his stricken brothers, by being the Levite or the priest rather than the Good Samaritan. One could argue that Gaeddert attempted to rectify what he saw as his Great War inaction by being a Red Cross volunteer during the Second World War and, even more, by working for the Mennonite Central Committee following that conflict. As MCC volunteers, Gaeddert and his wife spent several years doing relief work, first in the Near East and then with Russian refugees in Germany.

Gaeddert's diary provides testament to the tension he felt during the Great War, a tension between doing some military service and doing nothing, between autonomy and solidarity, between a singular and a corporate conscience. At times, the entries in Gaeddert's diary are maddeningly spartan, providing few details of his days beyond what becomes his characteristic refrain: "Hauled Garbage." Yet the

150 • *Writing Peace*

oft-times sparse nature of his entries provides an accurate reflection of life at Camp Funston where, at least for the first five months of his detainment, Gaeddert's days revolved around sanitation detail, a monotony broken only by all-important letters and visits from home. Gaeddert's diary entries also show his increasing discomfort with doing sanitation work, then the momentous decision to cease working, followed by the boredom precipitated by having nothing to do—not even the garbage hauling which in itself had been stultifyingly tedious. This pattern reflects clearly the idle life Gaeddert experienced in camp, punctuated by moments of indecision and by provocation from military authorities, colored always by the "thots" of home community, school, and family.

In many ways, Gaeddert adheres closely to the conventions of diary writing and to the "unrhetorical Mennonite rhetorical style" outlined by Al Reimer in *Mennonite Literary Voices*.[25] Still, readers might sense in places that the young Gaeddert wished to move beyond the bare language of his literary and denominational forebears; he seems at times to toy with his own prose style, as with the sudden appearance of the refrain "Ha Ha!" in both his diary and letters—and its equally sudden disappearance. Nevertheless, for the most part Gaeddert relies on an unadorned rendering of experience as he attempts (and sometimes fails to sustain) the objective reporter's voice of a fledgling historian. Gaeddert's diary at times becomes a commonplace book as well, for he copied into it letters he had written, a military notice he read, even a puzzlingly racist piece from the camp newspaper, the *Trench and Camp*: puzzling, at least, because we must wonder why Gaeddert felt compelled to duplicate it without commentary. At any rate, Gaeddert was clearly familiar with a diary's conventions. His own text shows he wished to make an accounting of each day, even if that accounting meant inscribing the date and nothing else, or the date and the briefest phrase ("Hauling Garbage") that said so much to Gaeddert about his experience, and says so much to us now.

Only Gaeddert knew why he failed to maintain this daily record after July 8, 1918. Nonetheless, it seems clear he wanted the narrative he told about his World War I experiences to have a distinct beginning and ending; Gaeddert's first and last entries corresponded with his induction into the military and his "first nite of Freedom" during his furlough. Yet although Gaeddert opened his diary with the September 9, 1917, entry, he in actuality did not receive his "diary book" until early October. On October 1, 1917, he sent a postcard to Krehbiel requesting "a day book or Diary book a good book worth having" for himself and several of his brethren.[26] Krehbiel noted on Gaeddert's postcard that he had written back to Gaeddert on October 4—and apparently sent the diary at this time. Once Gaeddert received the diary, he felt compelled to recall the previous month's momentous events in writing: his conscription, his "tragic farewell" at the McPherson train depot, and his first weeks in camp. The diary's beginning was therefore as its end: Gaeddert endeavored to provide the complete narrative of his military camp experience by covering several days' entries at a time, thus telling his whole conscientious objector story from the first day until the last.

In 1962, Gaeddert donated his Great War diary to the Mennonite Library and Archives in North Newton, Kansas, where it joined a sizable collection of World War I material. Gaeddert died ten years later. His diary, his 1967 interview, and his letters to Krehbiel remain as artifacts that clearly trace the Great War journey Gaeddert made as a General Conference Mennonite. They show a man attempting to discern what a nonresistant witness might look like; what Christ would have Mennonites do in military camps; what service an objector could conscientiously render. During the Great War, Gaeddert followed his brethren, who had themselves embraced the gospel's teachings about resisting not evil and loving one's enemies, and who had themselves asserted that those teachings dictated absolute objection to working under military authority. Fifty years later, Gaeddert believed Mennonites, in sincerely trying to embody a nonresistant witness, had missed part of the New Testament: the story of the Good Samaritan, who saw and saved his supposed enemy lying wounded by a Jericho roadside.

Text

The original diary book, preserved on microfilm at the Mennonite Library and Archives in Newton, Kansas, served as the copy-text for this edition. No other versions of Gaeddert's diary exist or were published; his only known publication about his World War I experiences was a letter he wrote to *The Mennonite*, a General Conference periodical, while detained at Camp Funston. The book that H. P. Krehbiel sent Gaeddert in response to Gaeddert's request for a diary was not manufactured for that purpose. It had no preprinted dates on its pages, no lock and key, none of the physical characteristics we often associate with a diary. Instead, Gaeddert's book seemed to be more a composition book, similar no doubt to those he had carried to the Bethel Academy as a student several years earlier.

The diary's lined pages were bound by string. The book had no margins save for an inch at the top of each page. Gaeddert rarely transgressed this margin but used all other available space, often writing in small print at the page's bottom in his effort to squeeze just a bit more on to the paper. He wrote on both sides of each page. Pre-printed numbers appeared on the upper outside corner of the pages, and because Gaeddert wrote on consecutive pages from one to sixty-five, we know that he did not rip out or destroy any part of his diary. Gaeddert's entries were remarkably legible, due in great part to his fair hand and his consistent use of dark ink.

The Diary of Gustav Gaeddert

Diary Book bought from H. P. Krehbiel Newton Ks. in yr. 1917.[27] Oct.third while residing at Camp Funston.

[1917]

Sept. 9. arrived in Inman at 1 o'clock P.M. from California trip. Received many greetings.

Sept. 10. Started my school. Enjoyed first days work.

Sept. 16. Attended D. C. Regiers wedding. Met many College friends.

Sept. 18. Received notice to come to Camp Funston. Had a farewell party at Lakeshore in evening.

Sept. 19. Taught school till noon. Said good-by to my pupils (a sad parting.) Then went to Hutchinson on school business came home at 5 P.M. Friends cousins and pupils came to say good-by to me. With tears in our eyes we parted.[28]

Sept. 20. Rose up early in the morning. Said once more good-by to brothers and sisters. Then went to McPherson where we then departed at 1 o'clock in the afternoon. Oh what a tragic farewell I had to endure when we left. [Page 2] Mamma and Marie especially took it hard.[29] Arrived at camp about 6 o'clock. Reported at Captain, handed our exemption papers to Captain. At eleven oclock I went to take a bath. Went to bed at 1 oclock. A.M.

Sept. 21. Came before Colonel.[30] He asked us few puzzling questions then sent us out and said he could not talk to us and told me I belonged to Supply Co made me feel worse.

Sept. 22 till Oct 11. had a fair time even though lonesome.

Oct. 14. Had a trial because of refusing to work on Sunday. Some boys were beat down by fist by the guard. I was left free at 8.45 AM.[31]

Oct. 15. Received our vaccination and inocculation of 5000 germs. The side is getting sore. Had a headache during the day.

Oct. 16. Was transfered from ninth Co 164 Depot Brig. to Dept. of Sanitation Bldg. 527.

Oct. 17. Hauled Garbage, was thru at 4.50 P.M. Than had a talk with H. P. Krebhiel, P. H. Unruh and P. H. Richert who explained to us more [3] in detail the conditions and our attitude toward them.[32]

Oct. 18. Hauled Garbage. a long day.

Oct. 19. Hauled garbage, Friday was a cold day. Got stuck with the truck.

Oct. 20. Sat. Hauled garbage. Enjoyed the time with Dave Goertz. Talked thru some practical problems.

Oct 21. Sunday. Hauled garbage till 10.30 oclock A.M. washed and then was surprised to meet my brother, H. T. Unruh, Otto Lowen, Burkhart, W. Voth in the Latrine. Enjoyed the time very much. Received greetings from friends at home and at College. The boys left at 2 o'clock. Met many other friends from Home. Rev. A. Dyck, John P. Franz etc.[33] I am thinking of home friends and folks whom I love so dearly and yet I may not be with them. H. T. Unruh had the misfortune of stepping into the ditch into the mud when he stepped off from the Automobile here in Camp Funston Ks.

Oct. 22. Hauled garbage. cold rainy day. many thots.

Oct. 23. Hauled garbage. Said good-by to Merle Vilven our truck driver who left [4] for Camp in Texas. At the farewell, his mood changed from a careless and indifferent attitude to a warm and true boy. His farewell words were: Be good boys and we shook hands with him and he further said, I hope this war will be over in 3 Mo. In the evening we sincerely waited for a pass to go home but had to go to bed dissatisfied. We were discouraged.

Oct. 24. Got up at 5.45 A.M. Ate breakfast then waited till 8 AM when we received our pass to go home. 24 hrs pass. We left to Junction city on interurban, took a hired Oakland six and were taken to McPherson for $26.70, left Junction at 9.30 arrived at McPherson 1.00 P.M. shaved and were taken home by Mr. Toews. 2.15 P.M. Reached conference at 3 oclock was at home greeted by sis. Annie & Earl. taken to church by John & John Franz.[34] Greeted there by father mother sis. & bro. & friends & relatives. Had a committee meeting. After that met many friends. Went home and had a good hearty homemade supper. In evening went to church, went home at 10 and had fine talks till 1.30 A.M. when we left for Camp again. [5]

Oct. 25. Thurs. Reached camp about 8.15 A.M. learned of situation here.[35] Tried to straighten matters up a little and presented best wishes and greetings to boys from confer. & also the work done for us was presented. Have no work to do will write & ans. letters.

Oct. 26. Friday. Had a day of rest, which resulted into a day of letterwriting and reading. Read the book "Should a Christian fight?" by Samuel H. Booth-Clibborn.

Oct. 27. Hauled Garbage again.

Oct. 28. Hauled Garbage. Sent Message or telegram to H. P. Krehbiel to come to camp.

Oct. 29. Met Krehbiel and Kliewer was off in afternoon.[36] Wanted to meet Krehbiel & Kliewer at Y.M.C.A. but failed on account of lack of patience in waiting. My mistake.

Oct. 30. Hauled Garbage. Quackers stopped working. A day of arrousement.[37]

Oct. 31. Hauled garbage. Restless day.

Nov. 1. Hauled garbage. Some more information was gathered from us in regard to what church we belong to.

Nov. 2. Hauled garbage. The 3 cent letter tax went in force another war tax. [6]

Nov. 3. Sat. Hauled garbage.

Nov. 4. Sunday. Had a big crowd here. An interesting Epoch making event happened here today. Rev. Mr. Krehbiel spoke in our mess room preaching the Doctrine of Nonresistance to us boys in the presence of Colonel Kilborne, Captain Cole, Liut Jones and other officers of rank. The privilidge was granted that services may be held in the mess room by Rev. Mr. Krehbiel and thru his permission or letter of introduction others may speak. The Heid famili from Okla were here visiting. It all together made me feel tired.

Nov. 5. Mond. Hauled Garbage. Paul was on guard duty i.e. fire guard. Was a windy day. Still having many thots concerning our work. Had a little talk with our truck driver.

Nov. 6. Hauled garbage.

Nov. 7. Hauled garbage. Received a letter from Prof. H. D. Penner

What Service to Render • 155

and from home felt better.[38] Had an election of chairman of Religious meetings. I was elected. [7]

Nov. 8. Thurs. Hauled garbage.

Nov. 9. Fri. Hauled garbage.

Nov. 10. Sat. Hauled garbage. Had quite a talk with driver Bauer.

Nov. 11. Sunday. John Thiessen visited me.[39] Had a fine time with him. Also saw Katie Krause & Miss Clark took a walk with Miss. Clark Sat. nite. Received a kind letter from Hans. & Dickie.

Nov. 12. Hauled garbage. long day

Nov. 13. Tues. Saluting exercise and had to run double time. Hated that.

Nov. 14. Wed. Hauled garbage. Paul was sick. Had Schmidt instead.[40]

Nov. 15. Thurs. Hauled garbage till Noon. Was off in the afternoon because Mamma, Marie, John, Jacob, and H.T. were here, had a very good afternoon. Talked about some practical life problems.

Nov. 16. Hauled garbage. Was asked once more to sign the payroll but refused to sign it. In evening our beds were moved and I was separated from Paul. [8]

Nov. 17. Hauled Garbage.

Nov. 18. Sund. Hauled garbage till 10.30 Last time or day with Bauer glad of it.

Nov. 19. Mond. Hauled garbage.

Nov. 20. Tues. Hauled garbage. Oyer told me he was going to quit working next day Nov 21.

Nov. 21. Wed. Hauled garbage. Long day with many thots. Oyer quit.

Nov. 22. Thurs. Hauled garbage. Deep thots and felt uneasy about the work.[41]

Nov. 23. Fri. Had to carry out our beds. New order. Waiting on truck. Still feeling uneasy about the kind of work we are doing. Good news creeping in slowly don't know whether or not to believe them. Received a pusseling letter from Hans.

Nov. 24. Sat. Hauled garbage. Chilly day. Decided in evening suddenly to go home got a pass and left at 5.39 P.M. had a dreary night's rest.

Nov. 25. Reached Inman at 7.45 A.M. was tired. Ate breakfast at George Froezes. John got me and went home surprized [9] folks. Later went to church surprized them. Had a splendid time. Told H.T's that I had decided to enter upon mission work. They were *very very* glad to hear that. Asked H.T. another important question concerning my plan or thot he decided in my favor i.e. the way I thot about it. In evening went along with H.T's, to Christian Endeavor, had another nice talk with them.[42] At Endeavor I learned the opinion of many regards their attitude they take in respect to this war and toward us.

Nov. 26. Monday. Expressed my feeling, at the table, to home folks and friends surrounding and in the afternoon I & Mary visited my former school, Now Miss Lohrentze's school found it satisfactory especially did I appreciate her treatment of the youngsters.[43] Order could have been a little better. Had a fine time. Was asked to say few words to pupils which I did. Car would not start had fun about it. Told Hans about our life here in camp. Stopped in at Grandma's alittle. In evening I was at my siss. Many questions were asked yet. Had a short seperate talk with Marie told her about my future intentions. [10] She told me how hard it was for her to see me go because we had always, and now again, had such intimate talks together and now she was alone. Left at 9.30 P.M. arrived here in camp at 7.45 A.M.

Nov. 27. Tues. Had to wash floor in forenoon was free in afternoon. Wrote letter to father and sent Thanksgiving cards to Hans & pupils.

Nov. 28. Wed. Hauled garbage. Received another letter from H. D. Penner. Nothing new has happened. thot of home & school.

Nov. 29. Hauled Garbage till 9.20 A.M. Had a fine Thanks giving dinner.

Nov. 30. Friday. Hauled garbage till 3 oclock P.M. Than had visitors: Miss Minnie Boese & Adolph and Miss Ruth Clark & Mrs. Clark. Had a fine time. Ate Supper together with them in Y.W.C.A. Received a box of candy from Minnie Boese.

Dec. 1. Sat. Hauled garbage. Inspection at 12.45 P.M.

Dec. 2. Sunday. Made up my mind to go home Sat. night and asked for pass of our new [11] Lieut Ray which he granted me.[44] (not true) Heard nice sermon of P. H. Unruh and Missionary from China. Inspired me fully.

Dec. 3. Mond. Hauled Garbage.

Dec. 4. Tues. Hauled Garbage.

Dec. 5. Wed. Hauled Garbage.

Dec. 6. Thurs. Hauled Garbage.

Dec. 7. Frid. Hauled Garbage.

Dec. 8. Sat. Hauled Garbage. Paul went home on 48 hr. pass.

Dec. 9. Sund. Hauled Garbage till 9 oclock. Helped Oyer in after noon and finished afternoon with letter writting. Evening listened to Rev. Crist. Cold day.

Dec. 10. Hauled Garbage. Cold day & snow.

Dec. 11. Hauled Garbage. Paul returned & brought butter, & sweater, & caps, and money from home. Busy with renewing the claim's on Exemption.[45]

Dec. 12. Wed. Hauled Garbage. Had bad headache in afternoon.

What Service to Render • 157

Evening filed my affidavits. Snow. Am tired and want to go to bed. Oyer received his discharge. [12]

Dec. 13. Thurs. Hauled garbage Cold day. Oyer left for home. Keenly felt his nearness and dearness to me. Went with him to the Depot and saw his happy face leave.

Dec. 14. Read in paper that no passes will be granted for Xmas. Was very much disappointed. Hauled Garbage. At noon I was called into the orderly room and was informed that my application for Xmas pass would be granted. Made me feel good but also felt for the others who may not go home. Some boys very much envy me—.

Dec. 15. Sat. Hauled garbage. were thru early.

Dec. 16. Sunday. Hauled garbage. Waited for trucks till 9.35. Bulletin posted a statement that no Religious meetings or gatherings of any kind are permitted in the barrack or camp. This did away with the Sunday Sermon and also with the Evening Bible class.[46] Was a weary and lonely Sunday. Read on Bulletin that could not take train going home. [13]

Dec. 17. Monday. Hauled Garbage. Received a welcome & kind letter from Hans.

Dec. 18. Hauled garbage. Had instructions in regard to saluting. was fine. Nice day longing to go home.

Dec. 19. Hauled garbage. Beautiful day. Received notice that only 5% can go home Xmas. Bad and discouraging news. Thinking often of home and friends.

Dec. 20. Thurs. Waited for trucks. Waiting in suspense for the decision who will go home.

Dec. 21. Fri. Hauled garbage. Received notice that my pass was cancelled. Wired or sent Telegram home that I couldnt come home. Was a long day.

Dec. 22. Suderman left on Xmas pass. Hauled garbage.

Dec. 23. Sunday. Hauled garbage till 10 oclock. Dr. Kurtz gave a sermon in Mess Hall. Helped Carl Schmidt to get a pass for funeral of his Sis. Went to Junction and found Lieut Ray then to Funston and saw [14] Capt. Tooley and finally Schmidt received a 5 day pass.

Dec. 24. Mond. Hauled garbage were inspected for Tuberculosis.

Dec. 25. Tues. Xmas. Hauled garbage till 10 oclock A.M.[47]

Dec. 26. Hauled garbage. Sec. Holliday. My sis. Marie was here Dec. 25. Had a fine time. Lizzie & Gus. Heid were here also. Was worried a little about Marie for when she left on Interurban she and Lizzie Heid went on car while Gus stayed behind. Have not heard whether she arrived home safe.

Dec. 27. Received card from Hans telling me she received card for pupils just in time. Hauled garbage. Came in to early. Suderman came

158 • *Writing Peace*

back. feels good. Waiting in suspense to receive pass for New Year.

Dec. 28. Friday: Hauled garbage. Notice posted which says that New Years passes will start Mond. 31.4.30 p.m. and be due Jan 2. 7.40 A.M.

Another discouragement. [15]

Dec. 29. 1917. Sat. Hauled garbage.

Dec. 30. Sunday. Truck was filled with wood had to unload it first and after that hauled garbage. Kinda got my goat. Answered Han's letter.

Dec. 31. Mond. Hauled garbage till noon. Will go home in afternoon. Waiting on folks.

[1918]

Jan 1. 1918. Tues. Spent New Year at home. arrived home Dec. 31 at 10:30 P.M. Many visitors. Some of my pupils, i.e. Lynda, Herbert, & John Buller, Cornelius & Frank Adrian. My aunts & uncles, H.T's and Froezes. Had a fine time. Left home at 12 oclock P.M. Jacob, John and H.T. brought me to Salina arrived here at 8 oclock Jan second. Talked about many a practical problem and one of these the mateing problem. Talked about many a question relating to the Salvation and Life after Death.

Jan. 2. 1918. Slept in forenoon. Hauled garbage in afternoon. Asked to attend Lecture on Venerial Disease in Auditorium.[48] Lecture was illustrative & sure interesting. [16]

Jan. 3. Thurs. Hauled garbage. Kurtz, Haskens, and other boys were sent to isolation camp. Answered letters.

Jan. 4. Friday. Hauled garbage. Was off after 3 P.M. Had a fine driver Eckhardt. Nothing new.

Jan. 5. 1918. Sat. Hauled garbage and a load of trash. Lots of dust. Ebert received a discharge. Received a Christmas present from Bartels girls my pupils. Was on guard duty from 3.30 A.M. till 5.30 A.M.

Jan. 6. Sunday. Worked till 9.30 A.M. Had services in the afternoon.

Jan. 7. Monday. Same work, no change, no sign of Peace. Had a long days work.

Jan. 8. Tues. Hauled garbage. Had my first Thyphoid inocculation and also small pox vaccination. Resulted in headache and sore arm and side.

Jan. 9. Wed. Had to work inspite of sore arm and side. Had lots of fun. [17] Was discouraged because I didn't receive any mail. Read President Wilsons Peace terms and seem reasonable. Hopes for future to bring Peace soon.[49]

Jan. 10. Thurs.

Jan. 11. Friday. Hauled one load of garbage to the incinerator than the truck gave out and had to be pulled in. Didn't work at all in afternoon. Had a fine talk with Boys.

Jan. 12. Delivered cans from yesterday. Was very very cold. A serious act was committed last night between 9-10 oclock. A supposed capt of 354 inf. is supposed to have killed 5 men, shot one and cut four with knife or hatchet and robbed bank in camp. A note has been found in orderly room of Capt. stating that before he would end his life he would do something real mean. We were searched 3 times in afternoon and had to stay in the barrack. Nothing but extreme necessary business was transacted. Capt. is supposed to have killed him self in Ft. Riley. [18]

Jan. 13. Sunday. Worked all fornoon and hauled another load in afternoon. Was done at 10 of 3.

Now I am going to write letters. Feel a longing in me to see my home, friends. No preacher here to give us a sermon so Sunday will be lonesome. Am sitting in Mess Hall. Oh those College days how lovely they were and now I am here in camp separated from my friends I loved so dear. Well it could be worse I have some dear friends here also.

Jan. 14. 1918. Monday. Hauled garbage & Latrine together with Serg. Cabiness. Old Mennonite quit working & also plain [. . .].[50] Was informed to appear before Major Smith tomorrow at 8 or 8.30.[51]

Jan. 15. 1918. Tues. Hauled garbage. In the evening I noticed the beginning of the mumps. Had a nice Bible class yet before I left. [19]

Jan. 16. 1918. Was taken to the Hospital. Had a rough ride. Felt somewhat uneasy & feverish.

Jan. 17. 1918. Was swollen [. . .] but still it hasn't reached the limit.[52]

Jan. 18. 1918. Thurs. Had the mumps right on both sides.

Jan. 19. Sat. Feeling fairly well.

Jan. 20. Sunday. Received 8 letters and one card. A fine long letter from Hans. She has various experiences to report in the letter. Were entertained by Manhatten ladies. Music & readings. Felt very lonesome. In evening had a nice experience with the boys about the Bible or rather religion.

Jan. 21. Monday. Was answering letters. Mumps were beginning to leave me.

Jan. 22. Tues. Feeling fairly well.

Jan. 23. Received my clothes and left the Hospital Sec. 7. Ward 22. in the after noon & went to 1729 Funston. [20]

Had considerable fever in afternoon and in the evening & night I had high fever. Slept but little all nite. Went down to the Latrine about 3 times to drink water during nite. Last time as I went and was on the steps I had forgotten what I wanted. Went down to the Latrine and sat down on the bench soon had to lay down and at once I began to sweat and I sweated till I was plumb wet the sweat just ran down and my worst fever was broken and I could sleep.

Jan. 24. Had my temp. taken & had 103 degrees fever at noon. Doctor was called and said I had Diphtheria and I was sent to Base Hospital Sec. 2 ward 46.

Jan. 25. My throat was pretty sore. All three Doc's said I had Diphtheria.

Jan. 26. Had my culture taken. Met with another boy who had [21] been opperated on appendicitis and they had cut his nerve running to his left leg, and consequently could not use his leg. He was very much concerned about it and was sent from one hospital to another because of the maltreatment received by the opperator.

Jan. 27. Sunday. Paul & Shierling came to see me and brought me a letter from P. H. Richert really explaining to us a few things. Made me lots of thots.

Jan. 28. Mond. Toews & Wiens came to see me and brought me letter from P. H. Unruh advising us to lay down. Felt somewhat indifferent. Otherwise I was feeling better. This very morning one of the boys died of Diphtheria. He had been a regular soldier for 4 years & was swearing considerable.

Jan. 29. Tuesday. Feeling fair. Not much of anything happening. Had my second culture taken. Fine experience with the Doctor. [22]

Jan. 30. Wednesday. Received clothes and could walk around. Felt very weak but helped to wash the beds. Light work.

Jan. 31. Was moved into another room together with Leib. He was from Missouri and knew Marie & Jess Loganbill very well. Had a fine talk with him in the evening.

Feb. 1. Friday. Received third culture.

Feb. 2. Saturday. Helped to wash dishes and was feeling stronger.

Feb. 3. Notice was given that my culture was negative. Left Hospital in the afternoon. Glad of it. Said good by to boys and left. Arrived at 527 and found it quarentined and had to bunk in 636.

Feb. 4. Monday. Asked for a pass but couldn't get more than a 24 hr. left that day at 5.30 P.M. on U.P. arrived at McPherson at 8.45. at Salina [23] I bought ticket and left it in the doorway at depot. Was lucky and found it. Conductor said I couldn't do that again once out of a Hundred times. Arrived home at 11.30. Had tire trouble & water trouble on the road. Marie & Jns. Cor. Heid & Lizzie Heidebrecht came to get me. Had a fine ride. Found Folks all looking for me. Talked till

1.15 and then went to bed.

Feb. 5. Tues. Got up at 8.30 about and ate breakfast at 9.30. Boys had all left for school. H.T.'s and Mrs. Froese & Hilda came at 11.15 about. Had a fine and dandy time. Oh it sure felt good to be free and together with Home folks. In afternoon H.T. Jno and I went to Newton. Was examined and found it to be Umbilical Hernia said Dr. Haury whil Dr. Smith said it was not Hernia. Dr. Haury gave me information how to treat it. Then we went to Campus. Say that was [24] lovely. Spoke especially with Prof. Kliewer about this business of quitting and he did not know whether it would be the best thing to do. Then spoke to Krehbiel & Richert. Shook hands with College Friends & Professors and especially with Fritz, Mandi, Minne Boese and Miss Kliewer. When Fritz saw me as I passed the boarding hall she cried out Hello Gus and then she laughed. Same old Fritz.[53] Finally Jno Thiesen couldn't stand it any longer & he took me to his room and we talked over the whole problem. Prof. Kliewer said that he was getting letters from all sides telling him that he sold the boys to the gov. and a mother had written him that she had always thot Prof. Kliewer was a Christian but she had found out different. Jno told me this also. That sure felt like home to be on the College Campus once more. [25] Left for home on 5.40 car. Had a fine talk with H.T. while going up and continued it while going back. Noticed especially how bro. Jno. was interested in what we said and sure made me feel good. Ate a sandwich in Burton and noticed that I had left the books on the car which I received from Jno. Thiessen. Arrived home about 8.15. Heidebrecht were there. Had all kinds of talks yet. Was undecided what to do, when I went bed, about the work. Father & H.T. didnt know whether it would be best to lay down everything. Went to bed together at about 1.20.

Feb. 6. Had sad fairwell greeting to all and I sure felt bad. Jno. brought me to McPherson. Arrived here at 1 oclock and found the barrack still under quarantine and 30 carriers. Paul left for detention camp went back to 636. Wrote letter to Prof. Kliewer.

Feb. 7. Didnt do anything. Wrote letter to Hans. [26]

Feb. 8. Fri. Was asked to go to Y.W. C. A. but they didn't need me. Read books & wrote letters.

Feb. 9. Sat. Helped to sweep & mop the room. Wrote letter to H.T.s. Heard the Emporia Glee Club.

Feb. 10. Sund. Helped sweep & mop room 636 and went to Sunday school. Didn't like it much Lieut. Lauterbach held meeting. To much war. In evening heard fine Sermon, given by Y.M.C.A. leader.

Feb. 11. Monday. Helped sweep & mop and received notice that my application for furlough was denied and stated *No* you had better stay here and take "Short quarter Master Course" You need it. Good joke. Ha Ha!

Feb. 12. Helped sweep & mop floor. Afternoon writting. Barrack 527 still under quarantine. 7 of us boys are bunking in Mess Hall in 636. Receiving fine meals. [27]

Feb. 13. Wed. Started to clean Mess Hall in 636. Wash tables. Some dirty job. Read Calling of Dan Mathews. Fine story. Received letter from E. W. Penner & P. H. Richert.

Feb. 14. Thurs. Scrubbed tables. Still in 636 but quarantine of 527 is lifted.

Feb. 15. Friday. finished the tables in fornoon and washed in the afternoon. Have moved to 527 again.

Feb. 16. Sat. Not doing any work but keeping quarters clean. Will read in the afternoon.

Feb. 17. Sund. Had Sunday school in forenoon—"The parable of the sower." Prof. Toews from Tabor College was here and spoke in forenoon & afternoon also Smith from the Dunkards.

Feb. 18. Mond. Visited Hog range in forenoon. Write & read in afternoon. Serg. Thiessen left our barrack to-day. [28]

Feb. 19. Tuesday. Another day of rest. Cashed the draft received from the Church. Boys wrestled in afternoon. Had an Arithmetic match in forenoon. Mohler will lead to-nite. Waited on letter but didn't come—. No news.

Feb. 20. Wed. Didnt do much of anything. Still no news & no letter.

Feb. 21. Thurs. No news, no letter. Walked up to the Hog range and took a few pictures. Received letter from Minne Boe.

Feb. 22. Washingtons birthday. Received letter stating of sickness of her father. Sympathetic letter. An extreme warm day.

Feb. 23. Sat. Washed Mess hall & windows in fore noon. Wrote letter in afternoon to Hans. Didn't read much.

Feb. 24. Sunday. Sunday school in forenoon led by College Senior Mr Engels from McPherson College very fine class. P.M. Met Ed Heid. and we went to Ft. Riley to visit Paul. Had to miss the Services in [29] the afternoon. Sorry, but I could not help it.

Feb. 25. Mond. Windy day. Read in forenoon and some in afternoon also played checkers. Are in need of some real work.

Feb. 26. Tuesday. Had a spelling class in forenoon.

Feb. 27. Wednesday. Nothing new has happened

Feb. 28. Thursday. Had a nice shower.

March 1. Friday. Received letter from Hans, interesting.

March 2. Sat. Oyer visited us in afternoon. Went up the hill afterward. Met with two girls Pauline Strauss Junction City R.F.D. #5 and Tillie Guegal Junction City. Had a nice chat with them i.e. Suderman Trowyer & Klassen. Took several pictures of them.

March 3. Sunday. Helped in kitchen till 9.15 then heard that Rev. P. H. Richert was in the Hostess House and could not yet receive a pass. Went to meet [30] him. Talked till ten than we went to get a pass for him and brought him into the barracks where Sunday school class was already in session. Had a nice talk with him and he seemed to be very favorably impressed and said that everything was pointing toward a change toward the better. Had a big rain. Paul & Dave were home.

March 4. Monday. Classes in forenoon and played ball in the afternoon. Wrote letter to Hans. Paul and Dave returned from home.

March 5. Tuesday. Started on classics. Played ball in afternoon had classes and singing in forenoon & after 5 P.M.

March 6. Wed. Wrote letter to Rosine. Received letter from H.T's & Jno Thiessen. Elard came out with us to play ball. Did something we shouldn't do i.e. set the beds of neighbor so it would break down by weight.

March 7. Thurs. Menno Nickle visites. Had spelling exam, made 92%. Got a scolding from Serg. Stanfield, [31] because of the noise after taps. We took notice of that. At 9.40 P.M. we saw the Auroraboreal Northern light in the Northeast. It had a very red aspect and would change to a streak of light crossing thru the center. Lots of yelling was heard by soldier boys. Some said it was more than mere reflection that it was a sign of a bloody war to come.

March 8. Friday. Spent day in our usual manner. Received letter from prof. Balzer.

March 9. Sat. Very windy day. Smoke pipes blew down. Made up my mind to go home. Left at 4.15 P.M. on the U.P. reached home at 9 P.M. Surprised folks at home, Henry and Albert came to the door when I arrived but were afraid to open it. Then John came and opened it and recognized me.

March 10. Sunday. Was in church in forenoon, heard Prof. Kliewer in forenoon, afternoon and in the evening. Professor was at our place for supper. Was pressed from all sides by friends & relatives. Left home at 10.35 P.M. [32] Talked with many friends but couldnt talk with all those I wanted to *chat* with.[54]

March 11. Monday. Arrived here at 7 o'clock A.M. Was tired, and headache was troubling me. Windy day.

March 12. Tues. Had classes in forenoon and played ball in the afternoon. Had an interesting Bible class. Burden and another man visited our class. Waiting on some news daily. Some boys were searched and their letters read.

March 13. Wed. Played ball in the afternoon. Had classes in forenoon.

March 14. Thurs. Had a neurological exam. Misunderstood Lieut in one question.

March 15. Fri. Rest of boys had to take neurological exam.

March 16. Saturday. Many boys went home among them Paul & Dave Jantz & Pete Neufeld.

March 17. Sund. Was K.P. all day. Rev & Prof. Hiebert from Tabor College spoke to us.[55] An interesting meeting. Gus Jansen wedding was held in Buhler church

[33] Sunday-nite. Bro. Pete & Lena from Okla were home.

March 18. Mond. Felt sick, feverish all day. Received Telegram from home that bro. Pete's were home to visit and want to speak to me. Tried to get a pass that day but got nothing but 24 hr. pass. Wouldn't take it yet applied for 48 hr. Had to send telegram home that I would not come that day.

March 19. Tues. Had classics & spelling in forenoon. Was turned down on my pass but Serg. promised to give it to me after checking in the stuff issued to us by Gov. Still feeling sick & feverish. Did not get my pass but old Serg. Stanfield says I may get it tomorrow.

March 20. Had classes in forenoon played ball in afternoon. Didn't get my pass.

March 21. Thurs. Waiting to be transferred but do not know at what time nor where we go to. [34] Received letter from Hans. Wishing to see bro Pete but it probably will not be possible.

Were transferred to 45 Co. 164 Depot Brig. Detention Camp No. 1 Funston Ks.[56] Officers were very kind. Am together with Goertz, Goertzen, Heidebrecht, Eichenberger & Guftavson.

March 22. Friday. Cleaned our tent and quarters thats all. Took a walk, enjoyed it. That's all we are supposed to do says Capt. Kintz.[57]

March 23. Sat. Tried once more to get a pass but could only get a 24 hr. pass. Capt. explained it to me very definitely. Tried to phone home but the officers at the Bell Station had a peculiar way of keeping me from it. They wanted me to tell them to what organization I belong, when I told them to the 45 Depot Brig. they wouldnt believe me and sent me out to inquire of my Capt. to what organization I belong. [35] I then sent a telegram home instead of writing and will never visit that Bell Station again if not absolutely necessary.

March 24. Sund. Bro. Pete & Father were here for breakfast. Had a nice visit with them, but it resulted in a sad parting. I noticed it before, but Pete broke out in tears when finally he said that it had almost broke Lena's heart when she found out that she could not see me. He grasped my hand firmly and said, "God be with you, not so, Gus?" and he cried and we could hardly part. I then went to my bed and cried for I could not keep from it any longer. I had to resist again when we parted for Pete could not. Had a fine prayer meeting yet and went to bed.

March. 25. Mond. played ball in forenoon and partly in afternoon. Had spelling class.

March 26. Tues. For first time played 6-0 gave the other side a 0. [36] In the afternoon had a 2 hr. walk. Received copy of the ruling from Washington.[58] It defines Non-Combatant service, but leaves question for Sec. Baker to decide what to do with us. P. H. Richert was here, called here by Kleinsasser on account of the 15% Non-Comb. They are all in the guard house.

March 27. Wed. Nothing new has occurred. Wrote a letter to H.T's. that I most likely will not come home for Easter.

March 28. Thurs. Was in tent all day. Had a fine rain. Had nice talk or chat with boys.

March 29. Friday. Good Friday had a nice talk with Pete Neufeld on the question of policeing up in the Zone which we were asked to do. Had many a thot about home. Heard that Uncle Abe Gaeddert had received notice and was to report for Service April 1. Had a nice crucifixion discussion or meeting in the evening. [37]

March 30. Sat. Had a nice little talk with Capt. Kintz in the morning as regarding our attitude toward the work in camp and asked him whether all this policing up was taken as belonging to our quarters. He did not answer it but said "I have charge of the whole zone now and do you think I will clean up the vacant part of it?" He intimated about the ruling that we would soon get it and we would than have to accept either quarter master, Medical or Eng. Corps, if not we would be put in Disciplinary barracks etc. We told him that the new ruling said that we need not accept any work which would violate our religious conviction. Received my first shot for typhoid fever i.e. first of third trial arm is sore. Received a fine letter from Jacob.

March 31. Easter Sunday. Was sick with a head ache all day because of the shot or inocculation I received Sat. Thot of home and friends and especially what the day meant for us it being Easter morning and celebrating it in [38] the camp or detention camp.

April 1. Easter Monday. sec. holiday. Nothing new happened except some of the boys were asked to sign the allotment cards and they were not present so I had to hunt for them in the woods along the Caw river. This meant that our permission was restricted to definite boundaries, on the South, the telephone line, on the East and West boundary of our quarters on the North the top of hill Rocks on top. This is due to some of the boys taking advantage of permission given.

April 2. Tuesday. Took a 2 hr's. hike over the hills, were tired and dirty when we arrived at the tents. In the afternoon they read to us the ruling and explained it. Lieut. Hickerson read and explained the ruling to us and was surprizingly kind in doing so. He read to us twice a part of number 2 about that, "will be assigned [39] to non-comb. military service as defined in paragraph 1 to the extent that such persons are able to accept service," etc. and 3 "on the first day of April and hereafter monthly," etc. Then he gave permission for us to question if we did not understand. Next he told us that we would be called into the orderly room according to alphabetical order and we should than answer whether we wanted to accept or not. If not, we were to give our reasons in short why not. Oh but how our brains did work. Beargen was called in first. Lieut Hickerson questioned us while another man took it down in short hand. When I was called in I saluted him & he returned and said, "which of these three services will you accept?" "None" I said. "None," said he. "Yes sir None," said I. "Because of your religious belief, that it is under the military establishment?" asked Lieut. "Yes sir, but because the teachings and principles of Christ forbid me too." [40] "That's all," Lieut. said, and I was dismissed. I forgot to salute him when I left. He was to kind indeed. Marvin Schmidt was transfered into our Co. and he also had to answer. He accepted Medical corps. Met him for the first time in the camp. Future will decide as to the hardships connected with it, besides those already received. May God but help us to do what is in accordance with his will.

April 3. Wed. Received a letter from father telling me about the Ordaination of my bro-in-law H.T. & sis. Annie. Told me how we were remembered in prayer and also at this occasion how Rev. P. H. Unruh had especially remembered me before God in prayer. I felt consoled and still home-sick when I read it. Answered Prof. Balzers letter and gave him exactly my opinion. It always takes special thot and exactness when I write to the Prof's or Committee. A certain Quacker also came to our Co. and has laid down all work. [41] He had been a military Police before for six mos., but when they started to use guns for this service he quit everything; thus is now with us.

April 4. Thurs. Nothing new occurred. It was a windy and dusty day. Suderman's brother is sick on Spinal Miningitis.

April 5. Friday. The article on furloughs appeared for the first time in the paper as it was finished by Maj. Gen. March, April 4. It is a wise and clear cut law. I sent it home right away and instructed father how to proceed in case I was needed for I certainly wanted to help in this line.

April 6. Saturday. A piece found in the Trench & Camp:
He doesn't know.
By H. E. Fisher.
"The man who doesn't know" is at one of the Camp Funston detention camps in the person of Seay, who can be fully described as six

feet three and dark, very dark, black.

Beyond the fact that he's in the army now, and that the meals at the camp are much to his liking, Lazarus confesses to knowing nothing. Where he was born, how old he is, even whether or not he is married proved questions fraught with deep, dark mystery to the colored lad, who is described as the most magnificently ignorant person in camp, by officers who attempted to fill out his personal record blanks.

"Where do you live?" was the first question that stumped this reverse prodigy, who stood scratching his woolly head in perplexity. "Ay do'n rightly know, boss," he replied. "Ah jes sorta mosseys aroun'."

Lazarus thinks that his parents are dead but wasn't certain enough to answer the question definitely. The question of whether he was married or not worried him, too. "Lawd, man, I jes do'n know, dassall. Dat woman of mine got uppity one [43] day and jes lef' me flat. Ah think she got a divo'ce, but ah ain't certa."

What was her maiden name?

"Now ain't that funny, boss? Ah jes plumb disremember."

He has forgotten where he was born, and he can't remember when. He doesn't belong to any lodge, he has no dependents and may be he had a best friend, but if so he's forgotten him. There fore, he points out there is no one to notify in case of any emergency.

Lazarus's ignorance is apparently real. To nearly every question his answer was "Ah jes sorta disremember, boss, dassall," given with all of the ingenuousness of his race. In despair
the recording officer finally put his last question, "What is your attitude regarding the war?"

"Lawdy, boss, ah don't know. Ah do'n suppose ahs goin' to do it much good."

And only the cook, who declares a man who eats like Lazarus can surely fight, disagrees with him.

---
[59]

Had inspection to-day. A splendid day. [44] Had a fine rain during the night.

April 7. 1918. Sunday. Rev. Amstutz was here and gave us a fine sermon. In the forenoon I went with him to Fort Riley to see a certain Showalter from Halstead then in the afternoon after services I walked with him to Camp Funston. Had a fine time.

April 8. Monday. Received a package from home and also letter. 30 boys were taken to Funston and once more tried.[60]

Notice on bulletin required me & others to write this letter: Funston Ks. April 8'18. Capt. F. J. Kintz. 45 Co. 164 Depot Brig.

Dear Sir:

The following are my reasons for objecting to accept any work under the three branches of service, Medical, Quarter master, and Engineers Corps, as declared by the Pres. to be Non-combatant military service:

The three branches of service, as mentioned above, belong to the military machine and as such are necessary to make the military machine efficient, and likewise necessary to carry on modern warfare; whose aim is to bring about peace by destroying the enemy. [45] My participation in this service would mean that I was playing my part to make this machine efficient i.e. to conquer the enemy at any cost. Therefore I cannot participate in this service, for Christ says in Matt. 5:44, "but I say unto you, Love your enemies, and pray for them that persecute you." Likewise, in John 8:7, when the scribes and Pharisees bring to Christ a woman taken in Adultery and question whether she should be stoned Christ says to them: "He that is without sin let him first cast a stone at her."

These Scriptures are well known to you Captain and as such need not be quoted; but they and others are the principles and teachings of Christ upon which the Mennonite Church founded its Doctrine some 400 yrs ago, of which church I am as member. Thus being trained and taught accordingly my conscience forbids me to participate in war in any form.

Sincerely

Gustav R. Gaeddert. [46]

April 9. 1918. Nothing much happened. Played ball in the afternoon. Received letter from Hans.

April 10. Wed. Some of the boys were asked whether they could do work at Fort Riley cleaning up. They rejected.

April 11. Thurs. In the afternoon Colonel Parker & also known as Judge Advocate spoke to us boys and tried to tangle up what we had by explaining to us the ruling like he did. Result was lots of thot but otherwise left conditions as before. He likewise threatened us if we would not change mind.[61]

April 12. Friday. Day of thot—.

April 13. Sat. Took hike in forenoon. Received my third inocculation and sec. vaccination. ans. Hans letter. Took almost 7 mo to fix me up on that. Side was sore but otherwise felt alright.

April 14. Sunday. Heidebrecht bro's & Edd. were here. Also Rev. Albrecht. Had a long talk with Albrecht. Brought me on old thots.

April 15. Mond. My thots and arguments were finally defeated and I felt good and thankful. Were taken out on a hike this afternoon, [47] best hike taken as yet. Also two more men came in Joe Walman & Kleinsasser from S.D. Felt good. George P. Stucky died Sunday morning at 7 oclock. Will be taken home tomorrow. He had the pluersy.

April 16. Tues. Took hike in the afternoon

April 17. Wed. Went to Funston in the afternoon to clean the barrack 1734 where we were suppose to move in the following day. Sailors lost some money $45. and boys were searched but money and purse was not found.

April 18. Thurs. Moved to Funston into barrack 1734. Remained in same Co. retaining same officers. Money & purse was found by Marion Schmidt in the trash box. A great give away by somebody. Put a black spot on our Company.

April 19. Washed Mess hall & had a good rain all day. It began to snow at 4.30 P.M. and snowed all night. [48]

April 20. Saturday. Still snowing at 9.30 A.M. Have inspection at 9. Snowed all day.

April 21. Sunday. Had no minister here to speak to us. Had Sunday school in the forenoon and our usual prayer meeting in the evening.

April 22. Monday. Nothing new occurred. Helped to clean the mess hall like usual. Some of the boys receiving the furlough blanks as filled out by the local board and have signed it.[62] I would refuse to do so because of certain statements in it. Jacob J. Tochetter received his discharge to-day because of mental deficiency.

April 23. Tues. Took a hike thru Ogden and for once saw the outside world again. Everything certainly looks fine.

April 24. Wed. Nothing new happening.

April 25. Thurs. Rained. Received letter from Hans and father. Learned that the furlough is not for us.

April 26. Friday. Boys took a hike but I was not along was [49] just then shaveing myself.

April 27. Sat. Learned that Bernhard Bartel is in the guard house getting along fine. Answered Han's letter in a questionable way.

April 28. Sunday. Dr. Kurtz was here and wanted to speak to us but it was forbidden him. He also advised the boys of their creed to accept some work.

April 29. Monday. Had Muster Roll.

April 30. Tues. Went home at 2.35. Reached home 7.30 P.M. Went to see my wheat & oats. Oats is fine but wheat looks slim. Also went to see Hans but she was not home. Had a fine time. HT's P.F.s also were home. Went to bed at 4.00 A.M.

May 1. Wed. Came back to camp at 1.30 Captain told us we should take up our bed and go to sleep.

May 2. Thurs. Worked in Mess Hall.

May 3. Fri. Nothing new. [50]

May 4. Sat. Open Sat. for ladies and also were well represented.

May 5. Sund. Rev H. P. Krehbiel was here. Couldn't speak because Serg. would not permit had received orders from Capt. not too. We went to find Major Smith but could not find him. Thru direction of information bureau H. P. Krehbiel spoke to the Capt. of M.P. who recognized him as a Co-member of him in Legislature of 1909 and gave him permission to enter the building and speak.[63] Orders of Capt. Kintz were contrary and thus he would not be permitted to speak. He recognized and appreciates our stand.

May 6. Mond. Took a hike and had fun with a squirrel.

May 7. Tues. Worked in Mess-hall.

May 8. Wed. Received letter from Hans which was interesting and more than that. It was conditional. Gave me many new thots.

May 9. Thurs. Assention of Christ. Worked in the Mess Hall.

May 10. Fri. Very windy day. [51] Answered the letter of Hans and tried to satisfy her in the questions put to me. Also did I give her my faults and explained to her how I looked at the problem did not finish it tho.

May 11. Sat. Finished the letter and had it mailed. Cleaned the Mess Hall. lots of dust in it. Other boys went on the hike. Waited to meet my Uncles & Aunts at fore oclock but they didn't come. Met them after supper and Paul & I got a pass and went along with them to Manh. had a fine time.

May 12. Sunday. Paul Henry & I slept in one bed. Had lots of fun. Met Ernest Penners sweetheart & Ernest Wiebe in Manhatten. Left Manh. at 9:15 and arrived at Funston at 10. Had a fine & explanitory talk with Katherine on this present problem. She seemed to be very much concerned about it. They left at 3. P.M.

May 13. Mond. Played a game of ball. Nothing new. Bartel is in our barrack now. Heard the Messiah thru the help of Hayden who furnished us with tickets. [52]

May 14-18. Have been doing my usual work otherwise things have been comparitively quiet. Two Galle boys, Harnley and several other fellows were transferred into this building but also transferred out the same week. Galle boys accepted quarter master work. Applied for a pass and also received it.

May 19. Sunday. Left for home at 5.45 and reached home 10.30 A.M. Was in church at Baptism in the forenoon; in after noon George Froezens, H.T's and likewise Dave Unraus were here. In the evening I visited with Hans and certainly had a fine time and talk with her. Left for Camp at 12.15 A.M. and arrived in Funston at 5.30 A.M.

May 20. Monday. Ernest Penner, Paul Barsh, Johnson, Warkentine, Klassen and about 18 others were transferred into our barrack. They all seem to be fine boys, and certainly were glad to see them come.

Some refused to accept any of the three branches of service while the other accepted either Medical or Quartermaster corps.

May 21. Tues. Boys went on a hike. A windy day again. Some of those boys who were transferred into our barrack were taken to Headquarters to explain their position.

May 22. Wed. Had a big rain during the night and another one in the morning. Received a book from John M. Horsh Scottdale Pa. "Menno Simon's life. to be used by all the boys in the camp."[64] The 89 Division is in mobilization now. Six train loads left to-day.

May 23. Thur. The Serg. slipped one over us when we carried the gun racks from the wood pile to our barracks. It taught me to be more careful. [54]

May 24. Friday. Ernest Penner and the other boys who accepted work were transferred to their respective places. Hated to see Ernest go.

May 25. Sat. John Gaeddert & E. O. Schmidt were transferred into our barrack. Both accepted work.

May 26. Sunday. Rev. P. H. Richert and prof. Hiebert visited us and we had a fine forenoon. Rev. Richert led the Bible class while prof. Hiebert spoke to us. In the after noon I wrote a letter to Hans but did not finish it because Ernest & Abe came to visit us.

May 27. Monday. Finished the letter I left undone yesterday.

May 28. Tues. Still raining about every night. Received letter from Hans. Boys have been and are still leaving fast. The 89th Division has left while the 92 is getting ready.

May 29. Wed. Sang in the morning. Intended to have my teeth repaired but did not. [55]

May 30. Thurs. Decoration day and Pres. Proclamation day. We observed it had a meeting from 11 A.M. till 2 P.M. Meeting consisted of prayer, singing, reading of Scriptures with comments on them by the speaker.

May 31. Friday. Curt Galle came to borrow shoes. Nothing new occurred.

June 1. Sat. Read a few statements in the newspaper regarding our future. What will be done with us. Asked for pass & received it also.

June 2. Sunday. left for home at 5.15 A.M. Reached home at 10.30 found mother in the flower garden picking flowers for decoration of children's day. Annie I got after dinner from Inman while George Froezens were at home for dinner while Mr. H. T. Unruh came in the evening being at Hillsboro having been asked to speak there. The feast was fair Walter sang a solo, was good. Met many friends and likewise P. K. Regier was home. In evening I went to see Hans found her sitting on the porch with her sis. brothers and nephews around her. [56]

Certainly enjoyed my time talked to her about the plans being made for us, which she herself had read already. Left her at 10.15 came home and found H.T. there. Mamma took it hard.[65] She is to dear to have her suffer like she does because of my absence, where I am. Left home at 12.15 and reached camp at 5.30 A.M.

June 3. Monday. day of rest & sleep and windy at that.

June 4. Tues. Had my money cashed at store wouldn't cash it in the bank because of the many false checks coming from soldiers that are leaving.

June 5. Wed. Quakers boys received the ruling yesterday of May 31.[66] I copied it and sent a copy to H. P. Krehbiel. Played a game of basketball in evening East against West. We beat them 11-6.

June 6. Thurs. Commencement week. The Western District Conference meets at College to-day.

June 7. Friday. Rumors begin to appear that a transfer can be expected at any time. Received a welcome letter from Hans.[67] [57]

June 8. Saturday. Notice was given to Jacob H. Suderman by Capt. Kintz that we would be transferred to Detention Camp No. 1. again.

June 9. Sunday. John Thiessen and P.K. did not come. What has happened to them I do not know. Met Lena Esau, had some pictures taken, altho in a different way that Paul and I had intended too. Received a letter from Jacob telling me that Marie is in the Goessel Hospital.

June 10. Monday. Waiting for orders to be transferred.

June 11. Tues. Left for Detention camp at 2 P.M. Packed everything in forenoon. Retained the same officers with the exception of some sergent's corporals and buck privates acting somewhat fresh all from the 58 Co our address likewise was changed to 58 Co. Detention Camp No 1.

June 12. Wed. Wrote letter to Hans. Had various experiences. Cut grass with pocket knife all day. Asked us to help put up tents etc. [58] At 3 P.M. we received the orders that it is to hot to cut grass ha! ha! some logic, took them quite a while to find out.

June 13. Thurs. Continued to cut grass but they asked us again to help build tents etc. In the evening Paul Boese & I went to the grove by means of permission and wrote letters to bro John.

June 14. Friday. Finished cutting and carrying away grass. Asked us to cut grass in the Verenal district. No! After noon we also cut the ditch of the road, slanting. Those corporals and private giving orders.

June 15. Sat. Was on K.P. duty, had a good time. Boys were asked to cut grass on the baseball dimond, after noon they were off but in forenoon had to remain on the hill till 11.30 A.M. ha! ha! No passes were permitted. We boys even had to stay back of the last row of tents, they said that we may catch spinal Meningitis germs if we would get to close to the highway ha! ha! Sudermans [59] bro. Paul Bartel, Wiens and others had intended to go home their cars had arrived but passes are not permitted. About 11 P.M. Jacob Neufeld crawling into our tent with the intentions to sew the trowers when so doing he was noticed; when he returned them Heidebrecht gave him a hasty shower leaving him to disappear almost unnoticed. This was a make up by Unruh and others because of false statements regarding Heidebrecht, telling them that he would get married Sunday afternoon.

June 16. Sunday. Had a fine Sunday-School lesson on the crucifixion of Jesus led by Hioth. In the afternoon, boys could not see their friends, confined. Had some fine waterfights to keep cool. Ernest & Abe came to see us.

June 17. Monday. Was on K.P. duty. Had lots of fun. Boys were sent on the hill again. Letter from Hans.

June 18. Tues. Declared my intentions to the Friends Service Committee to join in the Reconstruction [60] work thru a letter. Recommended Prof. Kliewer Rev. Krehbiel Rev. D. D. Unruh and John Thiessen for the persons to recommend me.

June19. Wed. Was on K.P. duty. Boys made their usual visit to the hills.

June 20. Thurs. Moved to another zone. My tent mates are Suderman Epp J.Miller, Hofstetter, and Naffzigger. gave the tent a good bathe. Retained the same address.

June 21. Fri. Our day in kitchen. Oh but the kitchen was dirty changed it from a—pen to kitchen by 10.30 A.M.

June 22. Sat. The boys finished the building of the Messhall. In the evening the captain gave us a splendid talk. Among other things he said that he had met us half ways and expected the same in return, also said he you will not be here a lifetime. Expecting us to build cornerstone. Commenting on the clean tents with few exceptions.

June 23. Sunday. Was on duty all day. Rained in forenoon. Wrote letter to H.Ts. Hioth could see his wife for a short [61] time but was asked to go back by the Major & Capt. Kintz. Expecting a change.

June 24. Mond. Lots of boys are leaving for the various camps again to-day. Among them Mr. H. H. Lohrentz, Sarahs cousin. Many tears will be shed again to-day. 8 more COs came in while 18 N.C's go out today.

June 25. Tues. 10 NonComb. and 1 CO came in today. Carl Richert and John Wiens among them. Worked in kitchen. Received letter from J. Thiessen.

June 26. Wed. Ans Han's letter also wrote letter to Lizzie Dick. Notice posted on the bulletin that our mail (outgoing) will be censored. Some buck privates are reading some of the letters.

June 27. Thur. 2 more came in today (morning)

June 28. Fri. Was requested to give my reason for refusing to wear the uniform.

To Capt. F. J. Kintz. June 28.'18

58 Co. 64 D.B.

Dear Sir:

In reply to your request [62] I present my reasons for objecting to wear the regulation uniform which read as follows:

Sec. of War Baker, has from the very beginning of the war respected men of religious convictions and principles and not asked them to do anything which would violate their conscience. Therefore I have not been required to wear the uniform.

Since I cannot conscientiously accept any military service, I likewise cannot wear the regulation uniform; because, if wearing it, I would be misrepresenting to the public and inconsistent to my belief. To the soldier, as a soldier, it is an honor to wear the uniform bearing its insignia and representing its purpose. Therefore, because of my position, with my objection to wear the uniform I avoid misrepresentation and remain consistent with my belief and the dictates of my conscience. Sincerely—[63]

June 29. Sat. Had general inspection in Kitchen by Major Capt. & Lieut. also tent inspection by Lieut. King. Worked in kitchen.

June 30. Sund. My day off, certainly had a fine rain during Sat & Sund. nite the tent leaked considerably floor was all wet and partly beds also.

July 1. Monday. Received letter from Hans. Our day in kitchen.

July 2. Received orders to move to Camp Dodge. Major general Woods inspected the camp. Left Funston at 4 P.M. enjoyed the trip immensely, arrived at Topeka about 6 P.M. at K.C. Mo. about 7:30 and in Camp Dodge about 9 o'clock.

July 3. Reached Dodge at 9 were taken thru the receiving station than finally to our home to be. In the afternoon we were marched before the Board of Inquiry composed of Major Stoddard Stone and took 8 to 14 at a time.[68]

July 4. I appeared before the Board asked me only how old when I joined Church and whether I had a certificate. Questioned Carl considerable. [64] Plett, and Troyer were put in Class 4.[69]

July 5. Fri. Was on K.P. We were marched to the place of the scaffold where they hung three Negroes because of rapeing a woman. Certainly was a tragic scene, several cooks fainted—awful. unhuman.[70]

July 6. Sat. Were told that the following day we were all to drill.

Ha! [. . .] all read to us a few orders which we had heard before only by different interpretation.[71]

July 7 Sunday.—Our first sermon given by Chaplin Smith—tried his best to convince the C.Os.[72] Quartett sang Secret [. . .].[73]

July 8-Aug. 27. Heard many a supposed to be sermon trying to convince us to accept non-comb work—failed completely all chaplins of the 88 division of Dodge and many a prominent Civilian minister has spoken to us during that time called us yellow dogs skunks and threatened us in different ways. The Sergeants and Lieut Dockey Wilson were always [65] very kind to us and the Sergs. have treated us with due respect. At first we didn't take any exercise—than we started with calisthenics continued that until finally we took hikes about Aug. 15 we started it ordered by General of the Camp. John Andres was the first one to be furloughed out. We always had our evening devotional meeting and a joint meeting every Thurs. and Sunday evenings. Good programs too. Lots of quartett singing everybody enjoyed it.

Aug. 28. David Goertz Elmer Jantz Paul Heidebrecht Jns Friesen Carl Graber and myself were furloughed out to Independence, Iowa State Hospital. left Dodge in evening to Des Moines together with Rec. Boys who left the same day for Phil.[74] Hated to part with them. Arrived at Des Moines at 9 P.M. Serg Neufeur accompanied us. Missed our train to Independence so we stayed over nite in Des Moines first nite of Freedom how good it felt too, not to be expressed in words.

Della (Balmer) and Ura Hostetler, 1917
Courtesy of Thema (Hostetler) Kauffman, Harper, Kansas.

Chapter Five

Ura Hostetler's Lonely Witness

Had Ura Hostetler lived in some other part of the United States during the Great War, he might never have seen a military camp. He might never have been forced to decide between being a soldier, beloved by the American people, and being an objector, accused of slackerism by his fellow countrymen.

Elsewhere, generous local draft boards had been gracious to married men, granting them dependency exemptions so they could remain at home, caring for their wives and families. But Hostetler lived in Harper County, Kansas. There, the draft board was far less lenient with married folk; it deemed Hostetler fit to fight and decided that his wife, Della, could subsist without his financial aid. A dependency exemption might still be available if Hostetler got his wife pregnant, a doctor in the community told him. The physician offered to help Hostetler earn an exemption should a pregnancy develop. That, however, seemed to the young couple too risky an endeavor to avoid conscription. And so Hostetler, married only seven months, left his "darling sweetheart" in May 1918 and journeyed to Camp Funston, Kansas.

At Camp Funston, Hostetler's longing for his wife was acute. Barracked initially with regular conscripts and then placed alone in a guardhouse cell, Hostetler's isolation only intensified his loneliness. He missed the woman with whom he had lived for a short while, and believed that leaving her and his family for the military camp was "the hardest thing I ever had been forced to do." Better, he wrote, that Della "go to her grave as to leave her by herself in this cold and cruel world. Then I would of known she was free from all grief and sorrow."[1] Without passes home to see his wife, his sole solace was the mail which came irregularly; her letters, though a comforting voice from far away, only made him tearfully "blue." Yet despite the aching loneliness he felt, a pain to which he admitted over and over in his diary, Hostetler believed that his presence at Camp Funston, and the presence of his objector brethren, had holy purpose: they were to do God's work in the military cantonment, carrying God's "message of love to a few hungry souls."[2]

Hostetler's Great War internment was relatively short, especially given the fate of those objectors who were detained from the draft's beginning until long after the war's conclusion. He remained in camp a mere three months, then was furloughed to an Iowa farm for another five. The diary Hostetler kept covers only his time at Camp Funston and Camp Dodge, Iowa, and so is in itself a rather brief document. Nonetheless, Hostetler's manuscript is compelling, as it so clearly describes experiences common to many Mennonite young men during the Great War. We can trace in Hostetler's words the isolation from home community that he and others felt, as well as his sense of alienation from the military world he was forced to enter. We can also recognize in the diary Hostetler's conviction that he was sent to witness peace to others—a conviction shared by many of his brethren. Finally, Hostetler's diary shows the remarkable encroachment of military language into the writing of a rural Mennonite pacifist, suggesting the power one community of discourse can have over another, even if that community's ideals still do not permeate the other. However brief his diary and detainment, then, Hostetler provided testament to the World War I life of the lonely witness transformed by his military experiences—a life and a transformation shared by other conscientious objectors.

In many ways, Hostetler's family history was prototypical of believers from the (Old) Mennonite Church in the United States. By the twentieth century, his ancestors had long been American citizens, having emigrated from Western Europe in 1738 aboard the *Charming Nancy*. His first forebear on American soil, Jacob Hochstetler, was Amish; he settled in south-central Pennsylvania among others of his kind to begin a new life, cleared the land of its heavy timber, and began the difficult work of being a frontier American farmer.

According to Hostetler family documents, Jacob Hochstetler had himself faced the hard decision of supporting or objecting to warfare in 1756 when, during the French and Indian War, Native Americans attacked his home. Hochstetler and his sons could have battled the intruders; Hochstetler's sons begged their father to let them shoulder their hunting rifles against the Native Americans. However, Hochstetler refused to fight back. As a result of his unwillingness to fight evil with evil, his house was burned, his son and daughter tomahawked and scalped, and his wife stabbed with a butcher knife. Hochstetler and two of his sons endured years of captivity by the Native Americans.[3] Nearly two centuries later, Ura Hostetler would be compelled to make a similar decision, to violently resist violence or to reject warfare. Though the costs of Hostetler's decision were certainly lower than those for his ancestor, the choice to remain nonresistant was still the same.

Born in 1893, Hostetler was the third of fourteen children. His parents, Henry and Salome (Slabach) had met and married in McPherson County, Kansas, in 1888. Like many (Old) Mennonites, Hostetler's parents did not vote or take part in politics; as was also typical among their Mennonite group, their family's long tenure in America made them competent English speakers, although in their home they also spoke Pennsylvania Dutch, a German dialect common among (Old) Mennonites and Amish.

At age 13, Hostetler became a baptized member of the West Liberty Mennonite Church located near Inman, Kansas. He remained an active member of the (Old) Mennonite Church until his death, though he joined the Pleasant Valley Mennonite Church in Harper, Kansas, several years after his baptism, when his parents moved all their possessions and their then-eleven children to Harper. Ura Hostetler would reside in and around Harper the rest of his life.

Following their move, Hostetler finished his education, graduating from the eighth grade at the Pleasant Valley School. By that time he was 18 years old; his pace was typical of Mennonite farm boys, whose strength was needed more on the farm than their heads were needed in the classroom. On the many days Hostetler was not in school, he was receiving an education from his father, learning how to farm the southern Kansas land, to raise livestock, and to construct buildings. By 1914, Hostetler was helping his father build concrete silos in Harper County, a business that gave him a comfortable income, a motorcycle, a Ford car, and enough money to convince Della Balmer to marry him; during their courtship, Della had said she would accept his proposal when he had saved one thousand dollars.

The couple married on Sunday, November 11, 1917, at the Balmer homestead. Although Ura and Della had known each other for some time and had been courting for four years, their official engagement was a mere two weeks long and was highly secretive. Hostetler's parents discovered there was to be a wedding only several hours before it occurred, having been informed of the couple's plans that morning, before church. Other guests were invited to the Balmer house "for dinner" and were surprised by the day's entertainment when they arrived. The couple's honeymoon was spent at the bride's house, where they were shivareed by youth from their church. Ura and Della lived with the Balmer family until January, when they bought a home in Harper and settled in for their life together.

Several months later, Hostetler was called to war. His draft notice ordered him to report for duty on May 26, 1918, only three weeks after his younger sister, Gladys, had died of typhoid fever in a Colorado hospital. Hostetler's conscription only compounded the sadness already pervading his family. In Anthony, Kansas, Hostetler joined a train car load of Harper County men traveling to Funston, though few of these were conscientious objectors. During the journey, Hostetler conversed with a recently baptized Mennonite from Crystal, Kansas, about whether to accept noncombatant work. Hostetler's friend said he would probably choose noncombatancy, as he was a smoker and needed his cigarettes; the man was convinced that smoking would not be allowed in conscientious objector detachments.

On the way to Camp Funston, the train stopped in Wichita for several hours, and the men were allowed to disembark and tour the city. When the soldiers returned to the train at 9:00 p.m., Hostetler remembered, they were "pretty tight," having celebrated their layover in saloons. While waiting to reboard the train, the soldiers "began to sing and carry on. I was pretty ashamed to have to be in that crowd," Hostetler said.[4] Later, as the train cut through the Kansas night toward Camp Funston, a drunken soldier careened through the cars, waking everyone up by shouting that he was looking for a collar button and then that he was seeking someone who obviously was not on the train. "He was so stewed," Hostetler said in a 1968 interview, "he didn't hardly know what he was doing."[5] For Hostetler, a small town Mennonite who socialized at church functions and community gatherings, this was all quite new, a bit amusing, and certainly frightening. Such was his introduction to the military.

Once at Camp Funston, Hostetler was initially barracked with regular conscripts because of a two-week quarantine imposed on the camp. Those first days were particularly difficult for Hostetler, who missed his wife and family and who also did not get along well with the other soldiers. The regular conscripts resented him, Hostetler believed, because he did not have to drill or stand inspection. Instead, he spent his time working at the YMCA, staying at his bunk studying the Bible, and visiting with the few other conscientious objectors who came by his barrack to see him in the evenings. The soldiers showed their antipathy for Hostetler by verbal taunts and stealing his clothes. They made him don the uniform he refused to wear and took pictures of him in the puttees and military shoes they crammed on his feet.

Officers did their own part to harass Hostetler, cornering him alone and trying to cajole him into dropping his conscientious objection and taking up noncombatant or even combatant work. The only thing that checked their abuses, Hostetler wrote in his diary, was fear; soldiers and officers were afraid of facing military discipline, should their mistreatment go too far. Although his diary might suggest otherwise, years later Hostetler remembered that even if some of his fellow objectors were physically and psychologically punished, he received little abuse. Or at least, he said, the mistreatment "didn't hurt me" as much as those who were more weakly constituted and could not bear the brunt of soldiers' taunts and officers' cursing.[6]

On June 11, 1918, Hostetler was brought before the company captain, who "talked to me and then cursed me and everything else."[7] Again, Hostetler refused to accept any type of military duty. He was removed from his barrack and confined to a cell in the stockade, presumably to protect him from the wrath of regular soldiers. Sitting in a solitary cell deepened his loneliness, as there was little to do and he was only one of two conscientious objectors interned there. In the guardhouse, "You sit there and wait, mostly," he recalled later.[8] He was observed constantly by armed soldiers who marched the confined men to the mess hall and followed them to the latrine. Those keeping watch, Hostetler remembered, were not wholly adept in wielding their weapons. One soldier, while unloading his gun in the guardhouse, slipped and shot a hole through the floor. "They sure think a lot of a fellow in here that they send a fellow along with a gun to protect you," Hostetler wrote in his diary, almost certainly with a touch of irony.[9]

After nearly two weeks in the guardhouse, Hostetler was transferred to the conscientious objector detachment, a camp of tents located almost a mile from Camp Funston on the banks of the Kaw River. In his diary Hostetler expressed a small sense of elation in this move from the guardhouse to his new company: after being confined to a small cell, he was finally receiving some physical exercise, finally breathing the fresh air of nature, finally having a "spiritual feast" amid his brethren. While in the detachment, Hostetler did little work beyond helping to build a shelter under which the objectors could eat, then cooking in the kitchen when his turn came. His diary during this time marked the transfers in and out of other objectors, noted who accepted noncombatant work and who refused, and affirmed Hostetler's belief that "God has us here for a purpose, we are just gathering up oil for future use."[10] Despite this conviction, Hostetler also felt the loneliness and idleness that plagued most objectors, who were confined to their detachment zone and relatively bored by the inactivity. The long June days were hard to fill, although the men spent hours on forced hikes in the hills surrounding Camp Funston and on singing and studying the Bible. Still, there was plenty of time for Hostetler to idle away thinking of home and of his "dear wife" Della.

On July 2, 1918, Hostetler joined the about 175 conscientious objectors at Camp Funston in a sojourn to Camp Dodge, Iowa, where they were to appear before the Board of Inquiry. They arrived by train at Camp Dodge on July 3, and by then, Hostetler had already formed the impression that officers at Dodge were more "hard boiled . . . worse then they were at Funston."[11] Hostetler received his hearing before the Board on July 4. Year later, Hostetler remembered that his time with the Board was "easier than some"; appearing with fourteen other objectors, he was only asked to what church he belonged "and a few things like that." Other objectors were not so gently handled, Hostetler recalled, as members of the Board accused them of "going after women and everything else," thereby questioning the depth of their religious convictions.[12] The strength of Hostetler's faith, however, was not scrutinized, as he was a documented longtime member of the (Old) Mennonite Church. He was was classified as 1-A, qualifying him for a farm furlough.

Though now ready and willing to work through the farm furlough program, Hostetler remained at Camp Dodge nearly two more months. Letters from his wife were welcome but irregular during this time, in part because of an illness that lingered with her through July and August, and in part because the move from Funston to Dodge disrupted the flow of mail to objectors. Hostetler oscillated between feeling "wore out and blue" and enjoying the company of the men with whom he forged fast friendships. His diary clearly expressed the tight brotherhood formed with fellow objectors; the departure of objectors for imprisonment at Fort Leavenworth or for re-examination by the Board of Inquiry was especially hard for Hostetler and those left behind. Hostetler wrote on July 20, 1918 that "Last eve. 9:30 14 of our No. were taken from us. Had a meeting before they left. The Lord really blessed me seemed like his spirit was there. Sure gave us inward pain to part with the brethern, not because we are afraid of them falling but because we love them. Tears started to come to my eyes as I bid some good by and Gods blessings."[13]

Those still at Camp Dodge awaiting their fates continued to worship together, studying the Bible and singing. Hostetler wrote that "We must work more for [God] we must do it now."[14] Mennonite ministers rarely visited the objectors at Dodge; however, according to Hostetler, the number of other ministers brought into the camp by the military increased. On one occasion, an army chaplain preached that the objectors needed to be patriotic by accepting service. Hostetler remembered that the chaplain "got all wound up and finally he just walked off he got so worked up."[15] No matter how much Hostetler believed his nonresistant witness was part of God's plan, no matter how uplifting the nightly prayer meetings, the summer must have seemed interminable. Military officers at Camp Dodge apparently made the summer only longer, their "hard boiled" orders aggravating objectors weary of abuse and idleness.

At last, in late August 1918, Hostetler was granted a farm furlough. On August 29, Hostetler arrived at a farm outside Mason City, Iowa, where he would spend the next five months toiling for a local farmer whose own son was fighting in Europe. Other objectors were also furloughed to Mason City, although none with Hostetler. He appreciated the work itself, which involved chores similar to those he had performed on his father's farm for years: cutting weeds with a scythe, threshing wheat, filling silos. In his 1968 interview, Hostetler recalled he had a "good farmer to work for" but living conditions on the farm were less than desirable. The house was disorderly, the farm was chaotic, and the food was downright bad. The farmer's wife, he said, "was kind of stingy I guess and she didn't cook too good. I said this man had it made. I think he ate some in town is what I think he did. Because he delivered milk every day. And so, he had a chance" to get away from his wife's cooking, while Hostetler was stuck on the farm trying to eat the wife's culinary disasters.[16]

At any rate, Hostetler's farm furlough provided one sure blessing: Della was able to live with him on the farm for a month, until the Armistice. Then, since "she didn't like it [living on the farm] and she didn't have to put up with it," she went home, assuming that her husband would soon follow.[17] The farmer, however, refused to release Hostetler until his own son returned from the army, over two months after the war had ended.

By the time Hostetler was released, the government had decided objectors could only be discharged from a camp within 350 miles of their home communities. And so, after Christmas 1918, Hostetler returned to Camp Dodge and then to Camp Funston to await the shuffle of army papers and his impending discharge. The objectors had been idle and anxious for home before, but now the three-week wait was excruciating. There was even less to do: no drilling, no orders, no demands to take up work and help the American cause. "We just sat around," Hostetler said. "That's all there was to do . . . It was three weeks sitting up here, the longest three weeks you ever seen."[18] Finally, on January 29, nearly three months after the armistice, Hostetler received his discharge. He could at last resume life with his new bride, his stint in the military forever behind him.

Hostetler returned to Harper and to a farm several miles outside of town, the first of three he would cultivate in postwar life. There, he and his wife began a family, six children in all. He again took up farming, seeing his family through the depression and beyond with earnings from the livestock he raised and wheat he produced.

Largely a self-educated man, Hostetler began a reading program. In the midst of farming, he would read several hours a day; the most perused text was, of course, his Bible, and he became well-acquainted with its contents. The Pleasant Valley Church remained his faith community and, as the consummate handyman, he took an active part in its building maintenance. After he retired from a lifetime of farming, he helped construct a new church edifice, providing volunteer labor until the project was completed. This was his life, founded on pillars shared by many Mennonites: faith, family, and farming.

Although Hostetler was far too old to face conscription when World War II came, his family was not untouched by Franklin Delano Roosevelt's wartime demand for America's men. Hostetler's oldest son, Lester, was ordered to register for the draft nearly twenty-five years after Hostetler had stood before a Harper County draft board and expressed his own conscientious objection to war. Ura remembered speaking with a member of the draft board about Lester's conscription, wondering how he could help alleviate his son's concerns about the draft. According to Hostetler, the board member responded by saying "I'm not going to give you any allowances. . . ." Frustrated by the man's reply, Hostetler told him, "Well, I'm glad for one thing, the United States government isn't the one who is going to have the last say."[19] Hostetler suggested that the final word would be left to God. As the matter turned out, Lester, like many Mennonite young men at the time, was drafted, but did four years of alternative duty with the Civilian Public Service in Colorado.

Ever the Christian believer, Hostetler was sure that God would favorably judge those who stood firm in their nonresistant convictions. Such blessed assurance was a significant feature of Hostetler's Great War diary. Throughout it, he reminded himself to remain thankful for the generous providence of God, which gave him friends and fellowship and "good grub." This same benevolent God brought objectors to Camp Funston "for a purpose." The objectors' time in camp was, first of all, an opportunity to "draw closer to [God] . . . espicialy because of the persecution some of us have to go thru."[20]

The belief that distress fostered a closer relationship with God would, of course, come naturally to a Mennonite whose own church history was steeped in persecution and the notion of suffering love. But beyond this, Hostetler believed that the objectors' presence in military camps provided the perfect chance to be peaceful witnesses amid men who "practice killing devices."[21] The camp became a mission field that he was to "harvest," by refusing any form of military service, by remaining true to his nonresistant convictions, and by passing that nonresistance on to soldiers and officers—if only by including that which "will do the [censors] good" in the letters he wrote home.[22] As a "soldier of the cross," his was a cause he "would dare die for."[23] The torments of a "hard boiled corporal," the futile orders, the boredom, and the idleness mattered little, for he was in camp to do God's "bidding," whatever that was to be.

This conviction would remain with Hostetler throughout his lifetime. In later years Hostetler believed his World War I witness—and that of other objectors—had been to some extent successful. Certainly, Hostetler realized, they had not convinced everyone to embrace nonresistance. Even after the war to make the world safe for democracy, the United States still engaged in battle, in Europe and then in Asia; in Hostetler's view, Vietnam was "the worst mess that our country has ever been in, in more ways than one."[24] Nonetheless, he thought that the experiences of Great War objectors such as himself brought far-reaching changes to America. In a 1968 interview, Hostetler observed that the Civilian Public Service program of World War II, war relief, the Mennonite Central Committee, 1-W alternative service during Vietnam, and even the Peace Corps were all a direct "outgrowth" of the struggle and persecution endured by Great War objectors. These institutions had made significant transformations in a war-torn twentieth century, Hostetler believed.

Maybe more significantly, Hostetler was certain that Mennonites and other pacific Christians from World War I had contributed to the well-being of the United States by upholding Christan values. Military men who had appealed to the objectors' patriotism argued that the objectors were receiving all the benefits of the soldiers' sacrifice for freedom but paying none of the costs; Hostetler reasoned that those who fought "were getting all the benefits Christianity provides in the country" but offering little in return. "You see," Hostetler said in 1968, "they're protecting us physically and say we are not contributing. What about a country that didn't have any Christianity?"[25] Only the objectors' Christian witness could sustain the light of Christ in a darkened country, a light that Hostetler felt certain provided more comfort and security than could any military effort. In this way, he thought Great War objectors were making the world safe from evil, their peaceful witness even more necessary, really, than the soldiers' bloody mission.

Yet even as Hostetler sought to enact a peaceful change in his war-torn world, so too was he inevitably transformed by his time in a military cantonment supporting the ethos of war's necessity. While at Camp Funston and Camp Dodge, Hostetler certainly retained the ideals of Mennonitism and of nonresistance. These were inviolate and he would not forsake them, even if many other Mennonites did. Still, as we read Hostetler's diary, we might sense small but perceptible changes in the ways he viewed his experience as an objector and, even more, in the language he used to describe that experience.

With time, his complaints about his military company became not so much the laments of a conscientious objector mistreated at the hands of angry officers; instead, they resembled the plaintive moans of any soldier. He protested that the mess was bad, that it made the stomach hurt, that the food "would of been allright if it hadn't been for the dog," a joke shared with others in his company.[26] Military lingo and acronyms also began to infiltrate the text: he wrote of "good grub," being on "K.P.," and having "mess detail"; he referred to his C.O. (meaning in this case his commanding officer) and the people who joined his "Co."; he even described the "policing" of a barn he did while on farm furlough. At one point late in the text, Hostetler provided a definition of military camp jargon: "'Where do you get that stuff' is a common expression used here when ever some body does something that he shouldn't."[27]

The language Hostetler employed, although seemingly a minor feature in a text rich with detail about his confinement, nevertheless suggests that the military effected some change—if only linguistic—among the objectors it detained. At the least, Hostetler's diary shows the force with which the discourse of one community can penetrate another, even if its ideas do not. Undoubtedly, when Hostetler returned to Harper and to his Mennonite fellowship, words like *mess, detail,* and *policing* no longer had currency; the discourse of the Mennonite community once again came to the fore, and the military language he picked up at Funston was just as quickly dropped. We can only surmise that Hostetler was not fully conscious of the military language he at times used to figure his experience, just as we may never wholly notice new words we assume from a variety of cultural lexicons. His lack of self-awareness, however, merely makes his use of military jargon all the more striking.

Hostetler's activity as a diarist did not begin with the Great War; he had chronicled the entire year of 1914 in similar fashion. After the war, he continued to write, sometimes keeping a diary, sometimes writing down family history and memorable life stories, on one occasion documenting Pleasant Valley Mennonite Church's past. Yet it is his World War I diary that remains his most significant work, even if he did not realize its importance when, during summer 1918, he described his loneliness and proclaimed his everlasting faith in a peaceful God.

As the diary's structure makes clear, Hostetler wanted this to be a narrative solely about the Great War. His first entry began with his arrival at Camp Funston and the last entry ended with his initial night outside the army, furloughed to an Iowa farm. He was an irregular diarist, and days passed between entries. Nonetheless, his writing was filled with details about his experience, and even more, about his emotional reactions to the experience. This was his personal Great War history, unencumbered by the story of his life either before or after conscription, providing an account of his experience and perceptions while in camp.

The original diary manuscript is now in the possession of Hostetler's oldest daughter, Thelma Kauffman, who still lives in Harper County, Kansas. A copy is available for public perusal at the Mennonite Library and Archives in North Newton, Kansas. This copy was given to the library by Kauffman many years ago. Apparently she, like other members of the family, had long enjoyed her father's stories about his Great Way journey. She believed that his diary about life at Camp Funston and Camp Dodge deserved a wider audience than those closest to him, who already knew the depths of his nonresistant faith and of his love for Della, his "dear girl."

Ura Hostetler died of respiratory disease in 1981. He was 87. Della had died fourteen years earlier, succumbing to heart failure in 1968. Both are interred in a Harper, Kansas, cemetery, near the Pleasant Valley Mennonite Church, which Hostetler helped construct. In the Pleasant Valley congregation the couple courted, and in it they raised their family. Such was the small but powerful radius of Hostetler's life, informed always by the Mennonite church and its beliefs, by his wife and by his family, and by the rich farmland he cultivated in Harper County. The Great War, and his military experience as a conscientious objector, had certainly drawn him outside this circumference, transforming him through exposure to a world he had never known. As his World War I diary shows, he desperately longed for the peaceful security of smaller boundaries, of wife and family, church and harvest. However, Hostetler's text reveals as well his conviction that he served a higher purpose, and that the God who called him away from Della to the military camp would be the same God who carried him safely home.

Text

Ura Hostetler's original diary manuscript serves as the copy-text for this edition. No other forms of the diary exist or have ever been published. A small red leather notebook, about four inches by six, the diary was in actuality an address or ledger book, judging by the letter tabs which lined the outside of its pages. The pages did not have preprinted numbers, nor did Hostetler care to number the pages of his text. At first, Hostetler wrote in pencil, although on August 6, 1918, he bought a second-hand and broken fountain pen for one dollar (as his diary indicated), and then used this to write his entries from then on.

The book had no lines other than a preprinted line marking the top, left, and right margins. Hostetler did not violate the top margin, although he wrote beyond the left and right margins printed on each page. On the book's first few pages, Hostetler inscribed addresses of fellow objectors and his own company addresses. He also jotted down the location of several key Scripture verses. The volume may thus have served several purposes, as an address book cum reference book cum diary.

In the back of the book, Hostetler included additional lists of objectors from Camp Funston and Camp Dodge. One list, in pencil, had ninety names; the other, in pen, had about two hundred names. Both lists recorded each man's denomination. A newspaper advertisement for Hostetler's silos, circa 1916, was sandwiched between the diary's pages. It read, in part:

> Carnegie can write a few words on a sheet of paper and make it worth $1,000,000. "That's Capital." ...

I have eliminated cheap material and construct the best Silo in the United States. "That's Progress."

My competitors will tell you that they construct just as good a silo as I do. "That's Gall."

Everyone who wants the best Silo and avoid future troubles, will have me construct a Monolithic Concrete Silo for them. "That's Good Judgment."

In the advertisement as in the diary, Hostetler revealed his humor, creativity, and self-assurance. And, by keeping the advertisement in the diary, Hostetler showed his characteristic longing to document his personal history—a characteristic shared by his eldest daughter, Thelma Kauffman, who has preserved her father's diary and made it available to scholars interested in Hostetler's Great War past.

The Diary of Ura Hostetler

Matt. 5: 39-40[28]
52
? John 18-36 ?[29]
Rom 12:17-21[30]
II Cor. 10:14[31]
(H OM, Eli Durkenson, Superior IA)[32]
Odebolt IA
c/o Adams & CO
Grant Milford Nebr.
Box 114 [2]
This book belongs to Ura Hostetler
Harper, Kans. R.1.
If lost and someone finds me return to owner and receive reward. [4]
conscientisus
William F. Leitsal
45 Co. 164 Depot Brigade,
Camp Funston, Kans.
7th Co.
164 D.B.
Detention Camp No. 1
58th Co.
Prov. Det. (Con. Obj.)
163 Depot Brigade
Camp Dodge, Iowa[33] [6]

[1918]

On May 26th 1918, I had to report for military duty, at Authority Kans. 1:30 p.m. This was the hardest thing I ever had been forced to do. To leave my home folks and a darling sweetheart wife. I would just as soon have seen her go to her grave as to leave her by herself in this cold and cruel world. Then I would of known she was free from all grief and sorrow.

Arrived at Camp Funston May the 27th at noon, it was almost impossible not to wear the uniform but thru Jesus our Lord I got thru, only after [7] having the uniform forced onto me, for several hrs. They put overalls into my sack and uniform on me but I changed when I got a chance, put overall and jumper on and uniform into sack. Why does God allow such man killing devices to be carried on and practiced as they do here?

May 28. When I reported for duty without a hat I was ordered up stairs again. (Thank God) Have nothing to do, but write and study Gods word and talk with him.

May 29. Wed. Sure had a time today about 200 [8] came and talked to me and tried to persuade me into it, some are real reasonable Commander done so too. This morn boys made sport of me, glad they enjoy it, put my leggings and shoes on, stood me up and took my picture.

I sure would like to have one.[34]

Received our first innoculations today. Glory to God some of us concientious brethern came to see me this eve, done me lots of good.

May 30. decoration day today. everyone is taking it easy not even bothering me. [9] Got orders to go up to the Y.M.C.A. & work till I get out of here, not so much to do, only sweep and clean up a little.

Lot of men are sick over their shots last night. Some fell over in retreat tonight. Got carried in.

Still no mail from home.

May 31. Still loafing at Y. Hurrah. I got a letter from home today sure seems good. Was just wondering why I didn't hear, when sure it came.

June 1. Got a new boss at Y. don't like him so well, he thinks I his nigger. [10]

Was pretty tired and blue today [. . .] almost had to cry just wanted one bit of home.[35]

John came over this P.M.[36] I would of tried to get my half holiday today but I didn't. Try next Sat. God is sending us such a pleasant eve.

June 2. Sunday. Went up to Y. and picked up paper took about an hr. Stayed for their services, had some good things.

Was lonesome in P.M. Had no where to lay my head. Ben N. & Shrock came over after supper had a real pleasant eve. [11]

June 3. Monday. Am cleaning again today kinda had the blues, but thank God for brighter future hopes. The boys took their first hike out on hill, they all layed down to rest too at noon Hr.

June 4. Sergeant tried to give me another job also to scare me about going to Leavenworth. Had sort of a mental ex. today.

Got my work about all done till noon, so I just [. . .] in P.M.[37] Wished for $10 to buy Della music box. I just got so lonesome this eve I didn't know [12] where to go or what to do haven't seen any of the boys since Sun. I spent another quarter for ice cream, I just had to do something to cheer me a little bit.

June 6. Thur. Well I bought Dell her box, won't she be overwhelmed with joy. No mail from home wonder what can be the matter? I am beginning to get suspicious about the boys having gone to Fort Leavenworth cause they haven't showed up since Sun. Got bawled out this morn. for scraping my shoe on floor, had to sweep [13] stairs and hall thanklessly, just like all my work. Della won't you write anymore. dear me!

June 7. Friday. Well I received the dearest letter today, I wanted to cry so bad I couldn't hardly read it. I felt kinda sick from my vaxination.

Got another shot in arm this eve. 3 fellows went down just ahead of me when they got shot.

Am expecting to see daddy and Jim Hamilton tomorrow.

June 8. Saturday. My the fellows sure did some grunting and groaning, were sick from their shots, not affect me a great deal. [14]

I layed in bed and covered up before breakfast and a sergeant chased me up. They are getting stricter all the time. This is inspection day and some guys don't like it cause I don't have to stand inspection, whenever they have to do something they don't like and I don't do it, it eats on them. A few are real good to me.

June 9. Sunday. Cleaned up a little and got down to read and here come papa, almost surprised me. Brought a letter from my dear wife and some pictures. Heard a good testimony from a converted Jew. [15] Had a good visit for once.

Bill & John came over. They are still here, expect to be transferred Tue. After papa left I wrote my dear blessed wife a great big letter, I really feel that I have many things to be thankful for, the future looks brighter, yea I can even see beyond this life.

June 10. Monday. Things blue just a tint today but wore off again. Sure got some good general orders today, has our future pretty well laid out of course we are not to see them I guess. This eve. the boys got another [. . .][38] [17] was going to dress me up. They pulled off my clothes and started to put uniform on me but were afraid, one fellow called them down; not to talk so rough.

If they knew what the general orders were they would be afraid to touch me. Received another letter from my dear dear wife.

Before I went to bed I took my clothes off and sat down to read some of those dear letters and the boys swiped my clothes. I couldn't find them so I told the sergeant, he said if he had his way about it I'd go without [18] clothes, but boys this mans clothes will come back tonight, I know he's h——to live with but he'll be taken care of sooner or later.

June 11. Tuesday. Done some cleaning up at the Y. didn't hurt myself as I stoped to write a letter. Went back P.M. A sergeant came after me had me before the Captain, had another chance to work refused. Then they brought me to the gaurd house. Not the worst place I have ever been in either.

They march us over to regular mess halls for messes. [19] Always get in first too.

June 13. Thursday. eve. the sergeant made a misscue and fired a shot into the floor. They sure think a lot of a fellow in here that they send a fellow along with a gun to protect you.

Don't hardly get enough work to do for exercise. Gets kinda lonesome.

June 14. Friday. Received our third shot today. Had strawberries for breakfast. Lot of other boys got overseas examinations but I didn't.

June 17. Monday. Well things are just about [20] as the same every day, I sure was a little homesick last eve. Feel better today. We are going to be transferred, Praise the Lord. Tonight we move. I think we'll get to other objectors. Had some pretty good talks with Mr. Phrasher since I'm in here.

June 20. Well got on a transfer at last. Had to walk about half way down then rode in an ambulance the rest of way. Phrasher signed up for non-combatant work. Was lucky enough to get in a tent with John H. [21]

June 23. Sun. Well I feel kind sad for I know my dear wife is heart broken because I did not get to come home. May the Lord bless and comfort her.

June 27. Well there are lots of things happening now days, went on 3 hikes already. Went over the hills twice once about 4 mi. back. It sure is good to get out to see nature. Paul Zook, Amos Showalter and 8 others came in here the other night all signed up but 2. I'm sorry to see [22] them give in so easy. One went back on his signature yesterday morn. Thank God. A few more came in last eve. About 40 more are coming today, a bunch of us moved 4 tents over here for them. They were to be here for supper last eve. but didn't get here so we sure had some supper. Had all we wanted and then some. But best of all we had a spiritual feast. Had an open air meeting. A devotional meeting. Sure like to hear [23] the prayers and testimonies. We learn so many good things—have meetings every eve. about 2 hrs. God has us here for a purpose, we are just gathering up oil for future use. When the bridegroom cometh may we have our vessels and lamp all filled.[39] Some times I think we idle away to much time don't study and pray enough every time we get tried we get drawn closer to Him.

My prayer is that all of God's children [24] may be drawn closer to him, and espicialy because of the persecution some of us have to go thru.

Am glad for the privilege of being here, I feel as though I was getting rich, not with money, but with unperishable treasures.

Yesterday Capt. Kintz put up an order to read all our letters before they go out, it is just one of his own orders, but I think we should write just such things that will [25] do them good.

June 28. Well received a dear old letter from my good old wife. We aren't allowed to write anything about military affairs (so here goes) in letters.

9 Hutterites came in last night, some got treated pretty mean, one got his hair cut, one almost got drown under faucet.[40] Holcroft came in yesterday.[41] 6 or seven came in P.M. Some are C.O anyway. Some have worse time than I did. Holcroft said they stood him up and pointed gun at him said say your last [26] Mennonite prayer tried to make believe they were going to shoot him just for their own sport. When I see him in meeting makes me think of the parable in Luke 7:41-49.[42] Also Downs. The officers Don't want us to criticize them in our letters but here I can.

Our censorer is sure a nice leutinant, awful nice about talking to us. Makes better feelings that way: Read the letters then forget them and I believe he will. I have no objections about it. Lucena (not spelled right) [27] is an awful nice corporal.

June 28. morn. This morn sergeant King sure started to rattle off our names at roll call.

Roots & King get kinda hard backed at times. Had two Priv. or corporals to take us on a hike yesterday P.M. They took us over north of Funston to a spring, went thru part of Funston. Some of the boys got ivy poison. One boys right side of face is swelled up badly (eye shut). I got a lot of chiggers. Had the article of war read to us again this [28] morn. Were ordered up the hill and before we got up were ordered down again for another lecture or something which we are waiting for now. Got dismissed don't know what they wanted.

June 30. Sun. There are about 175 C.O.s. with the few NonCombatants. Last night 5 came in 2 took work. Ralph Troyer was in the bunch they made him take a cold bath, chew soap, kicked him several times and slaped him with a 3 in board, while naked. 2 Horst boys came this [29] morn, four in bunch 2 took work, those that accept go into other zone, they get to come over here to eat. 3 of the boys this morn. didn't get any hats and Capt Kintz gave the sergeant that brought them down here a jawin for it too.[43]

Am glad to see a few firm ones. Ralph Troyer wouldn't sign a thing except his clothes slip where he received clothes.

We sure had some rain last night these tents leaked like seines. Piled our stuff up and covered over with slickers. Pete Schrock didn't have [30] a slicker so he got under with me, the wind just beat it in. The floor was all wet by time it quit raining. Had a pretty good talk about education last night. Formal and real.

July 1. last eve had a good meeting. Job Becker sure gives some good testimonies. Said he felt shaky before he got up but the best way to do in that case is to get up and shake it off, or shake the devil off. Sounded funny, all laughed but was the most truth in it cause it came from the heart. [31]

Went on a hike this P.M. Were over on hill north of Funston got a good view of Funston.

Today 3 boys that had signed up for work, came back. They had been to Fort Riley, but refused to work as they had been deceived into it. Got some more Hutterites to night. They sure are all stickers. Thank the Lord. Have a move coming tomorrow, some report of going to Camp Dodge, don't know for sure yet where. Received some stationary from home today. [32]

July 2. Today we sure got to move. Had orders at 11:00 to be ready by 2:00. Loaded our baggage on four trucks all marched to Funston. There got on train for somewhere. Don't know where. Are on our way rejoicing now.

July 3. Well we arrived at Camp Dodge Iowa at about 9 oclock this morn. Had some time coming came thru K.C. Had guards along couldn't buy a thing. They chased every body away. Some tried to mail letters but didn't get by. I believe 2 did. Sure handled my baggage some rough. [33]

Had another time here had to line up got through another mill line operation to get assigned to our quarters. They waited outside of barracks for several hrs. to get baggage checked away. Sure was dirty. Didn't get done till marched us off to Y.M.C.A. to appear before the board, didn't only about have appear yet so far. Some of our orders are hard boiled by the time we get them, worse then they were at Funston. Pray that things will be all right by and by. We still are enjoying many blessings.

July 4. We were marched up to Y.M.C.A. to appear before board some sure had a hard time of it but I believe the Lord was with us. Some will be tried harder then some but may that just be the means of drawing them closer to God. Fourteen of us went in at once. Had 5 that they questioned hard four got put in Class 4 one in Class 2. Guess rest of us in Class 1A.[44] Thank God that we may have the privilege for farm work. It was 1:30 till we got back for dinner only done a little bunk fatigue rest of day.

July 5. This morn. they marched every one in [35] camp out to witness the hanging of three negroes. They can lead a horse to water but can't make him drink, some didn't want to go because they refuse to drill, leutenant said they didn't have to drill just going out for a walk. I and guess a lot knew where we were going as I heard about it last night. It is awful how hard some peoples hearts get. They had to carry out four negroes troops that watched and two more went into histerics when fellows went up on platform. I wasn't going to see it [36] but just happened to glance a second when they started to drop. Took eyes off right away. Perhaps they had repented of their sins and went home to Jesus. That is my prayer. They were praying as they walked in. We were about 40 rds off from scaffold.

Every body stood in attention. The negro troops took it hardest. They all negroes removed their hats when the led the victims past. As for my self I would of rather been one of the victims than the man who released the lever. Droped about 9:10 A.M.[45] [37]

Today is the time to accept salvation. Why do so many put it off. Wish I could impress everyone to take the stand today as we don't know what a day may bring forth. Saw Jim Troyer up at Y.M.C.A.[46] Has been here about 2 wks. He still is drilling but expects soon to get to truck driving, has had one trial or examination for it. They still press us as hard here as they possibly dare. They were going to make us drill but I don't believe now that they will. Salmon told our ser-

196 • *Writing Peace*

geant and leutenant [38] yesterday that at Funston we demoted several officers just like you, (which they did,) and it kinda quited our officers down a little.⁴⁷ Last night the sergant made us put lights out at 9:00 Pretty soon corporal comes and wants to know who put the lights out. we told him he cused a little and says there are no such orders, turn them on lights don't go out till 9:45. Some just act as spiteful as they can but maybe we will get them broke in after while. Am afraid they take to many privileges, may get in bad for it too if they hold us to tight. They have lots of C.O.s here [39] and they keep them to close, can't get no information, therefore they just use them about as they please. Had 13 in gaurd house for 2 mo. already wont even let them have prayer meeting. Praise God they can't stop us from praying also we had a prayer meeting last night.

July 7. Sunday. eve. Well we sure have many things to thank God for. Chaplain of this Brigade held meeting here this morn at 8:30 We got some real good things from it. Had Sun. school at 10: I sure was touched today guess I have homsick some song Holy, Holy, and Moment by Moment sure made me think of days [40] gone by and those gone to that heavenly home. Wished I could get there myself so as to get away from this cruel old world, but God has a work here for me to do. behold the feilds they are ready for harvest and the laborers are few. Fit we few, ready creatures to do thy bidding here and may we be able to carry thy message of love to a few hungry souls before it is to late.⁴⁸ Chaplain wants to make soldiers out of us. Thank God we are soldiers of the cross already and would dare to die for our cause.⁴⁹

I wrote Della a letter today had to stop writing for crying. It has been a week since [41] I heard anything from her. Yesterday the officers went thru all our reading matter took a lot of it to censor it. Took all German literature.

Had a real chicken dinner today for dinner I ought to get fat here as I feel pretty healthy, have fine weather plenty of sleep and eats.

July 10. Well we got our first mail yesterday. Then I didn't get a letter from wife, one from R. M. Weaver. Boys got a lot of packages. Also yes went to an illustrated lecture on sexual hygiene. It sure was good showed different cuts of diseased organs etc. of health, homes and families and vica verse. [42] Hutters didn't even stay in to take it all in.⁵⁰

They also took us out where the soldiers come together to learn some patrotic songs. Had some band music and saw negroes dance. I don't approve much of some of their songs. Some are all right. I worked on K.P. Mon. sure got all I wanted. to eat and work. This morn we went out here in front to take some physical exercise, sure does one good wish we would of taken them all along. Wished for a trapesse or over head ladder many a time. Boys play base ball, I like to watch [43] but believe I ought to help as will do me good. I admire some of it when played in good humor, but not as rival teams as world mostly plays.

Well I done some singing this morn, sure had some tune but had songs from heart. Hutters got some talking to yesterday. Got some new orders we have to bathe 3 times a wk. and report. It is a good order.

July 12. Received 3 letters from Della dear today. My poor dear girl has got the mumps.

July 16. Had to work on KP. again Sun. Missed all the meetings thru [44] day till eve got part of it. Had a good meeting last night. Yesterday crowded our bunks together and put about 40 more into our barrack. The bunch that was once in barrack east of us. Can talk to them now. Thank God for his faithful few.

July 18. Received a letter from Della today stating that her mumps are worse again. Sure hurts me to know that. Could not help but write her a rebuking letter, I love her and know she will respect me for it. My dear darling. May God bless her. [45]

Tomorrow 12 are going to be sent to Leavenworth for retrial.

They are getting stricter all the time got an order now that there will be no sitting on bunks between 7 and 12 A.M. In barracks by 9:45 P.M. and in bed by 10 p.m. Hutters got a good many talkings to already. They are awful hard at it trying to persuade us into work. Take us by bunches and singly talk to us.

July 20. Last eve. 9:30 14 of our No. were taken [46] from us. Had a meeting before they left. The Lord really blessed me seemed like his spirit was there. Sure gave us inward pain to part with the brethern, not because we are afraid of them falling but because we love them. Tears started to come to my eyes as I bid some good by and Gods blessings. Some of those songs mean so much to me. Holcroft & I put arms around each other walked around in yard, sang some songs kinda to ourselves and talked about some blessed [47] experiences, while the boys were being lined up to leave. Our whole bunch seemed to be out watching. This is a song I would of liked to sing to them as they left, but didn't for various reasons. God will take care of you, Onward Christian soldiers marching as to war, with the cross of Jesus going on before. Many such blessed songs. Thank God for them. Wonder how Della dear is, haven't heard how she was since Tue. Hope and trust she is made well again by this time. God bless her. [48]

July 22. Monday. Well I feel very much to wore out and blue today. Can't read to do any good, Haven't heard from my dear wife since Thur. Almost every day someone gets or writes a letter that they get a bawling out for. Yesterday eve. we had a pretty good time working in K.P. Some of boys were afraid of our supper, spuds and chicken. Chicken must of been a long time on road. It would of been allright if it hadn't been for the dog, as one fellow said, made me laugh till my stomach nearly [49] busted, I worked on K.P. That's why it hurt my stomach. Also two Chaplains held meeting for the boys while some of us peeled spuds on out side One fellow talked so loud and fast one fellow said he's afraid he peters out. One fellow went to listen a little on out side of barrack, came back an asked if there was any religion there, he said there is in his language. Guess he was right any way it struck my funny bone and I had another stomach buster. Also one soldier in [50] another barrack heard the preaching, and yelled out shoot the other barrack too. They asked for conversions but didn't get any. Such a bunch of yellow backed heathens as we are thought to be.

July 23. This morn some civilian Anti Christ was here and talked to us something awful. May God show him the light before it is to late. He left off talking awful sudden and left after he had talked a long while. Claimed to be a minister of the gospel?

July 24. Wed. Today 8 of us got to go after some clothes line posts and it sure was a [51] picnic for us, went out about 3/4 mi. Sat under a tree for about an hr. easy it was a treat, got two hickry posts and another kind don't know what kind I don't know half of trees here, is rolling all along and blue grass on ground sure fine works of God.

We sure had a laughing fit tonight. Hutters think it sin to laugh loud and Holcroft laughed till it sounded like it hurt him. I know it hurt me, my but how I had to laugh.

July 25. Well I got a letter from home and John Jim. Della the dear thing [52] thought I was on a move because she didn't hear so long from me. Didn't sent letter as she thought it would go to different address.

Worked in latrine today.

July 27. Yesterday I received such a sad letter from Della. She was oh so sad I did unjustice to her Oh God forgive, then, Oliver gave her such a talking too that it just broke her dear little heart, May God bless and comfort her.

John H. sure is a roamer and reports he knows all the latest all the time. Tonight he said [53] they are going to starve us, I always get plenty such as it is, but they cut down some on extras.

Am reading in old testament at present, some parts are sure interesting and good.

July 31. Well time is passing slow I get blue and homesick at times. Our eats have improved a little. CC Jenson said once to the cook when he had his slim mess this is just about enough to take to his quarters, he was going to raise a howl next meal if things [54] didn't fare better and sure enough have been getting better since that.

This morn. sergeants over slept I guess any way we didn't have any roll call.

They only gave us physical exercise once a day this week, guess they are getting like us tired and lazy cause they haven't anything to do.

August 2. Fri. eve. Am feeling rather blue and discouraged. Don't get any mail, none since Sun. Surely seems like they are holding it back. Can buy candy, now. boys' [55] sure are getting it anyway. They began to smuggle it in before so it isn't much diff.

Worked on K.P. again yesterday didn't have it so hard as I got in the dining hall, dried dishes. Sometimes get a few extra eats sliped out to us for helping our best friends peel spuds when they are on K.P. We had such a good lesson on giving the other night. I like the way the boys show an interest in the meetings couldn't hardly close as each one wanted to say something surely Gods spirit was there.

Had a good sermon [56] meeting last night Welcome Smith almost preached a sermon. Glad we have such good workers with us. Would to God that I would feel better, but seems like nothing can take the place of my loved one. Dear Girl.

August 6. This sure is one dusty day. I bought me a broken fountain to day but it writes anyway ($1.) Yesterday we had such good meetings Had some good talks on character building then in afternoon Chaffen gave us a talk used as a subject disobiedience. Used Saul for an example when he didn't kill all the Spoil. Sure had a touching [57] lesson. In eve studies a chap in Gala. Holcroft & I helped peel spuds till about 8:45 so we missed the singing & prayer. Tomorrow we are in for latrine police. He & I are sure some team hang together pretty good. The bunch of C.Os. that were in the gaurd house were taken out and put into our Co. Praise the Lord. There is lots of unjust things going on. Capt. Day got his orders Sat. to take them out.

Bill L. was down there at the time, he received his money statement and got called up to give to Y.M.C.A. or Red Cross.

August 9. Been having some experiences. Have been breaking in a new corporal, sure [58] was hard boiled for a few days, but he got call over the carpet for it too. He was going to make the Hutters cut their hair, but didn't succeed. He took one over to the top sergeant but he wouldn't even consider the case, he said he was going to take him to the commanding officer but stoped when he came to sergeant. Also Capt Day got himself into deep water kept those C.Os. in gaurd house without any orders or cause. Am afraid he will have a hard row to hoe.

The gaurd house prisoners had to clean up for lice the other day, 50 prisoners and fifty gaurds to take [59] them to the latrine. Today they made two gaurd house fellows eat outside but, before they got thru eating they took them in guess leutinant got scared of his bars. Co. B. tried to keep us from using the latrine during drill hours, but they sure got sliped up on it.

August 13. Well at last, today we put in our applications for farm furloughs. The day is drawing nigh.

Our eating co. moved two blocks north and other barracks are all filled with negroes now. Are going to get our own kitchen about tomorrow, even if I'm on K.P. with Grant, Hollcroft, & 2 Horsts. [60]

Our hard boiled corporal gave us a play tonight composed of two actors, (Stahl and Himself)(Bacheran) Two scenes and three acts. Gave Stahl a raking cause he didn't walk in rank coming from supper. Last act Stahl says, I'm not mad at you. (B) I don't care you will have to march in rank or I'll hire some of the boys to rape you. Hollcroft nearly bursted laughing again it sounded funny but realy how vulgar some mens minds are to always think of such stuff.[51]

August 15. This morn we cleaned up a kitchen for ourselves are going to start tomorrow and do our own cooking. [61] Worked on K.P. again yesterday. Had a pretty good day of it. The cooks left after supper and depended on us to clean it up and every thing that way, guess they realize we are pretty good worker any way they make some such remarks sometimes. One cook was heard to say he could do more with half doz of us fellows than sergeant could with 25 of their detail.

August 15. Had such a splendid good Mass meeting tonight. Redeeming the Time. Guess cause we needed it is why it was so good. May God help us make better use of our time. [62]

August 16. This morn went on our first hike Had orders to take hikes every day. Guess they want to toughen us up for farm work. We also learned what you would be in the future you have to be now. if you expect to serve God later on and work more for him we must do it now also. *Let your words be honest few and well chosen.*

August 17. Had some rain tonight. while our meeting was on.

Lightened & thundred poured down water. Lights went out something got wrong with it somewhere cause of electric storm. [63] Had a praise service then as the result of the darkness. Never stoped us any way. God can bless under all conditions. I had another spell of homesickness. I just wished so much for a little bit of love from dear Della.

August 19. This eve John Andrews got a furlough. three Mo. A farmer came right in to get him, lives about 30 mis out.

August 21. Every thing is all excitement about being furloughed nearly all the boys wrote to have some one to apply for them for a temporary furlough till Nov. 15. Hope I get one home as Della needs me so bad. had an earache Sun. O the dear girl has to suffer so. God grant I may soon see her. [64]

August 22. Today is a day long to be remembered. The top sergeant (Nefener) went with us on our hike, he never gave us any orders let us march any old step we wanted too, and took us to the river and nearly every one went in swimming. Sure had a picnic.

Enjoyed it very much. Are getting very good treatment at present and also extra good grub since we have our own mess.

"Where do you get that stuff" is a common expression used here when ever some body does something that he shouldn't. [65]

August 26. Sat. only twelve boys got furloughed looks like there is hope left, four today and maybe some more before night.

August 28. Today got a short farm furlough.

Char. Hollcroft, Grant Hochstetler, John Hamilton all got to go to Mason City Iowa. Arrived here on Aug. 29 3 A.M. Got us a bed, next day got located. My man got me before dinner. The first thing I had to do was police up the horse stable. Cut weeds first day.

Went thrashing rest of eve. Beats Army life all allow.

*John T. Neufeld, c.1921.
Courtesy of Dr. Elvina (Neufeld) Martens,
Elkhart, Indiana.*

CHAPTER SIX

Behind Prison Walls: The Diary of John Neufeld

Darkness shrouded the Kansas countryside, obscuring the amber of its July wheat fields. Yet John Neufeld no doubt could recognize the familiar landmarks of McPherson County. His family's farm was only three miles away from where the train was passing.

It was 1918. Neufeld had not been on the farm in quite some time, having been detained at Camp Cody, New Mexico, as a conscientious objector. He had not rubbed the growing wheat shafts between his hands; had not lingered outside on a muggy summer night, watching fireflies and hearing crocuses; had not enjoyed a Sunday afternoon with his family. Shackled to his cousin to prevent him from fleeing, Neufeld could only watch his community pass by and dream about the summer he would not have, as the train in which he was riding chugged away from the comfortable surroundings of home toward a more ominous destination: the Fort Leavenworth penitentiary.

As Neufeld later recalled, "It was night time in more ways than one, when we passed the very familiar crossing over which we had so often traveled to church."[1] Although Neufeld passed within miles of his sleeping family, he was completely isolated. A pane of glass separated him from everything he knew and valued, a separation soon to be symbolized by the prison's thick walls. At one time, Neufeld's church would have been shocked and outraged if a beloved son had been placed in handcuffs and thrown in jail. But times had changed. Mennonite young men had become as common criminals to the American populace, shackled and placed under armed guard for refusing to bear arms for the nation.

Neufeld's First World War experiences are emblematic of the treatment suffered by the most unfortunate objectors. In 1918, he endured physical and verbal abuse, then imprisonment. Sent to a camp with a small conscientious objector population, Neufeld was beaten for disobeying an order to drill, was convicted by a biased court, and was sentenced to fifteen years of hard labor at Fort Leavenworth.

Other Great War objectors would fall victim to graver physical mistreatment than Neufeld; others would receive harsher sentences. Yet Neufeld's "Diary" is likely the only holograph still available that provides a firsthand account of the trials, both literal and figurative, suffered by imprisoned objectors of the period. If for this reason alone, Neufeld's text deserves inclusion here.

Neufeld's rather brief Great War document sits somewhat uncomfortably amid diaries written by Mennonite conscientious objectors of that era. In many ways, Neufeld's work is unlike other diaries; his text does not conform to the conventions of a diary, having no pattern of regular entries detailing day-to-day activities. Neufeld's "Diary" follows more closely the model of spiritual autobiography, but with dates marking the import of various events. On the other hand, Neufeld's text was apparently not written in one sitting. Instead, it was constructed serially over the course of his imprisonment, more in the spirit of the diary. Neufeld's "Diary" (as he titled it) must therefore be seen not so much as a traditional diary but as a serial narrative, holding in tension the conventions of diary and of narrative autobiography. Through this unusual document, Neufeld tells a story of abuse and imprisonment, and of his own spiritual victory over what he saw as the laughing devil of injustice.[2]

The Great War journey Neufeld took to Camp Cody, New Mexico, was not his first time away from his kin and church folk of Inman, Kansas. By the time he was drafted in June 1918, Neufeld had already spent several years working with the General Conference Mennonite Church as a missionary, erecting buildings for Native American missions in Oklahoma and Montana. Neufeld's decision to dedicate his youthful energy to Mennonite missions was not unusual; like most Mennonite conscientious objectors, Neufeld's upbringing was steeped in the church, and his life plans were based on service to it. In Neufeld's case, however, Christian ministry in the General Conference Mennonite Church seemed almost ordained. His grandfather Heinrich Toews, a late nineteenth century immigrant from Russia, had been pastor of Inman's Bethel Mennonite Church, a position then assumed by Neufeld's father, Abraham, who was pastor of the congregation during the First World War and after.

Although Neufeld would not become pastor at Bethel following the war (that would be left to a brother), he too would become a minister, as would his son and three sons-in-law.

The Great War and conscription provided the only real disruption to Neufeld's lifelong service to the church. In June 1918, he was called away from the mission fields of Oklahoma and ordered to report to Camp Funston, Kansas, along with several other Mennonites from McPherson County. When he received his draft notice, Neufeld made what would prove a momentous decision. Wanting to be with a cousin who was traveling to Camp Cody, Neufeld asked that he also be sent to New Mexico. His request was granted.

The New Mexico cantonment was home to a small objector population under the command of misguided or perhaps misinformed military officers, who often ignored Newton Baker's orders to segregate objectors and to treat them with "tact and consideration." Had Neufeld gone instead to Camp Funston, where by now more than 150 objectors were detained, his imprisonment might well have been avoided—although even there freedom from abuse was not assured.

Neufeld and his cousin Abraham F. Neufeld left the McPherson train depot for New Mexico on June 26, 1918. Neufeld noted that fourteen other men from McPherson also made the journey, although most were not objectors. The train traversed the southern edge of the Rockies, reaching the camp two days later.

By the time of Neufeld's arrival, one year after conscription had begun, there was already a long record of objector mistreatment at Camp Cody. One Mennonite, Daniel Miller, had been the victim of a mock hanging there. According to historian Gerlof Homan, soldiers placed a noose around Miller's neck and threatened to lynch him. Yet the camp's adjutant general wrote in his report that since the soldiers were only playing a "practical joke," and since Miller had not "actually been hanged by the neck," no mistreatment had occurred.[3]

Officers at Camp Cody often wheedled work out of objectors, asking them to "volunteer" for veterinary or hospital duty but not informing them that their volunteer work made them liable for overseas duty. Courts-martial were legion at the camp; despite its small size, more objectors there received prison sentences than at all but three other cantonments during the war. Such abuse could apparently go unabated because of Camp Cody's remote location, which made it hard to hold the cantonment's officials accountable for their misdeeds. Moreover, without regular visits from Mennonite leaders, conscientious objectors were often left to fend for themselves against an overtly hostile camp population.

This was the environment into which Neufeld stepped when his train reached its destination in late June 1918. Upon arrival at Camp Cody, both John and Abraham Neufeld immediately sought an audience with officers to whom they could announce their pacifistic stand. However, the officer of their company was always sleeping or absent, Neufeld wrote, and a meeting was never granted. Instead, Neufeld and his cousin were placed in a regular outfit, along with two other objectors. As with every objector before him, Neufeld was urged to wear a uniform, to drill, and to take up noncombatant duty. When he and his cousin refused, they were threatened with the stockade, a court-martial, and imprisonment. Because they had already witnessed the treatment given another objector who would not wear a uniform, they knew the officers were not making idle threats.

Both Neufeld and his cousin decided they could cut wood, at least for that first day, and that they could probably drill. Neufeld later wrote to H. P. Krehbiel (and in his diary using similar words):

> [We] participated in Military drill at three different times. Our Idea was, when we came to camp, to try and make our stand clear to the officers and try to avoid disobeying their orders and to make as little trouble as possible. We had therefore also put on the uniform, although under protest, and had worn it for a part of a day.[4]

Neufeld probably did not realize that by giving the army an inch, he was encouraging it to take a mile.

Military officials asked for more on Neufeld's first Sunday in camp, when he and his cousin were ordered to cut wood. They refused, arguing that the military could not lawfully make them work on the Sabbath. Dragged before company officials, Neufeld was cursed vehemently, and the company's noncommissioned officers were ordered to beat the objectors should they disobey commands again. Neufeld was then demanded to do small chores as a test of his obedience. Knowing now the price of insubordination, he complied with orders and completed the tasks.

Yet Neufeld soon began to feel uncomfortable about the concessions he had made. He realized that military officials did not recognize his conscientious objection and were not offering him the rights granted objectors by Secretary of War Baker; instead, Neufeld believed, Camp Cody officers were "dragging" him further into the military.

Lacking the immediate counsel and wisdom of a Mennonite leader, Neufeld and his cousin had to decide for themselves whether they would continue drilling and working in the camp. Early in their second week as conscripts, when soldiers were issued weapons with which to drill, both Neufeld and his cousin decided that they could no longer acquiesce. Under the circumstances, Neufeld later wrote, "We decided . . . that it was best for us to refuse to do any more military work. Accordingly after having laid the matter before God in prayer, many times, asking him for help, we refused to go with the company for drill."[5]

The response to Neufeld's decision was swift and severe. When he stepped apart from the marching platoon on July 2, 1918, he was grabbed around the neck and shoved to the earth by a drill sergeant. Neufeld was pulled back up, and a corporal was ordered to force him to drill. Neufeld again refused. He was punched in the face, then thrown once more on the ground and kicked repeatedly.

By this time soldiers had ceased their own drilling to watch the excitement. They surrounded Neufeld and his attacker, jeering at the objector and cheering the corporal to continue. Neufeld's only protector on this occasion was a Lieutenant J. S. Beaves, who ordered the melee to cease: not because he was sympathetic to Neufeld—he in fact told the wounded objector that he found his type "disgusting"— but because Beaves figured "there wasn't use in hitting a man" of Neufeld's demeanor.[6] The lieutenant dragged Neufeld before Major S. B. Philpott and reported the incident. Philpott commanded the objector to "Go and Drill as ordered by your Officers." When Neufeld again refused to comply, he was put under arrest and sent to the camp stockade.

Two weeks later, on July 17, 1918, Neufeld went to trial. First Lieutenant Robert Waring served as Neufeld's counsel, although he did so without sympathy for Neufeld's conscientious objection and with little knowledge of the case, having met his client only briefly before the trial proceeded. At the trial's opening, Neufeld pleaded not guilty to the charge of willfully disobeying orders. The prosecution then called as witnesses Lieutenant Beaves, Sergeant Myron Clark, Major Frank Lund, and Major Philpott, all of whom testified that Neufeld had openly disobeyed officers' commands to drill. The evidence voiced against Neufeld seemed insurmountable, given that only Neufeld and his cousin—also in the stockade and awaiting sentence—were allowed to speak for the defense.

When Neufeld finally took the stand, he admitted under cross-examination that he had disobeyed the order given him, but said that the order itself had been unlawful because "it contradicted the order of the War Department of May 30th . . .[which] says that no person after he has made known his position as a conscientious objector shall be required to participate in drill, in any form, that is contrary to his conscience."[7] Neufeld argued that he had several times made his stance known to officers, and was therefore within his rights to refuse drilling.

If Neufeld was a sincere conscientious objector, he was well inside lawful bounds; he had refused to do something that, according to executive order, he was not compelled to do. Neufeld's counsel argued that the court must therefore prove Neufeld was insincere in his objection to war, defying officer commands for reasons other than conscientious scruples. Only in providing such proof could the court legally sentence Neufeld to Leavenworth.

So, during the trial, the prosecution aggressively sought to deconstruct Neufeld's conscientious objection, hoping to expose him as insincere, defiant, and worthy of a lengthy prison term. The prosecution bombarded Neufeld with questions about his church membership, his ethnic heritage, and his father's occupation. Neufeld was challenged to explain why he would willingly accept a farm furlough—and abet the military machine by raising produce—but would not work as a noncombatant in camp. He was asked whether he supported Germany or the United States in the war and, if he wanted the United States to win so badly, why he would not fight for her cause. Then in its coup de grace, the prosecution called First Lieutenant Ben Wood, a military psychologist who had administered Neufeld's psychological exam. Wood surmised that Neufeld was highly intelligent and that "a man of his intelligence" cannot be but "conscientiously dishonest," a sentiment commonly held and often voiced by military authorities.

Having spoken with Neufeld for two hours and gauged his responses to various questions, Wood reported, he could confidently measure Neufeld's sincerity as an objector. In a lengthy soliloquy, Wood provided reasons why Neufeld was insincere. Neufeld would do farm work, although he knew farming helped the military; he affirmed that killing was wrong, but would not pass judgment on others who killed, leaving such to God; he admitted that the United States should win the war, and that he "was willing or desirous to see other Americans do something that his conscience tells him is wrong"; he believed that God would punish Germany for its atrocities. Further, Neufeld voted, and taking part in American politics implicated him in the present war; he paid taxes, but would not buy Liberty Bonds and was therefore hypocritical; he had agreed to wear the uniform, even though he said it was against his conscience to do so. For these "salient reasons," Wood asserted, Neufeld was hiding behind the guise of conscientious objection "for the purpose of escaping the service which he knows is his duty to perform."[8]

Although Lieutenant Wood had been a witness at twenty-three similar trials, and had testified each time that the accused was insincere, his conclusions were convincing to the court. The prosecution rested its case, and Neufeld was sentenced to fifteen years' hard labor at Fort Leavenworth Penitentiary.

Seven days later, Neufeld and his cousin, who had been sentenced to five years at Leavenworth, began their trek to prison. On this journey, ironically, they rode in Pullman sleeping cars rather than uncomfortably bohemian troop trains. A sergeant and a private guarded them during the trip, which took them through to Kansas City, and then to Leavenworth. Their guards were kind to them, Neufeld reported, only handcuffing the prisoners at night "so we might not get the idea of running off or jumping off the train." The objectors were also shackled on their march through Kansas City's Union Station, with an armed sergeant walking twenty feet ahead and another "rooky private" following them, Neufeld wrote, "fully armed, so as to be ready for any emergency."[9] The manacled march under guard was an interesting experience for the rural Mennonites but one Neufeld found "amusing" only because of its incongruity.[10]

Prisoners and guards reached Fort Leavenworth at dusk on July 25, 1918. Before Neufeld and his cousin entered the penitentiary's imposing iron gates, a sentry told them "to take a good long look outside as we might not get to see the outside world for some time."[11] Inside Leavenworth, Neufeld was led through a series of steel doors and into the penitentiary's dark basement, lined with cells. He was strip searched to ensure that he had no concealed weapons, was issued prison clothes, and then was placed in a locked cell by himself. As the steel door clanked shut, Neufeld wrote later, he "surmised that the devil laughed and said 'Well, that's the end of those two Conshies [Conscientious Objectors].' Or perhaps he called us 'Yellowbacks.' But the Father in Heaven said, 'The end is not yet.'"[12]

During the first few days of prison life, Neufeld went through a series of physical and psychological exams. He was then placed with the "fifth gang," a working unit that left the prison grounds each day to toil under guard in the nearby fields. The fifth gang was comprised of forty to fifty conscientious objectors, men of "good moral character" who could be trusted outside prison walls. It was, Neufeld wrote Krehbiel in 1919, "a nice bunch to work with . . . free of the roughness in language and action so common in the army and especially among prisoners from the army."[13] Neufeld's workday began with thirty minutes of drill, an activity he felt he could now conscientiously do because he was "free from the army." Farm chores followed, from threshing to filling grain silos. At the completion of his day in the fields, Neufeld was allowed to take books from the prison library to his cell, or he could spend the evening reading his Bible.

On Saturday afternoons, J. D. Mininger of the Mennonite mission in Kansas City held church services for imprisoned objectors. On Sundays, Neufeld and others attended the regular prison service, a brief gathering that included Scripture, singing, and a short message. Neufeld found these opportunities for worship an encouragement, as were the visits from Mennonite ministers and conversations with fellow Mennonite objectors. Occasions for fellowship with other objectors were indeed more common than they had been at Camp Cody, for the objector population at Leavenworth was substantially larger than at the New Mexico cantonment. According to Homan, at the beginning of Neufeld's incarceration, there were around 250 religious objectors, a number that burgeoned to 350 by the end of 1918.[14]

For the most part, Neufeld was treated well in the early period of his detainment. His most serious hardship came several months after he arrived at Leavenworth, when prison officials ordered the fifth gang to work on Sunday—something not previously expected of religious objectors. Thirteen men, including Neufeld, refused to work, and guards handcuffed these men to those who had followed orders. The entire fifth gang was marched out to the fields in shackles. Once outside the prison walls, the men who would not work were handcuffed to posts. Although they were supposed to have their arms manacled above their heads via a rope to induce grave discomfort, a rope could not be found, and so they remained cuffed to the post. The others began working.

Thirty minutes later, an executive officer arrived and demanded again that the men take to the fields, arguing that the penitentiary—with the backing of Washington—did not offer religious objectors the provision of a Sabbath. Again the men refused. Shortly thereafter, matters began to work against the guards. The farm machinery broke down, and the day's chores could not be completed. Still in handcuffs, the men were marched back into the prison, given bread and water for dinner, and returned to their cells. Nothing more was ever mentioned about that day's insubordination. "God had kept his promise," Neufeld wrote to Krehbiel about the event, "and had brought to naught the plans of men against his people and against his word."[15]

In late fall 1918, Neufeld was granted star parole, a privilege given only the most trustworthy prisoners who were not considered a threat to escape or to perpetrate more crimes. Neufeld left his prison cell to live in a small building adjacent to the prison dairy, where he then worked. He recorded in his diary that "the work was not hard and such as I liked pretty good."[16] The living conditions, however, were not so congenial, Neufeld noted. The floors were "partly only dirt" and the building lacked the necessary weatherproofing to keep out the chilly Kansas winter. At any rate, Neufeld believed his "unsanitary" prison home may have weakened his immune system, making him susceptible to the diseases raging through Leavenworth. He fell victim to influenza and then to diphtheria, although he quickly recovered from each illness. Others at Fort Leavenworth and elsewhere, of course, were not so fortunate.

In a decision that was met with public outrage, Secretary of War Baker began to reverse conscientious objectors' sentences in early January 1919. The flood gates where opened by the release of 113 prisoners, Neufeld among them. Rumor of his impending freedom reached Neufeld while he was still convalescing in the prison infirmary for diphtheria. Afraid that he might not be granted a release if he were still in the hospital, Neufeld petitioned his way out of the infirmary although he was not fully recovered and still weak. Several days later, he went through the process of discharge and, along with 112 other objectors, marched back through the penitentiary's iron gates. They were a "rather rough looking bunch," Neufeld wrote Krehbiel. They wore old civilian clothes held long in storage or given them by the prison—apparel which, Neufeld wrote, "lacked the buttons so necessary on clothing."[17] Their appearance little mattered, though, for they were free.

The next train ride Neufeld took through McPherson County, Kansas, was far more pleasurable than that of the previous July. This time, the train stopped in McPherson—not in the dark but under the chill sun of a January morning. Neufeld, no longer immobilized by manacles, stepped off the train and back into his home community, putting the war and the penitentiary forever behind him. His parents, whom Neufeld credited with having "done much to open up the prison doors by their prayers," welcomed him back to the farm in Inman.[18]

Like many objectors, Neufeld returned home without any overt bitterness—not about being treated as a criminal, about the time wasted in a cement cell, nor about the apparent injustice of his sentence. Although he had spent six months in prison, Neufeld saw goodness in the experience, as the diary's conclusion suggested: "My thoughts are best expressed in the words of 1 Samuel 12:24: 'Only fear the Lord, and serve him in truth with all your heart: for consider how great things he hath done for you.'"[19] The prison sentence had, after all, allowed him to extend his mission field, to express through his suffering and persistence the foundations of his faith and his certain conviction in God's everlasting providence.

After the war, Neufeld continued to live and work in Kansas. A year after release from prison, Neufeld left his agrarian Mennonite existence again, traveling to Chicago with $125 and the address of several Mennonite churches in his pocket. Having worked for years in the building trade, Neufeld believed God had directed him to study architecture, and the Chicago Technical College seemed the most appropriate place to pursue his vocational interests. Once in the city, Neufeld traversed the city on a series of trolleys until he found the doorstep of the Mennonite Bible Mission. At the mission door, a daughter of Rev. A. F. Wiens answered, then informed her father that a soldier was waiting to receive an audience. "She did not know," Neufeld later wrote, "that I had accepted a fifteen-year sentence because I did not want to be this kind of a soldier."[20]

Nonetheless, the introduction to A. F. Wiens was fateful. Shortly thereafter, Neufeld made the Mennonite Bible Mission home, teaching Sunday school and attending Sunday and evening services. On May 28, 1922, two years after his meeting with Wiens, Neufeld married the pastor's eldest daughter, Catherine. Together, the couple would have five children.

That same year, in 1922, Neufeld completed his architecture studies and began seeking ways to use his education on the mission field. To Krehbiel he wrote of his desire to continue working in missions, asking also for information about where and how he could apply his skills. His central wish remained carrying the Christian message to the unsaved: "[I] wish to say that I realize that the spreading of the gospel should be the main and only object of mission work and to help with that is my only object. To save souls for Christ."[21] For the time being, Neufeld worked in the Chicago architecture community, as a correspondence course instructor for Chicago Technical College, as a writer for the *American Builder*, and for the Methodist Bureau of Church Architecture. Neufeld and his wife stayed active in the Mennonite Bible Mission, building a home close by so they could remain more integrally involved in its work.

That active participation took a more official turn in February 1936, when Neufeld was ordained as a Mennonite minister, then became pastor of the Mennonite Bible Mission, later named the Grace Mennonite Church. Neufeld remained immersed in the Mennonite community, though the Mennonite population in Chicago was, of course, more widely dispersed than that of Inman, Kansas. He served on various Mennonite committees in Chicago and in Illinois, working as well with the Mennonite Biblical Seminary and several ecumenical councils. He was also deeply involved in the lives of Chicago's unchurched, believing the Mennonite Bible Mission should be "a lighthouse by the side of the road where the race of men go by."[22] When Neufeld died in 1961, after a long illness, he was remembered by the Chicago church community and by the greater Mennonite church for his forty years' service to both.

Shortly before his death, Neufeld published a series of essays in *Missionary News and Notes* detailing his four decades on the domestic mission field. In the essays, Neufeld did not directly establish a connection between his World War I experiences and his lengthy mission career among the Chicago needy, though he affirmed that the connection was there. Neufeld believed God led him from the bondage of prison to the city—that the shackles of prison only prepared him to help others remove their own shackles of poverty and despair. During his time at Fort Leavenworth, Neufeld had been forced beyond the warmth and comfort of the Mennonite community, and had been placed among the nation's outcasts; indeed, he had himself become an outcast. The experience had increased his compassion for and understanding of others of what he termed the "criminal kind," who were yet "always well to get along with."[23] A lifetime of farming in Inman, Kansas, would probably not have given him the long view of humanity afforded by six months in a federal penitentiary. That view, in turn, provided him the passion—and the compassion—for his transformative ministry in Chicago.

Although brief, Neufeld's Great War story offers compelling testimony to the trials faced by many First World War objectors, while his life's story shows how such trials propelled one Mennonite to leave his home community for a successful career as an urban missionary. As readers, we may wish that Neufeld had told more: that he had offered greater detail about abuse at Camp Cody; about being tried by a partial judge and represented by unsympathetic counsel; about being treated as a criminal for the conscientious—and at that point legal—choice to refuse drill. Still, Neufeld's serial narrative remains valuable for revealing the depths of America's wartime fervor: a fervor that caused military officers to beat and arrest objectors, a fervor which impelled citizens to outrage when imprisoned objectors received amnesty long before their sentences ended. Neufeld's short "diary" shows as well one man's gratitude for God's providence despite the punishment given him—even if that thanksgiving must be expressed in shackles and from behind prison walls.

Text

The original holograph, held at the Mennonite Library and Archives, serves as the copy-text for this edition. Neufeld's diary never reached publication, although the author did write about his First World War trial and imprisonment for *Missionary News and Notes*, in a series detailing his mission service in Chicago. The only other extant version of Neufeld's text is a typescript housed in the John Neufeld collection at the Illinois Mennonite Heritage Center in Metamora, Illinois; it is not clear who created the typescript, or for what purpose.

Neufeld's diary was kept on a medium sized steno notebook, about five inches by ten inches. The notebook's pages, bound by string, are lined. There is a one inch space marking the top margin of each page, a space Neufeld transgressed only a few times in his text's construction. Although there are no pre-printed dates or page numbers, Neufeld included his own, numbering each page in the upper right hand corner. He wrote consistently in dark ink, oscillating between a fine and a medium point pen throughout the text.

At some point, Neufeld felt it necessary to revise several portions of his document. Entire paragraphs have been crossed out, with interlineations inscribed above the canceled passages. It is difficult to ascertain when exactly Neufeld made these revisions, though they are clearly authorial, being written in the same hand as the diary and as Neufeld's letters from the time. Because the interlineations have been deemed authorial, they are retained in the text.

The Diary of John Neufeld

[1918]

History of my[24]

Registered June fifth 1917.

Filled out questionairie in January 1918. Claimed no exemptions.

Feb. 27. Came home from Okla and was given physical examination. Appealed to medical advisory board and was given another physical examination.

Was passed for full military service.

June 24. Called to report for camp to go to Camp Funston. Changed with another friend that I could go to Camp Cody June 26. [2] In order that I might go together with my friend and partner A F. Neufeld.

June 26. Left for Camp Cody New Mexico together with 14 others from McPherson and arrived in Camp Cody on the morning of June 28th—1918.

We were put in twelfth Co June casual camp.

There were two other objectors in the same co. besides my cousin Abram Neufeld and myself. One of these took up noncombatant work or wanted too after passing the three weeks in the casual camp. The other one was sent to Ft. Riley later.

We made known our stand to the several officers as best or as [3] soon as we could. Although one of the officers usually was either asleep or absent from his tent so that we never got to see him. The other officers did not pay much attention to our stand. One of these gave orders once to give us kitchen work till our matter could be fixed, but we were taken out for drill with the other men just the same. The other officers told us that it was either for us to accept noncombatant work or go to the stockade and be courtmartialled.[25]

When we told them that we were willing to go to the stockade but protested to the brutal treatment as we had seen it given to [4] another men in our company Sheldon Smith who refused to put on the uniform.[26] They gave us to understand that we could expect the same thing and that that was the only way they would send us to the stockade. The close of this interview was that we were sent to the woodpile to cut wood. We cut wood that day and also several other times.

The first Sunday I did a little kitchen work voluntary.

That same Sunday in the afternoon they called us two boys out and ordered us to cut wood, telling us that we had [5] disobeyed their order, but they would not tell us which order we had disobeyed.

We refused to cut wood telling them that as it was Sunday we could not do any other work than was neccessary such as kitchen work etc.

They took us up to an officers tent but as the officer was not there they left us go back to our tents.

That eve. the officer called for us and told us in about these words (as near as I can reccollect them.

Officer: Did you today disobey an order given by one of these noncommissioned officers?

Our reply was "We did sir" and we started [6] to tell him why but he stopped us and said "I want you men to understand that when you are told to do some thing by these noncommissioned officers, I want you to do it. I don't care what your d— religion is" and to the noncom officers he said "if these men ever disobey your orders again I want you to lick the s—out them till the do it."

Then turning to us each seperarate he said "did you understand what I said?" to which each of us replied "yes sir!" Then to the noncommissioned officers "did you understand that?" to which they replied in the affirmative. The next morning we were given all kinds of little odd jobs before the [7] regular drill.

We had by this time participated in military drill at three different times. Our Idea being when we came to camp to try and make our stand clear to the officers and try to avoid any open disobediance, trying to avoid as much trouble as possible. We had also put on the uniform although under protest, and had worn it some. We however found out that they did not listen to our appeals nor counted our noncombatant papers or church membership papers for anything but thought they would drag us along as others.

Therefore we decided, under conditions like these, that it was best for us to refuse [....][27] [9] but this ordeal did not last long as lieutenant Beeves came out and told corporal that there was not use in hitting us again.

Then the lieut spoke to me and told me that I could imagine that he was pretty disgusted with me. Wherenfor, I answered him that I had tried to avoid the incident and had made known my stand to him and other officers. And I had gone as far in military work as my conscience would permit me.

He therefore told the corporal in charge of me to bring me and the other men who had also refused to drill, and follow him. [10] While going off the drill ground, the lieut. met Chislett commander in chief of [...] camp and reported our case to him. Major Philpot as commander in chief ordered us to go and drill as ordered by our superior officers to which we replied that we could not do it.[28]

He then ordered L. Beeves to take us to his office and read the articles of war to us and if we would then still resist in our stand, to make out charges against us and take us to the Div. headquarters.[29] Which he did. This was about [11] the 2nd of July. We arrived in the Div Stockade nearly noon and were put to cleaning up. After we had been entered as prisoners we worked here for one week, getting along fairly well, when our charges were read to us and the date of our trial set. We were asked whether we had any choice of someone for our counsil in our trial to which we replied we had non. Then they asked us whether they should get someone for us, which we told them would be allright to us. A week later we had our trial, this being the 19 of July.

Our defendent or counsil introduced himself about 15 min [12] before our trail. Asking us several things about our cases.

He told us that we would do the best he could for us, but that he really had no sympathy for us.

The proceedure of our trail by court martial can be seen from our copy of the court proceedings.

July 24. About a week later we were ordered to pack up or goods to go to Leavenworth.

Our treatment in the stockade had been fairly good with the exception that the man Sheldon Smith was beaten up pretty bad when he refused to work around camp [13] When receiving our goods out of the stockade office we found out that we were short some of our property. My partner was short about seven dollars in cash money and a watch valued at about seven dollars. I was short a new fountain pen. These goods have never been found. Although through reports we have heard that Sargent Reharn who was one of those in charge of the stockade has been sent to the federal penitentiary for taking property of some other prisoners.

A sargeant and another private were put in charge of us and we were sent to Leavenworth.

[14] We were very glad to be sent away from Camp Cody. (Two of us were sent AFT and myself.) We thought that although prisoners yet we would find work in Leavenworth in prison that we could do with a free conscience. My partners sentence was five years at hard labor and mine was fifteen years, but we never entertained the Idea that we would have to serve the full length of our sentence.

Our treatment on the way was fine. We had sleeping quarters and were allowed fifty cents a meal. We were hand cuffed only for the night and when we arrived at Kansas City. Our sentries in command [15] were very kind to us.

The experience of marching through Kansas City Handcuffed was new to us but we considered it mostly from the amusing side of it.

Leavenworth.

Before we entered the prison gates a sentry told us to take a good long look outside as we might not get to see the outside world for a while.

This however did not come true as we were outside the gates again after two days, although for work under guard.

The reception at the D.B. was better than we had expected. We were again spoken to at least [16] in a kind way (Although this is not always the case when prisoners are received).[30]

A sentry told us that they had allready 250 CO. This cheered us up very much as a man always likes when in trouble. The next day and the few days after this were spent in dressing in and taking our life history and physical ex etc.

We were put on thefifth gang for work. This gang we soon found out consisted of only C.O. usually 50 in number. And was not guarded heavily usually from 1 to 2 guards.

As they were all C.O. we did not have [17] any of the rough language that is so common among the general prisoners. This gave us a nice bunch to work with.

The first month of work was pretty steady for us as we were required to take 30 min of physical drill in the morning before we went to work. We usually were out for drill at six oclock having finished our breakfast by this time.

The food also was quite a change off from what we were used too. But all this was not anything to be worried about as we were now free from the army never being bothered about accepting service the plague of always being tried to get to accept [18] It was, stand in line before meals, march to meal, march out for work. Standing in line before going to work, stand and wait in the barbershop in the store room while receiving mail, while getting writing paper etc. In day time we did our work and at evening we could sit or lay down in peace with a book or paper. The library was a great help to me. Here we could get books to read.[31]

One tirsome task in the D.B. was the standing in line.[32] It was always, line up for meal, marchout, line up in the storeroom, line up for supper for work, line up for count and with lining up always was waiting, standing in line, from 15 to 30 min.

On Sunday forenoon we always attended the general services. The services were always short, good Scripture readings were given and quite a bit of singing. [19] We however soon received some visits from our own ministers which inspired us very much. When coming from these meeting I always felt like I really was getting along very good and had courage to go on whatever might happen.

Among the other ministers that visited us were. Aaron Loucks, D. H. Bender and H. P. Krehbiel.[33] Several others had been there before I was in the D.B.[34]

Later on when permanent services were arranged for Rev. Miniger from Kansas City always spoke to us on Saturday afternoon.[35] Also the brethern. H. R. Voth, P.H. Unruh, Daniel Kaufmann and others shared at some.

All of these services were very helpful to me and also I think to everyone.

[20] After I was at the D.B. about 3 months I was given star parole. This allowed me to work outside the gates without guard. I was given a job at the dairy barns and I had to move out there. We stayed in a building near the dairy barn. The work was not hard and such as I liked pretty good.

My partner AF Neufeld was by this time in the Hospital. He stayed in the Hospital nearly 7 weeks in which time we did not get to see each other, only a few notes passed. Soon after he came out he was sent to Camp Dodge, while I was held. I was in the prison hospital twice. At the first time I had the flu [21] and was in three days. The treatment was good, considering the many sick people they had to attend too. The second time I was in on account of Diphtheria. This was in January. The cause of this sickness was perhaps the unsanitary conditions in our building at the dairy barns. Our floors were partly only dirt floor and the building was not weatherproof. I had only a slight start of this disease and needed to stay in the hospital only 4 days.

While I was in the hospital I first heard the news that 113 CO were to be released. [22] This caused me to be in a hurry about getting out. I got out about the 23 of January. When I came out of my ward I read in the paper the list of names and found my name in it. This was a thing hard to believe. We had heard so many rumors we could hardly believe these. I went back to duty although I was weak yet with great hopes.

Saturday the 25th of January. My father visited me for the 3rd time.

We both were attending the services and Bro Minninger was just telling how the apostle Peter had been freed from prison bond, when an [23] orderly came in and read a notice for a bunch of us to report to the executive office. I had to leave my father but it was with the best hopes that I would soon follow him home. From this time on till Monday noon was spent in waiting for the different papers that had to be made out and a little physical examination. On Monday Noon the 113 were all outside the gates in civilian clothes.

Our clothes looked rather raggy. Those of us who had our own clothes wore these although they were not in the best of condition having been tucked away for several months. Those who had no clothes were given old clothes, some of these made a rather peculiar sight.

I happened to be in the last bunch that left the prison. They were turned out in bunches of ten.

[24] We were marched through one gate with a sentry. Then the other outside gates were open and the heard for the last time the word, forward march to which we have not heard the word "halt" yet. Our feelings were such it cannot all be expressed. We were glad to get out, and on the other hand sorrow to leave behind us over 3000 other prisoners who would value their freedom just as much as we did. I can say that all the other prisoners that I met in the last few days were all glad and rejoiced with us. Of course they would have liked to go to, but I have noticed nothing of the hatred feelings that the papers were so full of. The hatred of the prisoners was toward the officers but not toward fellow prisoners. [25] During all the time that I was in the D.B. I have heard and noticed very little ill feeling toward the C.O. Although there were among these prisoners many of the criminal kind yet they were always well to get along with.

The reason perhaps was that we shared their fate with them and were not given any priviliges whatsoever.

I arrived home the morning of the 27th of January after having visited in Kansas City at the mission of bro. Minninger yet.

My thought now is best expressed in the word of 1 Samuel 12-24

Only fear the Lord, and serve him in truth with all your heard: for consider how great things he hath done for you.

Jacob Conrad Meyer, 1918
Credit: J. C. Meyer Photograph Collection,
Hist Mss. 4-206, Mennonite Church USA
Archives—Goshen, Indiana.

CHAPTER SEVEN

Jacob Conrad Meyer's Legacy: The Great War and Beyond

The regimental medical doctor, a Harvard man with little time or energy to waste, wanted to speak with Jacob Meyer. Never mind that the Spanish influenza which had already ravaged the U.S. countryside was now raging through Camp Sevier, South Carolina, bringing low and in some cases killing the once healthy soldiers. Never mind that the fighting in Europe was nearing a crucial stage and able men were needed, fast, to help press the Allied offensive and bring the war to a conclusion. Those things surely mattered to the good doctor, but not at this moment. The physician had heard from a sergeant that another Harvard man was haunting the dusty streets of Camp Sevier, and he wanted to meet his fellow Ivy Leaguer, perhaps to reminisce about the hallowed brick walls of their esteemed alma mater.

Jacob Conrad Meyer was probably not as the doctor imagined. The man standing before him on October 20, 1918, was not wearing a soldier's uniform, but the simple and well-worn work clothes of a common civilian. Further, Meyer was no ardent patriot but a conscientious objector, and an Amish Mennonite one at that. The physician was, no doubt, suspicious. Had not the incredulous doctor heard, after all, that Mennonite objectors were ignorant and illiterate, intellectually inferior farmers who knew their Bibles but little else? How then could one of these be a Harvard graduate, holder of a Phi Beta Kappa key no less?

The doctor upbraided the fellow alum standing before him, reminding Meyer that citizens were called to fight and improve their world by whatever means necessary. He told Meyer that all objectors were ignorant, implying that present company was included. An hour-long discussion followed, with the doctor asking questions and the objector providing, through what he felt was rational analysis, the arguments for his pacifist beliefs.

After the interview, Meyer reported, the regimental doctor's mind was changed. Although he would no doubt continue to heal soldiers to make them fit for fighting, the doctor was now convinced that no man could be both ignorant and a conscientious objector, as the nonresistant stance required the reasoning skills of a well-trained mind such as Meyer's.[1]

The discussion Meyer had with the physician was not unusual. Throughout his five-month detainment during the Great War, Meyer was often called before men who could little believe a Harvard graduate might also be a Mennonite objector. In a way, Meyer became somewhat of a novelty, put on display as the marvelous anomaly among the supposedly "bovine-faced" and "stupid" objectors who populated United States cantonments. Men like the Camp Sevier doctor had to see for themselves the articulate and intelligent Mennonite who claimed to be an objector. When Meyer was placed before them, he was frequently derided for so grossly misusing his academic gifts, by failing to give his tremendous talents to his country and to the war. It was too bad, the Board of Inquiry's Major Walter Kellogg told Meyer, that a man of obvious intelligence felt compelled to take such a position. Other military officials were quick to echo the Major's assessment.

To be sure, Meyer did defy a good many of the stereotypes about Mennonite conscientious objectors that flourished during the Great War. Most of his fellow Mennonite objectors had little education, though not necessarily little intellect. Some could not read nor write competently in English, if at all, and could not clearly articulate the basis of their nonresistant faith, even as they understood completely the Bible's imperative that they remain nonresistant. Many had seen little of the world beyond their farms and families, and would see little more of it following the war's conclusion.

Then there was Meyer, who by the time of the Great War had already earned a B.A. from Goshen College, an M.A. from Indiana University, and an M.A. in history from Harvard; who, though versed in German could also speak clearly and well in English; who, during the war, read voraciously, from H. G. Wells to Homer, from Kant to George Eliot; who could justify his objection to war not only using his Mennonite upbringing and the Bible, but with philosophy, history, and literature as well; and who had already seen a great deal outside his small farming community and would see much more after the war had ended. Because of the differences between Meyer and other objectors, Meyer became a sort of dog-and-pony show in his cantonment, explaining his beliefs again and again to bemused military officials and, on a few occasions, convincing his auditors that the objector's way was not only righteous, but also right.

These meetings with the military brass afforded Meyer a unique opportunity to share his peaceful witness, something he recognized. Like other Mennonite objectors, Meyer felt that God had called him to the camp for a purpose. He believed further that his education and his erudition gave him the tools necessary to make his testimony more widely heard. His status as a Harvard graduate and his polished demeanor gained him the respect of his officers, who in turn were more willing to listen to Meyer's arguments about the evils of war, and who were impressed—if not convinced—by the reasoning Meyer provided. In turn, because the officers respected and trusted Meyer, they offered him freedoms not granted the other objectors. For these reasons, Meyer's experiences during the Great War were much different from those of the objectors who had little freedom, who received no respect from their officers, and who could only ineffectively attempt to make their stance understood or appreciated.

Meyer's wartime diary documented this unusual life. His diary told another Great War story, showing how prized a commodity education was in military camps, and how it brought even an objector a certain regard. At the same time, Meyer's diary suggests that despite the esteem granted him, he remained trapped by a system that refused to honor his conscience. He remained victim to soldiers' taunts and the petty slurs of officers; remained separated from his family and community; remained idle and all but useless, his mind and energy frittered away in detainment, his longing to do reconstruction work stymied by governmental red tape.

In addition to tracing Meyer's Great War journey, the diary recorded the beginnings of an important movement in Mennonite circles. Meyer's criticisms of the church and its role during the war found voice in his diary, as did his hopes of creating new avenues of activism within the church. The discontent of persons such as Meyer helped lead to the eventual creation of the Mennonite Young People's Movement and to a transformation in the church.

Despite his advanced education, Meyer came from a background somewhat like that of other Mennonite objectors during the war. He was born and raised in Wayne County, Ohio, an area densely populated by Mennonites, where still today Amish may be seen driving their horse-drawn buggies down rural roads. Like most Wayne County Mennonites, Meyer's parents were farmers, though his father, Jacob G. Meyer had been a machinist in the Alsatian city of Mulhouse and learned about farm life only after his immigration to Ohio in 1872. Six years later Jacob G. Meyer and his first wife began farming 78 acres of flood plain that Meyer termed the "swamp farm." Except for a brief period after his marriage to Mary Conrad, when the couple lived elsewhere, the "swamp farm" was home to the Meyer family and the place where he and Mary raised twelve children, including their son Jacob Conrad, born in 1888, and three from Jacob G. Meyer's first marriage.

Jacob G. Meyer assimilated to America much as had many other progressive Amish Mennonites who emigrated in the mid-nineteenth century. He began to learn the English language, though he held as well to the French and German of his own upbringing. He adopted some modern technologies, though also remained separated from much of America by his life in a Mennonite-dense area.

Meyer's family played an active role in the Wayne County Amish Mennonite community. They attended the large Oak Grove Amish Mennonite congregation, where his father's cousin J. S. Gerig was the bishop. The congregation has been considered by Mennonite historian James Juhnke to be "one of the most volatile and innovative of all Amish and Mennonite congregations."[2] In the 1890s, the church was not only among the first Mennonite congregations to hold revival meetings, but according to Theron Schlabach, was also one of the first Amish congregations to allow "meetinghouses, Sunday schools, cooperation with 'old' Mennonites . . . [and] adjustments in attire."[3] Thus Meyer grew up amid Mennonites who surely informed his own progressivism, as well as his adherence to the church's central doctrines, nonresistance certainly among them.

Encouraging the education of its young was an important part of Meyer's congregation; indeed, James Lehman's official history of the Oak Grove congregation argues that Oak Grove Mennonite probably sent more of its youth on to higher education than did any other Amish Mennonite or (Old) Mennonite congregation of the early twentieth century.[4] Meyer joined a large wave of Wayne County Amish Mennonites who attended Goshen College in northern Indiana. Meyer's roommate and many of his classmates at Goshen would later be conscripted during the Great War, and a few—as Meyer's diary noted—received Leavenworth sentences. While war raged in Europe, Meyer earned a B.A. degree from Goshen. After graduation in 1916, Meyer pursued graduate studies at Indiana University in Bloomington. In 1917, he joined millions of American men in registering for the draft, receiving the lottery number 4,124,743. The high number assured Meyer he would only be called to war if the fighting were prolonged, but also convinced him that his future was uncertain; it was best not to make long-term plans, as his country could conscript him at any moment.

Nonetheless, in September 1917, while many of his friends set out on their journeys to military camps, Meyer enrolled at Harvard University to begin studying for an M.A. degree in history. While he was there, Meyer met William Channing Gannett, a preacher and poet whose wife was a Quaker and whose sons were active in reconstruction with the American Friends. During a January 6, 1918 meal with the Gannetts, Meyer discussed pacifism with his new friends, as well as the current struggle of conscientious objectors in military camps.

The conversation with the Gannetts was a transformative moment in the young man's life. One day after his meal in their home, Meyer wrote to his friend Esther Steiner: "I am struck more and more every day by the fact that Mennonites are not the only pacifists and probably not the majority in most places." Although he saw a future in the military looming, although he knew he soon would need to make choices about wearing a uniform and working in the army, Meyer felt assured of God's guidance: "I hope never to meet a situation in which it will not be possible for me to say 'In this situation my Master did not go before me.' If hope cannot meet the situation how could despair do so?'"[5]

The new year, the impending arrival of a draft questionnaire from the government, and his relationship with the Gannetts brought these thoughts to the fore, compelling Meyer to make an important life decision: he too would toil in war relief work as did the Gannett boys. And so, in March 1918, he began the application process to join the Friends in France.

Throughout the first months of 1918, Meyer continued his graduate education at Harvard, completing "theses" and studying for exams. He took an active role in Boston church life, but because there was no Mennonite church at which to worship, he attended other congregations and was invited to speak at a few. His most interesting visit was to the "Christian Science Mother Church," where he heard Mary Baker Eddy's peculiar interpretation of Scripture. Meyer was concerned with the militaristic message spoken in Boston's pulpits, and worried that when he was discovered to be "one of those detested Mennonites" he would be castigated. This fear was never realized.[6] His pacifism did cause him some difficulty at Harvard. He turned down a position as president of the Harvard Graduate Society because of his nonresistant stance; since it would fall upon him to introduce militant speakers visiting Harvard, including Theodore Roosevelt, Meyer felt he would be unfit for the task.

For the most part, life continued apace. Yet for Meyer and his classmates, the specter of the army always loomed ahead, making studies difficult. In a letter to Steiner dated March 17, 1918, Meyer noted that grades were reported lower throughout the university, compelling Harvard's professors to "campaign" at young people's meetings to "stir up interest" in studies. However, Meyer wrote, "Too many people are not interested in their [school] work because they are thinking of war and the draft. This may give them a new view of life. They may see new realities."[7]

Although Meyer continued to do "fine" on his exams and essays, he began refining and strengthening his case for conscientious objection, all too aware that a strong argument would soon be needed. At the same time, Meyer believed he could not decide with any finality what he would do if drafted. He concluded that he might not wear a uniform, and that he probably would not accept any work. Yet he told Steiner, "I cannot express an opinion in so summary and definite a manner for *I have not been there* [in a military camp]."[8]

Though still hoping to be accepted by the American Friends Service Committee, Meyer discovered that because his father had been a French citizen when he emigrated from Alsace and because Germany now controlled the region, getting a French visa would be difficult. This, in turn, would make a relief assignment unlikely.

Around this time Meyer also heard a rumor that he would be drafted on May 25, as would his younger brother Elmer. Meyer arranged to take exams early if necessary, and discovered he could still graduate from Harvard even if he was called before the school year's end. Meyer decided to stay in Massachusetts until the government ordered him otherwise, but his mind was not wholly on his studies. To Esther Steiner he wrote, "School work is going as usual except as we fellows here who are to be called soon say it is very interesting when we think that each day might be our last one at Harvard. . . . The glories of the last day of school are a halo about us constantly."[9]

The rumor about being drafted before the school year ended proved to be unfounded. Meyer finished his degree in early June 1918. He departed quickly for Ohio and home without taking part in graduation ceremonies, for a new rumor was afoot: he would be called to camp by June 25.

On his way home from Boston, Meyer stopped in Philadelphia to see Samuel Bunting, the head of the American Friends Service Committee. There he also visited the French consul in an attempt to secure a visa, but was unsuccessful. Back in Ohio, June passed and Meyer remained at home, waiting for his number to be called. While he waited, he continued to seek a clear way to do relief work, requesting a passport and then receiving a release from his local board so that if possible, he could leave for France before being drafted. Time was running out, however, and Meyer knew he would soon be ordered to camp. In a final act of desperation, he wrote Secretary of War Newton Baker asking for help in getting a visa and clearance to go abroad. The letter to Baker was too late. When reading the Wooster, Ohio, newspaper in mid-July, Meyer discovered that he would need to report for military duty on July 26.

Meyer spent the day before departure visiting in his community, saying farewell to friends and family. His parents held a party for him and for Clair Moine, another Mennonite man about to leave for camp. On July 26, his parents drove him in the family car to Orrville, Ohio, where he joined others in a caravan of six troop trains bound for Camp Jackson, South Carolina. Saying farewell to his aging parents was difficult, Meyer later noted. In 1965, he wrote that he had tried to alleviate his parents' concerns about his future by refusing to shed "a single tear" and by "smil[ing] as I waved the last goodbye."[10]

The following day, while his train was parked in Augusta, Georgia, he wrote to Steiner,

> It is quite an experience to leave home for camp. I have concluded that the hardest part of the experience is for parents and for brothers and sisters. The one who goes is generally young and that is not true of many parents. Then too brothers and sisters seem to think one is going never to return. Of course this may be true but is that the most important? Is it as much how long we live as how we live? My mind centers on the latter. Do not forget the young men who must face some issues in the next few days. Pray not so much that we may not be tried out as that we may prove worthy the name which we profess. If we are to be in the front line in the fight for the ideal of Christ may we be spared the disgrace of not being faithful.[11]

Even before arriving at camp, Meyer knew what his mission would be: to serve as a witness for peace, fighting not against evil but battling for "the ideal of Christ." Still, the battlefield language he used—standing on the "front line" of this holy conflict—provided an interesting contrast to his pacific goal.

Troop trains pulled in to Camp Jackson in the early morning hours of July 28, 1918. Because of the general quarantine in camp, Meyer was placed in a regular barrack and so separated from many of the other "Wayne County fellows" who had traveled with him to South Carolina. Meyer had little trouble maneuvering through the demands of army initiation. When he refused to accept a uniform, an officer made a snide reply but caused little more trouble; when asked to drill, Meyer abstained and was politely dismissed; when inoculated, Meyer remained steady while other soldiers fainted around him. A psychological test proved a "cinch" for Meyer, who was also filling the idle time of quarantine writing letters home for the illiterate soldiers in his barrack.

After one week at Jackson, Meyer reported to Steiner that camp life was interesting. Food was good, even if pie and cake were "unknown quantities." Living in a tent was an aesthetic pleasure, reminding one of the beauties of a simple existence. Soldiers were as all other men; some were kind, worthy of friendship, some "foolish and fickle." At any rate, Meyer observed that the soldiers whiled away time in barracks doing "such stunts as boys are likely to do," smoking and playing cards, reading and conversing. True, some of his barrack mates and officers "laugh a person to scorn" for his conscientious objection, but that mattered little to Meyer, for he had already experienced ridicule and surely would again for holding such an unpopular opinion. "A really big man," he wrote, "can appreciate more than one view of life in a philosophical sense, but some thimble-brained folks think they possess the key to all knowledge and so they can show their ignorance and lack of intelligence by taking a scornful or humorous view of that which is beyond their mental horizon."

Unlike other objectors who felt the weight of their officers' derision too heavy a burden, Meyer believed in the early weeks of conscription that he would sustain an optimistic perspective, and would not find being in the military a horrible experience. In fact, life at Camp Jackson was so agreeable to Meyer that, he wrote to Steiner, "If I could convince myself that the salvation of this old world lay in the application of physical force as is done on the field of battle I think I would make a capital soldier."[12]

On August 12, 1918, Meyer was transferred to the conscientious objector detachment at Camp Jackson, and was again among brethren. There were about one hundred objectors at Camp Jackson,

Meyer reported, many of them Quakers from the East Coast. Three days after the transfer, Lieutenant Hugh L. Caveness, no doubt impressed by Meyer's trustworthy demeanor and clearly established intellect, gave Meyer a permanent pass which allowed him to leave the objector barracks whenever he wished, and provided Meyer free access to any part of Camp Jackson. In 1967, Meyer admitted he was probably the only conscript to receive such a pass at any of the three camps in which he was detained.[13]

Because other objectors were confined to barracks and under the watchful eye of armed guards, Meyer was often sent out to run their errands: to deliver mail, to check out library books, and most often to buy goods from area canteens. He quickly became a liaison between objectors and military officers, typing up governmental reports for his lieutenant and doing military clerking duties while also voicing the objectors' concerns to officers when necessary.

The dual roles little troubled Meyer. He remained steadfast in his nonresistant convictions but believed that he should still, to some extent, contribute to the army which held him—provided that he wore civilian clothes "so no one would mistake me for a soldier or am in camp by choice."[14] In making this decision to perform some chores for military officers, Meyer cited 2 Thessalonians 3:10 (KJV): "If any would not work, neither should he eat." He continued to hold this position during his five-month detainment, and received kinder treatment from officers because of it: so kind, in fact, that officers allowed his mail to be posted without censor, unlike all other objectors in the cantonment.

While at Camp Jackson, Meyer continued his efforts to go overseas with the American Friends Service Committee. In early August, he received a letter from Frederick P. Keppel, assistant to Secretary of War Baker, replying to the July missive Meyer had sent Baker. The letter reminded Meyer that, under penalty of law, he must report to camp when called—an irony of sorts, given that Meyer was already in camp. Keppel also enclosed the executive order of July 30, 1918, an order that made it possible for conscientious objectors to serve outside the military's authority. Officers at Camp Jackson were impressed that Meyer was corresponding with such a high-ranking military official; because no one else apparently had a copy of the order, officers often asked to borrow Meyer's document. The letter from Keppel had arrived too late, however. Meyer was already in camp as an objector, and so he would now have to receive the appropriate classification from the Board of Inquiry in addition to a visa if he wished to join the Friends' relief effort.

The Board of Inquiry was slow in coming to Camp Jackson, prolonging Meyer's tenure as a detained objector in sandy and hot South Carolina. Not much was happening at the camp, apart from the constant preparation of soldiers for battle. Thus, like so many other Great War objectors, Meyer reported feeling lazy and useless, even as he ran errands for officers and bunkmates. In a letter to Steiner, Meyer said, "If you know what laziness in Ohio is just multiply it by ten and then double it and you have it at about the degree at which we have it."[15] Like objectors at other camps scattered across the United States, those at Meyer's cantonment attempted to stave off idleness by taking hikes, singing, studying their Bibles, and writing letters or reading. Meyer especially indulged in the latter pleasure, finding at the YMCA library books that could readily complement his education. However, objectors who could not read or write were legion at Camp Jackson, Meyer said, and so did not have that diversion to entertain them, save when a literate man could provide help.

In October 1918, officers ordered that Meyer and other college-educated objectors create a school in their detachment. The officers believed the objectors "abnormal" and "lacking in education," and were convinced a school would serve two purposes: it might keep objectors busy while also providing them the education they sorely needed. Some of the men in Meyer's company opposed the idea, although Meyer did not say why. Still, the school went forward. Meyer and James Steer, a Quaker from North Carolina, ascertained the educational level of the objectors and then constructed a curriculum heavy in liberal arts, with typewriting and bookkeeping added as vocational components.

Meyer visited the camp library to compile reading lists and prepared lectures. His college and graduate school background must surely have proved useful in this endeavor, although Meyer already had teaching experience, having been an instructor in a one-room schoolhouse at the age of fifteen.[16] At any rate, by October 27, 1918, he was lecturing on "the development of civilization."

Whether the school proved a successful experiment remains unclear. Meyer worried that when men were sent out on furlough, the school would "break up." However, he wrote to Steiner, "I think I shall try to keep it going for there are several men here who need it badly. Naturally it is not an easy matter to interest some of the fellows here but that only makes our part of the work greater."[17] Yet, as time went on, mention of the school disappeared from Meyer's diary. One must wonder if, true to Meyer's concerns, it disappeared from the cantonment as well.

Meyer finally appeared before the Board of Inquiry on October 26, 1918, just two weeks before the armistice. In preparation for the hearing, Meyer and his detachment were transferred from Camp Jackson to Camp Sevier, outside of Greenville, South Carolina. The Spanish influenza had Camp Sevier in its grip, and soon many of Meyer's brethren were stricken and sent to the hospital. Meyer, who escaped affliction, cared for those convalescing in the surrounding tents. The flu caused a spiritual crisis for many objectors, who worried about death and the possibility of perishing so far from family. They wondered whether their bodies would be shipped home, or would be buried in anonymous military graves. "The sight of the hearse several times a day, as it passed our camp site did not make the picture more cheerful," Meyer admitted to Steiner.[18] Much later, Meyer wrote that, in an attempt to "keep the gloom from causing the very disease about which" the men worried, he had tried to humor his fellow objectors. At least one man, however, thought that Meyer was "going too far" in joking about their "condition."[19] Although Meyer several times received word from home that a community member had died from the Spanish influenza, most of the men in the detachment survived. By the end of October, when the Board of Inquiry appeared at Sevier, the disease had all but vanished from the camp.

Objectors at Camp Sevier were examined on October 26 only by Major Walter Kellogg, the other two members of the Board having attended to duties elsewhere. Despite Kellogg's clearly voiced belief that Meyer's intelligence was wasted on conscientious objection, Meyer respected the Major, adding this postscript to his diary: "Our experience before Major Kellogg was one that impressed most of us. He seemed to get more out of the men than an ordinary person would."[20] Kellogg classified Meyer as 1C, thereby recommending him for reconstruction. The way was once again open for Meyer to do relief work overseas. "Now I hope I shall be able to eat my Xmas dinner in Paris," Meyer wrote Steiner after his interview with Kellogg.[21]

A quick departure to France was not to be, however, as governmental red tape and continued difficulties with the French consul in Philadelphia kept him at Camp Sevier well past the armistice. Members of his group left for farm furloughs or for reconstruction work, but Meyer remained with a small band of Ohio objectors. Partings, Meyer admitted to Steiner, were difficult: "Since we have been together for some time the fellows who leave find it rather sad to leave the rest of us. Those who stay all plan on going out soon too when they see someone go. So every change makes a break into the monotony of camp."[22]

During November, Meyer spent his days clerking for the company lieutenant, writing up discharge papers and gathering military records for those still detained, hoping all the while for word of his own departure. In mid-November, Meyer even became "chief officer" of his detachment for a week while the sergeant was on leave, and so had to call roll in his company, march the men to meals, and supervise any work they did around the camp. He became in many ways indispensable to the officers in charge of objectors, helping them to dig out from beneath the heavy pile of paperwork which kept them in camp. His invaluable assistance, he feared, would push his own discharge far into the future, as his officers would not let him go so easily when the time came.

Although Meyer attempted to sustain his energetic optimism, military life was starting to wear him down. He found his lieutenant lazy and unproductive, more interested in playing checkers than in speeding the discharge process. In fact, the entire army was ineffectual, Meyer complained, with its mounds of forms to complete. Records—like his own—were inevitably lost or misplaced, compelling men to go through the rigors of inoculation again, or keeping men in camp long after a discharge was due them. To make matters worse, the officers had once more started pushing the objectors to accept work in the camp, with the threat of the stockade should they refuse. The demand seemed unreasonable, given that the armistice had been signed, that the men had already been deemed sincere by the Board of Inquiry, and that the objectors were only waiting to be furloughed or discharged.

Thanksgiving passed and Meyer was still at Camp Sevier. Now Christmas was rapidly approaching, and his hope of celebrating the holiday in France, or even at home, was waning just as quickly. Meyer continued to write discharge papers for other men but could not type up his own. Finally, word came that the last "Ohio boys" at Sevier would be discharged, but only after first traveling to Camp Zachary Taylor in Kentucky: the government had decreed that men should be discharged within 350 miles of their home communities.

On December 23, a train pulled out of Sevier for the long journey to Kentucky, arriving at Camp Taylor on Christmas Day, 1918. Meyer and his friends spent Christmas receiving inoculations and medical inspections, taking as well the brunt of criticism from unfamiliar officers and soldiers. One day after his arrival at Camp Taylor, Meyer found his brother Elmer, who had been an objector in camp for six months. Together, the brothers waited—and waited—for the opportunity to go home. Although officers had promised Meyer he would be at Camp Taylor only twenty-four hours, a week passed before he received his discharge and boarded a northbound train. He arrived back in his home community on January 1, 1919.

Meyer did not receive a hero's welcome; when he arrived at his parents' house, they were away at funerals for local influenza victims, so he immediately began to do chores on the family farm. This was the momentous conclusion to five months in the army.

Because of his release from the military, Meyer was not required to do reconstruction in France. However, his desire to participate in overseas relief continued, and war-torn Europe certainly continued to need volunteers. After fighting with the Philadelphia consul over a visa, Meyer finally received permission from the French consul in New York to travel. He spent January 21 to February 4, 1919, in Philadelphia, awaiting passage to France.

On February 5, Meyer boarded *La Lorraine* bound for Le Havre. Among his fellow passengers was Theodore Roosevelt's wife, Edith, making the voyage to France to visit her sons' graves. The winter journey across the Atlantic was difficult, and one man died in transit. A week in Paris followed the docking. Then Meyer and other reconstruction workers were sent to the heart of wartime destruction, in the Verdun sector of the Hindenburg Line. Verdun had been destroyed completely, Meyer later recalled, and "not one house . . . was fit for habitation."[23] Meyer spent the next year building homes for war refugees, repairing as well the infrastructure that had been obliterated by the battles on the Western Front.

Reconstruction work was not Meyer's only concern while in France. He is no doubt remembered more by Mennonite historians for his involvement in the creation of the Young People's Conference, a role he assumed long before leaving for his overseas assignment. In the latter months of 1918, Meyer had begun corresponding with other young Mennonites, many of whom were likewise detained in military camps and who were disappointed with the actions of their church leaders during the war. Some were concerned that they would be excommunicated from the church for wearing uniforms or accepting noncombatant jobs in military camps; some were upset that their ministers offered no encouragement or support while they were confined.

The confusing and often conflicting advice of church leaders also frustrated objectors, who had in Meyer's estimation been ill prepared "to witness to military officials." The wartime espionage and sedition laws had made matters still worse, Meyer noted in 1968. Those leaders "who attempted to advise the young men" were subject to possible legal penalties.[24] Meyer summarized his complaints in a letter to Steiner:

> I know there is a Mennonite Committee now, but it seems to me it has not done a thing for the boys at Camps Sevier and Jackson. And as far as I am aware it has not done anything for the boys overseas in Reconstruction Work. Do you think that is giving the boys a square deal? I meet boys in camp who have not seen anyone from home or a representative of the church since they came to camp. They need encouragement.[25]

Although Meyer could "see only one side" of the issue because he was in camp, he still felt sure some Mennonite leaders had disappointed their young men—a claim he repeated in 1967.

Of perhaps equal concern to Meyer and other objectors, however, was what they perceived to be the church's insularity, its seeming concern only with its own purity. Young Mennonites who had spent time outside the small confines of their home communities, either in college or cantonments, believed the church needed to more successfully reach out to, rather than withdraw from, the "worldly" kingdom. It seemed to Meyer that church representatives, in their Great War battles with the government and with one other, had suggested otherwise: that they had encouraged Mennonite objectors to stand completely apart from other men, causing objectors to become almost insufferably self-righteous in their nonresistant stance.

Meyer had taken a different tack while conscripted, and he was convinced that more Mennonites should express Christ's message by immersing themselves in the world and its suffering, rather than removing themselves from it. Mennonites needed more actively to practice a social gospel, Meyer believed, and "help[ing] to alleviate the results of the First World War" was one place they could begin.[26] Yet while the Quakers had quickly developed a much-needed relief organization during the war, the Mennonite church had done little, if anything, to provide assistance to war refugees in Europe. Any Mennonites wishing to do relief work had to operate through the American Friends Service Committee, without encouragement or support from the Mennonite leadership.

Meyer, although assigned to France by the Friends, hoped to change that. While still at Camp Sevier, Meyer was appointed chairman of a group of objectors proposing to construct an independent Mennonite relief agency. On November 24, 1918, amid his correspondence with others interested in developing a Mennonite agency, Meyer wrote to Steiner:

> I think this is an opportune time for the Mennonite church to prove her stand. To do so I think the Mennonites should take up some of the Reconstruction work themselves. I feel sure I could find a large number of young men who would go as soon as they get out of camp. They hesitate about going under the Friends Organization. And why should the Mennonites not do some independent work? I think there is material in the church that should be used in this way. Some one suggested to me that the young men should be given the opportunity to work under a committee of the church. I replied that I am in favor but I see no reason why the young women should not be admitted on equal terms. There are some forms of social service where a young woman could be of much more use than a young man.[27]

This desire to involve young people in a Mennonite relief effort remained with Meyer after his discharge from the military. Before traveling to France, he continued to write Mennonite leaders and fellow objectors interested in war relief, outlining the difficulties young Mennonites were experiencing in the church and proposing the creation of a relief agency. Writing in the (Old) Mennonite periodical *Gospel Herald*, Meyer implored his church to sustain a peaceful witness, even though the world now lived in peace: "Now that the actual fighting has practically ceased, the supreme moment for action has come for all who profess a belief in the doctrine of nonresistance."[28]

Unfortunately, Meyer's departure for Europe, so long anticipated, arrived with his dream of an independent Mennonite relief agency unrealized. In France, Meyer and other Mennonite objectors working in reconstruction began meeting and worshipping, sometimes hiking twenty-five miles one way to gather. Together, the group drafted a letter to the *Gospel Herald*, suggesting what the church could do in its development of a social and mission agency, and challenging Mennonite leaders to take on the task. In June 1919, Meyer spoke to a gathering of Mennonite relief workers at Clermont-en-Argonne, voicing again his beliefs about the Mennonite church and its young people: that Mennonite youth wished to enact—through their engagement with the world—the Beatitudes found in Christ's Sermon on the Mount; that the church needed to provide avenues for its members to express the Christian message; that without those avenues, young people felt their energy was wasted.

Energized by speeches of Meyer and other relief workers, those present developed a constitution for a new Mennonite group, "The Mennonite Young People's Movement." The constitution called for international Mennonite cooperation and, as Gerlof Homan summarizes, proposed "that the new organization's purpose was to deepen the spiritual life of the Mennonite church, to study Mennonites' social responsibility as it had been experienced during the war, to promote Christian education, to provide relief and reconstruction, and to inspire young men and women to consecrate their lives to the conservation and extension of the principles of Jesus Christ."[29]

To that end, several Young People's Conferences were held in the United States, in 1920, 1922, and 1923. The group's message found voice in *The Christian Exponent*, a periodical published from 1924 to 1928. By the end of the 1920s, however, the movement had waned and the periodical folded, as financial difficulties and disruptions in church polity proved overwhelming for the organization.

For his own part, Meyer had galvanized church leaders by persistently challenging them to explore the creation of an independent Mennonite relief agency. The Mennonites never did see Meyer's vision clearly in France, and the American Friends Service Committee remained the primary channel through which Mennonite men and monetary resources flowed. Only in 1920 did the Mennonites create their own relief agency, the Mennonite Central Committee (MCC), formed to provide relief to Soviet Mennonites. With time, however, MCC became a cooperative effort to alleviate suffering not only in the Soviet Union but in other nations. It continues today as an important Mennonite agency intent on practicing a social gospel, just as Meyer had hoped would happen.

Following his time in France, Meyer returned to the United States and taught for several years at Goshen College. In 1923, he married Esther Steiner, a college friend to whom he had written so often during the war. That same year he joined the faculty of Western Reserve University, and in 1924 he completed his Ph.D. in history from Harvard. He remained a professor of history at Western Reserve until retiring in 1959.

A consummate historian interested in the preservation of artifacts, Meyer saved a great portion of his lifetime correspondence, his lecture and reading notes, and a good deal of genealogical information he had uncovered. Housed at the Archives of the Mennonite Church in Goshen, Indiana, these documents trace the remarkable life of an academician who served also as a lay leader for his church, goading it into greater engagement with the world.

In the 1960s, Meyer returned to his Great War diary and correspondence with the intention of publishing an abridged World War I diary in the *Mennonite Quarterly Review*. Blending together passages from his diary and from letters written at the time, "Reflections of a Conscientious Objector in World War I" was published in January 1967. Despite its diary form, the *MQR* article did not wholly reflect the nature and spirit of Meyer's diary, given the author's own freedom to, as the journal's editor explained, "change wording and to shift materials from a strictly chronological order into topically workable blocks to give a representation of his experiences in shorter space."[30]

Meyer himself believed such revisions of his diary were necessary if the text was to be understood. The diary was written in "cryptic language," Meyer admitted, so that "no one inside or outside the camp would be involved in case the officers decided to confiscate it." Too many times in camp Meyer had been asked who gave him ideas about conscientious objection. Military officials hoped that by probing Meyer for information, he might implicate others who had violated the Espionage and Sedition Acts. Meyer refused to name names, either in conversation or in his diary.

That he felt it necessary to write his diary in an enigmatic way only adds to the importance of his text, showing how constricted the objectors' lives were in U.S. military camps. Though granted many more freedoms than other objectors, Meyer still feared indictment of himself and others should he openly state his feelings regarding the war. With this shadow hanging over him, Meyer avoided expressing his true thoughts, even in a diary, which by its very nature should allow for personal honesty.

Still, decoding the cryptic language is not necessary to appreciate Meyer's World War I text. His diary readily notes the ways in which his intelligence, leadership capabilities, and his friendship with officers shaped his experiences at Camps Jackson and Sevier, making his detainment by the military much more positive and less oppressive than that of other objectors. At the same time, Meyer's diary also shows the ways his was an experience like that of other objectors: he was scorned, forced into confinement and idleness, and constantly pressured to violate his conscience, despite his intelligence, his leadership, and the conciliatory relationship he established with officers. Finally, the diary reveals Meyer's increasing frustration with his situation and with his church, as well as his longing to enact change among Mennonites and his belief that Mennonites, in turn, should be transforming a bloodthirsty world.

Meyer died in 1968 after a successful career as a professor, after raising three children, and after a lifetime of activity in the Oak Grove Amish Mennonite congregation. His name is briefly mentioned in Mennonite history books as the activist and "insurgent" leader who, according to James Juhnke, "stirred" Mennonite youth following the war,[31] and pushed the Mennonite church in directions it might not have intended to go. Yet Meyer's diary suggests that he should also be remembered for another reason: he was able to transform the militaristic men he met during World War I, just as he to some degree encouraged the church's transformation.

Certainly it must be said that the officers who demanded an interview with the Harvard Mennonite did not drop their weapons, remove their chevrons, and take up a bunk in the objector barracks. As Meyer noted, however, many with whom he spoke were in some way changed. Meyer exploded the familiar Great War myths about ignorant farm boy objectors, showing that the nonresistant stance was one an intelligent man could embrace. Although during the war Meyer wanted badly to do reconstruction in France, he also recognized that witnessing to others in his military camp "may be the place which God intend[s] me to fill."[32] Those who met Meyer at Camp Jackson and then at Camp Sevier may have been as incredulous as the regimental physician who could little believe a Harvard-educated scholar could object to war. That Meyer proved otherwise became his testimony, the place God wanted him to fill. This Great War witness, too, must be seen as his legacy.

Text

Although a version of Jacob C. Meyer's diary was published in the *Mennonite Quarterly Review* in 1967, the original diary manuscript is used as this edition's copy-text. The *Mennonite Quarterly Review* edition was heavily edited and revised by Meyer himself, yet the author's 1918 holograph more clearly shows his feelings and perceptions about the Great War at the time of his experiences, rather than fifty years later. Because this edition privileges immediacy as the special province of the diary mode, retaining Meyer's original manuscript seemed significant. Both the annotated typescript of his diary and the *Mennonite Quarterly Review* article proved valuable in expanding or clarifying information found in Meyer's diary; when useful, this information has been included in endnotes.

Meyer's diary manuscript is part of an extensive Jacob C. Meyer collection at the Archives of the Mennonite Church. In actuality,

Meyer kept three diary books during the Great War: one covering the period July 25 to September 22, 1918; another from September 23 to November 4, 1918; and a third from November 5 until December 22. A fourth and fifth book detailed the end of his conscription and his journey to France with Friends reconstruction. This edition prints only the entries Meyer wrote until his discharge and return home from military camp, ending with the entry for January 1, 1919.

The first two of Meyer's three diary books were similar in appearance to a stenographer's pad or reporter's notebook: oblong, narrow, and with a cardboard cover bound to the pages with string. The pages in both books were lined, with a one-inch unlined space at the top of each page. This margin Meyer mostly ignored, save for the first page in the first book, which began on the first line. Meyer thus filled the pages completely, writing from one edge of the page to the other, and from the top of the page to its very bottom. There were no preprinted page numbers or dates in either book, nor did Meyer number his pages—although, of course, he dated every entry.

Meyer most likely bought the third diary book at a Camp Sevier canteen. Its cover has a large illustration of the American flag with the words "Old Glory" drawn in ornate fashion. The third diary is a composition book, as the printing on the cardboard cover's bottom indicates. This book has a cloth binding, and was perhaps more substantial in construction than the first two, though after eighty years the cover also betrays its wear and the back cover, on which Meyer wrote his final entry, is taped together. As with the first two diary books, Meyer covered every possible space with writing, filling the one-inch margin at the top of each page, and writing from the paper's left edge to its right. As with diary books one and two, Meyer wrote in heavy dark ink. This and his fair hand make most of his work easily decipherable. Usually, his writing only becomes difficult to read when he seemed in a hurry to complete an entry or was composing under a candle's dim lights, the electricity having gone out in his cantonment.

Because Meyer did not wish to expose his friends to legal liability should anyone confiscate his diary, he often resorted to the use of abbreviations when writing about those outside of camp. When the people about whom Meyer wrote are deemed significant to understanding his text, their full identity is revealed in the endnotes. Otherwise, the reader should consider the abbreviated names as referring to friends and correspondents from Goshen College or from Meyer's home community. Other "cryptic" language has been left undecoded, so that the reader might understand and appreciate

Meyer's writing as it was in 1918, while he was detained. Passages that seem especially enigmatic are explained further in notes.

The Diary of Jacob Conrad Meyer

[1918]

July 25. Thurs. To Sterling to get can supplies.[33] S. A. Slemmens gave a red cro kit. Visited at J.S. and John Gerigs.[34] Also at Emmet Yoders and Christ Conrads. Ed Moine, Erzula Rich, Cy's D.S. and Noah Schrocks and C. H. Korbels called in evening. Farewells.

July 26. Fri. Trip to Orrville. Tire trouble. Farewells at Orrville.[35] Trip to Covington and partings on way. Thru old Kentuck.

July 27. Sat. At Knoxville for breakfast. Mules and cotton in Ga. Stop at Atlanta also at Augusta.

July 28. Sun. Arrival at Camp Jackson. Weary. One man fell out of train. Assignment to company. Separations. A sort of lonely day because of tired feeling. Many new acquaintances. The early morning bath. First day in camp. [2] Many experiences. and examination. Most of men sore armed by evening. Several men fainted. C.O.'s questioned.

July 30. Tues. A warm day. Very little rain. Most men took uniforms. Four of us did not. Instructions read to us by Sargeant Springer.[36] Picture of group taken in evening. C.O.'s told to leave ranks when salute of officers was practiced. Treatment by officers and non-coms very good.

July 31. Wed. After breakfast tents were furled and bunks prepared for inspection. Report or rumor that a safety razor was lost or otherwise removed. 44 men of company called to leave the group. Among those were all the men in same tent as myself. The rest of us given military instruction. Later we stretched up tents and move to barracks. Schie and I together.

[3] A heavy rain caused change in weather. First night's sleep in barracks: *good*.

Aug 1. Thursday. Reveille 5:45. Breakfast or mess at 6:00. Clean up around barracks. I was detailed to go to personnel office. Reported but worked nothing. Asked to report next day 9:00 a.m. at depot to take care of Chicago men. Sing in afternoon. Supper. Studied some French. Wrote several letters & cards one for Mr. Guy Mack who is an illiterate from Wooster Ohio. Several of us went to infirmary to have tooth and shaving brushes sterilized; nothing doing. Cloudy evening.

Aug 2. Rain. Not many calls to line up. Due at Station at 9 o'clock a.m. Prepared tags for new arrivals. Ordered to appear at 7:30 p.m. to help locate 2500 Chicago men to arrive. Bring blankets to sleep. In the afternoon took Psyc. [4] exam.[37] Two slow men led the ranks in going. Schie and I led them back post-haste until halted by commander. On double quick he again put on the brakes. Arrived home safe. Exam a "cinch." Rearranged in squads. Sargeant Springer commander of my squad. Several C.O.'s sent on detail as Kitchen Police. They refused. Schie & I thought we would at least take regular turns.

Aug 3. Saturday. Nice day: Cooler than usual. Worked down at station on the force that registers new arrivals. All I had to do in a.m. was to write complete names, addressess and assignments in camp of several companies. Questioned as regards my C.O. position.[38] No difficulties. Dinner. Sent to Y.M.C.A. at 12:30 [5] by Sargeant Oakley. Ordered to do messenger service to 42nd Co. Back to Y.M. In a group of young fellows in line for Psyc. or Trade test service. Lieut passed me and several of us were given instructions. All O.K. until C.O. question was raised. Shall I accept uniform and a good position? Why or why not?[39]

Washed after supper. Sat. p.m. holiday but not so for me. No mail from home. Feeling fine. Schie very anxious to see his bro. I was anxious to know what became of other Wayne Co. fellows. No use to worry or complain. First week in camp almost over. Experiences were great. No very trying ones. Fine treatment by most officers. Very few exceptions. [6]

Aug 4. Sunday. Not much doing. Taken over to get second inoculation. Postponed for Monday 8:30. Y.M.C.A. meeting at 11 oclock. Chaplain Murray talked. Fine dinner. Wrote letters in afternoon. No mail. Read some. Not very ambitious. Taken out to pick up paper etc after supper. Lieut did not come so we did not work at all.

Aug 5. Monday. a.m. Breakfast fine. Inoculation. Three fellows fainted. All felt it more than first shot. Called before Captain Devers as a C.O.[40] He explained the stand of the army as regards C.O. men. Work in barracks such as cooking and cleaning up required of C.O. men. Also saluting. Men who refuse this sent to tent. I was permitted to stay in barracks.

[7] Opinion of Capt. Devers extraordinary. (He gave us the regulations from laws.) A fine, clean, honorable, man. A worthy captain a credit to his country.

First mail from home. Letters from Zarraga, Giosa and a card from Harley. Most fellows pretty tame over second inoculation. Nothing special in evening. Schie took a sweat. Longshore rather sick.

Aug 6. Tuesday. Felt pretty good when I awoke. Not over the effect of inoculation however. Weather reported 115 in shade. Letters to Harry Liechty, Noah Schrock, S. J. Bunting, D. F. Meyer.[41] Received a letter regarding C.O. men.[42] Wrote a "love letter" for Mr. Guy Mack. Some experience. Also [8] wrote a letter for David Baker. He needed money & tobacco and could not write. Anxious to learn. Schie had several interviews with Capt. Devers. He decided to take uniform if case could be settled. No uniforms to be had. Schie fixed another auto for the officers.

Made a desperate attempt to locate Albert Schie & Clair Moine. Not successful. The day seemed rather long because we were so unambitious and sleepy. Anxious to know what would happen in the morrow for we are due to work again in the p.m.

Aug 7. Wed. A very hot day. Water scarce. On duty policing and cleaning up the grounds. No work to speak of all day. Holiday in p.m. Inspection in a.m. for genital diseases. Some men ordered to hospital for circumcision. C.O. men ordered [9] to appear before Captain Devers. Capt. showed many favors to me. Said he would recommend me for overseas service in A.F.R.U. Showed him order from Sec'y of War which I read on day before. Second Lieut. asked about Phi Beta Kappa. Also asked about ancestry. Capt. Devers said his ancestry also Alsatian.

Read Roosevelt's book "America and the World War" in p.m. Discussed C.O. position with Longshore et. al. All agree that there may be something in it. Why not work at some kinds of work? Difficult issue.

Report of quarantine extension on account of measles or scarlet fever. Not unite us if rumor is true. Schie before captain decides to take farm work. Wrote letter to Bunting also to D. S. Gerig. [10]

August 8. Thursday. Went to Dentist after getting an order from Company surgeon. Date for Saturday 7:45 a.m. Weather not so extremely hot. Quarantine for measles or Scarlet Fever at noon. Read "Bosworth's "The Christian Witness in War; Bushnell's "The Character of Jesus: and the letters and conversations of Brother Lawrence—a Frenchman of long ago.

Wrote a "love" letter for John R. Hughes to Blanche Tyler. Brief discussion of C.O. position with Mr. Stork of Toledo. Discussed the divorce question with a Toledoan whose wife deserted him—as he says—before he came here.

Letter from Sister Clara in p.m. It told of [. . .] at Sam Detwilers. Mr. Detwiller in Class I. Nettie [. . .] in [11] Wayne Co. Husband in Camp. No work all day except helping to police around Y.M.C.A. in evening. Began to read H. G. Wells "The Soul of a Bishop" in evening. Schie rather anxious to get to doing something.

Health fine. Spirits good. Plan to go to foreign relief work still held in suspense. Answered letter to E.A.S.[43] Treatment fine.

Aug. 9. 1918. Friday. On duty stringing beans for two hours in morning. Read H. G. Wells "Souls of a Bishop." It is a study of a bishop who begins life anew. One who sees the error of his way. The need of a practical spirituality.

Letters to V. S. Ram & O. B. Gerig. Also to J. S. Gerig enclosed in Schie's letter to Sadie. Schie got two letters. His first news. Chocolates to come for Schie soon.

[12] Played ball in afternoon. Rather vigorous exercise in Carolina heat. Thunderstorm seems approaching. Artillery practice heard.

Water scarce. Inspection for tomorrow announced. One man comes to our barracks from hospital.

Spirits fine in p.m. Ambition at low ebb in forenoon. War news favorable to allies. No move to C.O. camp in sight: Quarantine still on.

Aug. 10. Saturday. Went to dentist. He pulled a molar for me after asking the advice of the captain (dentist). He was only an assistant who took the place of an absentee. After pulling the molar, for which purpose he made four hypodermic injections, he filled a wisdom tooth. It took almost two hours. Blood and saliva caused trouble. In P.M. Schie [13] and I got first permit to go to Y.M.C.A. I got two books "Alice of Old Vincennnes" and "God the Invisible King" by Wells. Had finished Well's book, The Soul of a Bishop, and returned it. Well's ideas not bad but not fitted for the common folk whose education is not such as even to appreciate the philosophy of Wells. A long stroll on Sat. eve out to the F.A.R.D. Field Artillery Replacement Camp. Saw the old boys especially Kline. Felt good but weak.

Aug 11. Sunday. Appointed orderly in personnel room. Cleaned up and stayed in room all day Tried to read and write but felt too weak and had headache. Attended Y.M. Bible Class and intended to go to evening Y.M. meeting but did not go. Schie got pitch on his shirt from a tree. That meant go home and wash. Retired early. Slept fine. Did not [14] know but had an idea that I would not spend another Sunday in Camp Barracks.

Aug. 12. Monday. Mess and policing of grounds. Called out and taken to "Sing" in Jewish Y.M.C.A. opposite Liberty Theatre. Back to barracks. Next to inoculation board. "Shot" for third time and vaccinated again. Back for dinner. Called to appear before C.O. officer. Transferred to C.O. Camp. Letter from Esther A—and a box of candy from Emma Smucker. Wrote to E.A.S. Mr. Schie, and Jennie. Bible Study.

Aug 13. Tue. Reveille and breakfast. A tear in trousers. Repairs. Furling of tent. Wrote letter to R. C. Stoddard Chm. Bd of Inquiry. Washed clothes. Dinner. Read in Atlantic. Studied French. In p.m. Andrew Miller and I got garbage can and supplies for our sergeant. Some boys refused to [15] work under a guard.[44] Orders from Lieut Caveness to make room for 8 new men. Holmes Co. bunch arrives. Base ball mitt arrives and is used. Met Y.M.C.A. man: ordered Napoleon's Life by Rose. Met Y-M. Chief and an officer of our company. They try to persuade me to work. Know about me thru Capt. Devers.

First day in C.O. Camp. Weather was hot

Aug. 14. Fine day but hot. Wrote and read in morning. Also went after wood. Letter to Major R. C. Stoddard. After dinner collected money for mitt and baseball. Played ball some. Studied French and read. Bible study in evening. In good spirits.

Aug. 15. Not feeling clear in head when I rose. Lazy and tired until noon. Did not read or study much all day.

Mail from Elmer, Clara 2 letters B.C. D.F. and Bunting reported the [16] arrival of passport at Phila.[45]

Lieut. Caveness interviewed me and gave me permanent pass. Went to Y.M.C.A. and Co "C" barracks. Letter informed me of death of Christ Conrad.[46] Wrote two letters one home one to B.C. Discussed the "South" and Negro question. Boys all interested in Am. Friends Reconstruction.

Aug. 16. Letter to R. C. Stoddard to inform him of passport. Read in Mr. Crewe's career by Churchill. Letter to Blanch & B.C.M. Worked in Kitchen. In p.m. went to Y.M. canteen and post office for other boys. Two trips. Bible class topic patience. Asked to help arrange new topics. Letter to Clara. In good spirits.

Aug. 17. Washed and made several trips to canteen. Candy the most important article of trade. Took money orders to post office for two [17] C.O. men. Bible service—Paul.

Aug. 18. Sun. Tried to have S.S. but Lieut ordered men to get tents. Bible service in evening based on S.S. lesson.

Trip to Hospital to see Ed Graber. Found him convalescing but lonesome. Also saw Wayne Co. boys in Co. "H." They were under quarantine. Schie and I together at hospital.

Aug. 19. Mon. Letter for E.A.S. Lester H. Elmer. Card to Mina. Several trips to canteen. Made large purchase of candy. Talked with new lieutenant in C.O. position. Seems to think C.O. men are stubborn. They refuse to stand at attention or at parade rest. Plans of new Lieutenant.

Aug 20. Tuesday. Rearrangement of tents and street meant work for almost all forenoon and part [18] of afternoon. Worked in kitchen about two hours. One man taken to guard house on account of a letter mailed surreptitiously (so rumored).[47] Helped get supplies from company mess hall. Read in Mr. Crewe's Career. Worked in a.m. Trip to Canteen for supplies. In p.m. a lecture on military law and regulations—by new lieutenant. At roll call and retreat several men refuse to stand at attention. Names taken. Major Carrier and Lieut Caveness give us a visit. Spirits of men good—weather cool in early morning. Boys look for [. . .] trials under the regime of new lieutenant.[48] Nofzinger goes to Personnel office on account of pay roll signing. Inspection during last two days very strict.

[19] Order not to spit or throw waste water in tents.

No mail for me but other men got some news which seemed very welcome.

Headache made me feel rather dull though my appetite was good. New arrangement of tent very favorable for me. Rumor that Major R. C. Stoddard will come in a week.

Aug. 21. Wed. Moving out and cleaning up in tent. Furling of tent. Inspection over and moving into tent. Baseball exercise. Read in Mr. Crewe's career. Men called out to get wood, others for psyc. examination and still others on account of pay roll.

To the canteen in p.m. and evening. Large orders. Candy $11.20 for day. No mail. Letters to N. U. Schrock and J. H. Conrads.[49] Cards to Tammy Graber and Harry Liechti. [20] Bible class in evening: Study of St. Pauls first missionary journey. The difficulty between liberal and conservatives. Barnabas, Paul and Mark. Haircut and shave. Several aeroplanes maneuvered over our grounds. Winslow taken away probably to guard house on account of letter.

Aug. 22. Orders to shake blankets as a part of morning clean up work. A short period of Baseball exercise. Miller taken away because of some difficulty which seems to have originated in his company. Several men refuse to stand at attention at retreat. Lieut. places them in last tent from which I and several others had been moved to fill up other tents. I was placed in tent with *Russelites*.[50]

[21]Martin H.D., Cecil, Hinshaw et al. under guard in last tent. Given bread and water for supper. My first night in new tent. A long interview with Lieut. He showed me order of Sec'y of War for June first. Are the men who refuse to stand at attention at retreat defiant or not? Section one or two.

The stand of the non resistant man discussed, Socrates, Savanoth, Roosevelt. The ignorance of the group discussed. What is to become of me and others? When does military law and civil law meet? Is standing at attention a military courtesy or a civil courtesy? When and where shall I serve? Lieut gave me manual of arms. Also told me to call out mail [22] other men anxious to know what our interview was all about. I tried to explain the clash of authority and order of Sec'y Baker. My impression was that Sec'y Baker's order is not easily interpreted. In a sense every man in C.O. camp might be classed as defiant yet that would make the order nil.—Bible Study. Paul.

Aug. 23. Friday. Cleaning up and moving bunks out. Baseball practice. Order men out to get wood. I was called out of rank and later asked to help seal letters of outgoing mail. Lieut. remarks as he reads "These men try to be martyrs yet they never had things better." A man called to ask men of a certain Co. to sign pay roll. When men came back from trip [23] to get wood they are called in but do not sign pay roll.

The men who were under guard in last tent given regular meals but segregated from us. Bath for all men.—Hoorah!

C.O. dog taken away. Some reports of men from several camps—Upton-Devers, Dix, Meade-Sherman, Grant, Taylor-Gordan-Jackson (?) furloughed to farms. My letter from D. S. Schrock reports Hartzler boys Leichty, Cora and Kurtz already out. Boys all much interested. Looking for Stoddard and Aaron Loucks.[51] Old order men asked to shave beards off. They explain their stand. Orders that inspection comes tomorrow. Read part of Silas Marner. One of cooks called me in to talk things over. He seems [24] sympathetic with my view though he may be a sort of detective. Who Knows? Moral is be a rational man at all times. Sincerity is never out of place.

Philosophical discussion with Jordan—Russellite. He denies a belief in Evolution. I try to explain to him that "like produces like" "no duplication" and "Survival of Fit" are the laws of Evolution. Those three laws he practically admits. He argues that species are fixed. I ask who fixed them? Who can classify animals or plants? Is sponge plant or animal?

Bible Class. Paul's second journey. Vision at Troas. Roman citizenship, claim at Philippi—At Athens etc. The place of women now & then. Old order men present for first time.

[25] After Bible Class, Russellites raise questions of Hell. Fire & Brimstone. Deny everlasting punishment. I take stand. Live right each day. Let the future in God's hand.

I also take view that after life is "disembodied memory" a figure of speech. Every day spent out of harmony with Infinite is lost forever, therefore hell is eternal suffering for a loss which is irreparable. God's justice and mercy demand that sin be punished. My opponent cannot but acquiesce but argues that I deny a literal hell fire. I explain that "literal and material" are terms not in any way applicable to the future existence. Finally lights go out and Russellites seem to be at end of their argument. They gain a point when I deny literal hell [26] fire but lose the whole case when I say time spent out of harmony with the Eternal cannot be made up and therefore punishment is everlasting–eternal, forever, time without end etc. No answer to my stand. On the whole the argument of all men here seem to be not their own but borrowed and bookish. Adams fall–Gods power over Satan and Future life seem to them the vital issues. I claim live right today. Trust God for the future.

Aug. 24. Inspection day. Bunks out policing about tents. Inspection of shaves, belongings etc. Several men asked to wash clothes and shave etc. Silas Marner. Big "Wash" in afternoon. Three trips to Canteen. $8.90 worth of candy. Many men taken away for Psyc exam [27] etc.[52] Apparently Major Stoddard is coming and this is done in view of his coming.

Read in p.m. Interesting. Bible Study. Lieutenant absent at retreat. A "subby" to take his place. Most men in pretty good spirits.

Aug. 25. Sun. "Pegram" a private acted as commander of police force in a.m. Hard to get men to work. Call for potato peelers. Toilet took a long time. Sunday school 10 oclock. A large crowd. Action rather than confession stressed.

Several men argue theology in p.m. Wrote letters to E.A.S. Adella, and Mrs. Felzer.

Return of C.O. dog. Poor dog. Courtmartialed: taken to stockade. Guards refuse to kill it. Sent to farm on "furlough" to live with [28] Negro. Bible study. Paul's third missionary journey. Bound to go to Rome.

Aug. 26. Mon. Reveille–breakfast and policing. Base ball practice. Men taken to get wood. I called to Lieutenant's tent. Asked to witness at courtmartial of several C.O. men who refused to stand at attention at retreat. I was asked to testify that a non-com told them to stand at attention. Trip to woods after poles to build railing around tents. I belonged to chopping crew. Lieut cut one tree. Negro gave us orders to cut no more. Trip home carrying timber. Asked to sign pay roll. I stated I would to avoid them trouble but I would send money to Sec'y Baker. Told to sign refusal roll. Did so with understanding.

[29] Read Silas Marner. Went to P.O. and Y.M.C.A. also canteen.

Read "Blue Bird" by Matenlick. Bible Study. Life of Paul. His trials. Discussed stand of our lieutenant with Lantz. Also question of rights of C.O. men according to order of Sec'y Baker.

Aug. 27. Tues. Washed in a.m. Most of C.O. men taken to bath house. Read "Blue Bird" and exchanged it for Kipling the "Light that Failed." The latter seemed interesting. Letters rec'd from Mrs. C.B.F.–E.A.M.–E.A.S.–C.E.M. and card from O.R.L. Bible class lesson on Pauls last trip to Jerusalem. His reception and imprisonment.

Aug. 28. Wed. Policing in A.M. Built a clothes line. Sent by Lieut. Avery to get mosquito nets. Pegram and I could not carry them all so we [30] Lieut sent a detachment under Pegram to get "nets." I bought a paper in first trip. Read in "Light that failed." Nets issued. Some fellows go to woods for "bows" on which to fasten nets. Several men called before a man from Phila. in presence of Lieut Caveness. I was first. He asked me my view as regards the C.O. position. He presented no new argument but re-iterated those which had been repeated to me over and over for years. In evening Lieutenants Caveness and Avery had several interviews. "Boys" report that prisoners are not to be fed in our mess hall as had been rumored. To canteen where a report that no buying in large quantities is allowed. I was successful to get almost all I wanted at second "canteen." Mailed a letter to E.A.M. and card (views of camp) to E.A.S. Got Iliad in exchange [31] for Silas Marner.

Bible Study Acts *26-27-28*. Lieut Caveness ask me for C.O. order of Sec'y of War. Returned it later. *Good night.*

Aug. 29. Thurs. Cloudy. Barnes absent at roll call. Sentenced to K.P. but refuses to work. Later sent to last tent by himself. The reason for the sentence no doubt was his reply when asked what he was doing. He said I'm p—ing. Vulgarity. Barnes on bread and water but I was given permission to buy candy for him.[53]

"War" in camp. The major who controls the area demands that the prisoners be fed in our mess hall. Avery & Caveness object. I was called in by Avery and interviewed Caveness came and I was dismissed for the moment. Caveness asks for my C.O. order of Secy Baker. Avery asks for further interview. [32] He wonders what my interpretation of "preparing food" is. He also wonders if K.P. men would work for prisoners. I said I thought they would for one day but not long. Finally new K.P.s come. C.O. K.P.'s sent out. Now no kitchen work for C.O. men. Avery explains situation. Two majors one over C.O. men and one over area. Second tries to take advantage because first is absent for 15 days. Much discussion. Area major calls Avery "down" before C.O. men. Avery & Caveness argue with major.

Mess kits issued to C.O. men. Both C.O. men and prisoners use kitchen. Avery asks for all C.O. orders etc in my possession.

We got bows for mosquito bars issued yesterday a.m.

[33] In p.m. went to canteen and P. office. Mistake in change by $1. Got the dollar from negro in canteen later. Sold six boxes of candy to boys. Also other things. Read Kipling "Light that Failed" Spoke to Willie Clark. Heard Rob't Stiener went home in anticipation of going to France. I asked Avery if Barnes could have candy. He consented.

Bible study. Thou shalt not lie. Why not? Mr. Steele from Tuscarawas County present. He had just come today and did not know of our segregation.[54]

First night under mosquito bar.

Aug. 30. Fri. Worked in a.m. Two trips to woods to get poles and boards to fix tents and grounds. Tried to write letter to E.A.S. Not successful in getting it written because I was [34] called out twice. Order that no boards be kept under beds.

In p.m. worked around tents and streets. Lining up in tents. Pegram & I plan to take bath after supper. Went to canteen before supper. Also brought several boxes of candy after supper while coming home from bath. The other boys went for baths with Pegram. Bible Study.

Aug. 31. Sat. On latrine detail. Finished reading the "Light that Failed." A peculiar ending. The hero dies on field of battle—blind. Men work on tents–lining them up. Schlabach (Levi) seems to be boss. Washed my crepe shirt and blue trousers.

In p.m. went to Y.M. to get some magazines. Also mailed letters. Went to lumber pile (waste) to get wall board for the fellows who [35] want them for their suitcases to rest upon. A heavy rain interfered with latrine orderly job. Trip to canteen for candy, bananas etc. Letters from J. B. Cresman, Mina and Mrs. Krabill [. . .]. Bible Study.

Sept. 1. Sun. Pegram calls roll. S.S. at 10:30. Mess sargent gave me pineapples extra for dinner. Argument with Jordan in a.m. on annihilation vs. death. Sunday school lesson on giving. In p.m. went to see boys of Co.H. also saw Frank Schie and *Glenn Gerig*. Talked with Ray Eschleman and Clair Moine especially. C.O. position and cap't of Co.H. Supper "not great." Bible study.

Sept. 2. Mon. Lined up tents. Worked almost all day. Read "Kenilworth" Several canteen trips. Canteen closed 12 n. to 6 p.m. Rush back to canteen after [36]

6 p.m. Logan berry juice etc. Trip to Y.M.C.A. in p.m. Reports that we are to be moved soon with depot brigade.

Sept. 3. Tuesday. Washed. Not thru when called in by Lieut. Call for volunteers to put clay in mess hall brought no result. Why not the question he asked me. All called out and the Sanitary order explained. Some few men volunteer. Three four horse (mule) leads brought. Some men work especially the "Amish."

In p.m. clay placed in tent of Lieut. And the tent of "Amish." I used Lieut gloves.

In p.m. at retreat Lieut. reprimanded in general those men who take the roll call as a joke. Trip to canteen and P.O. twice. Saw the Schie Mr. Mack and men of Co. "H."

Letter from O.B.G. reported Steiner, Stoltzfouz and Oswald on way to France. OBG mess Sargeant. Gerber cook. Bible study [37] in Galatians. Are heathen lost? Class letter came Sept 2.[55]

Sept. 4. Wed. Answered class letter. Men who did not work yesterday called on to dig latrine and do other work. A warm day. Did some figuring for the cook who is doing work in cooking school. One of the prisoners who worked on ditch fainted and was carried away.

On eve of Sept 3d mosquito bar inspector called. Asked Gobel what good "his bar did" if he kept his face uncovered. When Weston was told to put up his mosquito bar he said "D'ye know who I am." Officer said. "Don't make any difference." Put up your bar.

Sept. 5. A fine day but warm. Several of men make mail box and furniture for Lieut. out of boxes from supply sergeant and a box I got some bananas in on eve of Sept 4. Very little real work done. In p.m. I read in Kenilworth as well [38] as Book of Galatians. On eve of Sept 4 Clair & I planned trip to see Warren Bodager. We took the hike on eve of fifth so I missed Bible study. I had at 4:30 p.m. an interview with one of the Henshaws (Sanford I think) on Committees for Bible Study.

Bought $2.75 worth of apples and $6.70 worth of candy from canteen. Mailed letter to Jennie. Rc'd a letter from E.A.S. from Sugarcreek. She seemed in good spirits after the Medina Convention.

Our call on Warren B. was a successful venture out. He is ass't mess sergeant and they had a banquet. Leavings—pie and ice cream "came" to us. We talked matters over—all in good spirits. On way home Clair and I had a sort of confidential talk on C.O.'s. Also met (Lewis?) Walter in same brigade as Bodager but in different [39] Company. He told of fall of Fred Marbach etc. During night I heard many men halted by guards. Conclusion Some strict orders from "above"

Sept. 6. Sale at canteen. I bought about $5 worth of soap and shoe polish. Bought Waterman pen for Mr. Andrew Miller. Clerk made extra change. Took my $5 for a $10 I had $5 extra and did not know how or why. Tried to cash N.Y. draft for Brenneman—must be signed by Lieut. Also failed to cash money order for Candle. He must first endorse it in full. Bought Parker fountain pen $4.00 value for $3.00. Sold it to McClure for $3.00. Got orders to buy many more but after supper the canteen clerk would not sell at 1/4 off except one kind of pen–the Edison. Bought [40] more soap, shoe polish, and such articles at reduction.

Sept. 7. Sat. Inspection passed off nicely. My tent group cleaned up street. To canteen to buy Moore pen fine point for Noah Beachy. Bought U.S. pen for Mr. Wenger. Exchanged it for his fine point in p.m. Returned $5.00 to man who made mistake on day before. Changed $10 check for Brenneman and $1 P.O. order for Candle. Washed on Fri. eve. rain on Sat a.m. made wash wet. Bought a pen for 150 for White. Trip in rain after supper to get $6.00 worth of candy at one canteen and $1.30 worth at another. Had bought $2.40 worth in forenoon. Rain all night a heavy bombardment kept us soaked a while. Good night to sleep. [41] Letter from E.A.S. told of experience getting home from Ohio.

Sept. 8. Sunday. Rain all night and Sun. a.m. not very agreeable in tents. Spent a.m. in S.S. writing letter to J. N. Smucker, and in cleaning up. Ice cream, cake, pie & lemonade for dinner. To Co. "H" in p.m. Paul C. Clair M. Schies and Eschlemans there. Returned to camp about 4 p.m.

Not a very interesting or pleasant day. Evening meeting held in tent no. two. Good attendance.

A good night to sleep.

Sept. 9. Mon. Damp in morning. I began anew at Kenilworth. Read from p 162 to p. 310. Greater interest than at first. We were not called out all day. Caveness called in a.m. Troyer trying to get furlough paper signed. I asked Lieut. Avery about taking a hike. He said boys could go for bath but no decision on hike. Bought Moore pen for Yoder. He [42] asked me to get a finer point pen which I did in p.m. While at canteen in p.m. met Caveness who asked me to take mail. Several packages. Four letters for me also a fountain pen which I had repaired. Sent Elmers pen home. Insured mail 10c. Bath after supper. Also second trip for mail. More trips to canteens than usual. $3.00 worth of apples. Many small articles.

Boys play ball in evening. Bible Class of great interest. What is difference between view and vision. Was Amos a real prophet? How recognize a prophet today?

Sept 10. Got up a little late after a good night's rest. Cool and damp morning. After breakfast I read in Kenilworth. Very interesting. Called out for a "hike" of about ten miles. [43] Very interesting scenery. Cotton field ready to pick. "Niggers" at work. At the end of trip boys discovered some "muscadine" grapes–a luxury. All men in good spirits on hike. But many tired after return. Sleepy bunch in p.m. I went to canteen. Bought tablets at a reduction. Second trip to buy fountain pens. 4 for $5 also about 35 tablets 2 for 15c. Third trip—all goods up to former price—no purchases of pens etc.

Lecture by Major Carrier on furloughs to farms and for A.F.R.U. To canteen to buy candy and other articles. Found three feather pillows. Left them at supply house. Other soldiers wanted them. Candy 6c a piece. A good supper. Trip to canteen after supper. Lieut Avery gave talk on farm furloughs—Sent [44] out my application for A.F.R.U. Bible class very interesting. Study of Amos completed. Hosea the next assignment. What about Zionism and messianic prophesy.

A visit from Clair M. He, Schie, J. C. & Ray Eschliman, Nussbaum & Eberly moved to regimental infrimary. Clair in good spirits. Hope to see him again soon. Some excitement regarding furloughs.

Sept. 11. Wed. Clear cool morning. A trip to canteen and Y.M.C.A. in a.m. Read Kenilworth. Some interesting parts. In p.m. long trip to canteen near Bodagers company. Candy sold 6c a box straight. Also bought other articles. To canteen after supper. Not much of great interest all day.

Bible class lesson in Hosea of great interest. Several new men came to C.O. camp—four of them and one on day before. Several [45] from Ohio. One from N.Y. Cornell man.

Sept. 12. Thurs. As usual except I washed a large wash. A lecture in mess hall by lieutenant. What about non-com work? The pacifists and their faulty philosophy.

Finished Kenilworth. Ending not very pleasing. French class began. Argument of soul of man. If man's soul is gift of God or a part of God, does God suffer in hell? Old stuff.

Letter from Gerig of great interest.

Bible class of interest. Hosea's charge against the priesthood. One *company* man who is a C.O. listened to our discussion and though not inside he really was present.

Sept. 13. Fri. A nice day. of much work in morning. Bath at 10:30. I went to canteen to buy some [. . .] and bought. Letters to Aruarraga, Clara M. Striad Miss Brosser for Gerig. Letters from Clara and Mr. Maxfield Howard. Card from Miss Wheeler. French class in p.m. Pretty fair work. Read some in Iliad during day. At 4 p.m. a trip to canteen.

After supper I played ball. Then discused heaven & hell ideas with Christadelphian. He and Russellites challenge the right of scientific interpretation of Bible. How can each man make his own God? How else can it be. Revelation or reason.

Clair and Warren call on me. Only a brief but very pleasant interview. May have been last in Camp Jackson. Bible class lesson very much interest shown. [47]

Sept. 14. Sat. Inspection. prepare to meet thy lieutenant. All o.k. Trip to see Warren B. Clair et al in p.m. with Schie who had come to our street by permission from a guard. We were playing ball. Schie and I go to the Co. "H" and see Graber in canteen. Next to see Warren, then to Infirmary to see Clair et al. They seem satisfied. On return I bought a suitcase and other articles.

While with Clair we discussed the Y.M. with a Jew.—a pessimist. Bible class well attended.

Sept. 15. Sunday. Fine day. Sunday school in a.m. "Witnesses for Christ." In p.m. I went to a little reunion at the barrack where Clair et al are located. Met Frank Schie and Warren Bodager with the boys. In the evening Bible class of interest Lieut scarce. "As we studied we got more light." A bath and I retired. [48]

Sept. 16. Mon. Read in Iliad. The first three books are good reading. Have not read further. Trip to canteen to get suit case and a large order. Major Carrier offers some boys a proposition—to farm on a very large farm of a company near Charleston S.C. Some object. The plan seems to be one which would make the furloughing an easy matter.

Sept. 17. Tues. Washed a big wash. Read in Iliad. Major Carrier and (Mr. McCrea) heard of farm furloughs called me in for an interview after dinner. He wanted to know my view. Made some rather sarcastic expressions about Mennonites. Men from Charleston here to size up our bunch of boys. The proposition is to ditch a large farm and eight men wanted by large scale farmer. Most of boys slow to accept. In sport some fellows "sell" the boys from [49] the block. Canteen work very heavy. Apples, bananas, $4.00, lemons, candy, stamps. New men in nearest canteen and prices good. Bought 11 prs. B.V.D.'s at 75c. Sold them all.

Bible Class on Luke. Ist chap.

French class of five. Great interest.

Sept. 18. Wed. Washed blue serge trousers and blue shirt. Rain in a.m. Read Iliad. Of great interest. A trip to Y.M. $2.10 in stamps in a.m. lost track of pass. Second trip to get pass which was at tent. Bought apples and Bananas then three boxes of candy at $1.20. In p.m. sent for 5 boxes thru Rockwell at $1.20. Went to get suitcase for Guthrie at $3.00. $1.50 worth of apples $2.00 stamps 3.00 suitcase. etc.

Weather fine but hot after rain.

Sept. 20. Fri. Read in Iliad 100 pp. Cloudy. Rained about 6 p.m. In p.m. made trip to canteen for candy. Some apples. Long day. [50] the other fellows were called out by fire whistle. French class lesson in stories of France. Letter from Elmer.

Sept. 19. Thurs. Read 100 pp. Iliad. Nice day. Several trips to canteen. No special developments. No mail. Furloughing proposition seems dead.[56]

Sept. 21. Sat. Inspection morning. Weather cold and men talk of winter. Hike after inspection. Saw a red head woodpecker. In p.m. went to canteen several times. Bought $15.60 worth of candy. Other articles about $8.00. In afternoon men bought views of camp for 20c from boy. Big sale. Reports of moving to Greenville again current. I had headache in p.m. Made on trip to stockade to carry mail after dinner. Saw our old friend Barnes. No French class this p.m. Read some in Iliad. Letters from Noah Schrock's, J. R. Allgyer, [51] O.R.L., Fannie Conrad. Card from Clara gave Melvin Rich's address.

Bible study. The divinity of Christ. The growth in wisdom and stature. Cold night.

Sept. 22. Sun. Cold morning. Tent 6 group rake street. S.S. at 10:30. Fruits of Christian Life. Call to mess. Food supply short. I got extra on ice cream. Some objection to dinner. Lieut brings his wife to Orderly tent. Some excitement. A trip to Y.M.C.A. to mail letters to Elmer. E.A.S. John Moine & E. E. Miller. Supper rather light was given an appendix of bread and molasses. I was among the lucky. [52]

This Sunday was a fine day but cool. I did not feel as well as usual but in general I was not sick. Clair, Warren, Ray Eschliman, Fred Ramier et al called on me in eve. Bible class conducted by Mr. Steere–I was quite late. Legain was taken away.[57]

[Beginning of Book Two]

Sept. 23. Mon. Cold morning. At 5:45 call of bugler for those due to move to Sevier. I arose and dressed. Alvin Breneman told me time so I went back to sleep. Before call for roll I met Frank Miller at latrine. He was not at all well—had not been for several days. On Sunday eve 22nd several callers at orderly tent on account of moving to Sevier. Mr. Legain was removed from our group probably to serve a 10 year sentence at Leavenworth. He had a court martial because he did not appear when called by local Board. Many rumors on Sun. eve. Clair, Warren, Ray Eschliman, Fred Ramier et al. called on me. Mess sergeant treated us with cream except Clair & Warren who came too late.

Finished Iliad Monday a.m. Also brought apples from canteen for fellows.

After dinner boys were called out–only those who had been recommended for farm work wanted to sign papers as to wages. All Boys went for bath. Then to office of Carrier only those for farm work in latter. [2] Carrier told them of their farm furloughs and their furloughs home until Oct. 2nd. Great excitement and many anticipations. "Home." Bible Study interrupted by bombardment of "taters" Pegram later reports it was due to our singing which interfered with violin music in Orderly tent. Retirement a little anxiety because of potato bombardment.

Sept. 24. Tues. Several early bugle calls. Moving to Sevier probably the cause. I was asked to escort men to "urine dump" and trash dump. Rockwell had left us on day before. Also looked after latrine orderlies.

Furloughed men prepare to go home. They hand in their goods. etc. Leave before noon. Some tears shed in the "parting." The boys who left for home were anxious to go home but some feared the "turtle farm" as [3] they nicknamed it. In the afternoon we prepared to leave for Sevier thinking we would go in the morning. By night we found out that we would not leave until Thursday morning. Since the 21 fellows left we felt a little lonesome but in pretty good spirits. Rumors were current that the men who had appeared before the Board but had not yet been sent out would be sent out ere we left for Sevier. Bible Study well attended for the size of our group.

Sept. 25. Wed. Cleaning up and policing. To trash dump and urine dump. Arranged for latrine orderlies etc. At trash dump one of the fellows found a U.S. granite cup which was given to me. Hurley found a traveling bag, several shirts, and other articles. The ten men who had appeared before Board were called out several times and all the arrangements were made to furlough them to a cotton mill [4] in Ritter South Carolina. The furloughs were not completely arranged until 8:00 p.m. At that time Caveness came to give them out. Lt. Avery was gone but Mrs. Avery was in Orderly tent. When the furloughs were to be given the fellows asked for extensions after Oct first. This was not possible. The question arose "Where are the men to go until Oct first." Money was scarce. Di Rienza (Vincent) said "I no got some money" "I don't know where to go." Finally Anderson,

Hurley & Gable left for home. Other seven stayed to go directly to Ritter.

A short session of Bible Class. Devotional entirely. Retirement with orders to get up at 5:00 a.m.

As for meals we got nothing until 10 a.m. Lt. Avery was to have arranged for meals but when Pegram took the fellows over I was left as [5] gaurd but when they returned they looked like hungry wolves. While they were gone I read several chapters in Luke. Even as it was we had gotten up late. Arrangements were made to have us cook our own meals for one day. Mess Sergeant and cooks try to get into kitchen but are ordered out and Harvey Hinshaw acts as Mess Sg't. A big meal at 10:00 and a second at 5:30 p.m. Before supper Lieut. Avery took emergency address of each man.

I made many trips to the canteen to get apples and other supplies. Returned back to Y.M.C.A. Also played horseshoe. Theo. Miller and I vs. Steer & Anderson. We beat them. I washed in morning and took bath at night. Some of boys climbed large ladder of Y.M.C.A. Had a short talk with Sgt Parrish. He had not been very kind to [6] the boys. During night I woke at 12:00, 3:00 and at 4:45. I called out the bunch. We slept fairly well but as we emptied our straw the day before we had poor beds. An extra blanket was issued to each man to keep warm. All goods ordered to be packed preparatory to moving to Sevier. I helped Major Carrier's orderly nail up a box while waiting to get a Reg. letter for Enos Moore. I finally got the letter after calling for it three times at the S70 post office and once at Jackson Circle office.

Sept. 26. Thurs. Up at 4:45. Brenneman and I called men. Policing up. Several men went to dump. General cleaning up. Cracker sandwiches for breakfast. To the train with goods. Some of us helped to carry the Major's goods. Staunton and I made last trip to old street. We picked up some souvenirs in Avery's tent. Post [7] card not properly marked. We tried to buy at Canteen, but man would not sell before 8 oclock. Off to station. A long wait. Maj Carrier gave us some of his hand baggage carried a hand bag until we boarded train. He was in car No. 3. I in No.4 and so as soon as I was on train I carried it to him. Off for Sevier at 9:10. Arrived at Columbia 10:10. Left Columbia 10:45. Arrived at Sevier about 5:30. A fine trip. We got a sandwich and an egg for dinner but we bought apples, etc from venders. On trip we watched my compass so as to keep straight. We met some men who made the trip from Camp Jackson to Sevier via Ford. On our arrival at Sevier we were met by about 25 guards and were escorted to our tents in the 47th Co. Some hike. We were called prisoners and kept in line for once. Several men almost gave out but we finally got [8] there. At first we could not get out of our tents but soon all guard was removed. Weston almost caused trouble by insisting on being out of the tent. We assigned the cots and had "some" sleep on the new folding field cots.

Supper was served in the 47th Co. Mess Hall. A very good meal and a fine reception. Some of our men helped to clean up in the kitchen.

A big rain interfered with our sleeping. A busy day with many events.

Sept. 27. Fri. Breakfast: A cloudy day. General inventory of stock by each man. Orders to move. Several men ordered to go to prepare the new place. The rest of us took baggage over to new site about 80 rods. Two trips. Tents set up and cots arranged. The whole day was spent in a general clean up. Caveness and Avery do the "bossing." A fine spirit [9] among the fellows. Every body works. Some arrange their own tents, while others work on all sorts of jobs. Division of men in tents causes dissatisfaction among some. Who shall sleep in tent with McCoy and Weston? Mess hall looked good but soon a mess s'gt and cooks moved in. Our fellows hoped to do their own cooking. Guards placed near us but not for our benefit exactly. The fence about our site was arranged. After a big days work we retired and slept fairly well. During the forenoon we had filled our straw sacks which made the sleeping more comfortable. I located in last tent with Diller, Moore (Enos), Miller (Andy), Brenneman, Brunk, Scheffel, and Lantz. Pegram asked me to move in first tent. I did not prefer to crowd anyone out and several fellows aimed to get into the first tent. [10] I helped K.P. in mess hall of seventeenth Co. at noon and in evening. Fine spirit among men.

Sept. 28. Sat. General work for big part of day. Cleaning up and making furniture for Lieut. At noon, Pegram and I played quoits with the two Lieuts. They beat us because I could not play. Pegram did well. About four oclock Lieut told me to have men clean up around our bath building. We soon did it up right. After supper Pegram and I went to canteen or store in Paris.[58] Some fine view of camp from Y.M.C.A. We bought over $13 worth. The reason I went was to get shoes for Harvey Hinshaw who had asked the Lieut about it. Upon our arrival home we found Lieut Avery gone with four fellows to look for lost baggage. Our goods were soon all sold out. [11]

I treated Caveness and left a treat for Avery. Candy cost me $1.00 per box and I sold it for $1.20. Lieut. Avery said we may start a Company Canteen.

On the whole we were well pleased with our new site and we all felt the better for the change. Of course our first reception was considered a joke by most of us. We had no lights in our tents but we put up one light in the Lieut. tent in afternoon.

Sept. 29. Sunday. Reveille when I was taking a cold bath. A big breakfast. Sugar visible on corn flakes. Tents furled after breakfast. General policing and clearing up. S.S. out doors tho it was pretty hot. Started a letter to J. S. Gerig. A big dinner. Brenneman asked to clean up officers mess. He fared sumptuously. Several others did K.P. work. Letter to mother and one to D. F. Pegram and I took a [12] hike to Y.M.C.A. and other part of camp. I K.P.d after supper and then I read some in Genesis. Retired early and slept soundly. Brunk said I snored.

Sept. 30. Mon. Fine morning. I did not take my bath before mess. We worked on our lot until 10 oclock and then I washed and took a bath. K.P.'d at noon. Then I helped make furniture for the Lieutenant. Avery brought his wife and we saw her as we tried out the typewriter table.

Several of the boys were sick; among them Diller Thomas & Moore (John). Shaved before retreat. According to appearances we will eat in our mess hall tomorrow. Diller used two of my blankets to keep warm.

Oct. 1. Tues. No place to eat breakfast on account of absence of light in our mess hall. A sergeant from 47 Co told us he would find us if we K.P.'d. We [13] did so. My job with several others was to make wood. After mess I left and worked at home. Some of the boys stayed to help clean up. Staunton made himself a sandwich and chef called him down: a chewing match followed. Our boys quit except Hockett who K.P.'d all day. A discussion between the Lieutenant of 47 Co. and Avery finished the matter.

Avery called me to go in search of 2x4 timbers. We made a stand for garbage cans after a long search for material. Next a wood box was planned. A fine dinner. Mess Sgt. made a fine speech. He spoke of our mess hall rules or plans. He even suggested that we say grace before meal. He made a capital impression. Mess Sgt and Lieut go for electrical appliances. When they are gone we clean up near bath house. Next we wired mess hall and our tent (et al.). After supper we finished the [14] mess hall wiring and tested several hundred lights in supply house just opposite our kitchen. Lieut. suggested that I quit work and leave some other fellow finish job. I asked a permit to go to canteen and went to Paris. Bought Candy, tablets and souvenirs. Found Y.M. used as hospital. Diller had been sent to Hospital in morning.

When I returned from canteen I gave Lieut some candy and then he gave out mail to me for boys. A box from home for Brunk. Started a letter for E.A.S. but could not finish it. Retired feeling ready to sleep after a long day. Felt fine. Had some [. . .] before noon.

Oct. 2. Felt fine upon arising. In the morning we built a wood box. Some fellows cut weeds. As on the previous day we put out all our blankets and kept tents furled all day. In the afternoon we cleaned up in our yard. Some of [15] the boys tried to get out of it. Among them McChase, Jordan, & E Mardfin. Noah Beachy felt sick so did also Pegram, Lantz, Moore Enos, Moore John F. I felt fine.

I went to Paris to take over 2 pairs of shoes for half soling. Bought three boxes of candy. We have fine meals and all went o.k. Intended to hold meeting in evening but decided it may not be best. Boys sang a while and I read in Book of Luke also in a book of Mr. Brunk "The Majesty of Self Control." I also read a part of Derstine's tract on Paul.

Oct. 3. Thurs. One week in camp. We had some fun by getting ahead of the line for breakfast. Our tent made good. We worked on our lot. Since Pegram was on sick list I was delegated to oversee a little. Not able to keep fellows at work before noon as I would like to have done. But in afternoon I made a success of it. We worked pretty hard [16] from 1 p.m. to 3:30 p.m. Before noon I got some repaired shoes and two boxes of candy. After dinner I shaved and took a cold bath. Another bath at 3:30 p.m.

Several fellows on sick list. Moore E. Moore J. F. Beachy, Noah, Pegram. Diller still at Base Hospital. Weather rather threatening but no rain. Lieut left around 3:00 p.m. but came back before "dinner." Pegram asked me to call the roll but he felt well enough to do it himself when the time came. After supper or dinner I went to canteen and shoe man to take shoes to repair man. Several of the boys from Elida got money from home church in checks. Can they be cashed? I thought they could not but with Lieut signature they possibly could. Letters to E.A.M. and E.J.M. Nice evening but rain was [17] threatening.

Oct. 4. Fri. Several fellows show the effects of Influenza: Among them Andy Miller, McCoy, Scheffel & Brenneman. In the forenoon such men as were able worked cutting weeds. Some are tired of job and call it Non combatant work. An extra big force in the kitchen because of inspection on the morrow. Levi Schlabach disgusted about carpentering without tools and lumber. Letter from E.A. Wrote him a new one for one of eve before was not yet mailed.

A big dinner—prunes. After dinner I was asked to get names of men and company assignments for Lieut.

Stockade prisoners worked near us. Report that a stockade to be built East of us. We saw some of our pals. Brunk got a letter in fine stationary.

Brenneman, Lantz, Miller "Andy" not very well. Fine stationery ordered by Corlot. Sold a gold [18] beveled card to Martin W. C.

In evening I made trip to get shoes and canteen supplies. $1 worth of stick candy, $4.25 worth of shoe repairs. Bible class planned but again postponed. General talk in tent in the evening on fine stationery etc. Most of fellows in good spirits. Staunton told me Lieut. may order all our furniture destroyed. Why not object. A good night to sleep.

Oct. 5. Sat. K.P. for me so I arose early. Worked pretty hard. Went to P.O. and Y.M. at 10 oclock a.m. Got money orders cashed for Pegram $10 and Scheffel $15. Also bought four books from Y.M. A sort of light dinner. In p.m. I went to Co. I and K for provisions. Read in Sabatiec's "France Today" Interesting. Lieutnant gave me identification card so to make collection of money orders possible. He wanted one of my books to [19] read when I came back in camp.

In eve I went to Paris to get shoes repaired. Also brought a very big order of candy etc. Letter from E.A.S. E.J.M. and Clara E. M. also from O.B.G. at Haverford. Diller came back from hospital. All sick in our tent but Brunk and I. I felt bad for Lantz and Payson Miller.[59] Brunk and myself slept outdoors all night.

Oct. 6. Sun. 1918. Had a good night's rest outdoors. After a fine breakfast I helped K.P. a little. Made a trip to Co. J. for lemons. Asked about my C.O. position. Not scorned in any manner. After breakfast I also tried to see that sick men got some "eats." Read Gen. 1-12 chapters. Read some in Sabatiec's France Today.

A fine dinner. After dinner I started to write my article for paper but soon Doctor came [20] and even before that we got order to put up a new tent for the sick. In fact we moved the tent in front of Lieut's tent to space beyond supply tent. Noah Beachy, "Andy" Miller, Enos Moore, Alpha Lantz and Marvin Hockett moved in to new tent. Dr. ordered four of them to Hospital. Lantz not sent. He said he thought he need not go. Dr. said it makes little difference what you think it is what I think Tempts. Beachy 104, Hockett 102. Moore 102. Miller 102. Lantz —. We made fun of Lantz, called him lazy.

Letters to E.A.S. J.B.C. Adella and O.B.G. Supper at 4:30. Retreat after supper. A fine evening. We expect to have a S.S. Walter Martin made lemonade for Lieut and wife. Mess Sg't took several pictures in camp. A rather somber atmosphere due to [21] influenza and removal of men to hospital. S.S. pretty well attended and a good spirit shown. "Conche"

Oct. 7. Mon. I felt rather "full in head." Of course I soon imagined that I was a victim. Hampton had a vomiting spell during the night. We worked with pick and shovel. I went to Post office to cash money orders for Levi Schlabach $30 J. W. Steer $50 Thomas $10 J. F. Moore $15 Hayes $10 Staunton $10. Also went to canteen and bought 1 box of chocolate candy and matches.

Read in France Today after I got back. Soon I felt very miserable so I quit reading. All afternoon the fellows told me I would be the next victim. Went to canteen twice in p.m. to get a few things and change for men. In evening we had Bible Study. Good interest. In afternoon I reasoned with Brunk & Diller about Goshen College. Tried to show them that [22] in my estimate J.E.H. was a victim of circumstances and a system.[60] Retired hoping to see the new day in good spirits. Monroe Schlabach to hospital.

Oct. 8. Tues. Cool morning. I did not know whether to answer roll call or not consequently I was "late" for the first time since in the camp. Ate a good breakfast and began to feel that I was pretty well after all. Then came work. Cleaned up Lieut's tent a regular job for me. Then helped to put out blankets and line up around our tents. A call to "assemble." Physical exercise. Rather hard on some of us who had colds but I stayed by them. Next came the first Lieut from Carriers office. We were again called out for foot races. Several groups raced. I came out second in the final-Steer the fasted man. Next we laid off for a little spell. A great big dinner. In the p.m. I went to cash money orders for Theophilus Miller [23] $30, Clarence Nofzinger $17.00 & Walter Martin $20. Postmaster and I talk on C.O. position. He was very congenial and hoped I would get to France.

After supper I went to Paris and bought 3 boxes stationary, hair tonic, candy etc. Arrived at home to find Beachy (Noah), Moore (Enos) and Miller (Andy) back from hospital. Monroe Schlabach and Hockett still at hospital. Returned men feel pretty good. They were placed in my tent so I moved while I was gone. I was moved to Holmes Co. Bunch.

In afternoon I put racks on our china closet. Just finished it ere I went to Paris. No longer mine when I got back from Paris. Felt pretty good all day. Had no Bible Study in eve. Postponed. Levi Schlabach not well in eve.

Oct. 9. Wed. 1918. Mardfin and Levi Schlabach off to hospital. Other sick men pretty well. We fed them at mealtime in their tents. In the forenoon we [24] swept our whole lot. Why? We did not know. I wrote a letter to L. E. Blauch. After dinner we built a frame for Lieutenant's tent and put it up. Major came. He asked me if I could keep books. Soon a report spread that we would be furloughed soon as Board was due shortly. Lieut. Avery asked me to get reports of men for Board. I lined them up. Then I got reports of sick men and those in hospital. Next I went to P.O. to collect a money order for Samuel Yoder. Written for $30 but [. . .] for $5.00 I could not collect so I sent it home for him. Bought stamps for Orderly. Also returned tobacco for Frank Miller. Good Supper. Fed sick people. Small attendance at Bible Meeting. Luke 6. Cool night.

Oct. 10. Thurs. 1918. Rose early and called upon sick. Also helped Harvey Hinshaw with cooking for one cook was indisposed and the K. [25] P's were sleeping. Cleaned Lieut tent after breakfast and feeding of sick and convalescents. Took physical exercise under Lieut commands. Great humor when I could not do a stunt.

Called in by Major. He asked me if I knew of any conscientious objectors in camp besides Mardfin. I first misunderstood but was soon told that other men were religious objectors. Pegram and I asked to classify all men as to religion. Over 20 Mennonites. Fixed up checks for Diller, Moore, Brunk, Lantz & Brenneman. These checks came from Elida Church for the boys. I asked Lieut. to sign them and in p.m. I tried to pass them. Cashed two Lantz & Diller's but others not. Finally I told boys they had better send them home. Too much trouble to cash them here. Brunk tried in afternoon to send his. Pegram said it was too late on account of the [26] censor. I saw to it that it was mailed at that time.

After dinner I had one shoe soled for Troyer 50c. Rubber heels for Brenneman (and nailing 60c same for myself 60c. Sent reply to letter from E.A.S. of same day. Also had letter from Clair Moine on eve before one from Harley. Read France today made a hasty survey of book. Called it good. Supper. fed the sick. Bible Class. Retired (to K.P. in morning).

Oct. 11. Fri. Called Frank Miller to K.P. with me. We had things in apple pie order before breakfast so that work was soon all off. I took Physical exercise. Rather strenuous. Duck Waddle interesting. Some of the boys cut wood.

In afternoon a bunch went to Co. J. kitchen. Wrote letter to Harley, J.E. Baked pies in mess hall. Second time K.P. for me. Pies baked both times. [27] After supper we cleaned up in fine shape. Mopped and scrubbed. The day was a busy one. Very tired by night. Retired after Bible study in good time.

Oct. 12. Sat. 1918. Inspection day. Hurry and hustle to clean Lieut tent, feed the sick and prepare for inspection. Wrote to father, D.F., Mr. [. . .] (Ind. U.1. class business) and Harley. Sent views of Camp

Sevier to Jennie.

After dinner trip to Post Office to cash two money orders for Mardfin $5 for Hampton $5 Arranged that Staunton could keep two books another week. Trip to Paris for apples candy changed check for Moore etc. Looked thru Hazen's "Modern European History." Meeting in our tent. [28]

Oct. 13. Saturday. Up late in a.m. One dozen at S.S. out doors. A good meeting. Fine dinner cake and fruit salad. Afternoon I planned to go see Monroe Schlabach but did not go. No one to give permit. Lieut gone also orderly. I sent letters to E.A.S. Clair, home folks. E.A.M. D.F.M. Felt tired in eve. Took care of sick after meals. Most of them improving.

Oct. 14. Mon. I washed in a.m. took exercise both in a.m. & p.m. I went to get money order changed for Brenneman and letter (of postage due) for Walter Martin. In afternoon I went to get personal mail for Major Carrier. In eve I went to Paris. Meeting was well attended. Sick improving. I saw Monroe Schlabach. He is in the Pneumonia ward but looks [29] well. My C.O. position is questioned several times ere I got to see him. Mail from Clara and Elisia.

Oct. 15. Tuesday. Sawed wood in morning. Then took exercise. Fed sick and cleaned in Lieut's tent in morning as usual. He and I discussed Peace plans. Wilson turned down Hun's plans. What next. Physical exercise. Read in Kant's Critique of Pure Reason. In afternoon we fixed stove in Lieut. tent. We also turned the tent. It took full force of C.O. men. H. D. Hinshaw got papers for Reconstruction work from Major Carrier.

I went to Paris in eve to get three sweaters etc. Meeting in Mess Hall in eve. Luke 9-10. Retired, to K.P. in morning. [30]

Oct. 16. Wednesday. 1918. K.P. for me as I arose early to go to Mess Hall. Fellows came ere we were ready. K.P. work went nicely. In a.m. I read in Kants "Critique." Lieut and Major came to kitchen. Sanitary inspector gave orders that all sweeping of grounds cease at once.[61] After dinner I went to Paris. Bought over $18 worth. Had orderlies shoes soled for $1.25. Bought 3 sweaters and sample of underwear. Some boys whitewashed mess hall in anticipation of the return of our Mess Sgt. Horton tries to sell his sweater for $6.50. Martin finally bought it for $6.00. Bible Class in Mess Hall. I got a letter from J.H.W. He was rather confidential about it. Some of us had [31] a long talk with cooks after Bible Study. Retired late.

Oct. 17. Thursday. 1918. Arose quite early. While sweeping Lieut's tent I got a chance to read a card from Clara. It told of death of J. J. Miller. In a.m. we dug in ground for exercise. I took cold bath and shaved. After dinner, Mausel (the cook) and I went to Post Office to cash a money order ($20) for Jordan. Next a trip to Paris. Bought candy had shoes repaired ordered underwear and bought other things. After supper I framed a picture of "Goshen girls." Had found frame in a.m. Someone had thrown it away as a broken mirror frame. Good Bible meeting well attended. Held in Mess Hall. Before supper I was moved [32] to old place. Next the question arose who is to move out of Holmes Co. Tent. Frank Miller decided to come to us and E. S. Jones moved to Pegram's tent. Retired. Read Kant.

Oct. 18. Fri. 1918. Felt fine upon arising. Big breakfast apples, butter, and pancakes. After breakfast Pegram and orderly went to Personnel office to get service record for Pegram. My job to get men to work. Major came and all men called in to report how long they had been in camp. I was asked to take the sick negro to infirmary. He was sent to Hospital. Read Kant. Dinner. Money orders and stamps. Orders for Hampton $15. Sam Yoder $40.00. Trip to Paris. Bought about $25 worth underwear, suitcase, [33] raisins paper etc. Exercise when I returned. I then went to see Monroe Schlabach but found he had been transferred to the Base Hospital ward 16 as a convalescent. On my return I reported to the Lieut. Major asked to see my "N.Y. American." It reported that Kaiser will surrender. Later I placed the blankets in Lieut's tent and got my paper. To Paris to get shoes for Frank Miller etc. Bible Study.

Oct. 19. Sat. Stormy night and cool morning. Harvey Hinshaw got a telegram from his brother from Comelly Springs N.C. He asked me to send the reply. I have been helping to enlarge the coal bin. Trip to Telegraph office. A young man from N.Y. got news of death of his sister. Trip to Paris with Lieut's shoes. Cost 25c. Also bought other things. A shirt [34] for Brenneman and underwear for Lantz. Upon my return the boys were all found in Mess hall filling out furlough papers. I did same. I asked major about Reconstruction furlough. He seemed to think the furlough could be granted with the Board of Inq. seeing me. I decided to write to Judge Mack. After noon I wrote to S. J. Bunting and Judge Mack. Talked to Lieut. about it. Next I was called before a Lieut to make any complaint as to our treatment. I made none. Next a trip to Post Office and Library for books. Next a trip to see Monroe Schlabach. Could not see him but report was that he was doing well. Read in Kant. Bible study. Started a letter for E.A.S. Night cool and rainy. Everybody moved [45] to dry spots in tents. Even Brenneman moved this time.

Oct. 20. Sun. 1918. Rain Rain Rain. good breakfast, chicken dinner. I spent some time cleaning Lieut's tent and then I was called in to lieutenant who is the Regimental physician. He asked me of my C.O. stand as a Mennonite. He a Harvard man was very broad in his view but he seemed to think men must fight to bring about higher ideals. Chicken dinner came soon after. I shaved and discussed C.O. stand with Pegram. After dinner I carried food to Weston & Levi Schlabach. The Harvard man wondered where I got my clothes. I said I purchase them with borrowed money. At first he said he could not see how I could class myself with the C.O. bunch. When we got thru he wondered how an ignorant man could die a C.O.

In the afternoon I wrote to E.A.S. D.S.G. L.E.B. Clair M. and [36] Mrs. E.M.Y. Sunday school in evening in our tent. Frank Miller built a camp fire to drive off the dampness. Smoke was predominating factor. The S.S. lesson was on Abraham's offering of Isaac. Many facts about the Supreme Sacrifice were brought out. After meeting Mardfin talked about C.O.s. Among them F. B. Sayre's brother.[62]

Oct. 21. Mon. Cloudy for a short time and then bright and sunny. We dragged over yard and levelled things up a little. After dinner I went to Post office and Library. Next I took a trip to Paris to get Watch crystal for Enos Wengerd. Also took shoes over etc etc. When I came back I read Kant and Driesers "The Power of Silence." Hausley the cook went to Comissary Dept. after raisins. He had $1.75 of my money. But it was invoice day so he got none. He kept cash to go in morning. He also carried my pen and wants to buy it. [37] A fine eve. I got a card from Clara telling of a girl who came to stay at D.F.'s home. A letter from E.A.S. reporting on car strike at Lima. Weather cool. Bible Study in Mess Hall.

Oct. 22. Tues. After breakfast we dragged the grounds thoroughly. Slim Hausley went to get raisins at commissary. I read in Drieser's Power of Silence. Lieut came for breakfast and told about exercise so I went out to take it. Slim bought 5 packages of raisins for 36c. I gave him 50c and sold them 10c apiece. I was called in to see Major. He asked me to start a school. Whole plan of furloughing seems changed. He told of the types of men. His idea that the men are abnormal and lacking in education. He wants them kept busy. I said how about equipment. He said that was up to me to make out list.

[38] Dinner after meal I explained situation to men. Some enthusiastic, some not much interested some few oppose the idea but say they will take some work. Steer and I find out the educational status of men. We plan a course and a curriculum. Steer, Stanton, Mardfin, Jordan and I to teach.

Curriculum

Reading. I Eng. Hist. & Geog. J. W. Steer

II Am. Lit. J. C. Meyer
Math I Fundamentals—Staunton
Math II
Algebra & Geom. Steer.
Hist & Civics J.C.M.
I. American
II. General
Geography J.C.M.
Gen. Science Mardfin
Agriculture I & II Mardfin
Writing Steer
Spelling Mardfin
Bookkeeping Meyer
Typewriting Jordan

[39] I told Lt. Avery and he O.K.'d them in general but was not sure about typewriters. I planned to go to Paris. Major halted me and asked about my plans. He O.K.'d them and said I should make list of needs.

Trip to Paris with Horton H. D. Hinshaw asked me to get a telegraphic money order for $25. Supper. After mess Steer and I did work of dean—we matriculated the men. Bible Study in our tent fourteenth chapter of Luke. Goodnight: P.S. a letter from Alma Wayne Nappannee Ind. A card from B. C. Meyer informing me of dishwasher at D.F.s. Letter from O.R.G. He to go to France soon in Reconstruction.

Oct. 23. Worked on texts for our school work. The librarian of the Camp library showed great interest. Also a trip to Post Office to send a pillow home [40] for Walter Martin and cash money order for Scheffel $15. Big part of day spent in looking after school. Bookkeeping a problem. Who to teach it. Bible study well attended.

Oct. 24. Thurs. I K.P.'d all day. We were quite busy. Major and Lieut ate dinner with us. In afternoon I planned to go to Paris but exercise interfered with going so I went after supper. Took shoes to repair man for Brunk and ordered crochet cotton and cap for me. Also bought some paper for school work. Rain made tent a damp place. No lights. I slept in the Mess Hall as did also Hampton. Frank Miller and Brenneman. Rain all night. In eve I wrote a letter to E.A.S. on stationary of Frank Miller. A sort of dreary night. [41]

Oct. 25. Fri. Rain, Rain, Rain. Almost flooded out except in mess Hall. Good eats all day. I helped some in Mess Hall. We started a Class in Algebra and one in Arithmetic. After dinner I went to Paris. Almost had to wade back. An officer got stuck in water with a motor cycle. Water in tents. After supper I went with orderly to see Fletcher Griffith and Monroe Schlabach about their records. Could not get into hospital on acct. of quarantine. Before supper I was called before Major. Report that Board was to come on morrow. All boys asked to see Major about records.

After supper I wrote a letter to E.A. and finished [42] one for E.A.S. Intend to sleep in my tent. Candle light the feature of interest these nights.

Oct. 26. Sat. 1918. Cloudy and rainy. We all prepared for inspection. I took a cold bath. Board came. Some excitement. Men called before Major Kellogg. I was recommended for Reconstruction work. Kellogg told me he was sorry to see a man of my intelligence taking such a position.[63]

After dinner I went to Paris. Got pictures, shoes for McClure and other things. Next I went to post office to send a money order to Chas. William Co. for $18.10. Collected Money order for Mardfin for $10. After supper I taught a class in Geog. Good spirit in class. Bible class not as well [43] attended as usual. After class Horton the cook expressed some views about C.O. Men. He expected them to be extraordinarily willing workers. He doubted the sincerity of some.

P.S. Our experience before Major Kellogg was one that impressed most of us. He seemed to get more out of the men than an ordinary person would.

Oct. 27. Sunday. Cloudy. Clocks turned back 1 hour. A very late breakfast because of it being Sunday. We generally eat 1 hr. late on Sunday so today it was two hours. Hinshaw got orders to leave for Phila. Horton and I accompanied him to the hostess house to find out train time. Slow train at 11 pm from Greenville. Fast train at 5+ p.m. Latter due at Phila at 11:55 a.m. Monday.

I went with Hinshaw to Paris where he took taxi for Greenville. Dinner. Sun began to shine. [44] each man could sign up so that the $2 laundry bill could be paid. The rule at Camp Jackson was 25c a week for laundry for all men. I said I'll take the money and send it to Sec'y of War. My whole am't would be $90 less $2 for laundry would be $88 to go to Sec'y of War. Charges Money order 80c, stamp for special delivery 13c. My plan is to give all the money back. Some think they will give it to Friends Relief Com. or Mennonite Committees. Many arguments pro & con.

In the afternoon I went to Paris to get some ordered goods. Also took over two pairs of shoes for Andy Miller & C. Diller. I gave a lecture on the development of civilization with special emphasis on the need of proper readjustment after each step [45] in the change. Good interest. After supper we had a French class and the Bible Study class.

Oct. 30. Wed. Rainy Morning. We got up earlier than necessary. Bugles not understood. I found out that the record of my vaccination and inoculations is lost. Trip to library and post office. I sent a long letter Adella. Also sent a box home for Moore, Enos. A big dinner. Blasting just opposite our camp to the south caused rocks to strike over tents and mess hall. After dinner I went to Paris to get shoes etc. It rained all the way. Major Carrier came and we made some wood for him to take along. In the evening Wm. Cecil & Ferdinand Hinshaw came to us from stockade. Also a new man from the school for cooks & bakers. [46] We had a French class, Steer Miller & I. Bible class well attended.

Luke 20.

Important event of day. Weston's bath while I was washing.

Oct. 31. Thurs. A nice day but a little stormy. Weather changed and became cooler. In the a.m. we built or began a latrine. About all of us took turn at pick and shovel. At noon I took in some wash of the day before. My bath towel was gone. I tried to find it. After a careful search I found that Staunton had it. Dinner. Some of the men lined up early. When the "soupe" blew Pegram faced us about and so I was one of the first men to mess.

After dinner I went to Post Office & Library. Then to Paris with "Slim." Then I went to the Hospital to [47] find Griffith & Schlabach. The former was reported improving; the latter was sent out in the morning but to the wrong place. No sooner than I had searched our lot than Schlabach was brought back.

French class after mess and then Bible Class.

While I was at the Hospital John F. Moore got a furlough and left for home to report in a week at turtle farm. Cecil and F. A. Hinshaw were sent to turtle farm today.

I had been in Post Office, Paris and Hospital in the afternoon.

Nov. 1. Fri. K.P. I got up early and helped to get breakfast. Cleaned up in Mess Hall in a.m. Wrote letters to Mrs. C.B.F. Clair M. and D.F.M. Mess Sg't asked me to mop floor [48] and clean up in front of Mess Hall. A good dinner. After eating I cleaned up inside the hall. Next I was called out to Lieut. tent to work on our Service Records. Five men went to get "shot" again. Many records for vaccination & inoculation lost. I found out I made A in the Psyc. test. My number is 4,124,743. Some very interesting remarks on service record cards. Many fellows fear they must take "shots" again and they resent it. Pay day seemed near.

After supper I went to Paris. Many soldiers shopping. When I came back Noah Beachy and I had a settlement from day before. I gave him $1 but we do not know if that settles it or not.

The Bible class was extra well attended and the spirit was good. We discussed the [49] Communion service. Many took part. Quakers vs. Mennonite view. I mentioned the different views—transubstantiation and consubstantiation. Platonic and Aquinian views of philosophy. Several men had been "shot" today.

Nov. 2. Sat. We expected inspection but it did not come: pay day the big feature. After dinner most of men got paid. I got $95. Lieut. Avery explained how we ought to start a company fund.[64] Several men joked about it. I went to Post Office and sent $95 to Baker. I paid for money order 30c. Registration 10c. regular postage 3c. all out of my pocket. Also cashed a $40 money order for Staunton. Got a $50 money order for him. He expects to send it to Baker. Later I went to Paris to get shoes etc. The main subject [50] of the day was pay. Several men worried as to what to do with their money.

After supper we built a camp-fire to keep warm. Had no Bible class but we sang some songs around the fire. Retired to a warm place in bed.

Nov. 3. Sun. Fine day but very cool. The camp fire was not quite out so we soon had a good warm place. Sam Miller built the fire. After breakfast we cleaned up. Pegram wanted tents furled. The boys objected and said it was not according to orders. Pegram acquiesced. We had Sunday school in our tent. The Temperance Lesson. Esau sells his birthright. Big dinner.

After dinner I wrote to E.A.S., J. S. Gerig, Leah, and Bernice L. Then I read in Hyde's Five Great Philosophies of Life. Frank Miller took my picture alone, with Lantz and with [51] Staunton. In the eve we had a camp fire. Bible study was well attended and some vital issues were presented. After the study we warmed up and retired.

Nov. 4. Mon. 1918. Fine day, warmer than Sunday but we had a camp fire in the morning. I read some in Hydes Five Great philosophies. Steer conducted the physical exercises. Later we made wood but broke the axe. Marvin Shore came to get arrangements made to go Phila. for Recon. work. During the morning there were several men who wanted me to send off their money to Secy Baker. I wrote a letter for Henry Beachy. Others used it as a model.

After dinner the Lieut. called me in and gave me work on service records. [52] First I was sent to Hospital to locate records of men who had been at base hospital Sevier before they were sent to Jackson. No success. After that I wrote on typewriter for fellows on furloughs all to locate records.

After supper I mailed letters for Lieut. as well as my own. At retreat I called roll etc.[65] Letters I mailed to E.A.S. Elmer. Leah. Bernice L. and J. S. Gerig. Also mailed money order to Baker for Staunton.

While in Lieut's tent after supper Sam Yoder was called in because of a letter mailed to Loucks about farm furloughs.[66] The reply caused the consternation. It was not given to Yoder.

Bible Study interesting. Newspapers look to peace. Pegram went out on a furlough and I called the roll.

[Beginning of Diary Book 3][67]

Diary from November 5, 1918.

Nov. 5. A fine day. We got up in good time and I called roll for Pegram was gone since yesterday. After breakfast we lined things up a bit. Then we took some exercise—Steer in command. The Lieut. came and called for help for a supply Lieut. About all the boys went I was asked to get a book from the Library on Military Correspondence for Avery. I got it and at the same time I took back about six books. One belonged to Staunton and it had money in it. I also got two money orders from Secy Baker one for Henry Beachy for $94 and one for Sam Miller for $93. Cashed a money order for $5 belonging to Thomas. After dinner the Lt. asked for subscriptions for new supplies for mess hall. Myself chm of com. Steer, Staunton and Noah Beachy on committee. We had some time but finally got about $34.50. We went into Lt. tent and he called in all who refused to pay up. Next we had [2] a rather long theological discussion. After that I went to Paris on a business trip. Got a Registry receipt for Staunton at the Regimental Post Office.

Horton, Steer & Staunton went to the Commissar Dept. to buy goods for mess hall. Not Successfull so Horton asked Lt. that he (Horton) and I go to Greenville on morrow. I bought a paper thru Hayes. Somehow I lost my towel today. All went well at retreat. Four K.P.s are required now. Bible class in Mess hall.

Nov. 6. 1918. Fine morning. We got up rather late and some were too late for roll call. Breakfast late because Brenneman got up late. The alarm did not go off on time. After breakfast we cleaned up and made wood. Major came before the Lieut. When Lieut came Horton and I got passes for Greenville to buy mess hall outfit. We bought $25.50 worth of goods and the transfer cost $1.75 so the bill was 27.75. We got back at one oclock. We could not [3] get much aluminum. Some fellows objected. Next came the rules. We had to tell the Lieut. that the fellows objected to company fund. We the committee spent all afternoon in Lieut's tent. Supper served on new plan.

After supper I was delegated to "watch" in orderly tent. Letters from D.S.G., Clair M. and Father. No Bible study class.

Nov. 7. Thurs. A Fine day. Moore (Enos) and Weston late for roll call. They were detailed to clean latrine. After breakfast general policing. Lieutenant came early. We got stoves and set them up in forenoon. Orders that men move out when there were seven in a tent. Some discussion about who is to move. After dinner I went to Post Office and Library. Sent a pillow away for Theophilus M. and a fountain pen for Andrew Miller. Also got 71c which the librarians found in a book which I returned for Staunton several days ago.

[4] During the day about ten boys were out on detail to help the supply officer. The Lieut. had the rest of us clean the supply tent, the bath house and latrine. He also ordered some ditching done at bathhouse and a stove set up for cook Horton now our Mess Sergeant. He told me to make a duty register and to have Hayes and Weston set as K.P.'s in turn. He asked that the detail for the supply officer be a regular order job. That all men go in turn. He said we would all be furloughed soon anyway.

I got no mail today. Bible class in the evening after orderly came back and relieved me in his tent. I type wrote a letter for Troyer to Montgomery Ward & Co. and one for myself to A. C. Moine. We retired in good spirits.

Nov. 8. Fri. Up in good time. All men out to roll call but Thomas was late. After breakfast we policed around tents. The [5] Lieut. called me in and informed me that I would be a witness at a court-martial trial of Barnes. Frank Miller & I went with Avery but there was nothing doing in the forenoon except that the judge advocate and the counsel for plaintiff and defense questioned us in a general manner. In the p.m. McCoy & Weston went with us for Barnes asked that they be at the trial as witness for the defendant. My call before the court came first after Avery. I told them, after the affirmation, of my station and rank. I was questioned regarding the roll call scene on Aug. about 29th when Barnes answered roll call by saying "I'm pissing." About three oclock Miller Weston McKay and I proceeded homeword. Later we heard that Barnes got 12 years.

I read in Hyde's "Five Great Philosophies" and finished it after supper. Also went to Paris after supper. Got some candy, pictures, and stationary. Weston preached in the mess hall. I arranged the duty roll for the morrow. Read in Bible. [6]

Nov. 9. Sat. Read in the morning. We rose on good time and prepared for inspection. A detail was made up to cut woods. I arranged the Duty roll. I helped several tent groups to get tents into shape for inspection. At nine oclock I called men out for inspection. All passed the personal inspection except Weston was told to visit barber. McClure had cleaned our bath house and he was ordered to do it over. One man was ordered to move out of our tent so as to reduce the number to six.

The company fund committee met Lt. Avery and some of "the" slackers were called in to give a reason why they did not pay. Steer and I were sent to Greenville to buy things. We left Paris on 11 oclock car. We bought 3 shirts & 2 suits underwear—crochet cotton-kerchiefs, sox, a suitcase and extra stamps—paper & envelopes, spoons, pitchers, a cap, candy, gloves etc. Got home about 2.30 p.m. with things O.K. Next after eating [7] I went to Post office with money orders as follows—one for Hampton $5, one for McKay $5. Also took books to Library and got three new ones by Tolstoi, Miller & Haekel. Supper. Later I went to Paris with pictures for Frank Miller. Bought candy $2.40, pocketbook 70c, and got some collar buttons grabs. Later I sold to Andy Miller who made money on them. Bible class in our tent. No one moved out. Pegram back from furlough.

---
[68]

Nov.10. Sunday. 1918. Fine morning. We got up late as is common on Sunday. I spent a.m. reading Millers Life of Christ. Taught S.S. Lesson—Jacob's Deception Genesis 27. Report of Hun Revolution current. I got a letter from Uncle Albert. In the p.m. I wrote to E.A.S. D.S.G. L.E.B.—a letter of consolation—and after supper to Uncle Albert.[69] Bible Class quite interesting. [8]

Nov. 11. Monday. 1918. Cloudy in a.m. I was on detail to make wood. As soon as that job was done the Lieut. called me in and gave me a job on service records. Steer & I worked there until four o'clock. Reports that peace was made current. Major and Lieut. now convinced that peace has come ere the two years were up. I went to Post Office and Library after four o'clock and to Paris after supper. Paris closed. A new man came to our group. He is reported to be a stockade man. Question now is when are we going home.

Nov. 12. Tuesday. 1918. Cold weather. In the morning I tried to help arrange the work about bath houses and latrines. Spent considerable time keeping warm in our tent. I had some typewriting to do for Lieut. and I got a letter from Ray Rick. I wrote him a long letter describing army life. Also wrote a letter to Bunting of the [9] Friends Service Committee in which I told him of my plan to got to France even though Peace had come.

After dinner I went to hunt up Mr. Griffith who was sent to hospital on Oct. 18, 1918. Report is that he is improving. I read Confessions of an Opium eater. After supper I went to Paris on business. Got three purses, candy and pictures for D. Frank Miller. Bible study on the Book of Ruth. Quite well attended and interesting.

Nov. 13. Wednesday. 1918. Cold morning. I helped clean up and get detailed men started. As soon as I thought it warm enough I got water in mess hall to wash clothes. Pegram called me for work on typewriter and I worked until noon and again in the afternoon until four o'clock on the furlough papers and insurance blanks. Steer I and Staunton helped some but could not run the machine. At four o'clock I washed my clothing. After supper I went to [10] Paris. Got some pictures for Frank Miller. Read of reported death of Crown Prince of Germany. Also article on Mennonites. Bible class. Book of Ruth Chaps III & IV. We discussed the social customs of ancient and modern times. Retired late.

Nov. 14. Thurs. 1918. Diller got up to build fire. Soon I had to get up to shut off stove for it was a rosy red up to the third joint of pipe. After breakfast I bought a paper. Report of death of Crown Prince not yet confirmed. I washed a shirt in morning. Had washed a towel, night shirt and underwear on day before. Arranged Duty Roster. Otherwise I did not work much until noon. Then I was called in to typewrite an order for the Hq. 156 D.B. accounting for every man in camp. Late for dinner. After dinner I helped clean up. A hint had come to the effect that a special inspector was due today. I helped peel Irish & sweet potatoes. Read French and [11] wrote a letter to sister Kathryn. After mess Hines and I went to Paris. Business at the photo man and shoe man. Bought candy which I sold about 3 for one cent. Bible class. I Cor. chap. I. I went to bed early for I was K.P. on the morrow.

Nov. 15. Fri. 1918. Got up early to K.P. We were very busy and at 9 a.m. I was called to orderly tent to typewrite. Got Sam Miller to substitute for me. We had much extra work on account of an Inspector whom we are awaiting. We sawed-off a pipe of the refrigerator with the meat saw. At noon Andy Miller got sick and Enos Moore took his place as a K.P. In p.m. I went to Post Office and Library. Cashed a money order for $15 for Walter Martin. Got two books from Library. Sent a card to Adella. Before supper we went to company "J" for supplies. After supper we cleaned up so that we were thru by 7:30. No Bible study. I read some in Charlotte Perkins Gilman "The Home." She is in a sense a revolutionist. She thinks woman ought not to be tied to home so closely. She gives many good ideas. [12]

Nov. 16. Sat. 1918. Reports that Development Battalion would be sent home first. Boys interested. After mess I was sent to the wood lot to see that the wood makers did a good job. I worked quite hard and we made more wood than usual. After we finished I shaved and bathed. Then I read a little before dinner. After dinner I went to Paris on business. I did not get Miller's picture, but I got some candy and a Literary Digest. The dealer gave me 40 pieces of candy which I missed in a box the time I bought candy of him before. Also got pillow material and sold the bulk for $3.00. I patched my trousers.

I read some in the Digest and in The Home. At supper "Hines" poured his soup on his lap. Prim also tried the same stunt. We spent the evening in tents for it was raining. The boys sang. I read. About seven o'clock the Lieut. Avery came and told us we would be sent home in time or three weeks. We "Ohio" boys planned a reunion of Ohio C.O.'s to be held near Orrville. After discussing the question a while, [13] Steer went home and we retired.

Nov. 17. Sun. 1918. It rained Saturday night so that it was wet Sunday. We had good light and heat so we did not mind the rain. We had Sunday school in the morning. I read some and wrote some letters. In the afternoon I wrote letters and read again in "The Home" by Perkins. I wrote to E.A.S. Elmer, Clair & Mr. Cyrus B. Felzer. Not much doing in camp. In the evening we had a discussion in our tent on Social Problems. Should a man hate his rival in Love? Steer and I said no. Love should be unconquered. After a rather long discussion we held Bible Study. Corinthians I Chap 2-4. In the Kitchen Loewen and Staunton K.P.'d until noon. Loewen got sick and Staunton got a substitute. Hines tried to tell how hard he could work. Moore said he could not understand so Hines explained. He is some windy. "Have you ever worked on the railroad?" was the questions of all questions for a day or two. Should K.P.s go on at noon or [14] in morning? Can a man stand it to work all day? Horton laughs at the idea of getting tired of work in one day.

Nov. 15. Mon. 1918. A fine sunrise. I was on the wood lot until called in by the Lieut. to do typewriting. I made several copies of orders regarding Henry B. Thomas et al. They were arrested as draft evaders and now the extra charge is taken out of their wages. I wrote a typewritten letter to E.A. and one to the Chas. Williams Stores. The latter was in regard to a delayed order. Next I went to Paris to get pictures for Miller (D.F.) I got $9.00 worth. Also paid a debt of 35c which I owed at the Carolina news store. We could not make the change before. I got Mardfins' trousers but had to wait on them. He did not like the work. Also got a box of peanut candy for $1.10 and a box of chocolate candy at the canteen for $1.20. Dinner. After dinner I cleaned up my suitcase in good shape and had Horton put on my initials. Gave him a 5c piece of candy to do it. He would take no pay. I sewed my [15] sox and shoes. The weather was quite cool. About 4:30 p.m. the workmen blew a stump out our lot through two wire fences. Rather dangerous.

An excellent supper. After supper we had a discussion in our tent on the tricks of a school boy etc. We retired late and Lantz and Brunk had a "tussel." Brunk took after Lantz and a shirt tail parade followed.

Report that Weston's discharge had come. I washed some clothing in the afternoon but I did not take a bath. Pretty cold for bathing. No Bible Meeting in the evening.

Nov. 19. Tuesday. 1918. A very fine morning. We made wood (our tent group) for the cooks and ourselves. Others make remarks about our wood-pile. I read the prophecy of Isaiah in part. The Lieut called me to do some typewriting. I answered several Memos and made copies of some correspondence regarding "Thomas" et. al.—men who as draft evaders made themselves liable to the gov't. I concluded that it was very difficult to pay anything to Uncle Sam in any other form [16] than ordinary taxes.[70] Pegram went over to Hospital to see Griffith but he was unsuccessful.

My tooth began to ache so that I was anxious to lay off but I did typewriting for the morning. In the afternoon I went to the Hospital to see how soon Griffith would be back in the company. I got a pass to Ward 15 and there I met Bowser—a Mahoning Co.? man. He seemed very anxious to see me and we located Griffith to whom I gave three letters. He asked me about a package. I think he will be back soon for he was not transferred to Ward 26. Next Bowser took me to the Operative Room where I met Graber (Ed) and a Diller from Bluffton. These three boys—Graber, Diller & Bowser—seem to be lonesome and exceedingly anxious to go home. My idea is that these boys should be visited by some-one.

In the forenoon I got two letters—one from D. S. Gerig and the second from the Friends Service Committee. Gerig was interested in knowing my exact address so he could write me on a kind of business.—C.O. men in the [17] Army. The Friends wrote that they still expect me to go but have no definite information on my case. My toothache continued and so I spent the evening lying near the stove warming my head. Weston told of his Love affairs. Several men came into our tent to listen to the conversation. Finally all retired but myself. I did not sleep all night on account of the tooth. I was on the ground with my blankets so as to keep my head warm.

Nov. 20. Wednesday. 1918. Got out early for I had not slept all night. Spent some time after breakfast in Lieut. tent on correspondence and Daily Roster. The latter was lost but I planned the day's work. Then I went to my tent with a sore jaw. The fellows got tent floors in this manner. A Capt. asked Levi Schlabach about our conditions. When told that we had no floors he saw that we got them. I warmed up my jaw from about nine oclock a.m. to 9 p.m. then I tried to sleep and by the next morning I felt pretty good. Letters from Mr. & Mrs. N.W.S. and Miss E.A.S. Heard that Abrm. Zook was home on furlough and that he was in Trade Test Dept. [18]

Nov. 21. Thursday. I felt better after the toothache experience. but did not feel like doing much work. The fellows wanted me to go to Paris and to Library but I went only to the latter place and that in the evening. I did some work for the Lieut. in the Orderly tent. In the evening Mr. Bowser from North Lima called on me as I was alone in the orderly tent. We discussed army life as it concerns a C.O. He seemed to feel that the Mennonite Relief Committee did not meet the issue.[71] I had been writing a letter to D.S.G. when he came and I finished it when he left. Slept well but got up tired next morning.

Nov. 22. Friday. Spent big part of day in office. R. P. Weston discharged and I did part of office work for that. Also wrote letters for Lieut. to men who were draft evaders. After supper Steer, Horton & I were in orderly [19] tent. Several orders came. I signed up for one & Steer for one. One of the men who brought the order said all C.O. men should be shot at sunrise. He never suspected that we were C.O. men—Steer & I. We talked things over. Horton told of his first impression of a C.O. when I and three others helped our cooks to start housekeeping in their tent. A ridiculous letter came for our Lieut. It was from a Mennonite who wanted to hire Eli Yoder.

I wrote six letters to send money to Secy of War for the Amish boys.

Nov. 23. Saturday. 1918. Cool damp & Cloudy. After breakfast I got out the detail men to saw wood etc. A special detail was planned to go to the Brigade Infirmary. It was made up of Brunk, Diller, Beachy, Hayes & Hockett. This was an experiment in our group. What are these men to do? Where are they going? Everybody asked. [20] I did not know. All I had been told to do was to arrange the detail. This caused a suspense until noon when the boys came back and said they had not worked. In a sense the mystery was not cleared even during the day. During the morning I worked in the orderly tent. The most interesting event of the day was the "Battle Royal" between Majors Carrier & Horton, regarding the starving C.O. men.

Someone complained about our board, I think it was Mangrin our orderly, or the Lieut. or Carrier. Major Carrier informed Major Mallon who informed Major Horton. The latter resented the roundabout manner of Maj. Carrier and called in Lieut. Avery. Soon Major Horton came to the orderly tent and had it with Major Carrier. Result. Horton our mess sergeant disgusted in trying to please everybody. C.O. men get extra big feeds. Many open belts about mealtime.

[21] Lt. Avery & Corporal Mangrin make out pay roll—work nearly all day. I had a haircut in p.m. De Rienzo came to us. He was not satisfactory to his boss at Ritter S.C. The "boss" seemed to try to impose on him. In p.m. Lantz and Diller imitate a dog fight and all C.O.s came out to see the fight. Several were disappointed.

While at supper Lt. Avery asked me to get out morning report so he could sign it on Sat. evening. Hines asked to go to Paris but was refused. I was given the right and made a large assortment of purchases.

I washed in the morning and clothes were dry by night. During the day the hopes for an early discharge were decreased. Reports were that we would be transferred first when the Company "I" was moved. [22][72]

Nov. 24. Sunday. 1918. I went on as a K.P. for the whole day. My associates were Prim, Hines & Loewen. Prim soon gave out and Hockett took his place. We had a big breakfast, a big dinner & a big supper. Things went nicely except at noon Acting mess sergeant Horton gave Hayes a severe "calling" for acting the hog at the table. After dinner Eggart Bowser & Gideon Amstutz came to see me. I went out with them for a hike. We walked out "past" the hospital farm. I got a ball of cotton in a field but I asked the "boss" for it. We talked over the C.O. proposition and the part played by Mennonite Relief Committee.

After supper the K.P.'s finished by five minutes after six. Record time. We had Sunday school and had an interesting discussion of the subject. How to win a brother. I wrote letters to Jesse Roth & Mrs. A. D. Krabill in the a.m. and one to E.A.S. in the eve. Retired. [23]

Nov. 25. Monday. 1918. I arranged to send out detail to Brigade Infirmary and to get the wood cutters etc. to work. Then I helped the Lieut. with the pay roll. We fixed it up and had the fellows sign it before noon.

After dinner the Lieut. called me and said the payroll was not good enough to hand in so we copied and corrected it. By four o'clock we had it complete. I then shaved and took a bath etc. After supper Henry Mangrin the orderly wanted some medicine from

Paris and so I got it for him. Also got other things for the fellows. I got a letter from father and one from Friends Service Committee. The latter asks if men who applied for Reconstruction work are still ready to go. From Paris I sent five Thanksgiving cards to E.A.S., R.R.S., Jennie, D.F. & Melvin R. G. When I got back we had a meeting of the Ohio boys to arrange for a reunion. Election of officers resulted [24] as follows. J.C.M. pres. Alvin M. Brenneman v.Pres. Enos Moore Secy. Retired in good time.

Nov. 26. Tuesday. 1918. Breakfast late because the cooks had hard luck. After I arranged the detailed groups the Lt. called me in to do the typewriting. During the forenoon I read Emerson's Essays on Self Reliance, Love, and Friendship. I was struck by Emersons individuality. Also read "The Heart of a Rose," and some poetry. After dinner I wrote a Roster of C.O. men for the Lt. on the typewriter. The Major came and I went to my tent. Wrote letters to Cressman and Clair Moine. The day was cloudy and cool but it rained very little. In the evening I went to Paris to take four pairs of shoes to be repaired. Theo. Miller went along and bought a sheep lined coat for $10. Later he sold it to Enos E. Moore. I got a letter from D.S.G. E. E. Miller and John Fisher regarding the Mennonite Relief Work.

Nov. 27. Wednesday. A nice day. We aired out blankets. I did the morning typewriting and then returned to my tent. Later I went to the Mess Hall to write my reply to the letter from D.S. [25] E.E.M. & J.F. which came the evening before. I got another letter from D.S.G. in the eve. As I see it the Relief Com. is not doing much and some are not satisfied.[73] Mr. Bowser came to our tent in the evening and I talked it over a little with him. Why should the Mennonite Church not get into this work? In the afternoon I went to the library and Post Office. I sent a cotton ball to E.A.S. and my letter to D.S.G. on the Recon. plan. I brought back several books for the C.O. men. In the eve. Levi Schlabach, Theo Miller and I went to Paris. They each bought a sheep coat for $10. I got the shoes which I had repaired. When I returned Lantz asked me "whom do you know at Col. Grove." He had a letter from E.A.S. from there. I also had a letter from D.S.G. The boys all teased me about my letter. Brunk feared I could not sleep & what not.

Bible study was late because of my talk with Mr. Eggart Bowser, Med. Det. B.H. Retired late but in good spirits. D.S.G.'s letter made me meditate. [26]

Nov. 28. Thanksgiving Morn. Rain, rain, rain. We got up late. Had no roll call but I had to typewrite the report for the Lt. when the other boys went to breakfast. After breakfast I went to the tent and read in Petrarchs Sonnets, and Isaiah. Also wrote some letters. During the day I wrote to Elmer, Joseph Giona, Lester Hostetler, Jesse N. Smucker and Ray Eschleman. A big dinner. Officers ate first. We had turkey, dressing, potatoes, celery, apples, peaches, cranberry sauce, giblet gravy, olives, bread, cake, jello, pumpkin pie, deviled eggs, nuts, "cigars and cigarettes." The major, lieut. & orderly and their wives ate for a long time and then took a supply along to the orderly tent. After we had finished the Lt. seemed to want to make a clean sweep of the apples, cake, cigars etc. but Horton failed his attack by hiding a good part of the goods.

I spent the p.m. writing letters. Supper after retreat. Just a cold lunch. After supper I mailed four letters and had one to mail the next day. A report from the Lt. indicates that we move across [27] the Railroad next Monday. Gill the orderly seems to think that Reconstruction men will be furloughed next week. I doubt if either of these reports is true. The weather has been rainy. Some of the boys seem a bit tired of camp life.

Bible study quite interesting. Corinthians 8 and the origins of Thanksgiving.

Nov. 29. Friday. 1918. A fine day. I helped to cut wood almost until noon. Pegram's tent caught fire and there was some excitement. Lt. ordered that fires should be left to go out during day. I shaved and bathed in cold water in p.m. Washed clothes in a.m. I read in Petrachs sonnets. I got a letter from E.A.S. and one from Bernice Lehman. The latter reports that films of swaps taken at Columbus Grove were not good. I wrote to E.A.S. Also to French Embassy and Albert Teachers Agency. Asked the Embassy if passport vise would be granted. Asked Teaching Agency if positions are open. After supper I was Paris. Got two boxes of [28] candy etc. etc.

Made C.O. roster of Buckeye boys. Cooks and Mess Sgt. report that Thanksgiving Dinner Cost $51.19. No Bible Study.

Nov. 30. Sat. Cloudy. After breakfast I got up a detail of volunteers to cut wood. We filled the box to the capacity. About eight oclock 18 men were detailed to go to the corral to do some work. Lt. Avery asked the fellows to let fires go out. When the 18 men came back for dinner they were not very well pleased with the treatment which they had rec'd. In the afternoon we were put to work replacing the Lt. tent by a new brown one. Just as we were ready to eat dinner the Lt. said we were to unload a wagon. It had about 20 bunks and four tents on it. This goods we placed in the supply tent after dinner. The Lt. told me how to make out reports in the morning because he was not going to be there. Kelly Murphy was assigned to our company in the afternoon. I wrote some forms to send money to Sec'y Baker. Also [29] a list of Buckeye boys with addresses. In the eve I went to Paris. Bible study.

Dec. 1. Sunday. Cloudy. I made out the morning reports. To my surprise I found that the 18 men at Whitehall were reported "on duty" here since Nov. 27. Where are they is a question we cannot answer. Sunday school in our tent. I read in Isaiah and in Genesis. Lesson. Joseph sold to Egypt. After dinner I wrote to N.W.S., Elmer, J. E. Harley & Ben. It sleeted in p.m. Bible study in evening. Cold night.

Dec. 2. Monday. A nice day. Some of boys objected to the new plan of sending them to work at Headquarters. There was considerable trouble in camp and I was almost discouraged because of the situation. I was busy for a part of time on wood detail and later on office work. We had Bible Study in evening. I had been to Paris with four pairs of shoes but the cobbler would fix none now. I came back with but three pairs of shoes so I had to go back [30] to Paris. I took films along for Hampton. He bought them from Sergeant Dooley and we are getting pictures from him. Dooley charged 10c a picture. We hope to get them cheaper. I bought oranges and apples and candy. Retired early. Cold night.

Dec. 3. Tuesday. Cold morning. I worked on wood detail until 10 a.m. then policed a little. The rest of day I spent in orderly office writing on machine. Report current that C.O. men are to be sent home soon.

Considerable agitation over new move to work men. Whitehall boys came to us. Had been delayed on acct of boss who was gone for a week when order came. The idea of sending a detail to Headquarters does not appeal to some men. The whole attitude in camp is one of slight depression on account of this work. The Lt. and Major seem to have but one alternative work or stockade.

Dec. 4. Wednesday. Nice weather. We began to eat in details of 36. The whole [31] group is divided into thirds and one third has to wait each meal.

I went out on wood detail but soon I was called back to typewrite an order for the Lt. One was an endorsement about Julius Huntley. Another was a Memo. to Hq. regarding conditions here. Pegram asked me to write a Roster of C.O. men for postmaster. Lt. Pegram and I discussed theology until Major came. He told how he put Whitehall boys to work. I left the Lt. tent when Lt. and Major began to play checkers.

From then until noon I loafed most of the time. I had some clothing to wash after dinner. Before dinner I gave out the mail and almost made a mistake. When I got to tent two I said "Wehr Lebt do" and to my surprise Lt. Avery was there all by himself.[74]

After dinner I helped carry tent floors for the new boys. Next I went on detail for Lt. at supply house. We hauled coal, two loads. I got my first impression of the detail work. [32] The Whitehall boys seemed rather worried because we worked so much. When I came back from detail work I helped stretch up a new tent for cooks. Next I got my $30 pay from Lt. Next we moved Brenneman to cooks tent. After supper I went to Paris. Walter Martin Loewen, & Hines were along. After we returned I sold my oranges candy etc. Also got pictures for Hampton.

Dec. 5. Thurs. The most important event of day was a report from Wash. D.C. that C.O. men be discharged. Maj. Carrier came over in the morning and was very anxious to see Lt. Avery who was over at Hq. The Maj. told Horton something but we knew not what. At noon I asked Horton about dishes. He told me some men would soon leave. After dinner Major Carrier came with the discharge orders. Lt. Avery asked me to write memo to Personnel office reporting men for discharge. Late that evening a return report came calling for all North Carolina men to report for Physical Exam. [33] We began to work on discharge papers.

Dec. 6. Fri. Discharge work all day. There were so many forms to get out that we got busy early in the morning. Steer and I with some help from Lassiter did most of the office work. Reports current that all men will be sent to within 350 miles from home for discharge. Buckeye boys may be sent to Camp Taylor. I was very tired by night.

Dec. 7. Sat. Steer and I got busy early and worked until 2 p.m. when the boys left for trains. They felt happy as larks. Pegram reported that they had a little trouble at Quartermaster Dept. but on the whole all went well.

Griffith (a negro) returned from the hospital Fri. eve. Sat. eve he refused to stand at attention. Sat. p.m. he preached to us almost under order of Lt. Avery. Some sermon in Mess Hall. After the sermon Lt. Avery left me in charge of orderly tent. I cleared away the old papers and arranged matters. Also [34] wrote two letters—to E.A.M. & E.J.M. Next Lt. Avery asked me to arrange paper to prefer charges against the four or six draft evaders. Steere and I worked at it after supper but it is a difficult task for the laws conflict.[75] Retired late and tired.

Dec. 8. Sun. 1918. A fine day. In a.m. I took a cold bath & shaved. Also taught S.S. Griffin the negro preacher attended S.S. and gave us a few amens but no disturbance. Lt Avery & Major Carrier were present at noon. After dinner I decided to write. I wrote to E.A.S. half the letter then Steer and I took a long hike to the Mts. Scenery very beautiful. After supper I finished my letter to E.A.S. and wrote a card to Mrs. D.S.S. in reply to a letter of Dec 7. Bible study quite intersting. Report to discharge Ohio boys. Great news.

Dec. 9. Mon. 1918. A very busy day on discharge work. Steer and I worked practically all day in Lieut. office. Adams and Hobson on discharge list. I got a letter from father and one from [35] Friends Service Committee. Former told of Uncle Albert on way to Iowa. Latter told of my "open way" to France. Pa also told that Clara & Adella had Flu in slight form.

Everyone worked up over reports but we were not sure just when we were to leave and no doubt we must go via Camp Taylor.[76]

Dec. 10. Tues. Steer & I worked all forenoon in office. Very much work but no sure evidence of our going out soon. Letter from Clair & and a card from D.F.[77] Read some in Veblen's theory of leisure class. Di Rienzo, Jordan & McClure may be sent out soon; their records are lost but we made temporary ones in place of the originals. Outlook for early departure not very good. Boys who worked at Hq. report a good day's work.

Dec. 11. Wed. Spent most of day in Orderly tent on records of Hobson & Adams who left at noon. Also worked on records of Di Rienzo, Jordan, McClure, Daniel, Cooper & Guthrie. All these men are to leave tomorrow. Ohio boys seem to be delayed very much. A report that we shall [36] go out soon because the C.O. detachment is to move to Camp Jackson Saturday. Major Carrier seems to think we may be held a while. Especially does he wish to keep the group intact. Lt. Avery prefers to get rid of all men as soon as they are available. Service records of several men came these last few days. Bible meeting on 1 Corinthians 15. Pretty well attended. No news for Buckeye boys.

Dec. 12. Thurs. Work in office again. Six men left today—Di Reinzo, McClure, Jordan, Guthrie, Daniel, & Cooper. William Shore, Thomas and Candle billed to leave tomorrow. They were draft evaders and their charges were set aside. Service records of Ohio boys came back from Personnel office in a.m. Thomas left at noon and had no idea when he would go home. Tonight he is almost certain he will leave tomorrow. After supper Steer & I were to Paris. Bible study 1 Corinthians Chap 16. A late report that Mardfin & Staunton should be ready to go at any time. [37]

Dec. 13. Friday. 1918. Rainy morning. When detail was to be sent out few men reported. Corp. Mangrin made remarks as to how he would make the men go. He himself is possibly the laziest man in the company. It does not look right for the C.O. men to be sent to work when it is so wet. But such is the life of a C.O.

Major Carrier & his orderly came to play checkers. What does Carrier do anyway? Nothing! seems to be the answer from C.O. men and Lt. Avery. Our chances to get out today are nil. here's hoping it will not be long. A letter from Camp Wadsworth Spartanburg S.C. reports that the Board of Inquiry was there and here we have Monroe Schlabach who ought to be interviewed and he is not reposted there. Such is army life. Today Candle, Shore and Thomas are to leave for home. That will make a total of 26 men discharged inc. Weston who went out on a disability discharge.

Dec. 14. Sat. Rainy day but the detail of C.O.'s went to Hq. anyway. I spent all day in orderly tent. Orders came for Staunton and Mardfin to go to Camps Dix & Devers. Lt. worked on our service records for [38] orders came whereby we are to go to Camp Taylor Ky. Steer & I spent the eve writing transfers to Camp Taylor. I had written the charges against McKay and they together with records for Mardfin & Staunton went in before 5:30 p.m. Hopes to get out soon good. Trip to Paris for Steer & I.

Dec. 15. Sun. 1918. Griffin preached in the forenoon. Some would not stay but I did. I think the Dr. heard him and he may get a disability discharge thru it. Staunton and Mardfin left for the train at 11:50. Got thru O.K. Lt. asked me to get report of goods turned in by men of Ohio early tomorrow. Cloudy day. No news as to where we should depart. Several of the boys took a long hike in the afternoon up to the mountains. We had Sunday school in the evening. Letters J.B.C. E.A.S.

Dec. 16. Monday. Rain, rain, rain. The Lt. had some of us to check up, and clean up the surplus mess kits. Major Carrier and his orderly came. Several reports that we would not go or that we would go [39] during the next week. No news except reports that we are to leave on the 23rd. The outlook was not good for a Xmas Dinner at home. A letter from Orie B. and one from D.G.G. Orie sailed at 10 a.m. Dec. 14. D.S. still interested in Relief Work. We had meeting in the eve. II Cor. 2. Griffith was present and took part. The theme was—sorrow or anguish vs. love as a means of salvation. I had a haircut by Steer. This day was a rather gloomy one. We all looked for news. Horton and Cavanaugh our cooks left. It seems everyone goes but the Buckeyes. I wrote to Albert Teachers Agency turning down the job offered at Marquette Mich for $1500. Also wrote to B.C. and Elmer.

Dec. 17. 1918. Cloudy in a.m. A detail of men went to police around Headquarters. I worked in the Lieutenants tent. We did the regular work and turned in 54 blankets and thirty bed-sacks at quartermasters. Avery sent me to get receipts. The officer laughed at me when I saluted. He thought I had just given up the uniform never thinking that [40] I never had one. No receipt was given but he said he would send one. Returning I got two books at the Library. Sent post cards to E.A. & Jennie. In the afternoon I made an inventory of our stock on hand preparatory to sending it to quartermaster. Everyone "downcast" because no news came for us to depart. I tried to laugh at our predicament. Wrote a letter to E.A.S. Had an interesting Bible Study class. I1 Corinthians 3. Also made a package for Hampton.

Dec. 18. Fine day. Did office work, then got goods ready for quartermaster. Some was wet from washing yesterday. I tried to dry it at our stoves. No news. Major came to play checkers. This is a daily occurrence. After dinner we took six barracks bags of goods to quartermaster. All O.K. except one belt missing. Avery threw his into the "bargain." McKay had to leave his shoes there because one other pair did not match. I went to Sub. depot Q.M. Capt. Kliber with the invoice tent. Next I went to [41] post office with intent to locate letter sent to Scy Baker. Had another inquiry made.

I rec'd a card from Library reporting a book due. I could not find it so Steer & I went to look into the matter after supper. We met Horton at Cooks & Bakers school. He informed us that he turned the book in that afternoon. He and Cavanaugh had taken it along. All O.K. Horton said they were to leave tomorrow. Steer & I went to Paris. Later we had Bible Study. Most of discussion was on hypnotism, sorcery, spiritualism, etc.

I had a letter from E.A.S. A report came to the effect that Harvey Hinshaw, Hurley and Marvin Shore had been recalled to C.O. Det. from Phila. Corp. Mangrin left for home.

Dec. 19. A cold day but very clear. I worked in office and on wood detail. Checked up on goods. Everyone wondered about orders. No news except rumors. I began to feel that we would be held here a long time. Read in Ethics. Not very busy. In the evening I wrote to Cressman and home. Bible study very interesting. [42]

Dec. 20. Routine of office work and wood detail in morning. No news until after supper when message came to leave Monday Dec. 23. 7:30 a.m. Before supper I had written Di Rienzo about some charges against him due to his being recalled from Ritter. Camp was all joy at our going. Shall we get home by Xmas? I fear no. Trip to Paris. Large pictures for $1.25 with Det. plainly visible. I ordered 13 of them. Bible study. II Cor. Chap. 5. A new atmosphere. We had all become downcast because of the long delay.

Dec. 21. 1918. Rain, rain, rain, No detail so every one was at home. I worked on records in forenoon. Also tried to arrange matters regarding mess kits etc. for our trip. Afternoon Steer & I went to Greenville to get some things. Got back in time for supper. I got a new pen with money $2.10 given me by the boys who are going home. Once before they gave me $3.25. After supper I had a long chat with postmaster. Then I asked all who are to leave into mess hall. We sold mitt & ball for 75c. Decided to give our mess outfit to Y.W.C.A. of Greenville S.C. [43] Also decided to give one pitcher to postmaster. A few men want souvenirs from the outfit. We also planned about "demeanor" on the way to Camp Taylor. All went well. All retired with light hearts except Monroe Schlabach is disappointed because he is not going home.[78] No Bible study.

[End Book Three][79]

Dec. 22. Sunday. Rainy in a.m. We prepared to leave. Emptied our bedsacks. No S.S.in morning. After dinner Steer, Enos Wengerd and I went out to rifle range. Next I went to Hospital with Bowser and Amstutz to see Graber. I found him in office. After that I went to Paris with Moore & Enos Wengerd to get oranges and pictures. Could not get the latter. We had Sunday school in the evening, Bowser, Diller (Elmer) and Amstutz were present. Retired late on poor bunks because we had no straw. During the day I wrote several memorandums. Also letters to Cressman & D.S.G.

Dec. 23. Monday. Arose at four and worked in office. At 7:00 a.m. we went to mustering office. Waited until noon then went back to the C.O. Detachment for Dinner. After dinner we were to report again at mustering office. [2] In the meantime we got our pictures of the camp. Nofzinger got a telegram reporting death of sister-in-law. He sent a return message and I sent one to E.A. at Camp Taylor. We reported in good time at mustering office and left Sevier at 2:30 bound for Taylor. All were in one car which was a tourist pullman for 47 people. Several carloads were disappointed but luck was in our favor.

Soon after we got started we got two loaves of bread for every three men. We did not move very fast and the trip is long since we are going thru Atlanta.

When seven o'clock came we all retired. Steer and I slept in the lower berth. Enos Moore slept above. We had a good night's sleep.

Dec. 24. Morning found us near Rome GA still raining. By noon [3] —about 11:30—we were at the Chattanooga station. There we paraded for about 20 minutes then we got some coffee if we wanted it—and boarded our car. The Red Cross woman gave us some cards but she wanted no money. We—Moore and I gave her 50c as a donation. I wrote one to E.A.S. The scenery is beautiful. We have seen Lookout Mountain.

Our parade was quite an affair. We took it all calmly and got along nicely. Left Chattanooga at 1:05 p.m. Soon Major Ward came into our car and called for all "soldiers" to assemble. He told about keeping the uniforms and wearing the chevrons. We were not considered soldiers. Are we in the army. I guess not. Beautiful scenery for 75 miles along a ridge. We had no dinner but ate some of our extra bread. Moore, Steer & I ate one loaf. At Oakdale Tenn. we ate supper—ham—tomatoes & bread. Reports that we are to arrive tonight at 10 p.m. A good nights sleep. Lantz & I slept in the upper berth we got thru night. [4]

Dec. 25. 1918. Arrived in camp at about 4 oclock but did not get off train until nine oclock. Then we went to Personnel Office. After roaming about we finally arrived at the Utilities Division at a Receiving Station. There I met E.A. We were given a med. Inspection and sent back for mess at about 11 o'clock. After mess we were again taken out to find a place. We located and had a little trouble getting a place for our trunks. We were "bawled out" some during the day but we were accustomed to it.[80] Finally all was settled nicely. We did not go for mess at noon and at night we got no food but we were not especially hungry. Things look well but we hope to get out soon for we want to go home. I wrote a letter to Adella. [5]

Dec. 26. 1918. A cold day with snow. We got breakfast and went back to barrack. We did the cleaning up and firing etc. The Lt. took four of us on a detail to get toilet paper. At noon the mess sergeant ordered us to wait until all soldiers were served. It seemed humiliating but we just went back after all others and got our food. The soldiers were silent except to discuss matters. We decided to go back for supper. After dinner we got an extra blanket apiece. I took a bath and shaved. While at it a man discussed our stand with me. I explained. He was sympathetic. At supper we waited until last. Some of the soldiers sympathized with us again. Abrm Zook and E.A. called in the p.m. and again at night E.A. came. We had a long visit. He gave me a box of candy. Several of us went for supper and though there was a large crowd we got well fed finally. After supper Emanuel called and brought some other fellows with him. He went back late and I retired. [6]

Dec. 27. 1918. I got up early and began to write a letter to J. S. Gerig. Some of us went out for breakfast. After mess the C.O. men were called out and taken to the C.O. of 3d regiment. He asked someone to come in. I went in and he asked me why I had no uniform. I explained. Then he asked about pay. Again I explained. He dismissed me and we all went back. They told us to stay around here. Steer & I swept our room. Then I wrote three letters, one to J. S. Gerig, one to S. E. Allgyer, and one to D. D. Miller. Ten boys were called out to work on a detail. That caused a little worry but we hope for the best. The attitude of the boys here around us is very good. I did not go to dinner but some of the others did. We generally plan to have a delegation, go in a meal, to witness that we are not afraid. In the p.m. all the boys seemed very much discouraged. We were called out and about one half of the group were named to go for physical exam. Report that our discharge is to be dated Jan first. 1919. Will we get home sooner? Very cloudy day.

In the eve E.A. & several C.O. men came to see us. Adam Mumaw was one of them. E.A. & I discussed affairs a little both in army and [7] out. We decided that the morals of an army man are not very good. What will be the effect of camp life on the civil life of the future. Retired late.

Dec. 28. 1918. About 3:40 a.m. two fellows came from Louisville drunk. Some stir ere they were settled. We got up rather late and went to breakfast. This was to be the last meal with the fourth Co. Things went pretty good lately. No yelling. Before noon we were taken to the orderly Room barrack. There we were roll called by our medical slips. All C.O. men got thru O.K. but only a few signed papers. Dinner at home in barrack for us for we felt our time was too short to go to fourth Co for there we had to wait until last. After dinner we again went to 3d. Co. Lt.—Lectured to us about discipline and records. He said we were due at 9 a.m. Sunday at the same place. Also Monday at 8 a.m. for physical exam. We went home and a transfer was made whereby are landed at the 3d Co. Hq. barracks. Seven C.O. men had been detailed ere we returned from the afternoon detail. After we settled at 3d Co. we were called out for retreat. Next came supper after which we were practically all listed for [8] K.P. work on the morrow. Steer and I went to see the first Sgt. as regards the time and also as regards the detail of the morrow. The fear that we would be detained by the transfer of the p.m. cast a slight shadow on our hopes.

Dec. 29. 1918. Went on K.P in 3d Co. We fed many men and got along nicely. Of course it was Sunday work but as long as I eat on

Sunday I suppose I ought to work. Several C.O. boys called on us among them Adam Mumaw. I got off in the p.m. and E.A. and I walked a long way over camp. The top sargent got me to sign transportation in the a.m. and another sargent got me to sign the pay roll after supper. Three of our men not on pay roll. We were asked to K.P. again Monday. We did not like to take a regular job but we felt ready to do our part. Several of the cooks, the mess sergeant and the top sergeant all wanted us to do it.

We were billed to have a Medical Exam in the forenoon tomorrow. Finally it was arranged that we were to K.P. a part of Monday. Emanual came over in the eve and we had a chat till time to go to bed. He brought several pictures with him [9] & was especially interested in one or two pictures of Josephine Lehman. She looks like Stella Detweiler if these were good photos. The whole attitude of the boys is rather strange—anxious to get home. Every transfer has made it hard for us until we get accustomed to the new place and its workings. Men who are over us do not understand. I am disappointed because of not getting out in time for the Elida Conference. Then too I do not like to go thru this breaking in again.

Dec. 30. Mon. On K.P. until 8 a.m. then we were examined. We wore our overcoats for the exam. Mine marked me as a C.O. and several of the men asked me about it.[81] I passed easily and never had any trouble. We passed thru in the order which we got ready. I could have been first but I left a soldier ahead. Back on the K.P. job at 10. The question arose as to K.P. work every day. It was finally decided that we get off tomorrow. Enos Moore talked to the Cook & Mess sergeant. The questioned him as regards his religion and the idea of not accepting pay. They bragged on our K.P. work. Some of our fellows helped to cook. Our whole idea was to try to get along for a few days for we expected to go home [10] very soon. When first we knew that our Papers were being made up we found out that our discharge papers were to be white like the regular soldiers. Why I do not know! Our order from Wash D.C. seems to be plain and clear that we are not to get those. We signed the transportation slips and pay roll on Sunday. Today we had the examination. Tomorrow we expect to sign the discharges and Wednesday we expect to leave. While we were in the mess hall the Lt. came. He asked about our clothes. I explained that we were C.O. men. Then the Capt. came. He told the cook that several hundred men would leave in the next few days. It began to rain toward evening. We finished up early and I went home. In my barrack I found E.A. and Dan Hostetler. E.A. brought me some mail from Mrs. Garnett who offers me a sweater. Also a letter from father, one from Lester Hostetler on Reconstruction Work and one from the Service Committee telling me [11] that I could probably sail Feb. first if I got to Phila about Jan. fifteenth.

E.A. Dan Host. and the rest of us had a good visit after which they went back and we retired. All the men in our barrack left today except the ones in our room.

Everyone is very anxious to go home. Each day makes us more anxious of course I have given up attending the Elida Conference for I shall get home too late even if we leave here Wednesday. Tomorrow (Tuesday) I expect to wash.

Dec. 31. I was off duty most of the day for I had K.P.'d twice in succession. We signed up a few papers etc. In the evening E.A. came to see us. He almost stayed with us but he preferred to go home and get some towels for Steer & I . Rain. Last night of year.

[1919]

Jan 1. Rain. All morning we stood in line carrying in blankets, mess kits etc. And getting money, ticket etc. [12] By one oclock we the Lousiville & Nashville men of whom I was one were to leave. About 11:30 they took us out first for a sandwich then to car. Three trolleys took us to Broadway station where we got discharges. At one twenty five we left for Cinci. Changed there at about 6 p.m. Columbus at 9 p.m. and got to *Jan.* 2 Orrville at 2:40 a.m. called for phone but found none. At three oclock I walked to Noahs. Called home and told them not to come after me so soon as I indicated in telegram from Col. Elida conference postponed.[82] I stayed at Noahs and D. S. Schrocks until noon except I went to Orrville with D.S.

Got home about 4 o'clock, worked on chores. Father came home from Canton funeral of Mary Graber. Ma and Jennie to funeral of Ida Steiner. Wrote letters in eve to Cressman, Azarroga, Service Committee, E.A. & Nofzinger. Very tired so I retired. Elmer went to Moine's. a dramatic club meeting.

Appendix

Editorial Method

As noted earlier, diaries present unique challenges for a textual editor. The diary is by its nature a private document. So the diarist may use abbreviations, symbols, and self-manufactured forms of punctuation. Because these may be confusing to later readers, the diary almost begs for standardization.

Yet to read this edition's diaries as historical texts requires that they be reconstructed as closely as possible to the original manuscripts. For the most part, then, I have resisted the urge to standardize. Misspellings, grammatical errors, abbreviations, and inconsistencies of style have been retained.

The editorial methods explained below are used for all four of this volume's texts because the texts each conform to the diary's conventions, and they are each written by men with similar pasts and experiences in Great War military camps. Any divergent editorial methods would render the texts too confusing—or far too different from the original manuscript—to be appreciated. When a diary calls for some alteration of practices outlined below, I report such in the "Text" section of that chapter. My goal has been to allow each diary to reveal the writer's singular voice, letting him speak his own unique view of history.

Canceled Passages

All the diaries have a fair number of canceled passages. Because the writers did not edit their diaries in the years following the war, these cancellations occurred as the writers composed and form no part of each writer's final intentions for his text. Therefore, they are not reprinted in the printed text.

Interlineations

Each text includes some interlineations. As with cancellations, these interlineations are deemed part of the original composing process rather than revisions made by the writers in later years; they are considered authorial additions. Interlineations are printed as part of the text without indication that such was added material.

Absent Material

In some cases, words, sentences—and in one instance an entire page—are missing from this edition's diaries. Where written material is missing from the original manuscript, or is obscured by imperfections on the page, such is indicated in the edited text with closed brackets and ellipses, as follows: [. . .]. An explanation in the textual notes indicates the nature of the missing material: whether it was the result of ink splotches, a missing or torn page, or indecipherable handwriting.

Underlining

Throughout the texts, each diarist uses underlining, most often for emphasis. Any portion of the original manuscript underlined by the writer appears in italics, following standard procedure. Material double underlined remains unchanged in the text. Datelines for each entry prove the exception to this rule and are discussed below.

Capitalization

Capitalization is inconsistent in all the diaries. Though conscientious about capitalizing proper names and places, the diarists did not always follow standard rules of capitalization at beginnings of sentences. Silently emending capital letters is avoided. Mistakes in capitalization remain. In a few cases where it is impossible to decipher a capital letter from its lowercase counterpart, the letter has been capitalized in the text.

Punctuation

As with capitalization, writers are inconsistent in punctuation, sometimes ending sentences with periods, sometimes with dashes, sometimes with no punctuation whatsoever. Because these inconsistencies remain an important part of each writer's character, and because they should be in no way distracting to the reader, they have not been emended, except in cases where the missing punctuation is part of a set and was probably omitted because of the writer's haste. Dashes in the text are represented as they appear.

Spelling

No attempt has been made to correct spelling in each text, even when it is clear that the author knew the appropriate form of a word but misspelled out of haste or carelessness. In most instances, spelling errors do not obscure the writer's intentions, nor will the reader find such mistakes distracting. Instead, misspellings may well offer insight into a writer's emotional state at the time and may alert readers to an author's unique writing style. If a diarist misspelled a proper name of a figure deemed significant, the correct spelling is given in an explanatory note.

Abbreviations

Some diarists rely more heavily than others on abbreviations, although all at some point abbreviate. Many of the abbreviations are easily identifiable by the reader. (For example, "C.O." means conscientious objector, except for the rare occasions when a writer mentions his commanding officers.) Abbreviations have not been expanded. Explanatory notes are provided in cases where abbreviations may be difficult to decipher yet are crucial to understanding the text.

Paragraphing

This edition attempts to retain each author's paragraphing practices, beginning a new paragraph when such is indicated in the diaries, even on occasions when one or two words constitute—for the writer—the need for a different, discrete paragraph. However, to ensure readability and to provide uniformity, indentations in each diary have been standardized.

Pagination

For the most part, the diarists did not paginate their own texts. To give readers a better sense of the pagination, the original page break is recorded within the texts by brackets, marking the beginning of each new page in the manuscript.

Datelines

The four diarists chose different methods for dating their entries. Some specify day, date, and year; others provide only the date; some include the day of the week. Retaining this vast array of datelines might confuse the reader and interfere with the diary's readability. Therefore, datelines have been silently emended and standardized for uniformity and easier referencing. Each entry has been dated by month and day; the inclusion of the day of week and the year appears only in entries where the writer himself noted such in his diary.

296 • *Editorial Method*

Remark on Endnotes

Explanatory notes in this edition are meant to amplify, expand, and enrich a reader's understanding of the text and its writer. The notes should not provide too much or too little information. Material for notes is gleaned from letters written by the diarists; from diaries and autobiographical sketches of others detained with the diarists; from taped interviews in the Showalter Oral History Collection; and from James Juhnke's *Vision, Doctrine, War* and Gerlof Homan's *American Mennonites and the Great War, 1917-1918*.

Diarists included here often wrote about what was important to them: the church family and community of which they were so vitally a part. Yet although these people certainly mattered to the writers, knowing their identities now, some eighty years later, would little enhance our understanding of the text or of the writers. Therefore, most of the names remain unidentified, except those who deserve especial recognition because of their unique relationship with the diarist or because they provide an important footnote to the writer's own story as narrated through the diary. In cases where names remain unidentified, the reader should assume—depending on the context—that the person is either a relative, a member of the writer's church community, or, most likely, a fellow conscientious objector or military officer.

Provenance

Two Midwestern libraries hold a majority of the archival material about American Mennonites and the Great War, including diaries, autobiographical sketches, and letters written by the war's Mennonite conscientious objectors. The Mennonite Church USA Archives—North Newton, Kansas houses an extensive collection of World War I artifacts. (Because the above name emerged after this book was completed, in the remainder of the notes the original name, Mennonite Library and Archives, MLA, is used.) MLA includes 270 taped interviews of Great War objectors, gathered in the Showalter Oral History project. will collection also includes the diaries of Gustav Gaeddert and John Neufeld, as well as the letters Gaeddert and Neufeld wrote to the Mennonite leader H. P. Krehbiel. These texts, the diaries as well as the letters, are part of a collection of Krehbiel's documents relating to his work in the First World War with the General Conference Mennonite Exemption Committee. MLA has a copy of Ura Hostetler's diary as well; Thelma Kauffman of Harper, Kansas, owns Hostetler's original diary manuscript.

Mennonite Church USA Archives—Goshen, Indiana (originally Archives of the Mennonite Church, AMC), also contains much Great War material, thanks in large part to the work of historian Guy Hershberger. In the 1950s, Hershberger worked tirelessly to gather documents about the Mennonite experience during the First World War. As a result, AMC includes documents from the Mennonite Church Military Problems Committee and from objectors. AMC holds Jacob C. Meyer's diary, along with his letters to Esther Steiner and the annotated diary he prepared for publication in the *Mennonite Quarterly Review*; these are part of the Jacob C. Meyer collection.

Notes

Chapter 1

1. George R. Brunk, "War," *Gospel Herald,* 19 April 1917: 42.
2. *Gospel Herald*, 20 May 1915.
3. Levi Blauch, "The Lesson of the War in Europe," *Gospel Herald*, 22 April 1915: 58. It is important to note that a few German-Mennonite publications expressed sympathy for their homeland, proclaiming the "flatly horrible" treatment of the Germans at the Allied hands—the "barbaric" Russians, the vengeful French, the economically jealous English. These and similar declarations of German allegiances would prove detrimental to Mennonites once war with Germany began, and were in fact surprising, coming from a seemingly pacific people who somehow reconciled their wartime support for Germany with their belief in nonresistance. See Susan Schultz Huxman, "In the World, But Not of It: Mennonite Rhetoric in World War One as an Enactment of Paradox." Ph.D. dissertation, University of Kansas, 1987.
4. J. L. Morrison. *Josephus Daniels: the Small-d Democrat* (Chapel Hill, N.C.: University of North Carolina Press, 1966), 79.
5. President Woodrow Wilson, "An Address to a Joint Session of Congress, 2 April 1917." *The Papers of Woodrow Wilson.* Ed. Arthur S. Link, et al. (Princeton, N.J.: Princeton University Press, 1983), 521, 525.
6. "Our Attitude," editorial, *Gospel Herald* 12 April 1917: 25.
7. See Theron Schlabach, *Peace, Faith, Nation: Mennonites and Amish in Nineteenth-Century America* (Scottdale, Pa.: Herald Press, 1988), chapter 11.
8. For a detailed discussion of this merger, see Grant Stoltzfus, *Mennonites of the Ohio and Eastern Conference From the Colonial Period in Pennsylvania to 1968* (Scottdale, Pa.: Herald Press, 1969), chapter 13.
9. Schlabach, *Peace, Faith, Nation*, chapter 11.
10. These groups included the Mennonite Brethren, Krimmer Mennonite Brethren, and Evangelical Mennonite Brethren, all of which shared a Dutch-Russian heritage; the Holdeman Mennonites, whose Swiss-Dutch ethnicity was similar to the General Conference Mennonites; the Hutterites, who had a South German-Austrian origin; and the Old Order Amish, Stucky Amish, and Egly Amish (or Defenseless Mennonites), who had a Swiss-South German background like the (Old) Mennonites.

11. John Higham, *Strangers in the Land: Patterns of American Nativism, 1860-1925* (New York: Antheneum, 1963), 195.

12. Albert Dieffenbach's editorial in *The Christian Register* became a typical ecumenical call to arms: "As Christians, of course, we say Christ approves [of war]. But would he fight and kill? . . . There is not an opportunity to deal death to the enemy that he would shirk from or delay in seizing! He would take bayonet and grenade and bomb and rifle and do the work of deadliness against that which is the most deadly enemy of his Father's kingdom in a thousand years . . . That is the inexorable truth about Jesus Christ and this war; and we rejoice to say it." Quoted in Ray H. Abrams, *Preachers Present Arms* (New York: Round Table Press, 1933), 68.

13. Ray Abrams's *Preachers Present Arms* (New York: Round Table Press, 1933) does a remarkable job of describing the civic/religious spirit dominating the American Great War landscape. He details especially the patriotic sermons delivered from the country's mainline pulpits, but explores as well the ways religious rhetoric infiltrated the American government.

14. Gerlof Homan narrates many of these stories of abuse in *American Mennonites and the Great War, 1914-1918* (Scottdale, Pa.: Herald Press, 1994).

15. Perry Bush, *Two Kingdoms, Two Loyalties: Mennonite Pacifism in Modern America* (Baltimore: John Hopkins University Press, 1998), 6.

16. Ibid., 7. Bush is here quoting Guy Hershberger as well, from *War, Peace, and Nonresistance*, 3rd ed. (Scottdale, Pa.: Herald Press, 1969), 160.

17. James Juhnke, *A People of Two Kingdoms: The Political Acculturation of the Kansas Mennonites* (Newton, Kan.: Faith and Life Press, 1975), 109.

18. President Woodrow Wilson, "A Draft of a Proclamation," *The Papers of Woodrow Wilson*, 182.

19. Daniel R. Beaver, *Newton D. Baker and the American War Effort, 1917-1919* (Lincoln, Neb.: University of Nebraska Press, 1966), 30.

20. Homan, *American Mennonites and the Great War*, 44-45.

21. Wilson, "A Draft of a Proclamation," *The Papers of Woodrow Wilson*, 181-82.

22. A Beatrice, Nebraska, Mennonite congregation wrote this to President Wilson on March 31, 1917: "During the year 1873, we sent several of our leading men as delegates to America to spy out the land and to inform themselves regarding the, to us, all important matter of freedom from military service. They were assured by high American officials, including President [Ulysses] Grant, that we would never have to fear compulsory conscription." Qtd. in *The Mennonite*, 13 Sept 1917: 1.

23. In December 1917, the government changed its policies to include others who were not religious but had "personal scruples against the war."

24. James Juhnke, *A People of Two Kingdoms*, 97.

25. Homan, *American Mennonites and the Great War*, 50.

26. Ibid.

27. Amish Mennonites were in agreement with their (Old) Mennonite co-denominationalists on this point, believing as well that their men should assume no military roles, combatant or noncombatant.

28. "Mennonites on Military Service: A Statement of Our Position on Military Service as Adopted by The Mennonite General Conference, August 29,

1917." Reprinted in the *Gospel Herald*, 6 September 1917: 420.

29. Juhnke, *A People of Two Kingdoms*, 100.

30. Quoted in Homan, *American Mennonites and the Great War*, 54.

31. E. E. Leisy, "The Martial Adventures of a Conscientious Objector." Unpublished typescript, Archives of the Mennonite Church (AMC), Goshen, Ind., 3.

32. John Hege, "Camp Meade Diary," unpublished, n.d.

33. Clarence S. Shank, *A Mennonite Boy's World War I Experience* (Marion, Pennsylvania: n.p., 1963), 9.

34. Noah Leatherman, *Diary Kept by Noah Leatherman While in Camp During World War I* (Linden, Alberta: Aaron L. Toews, 1951), 5.

35. Jacob S. Waldner, "Diary of a World War I C.O., A Hutterite," Translated typescript at AMC, 4.

36. H. C. Peterson and Gilbert C. Fite, *Opponents of War: 1917-1918* (Westport, Conn.: Greenwood Press, 1957, 1986), 14.

37. A. B. Hart and Herbert R. Fergleger, *Theodore Roosevelt Cyclopedia* (New York: n.p., 1941), 100-01.

38. John Whiteclay Chambers, "Conscientious Objectors and the American State from Colonial Times to the Present." *The New Conscientious Objection: From Sacred to Secular Resistance*, John Whiteclay Chambers and Charles C. Mosleos, eds. (Oxford: Oxford University Press, 1993), 33.

39. Sarah D. Shields, "The Treatment of Conscientious Objectors During World War I," *Kansas History* (Winter 1981): 255-69.

40. Waldner, "Diary of a World War I C.O.," 3.

41. Quoted in Shields, "The Treatment of Conscientious Objectors During World War I," 261.

42. Ibid.

43. L. A. Dewey to Aaron Loucks, 29 September 1917. Reprinted in the *Gospel Herald*, 11 October 1917: 523.

44. Adam H. Mumaw, "My Experiences as a Conscientious Objector in World War I." Unpublished typescript, Menno Simons Library and Archives (MSLA), Harrisonburg, Va., 6.

45. Ura Hostetler, "Diary of World War I," 29 May 1917; 10 June 1917. Copy in Mennonite Library and Archives (MLA), North Newton, Kan.

46. Quoted in Donald Johnson, *The Challenge to American Freedoms: World War I and the Rise of the American Civil Liberties Union* (Louisville, Ky.: University of Kentucky Press, 1963), 31.

47. Quoted in Frederick Palmer, *Newton D. Baker: America at War* (New York: Dodd, Mead, 1931), 342.

48. Ibid., 31.

49. Norman Thomas, *The Conscientious Objector* (New York: B.W. Huebsch, 1925), 94.

50. C. E. Kilbourne to Aaron Loucks, 16 November 1917. Copy in MLA.

51. Gerlof Homan, "Mennonites and Military Justice in World War I," *Mennonite Quarterly Review* 65 (July 1992): 366.

52. Walter Guest Kellogg, *The Conscientious Objector* (New York: Boni and Liveright, 1919), 84.

53. James Juhnke, *Vision, Doctrine, War: Mennonite Identity and Organization in America, 1890-1930* (Scottdale, Pa.: Herald Press, 1989), 234.

54. "Some Live Questions," *Gospel Herald* 1 November 1917: 633.

55. "Things We Have Seen and Heard—and Think," *Gospel Herald* 4 October 1917: 489.

56. Waldner, "Diary of a WWI C.O.," 3.

57. Emanuel Swartzendruber, "Nonresistance Under Test." Unpublished typescript, AMC, 6.

58. Cliff Landis, "A Soldier for Christ." Unpublished essay, AMC, 1973, 3.

59. Leatherman, *Diary Kept By Noah Leatherman*, 6,8.

60. H. P. Krehbiel to Gustav Gaeddert, 21 January 1918. Microfilm copy in MLA.

61. Homan, *American Mennonites and the Great War*, 123.

62. "Western District Conference Resolution," 25 October 1917. Microfilm copy in MLA.

63. "Executive Order," 20 March 1918. Microfilm copy in MLA.

64. Homan, *American Mennonites and the Great War*, 131-32.

65. Quoted in J.S. Hartzler, *Mennonites in the World War or Nonresistance Under Test* (Scottdale, Pa.: Mennonite Publishing House, 1921), 122.

66. Adam H. Mumaw, "Second Company Development Battalion." MSLA, Harrisonburg, Va., 7.

67. Hostetler diary, 23 July 1918.

68. Ibid., 10 July 1918.

69. Mumaw, "Second Company Development Battalion," 9.

70. Hostetler diary, 4 June 1918.

71. Juhnke, *Vision, Doctrine, War*, 342.

72. Shields, "The Treatment of Conscientious Objectors During World War I," 267; Gaeddert diary, 25 April 1918.

73. Quoted in Shields, "The Treatment of Conscientious Objectors During World War I," 267.

74. This is the number provided by Kellogg in *The Conscientious Objector*, as reported by the Adjutant General's Office. In his article for *The Columbia University Quarterly*, Harlan Stone put the number of conscientious objectors appearing before the Board at 2,300.

75. Kellogg, *The Conscientious Objector*, 27.

76. Harlan F. Stone, "The Conscientious Objector," *Columbia University Quarterly* 21 (October 1919): 262.

77. Kellogg, *The Conscientious Objector*, 54.

78. Mumaw, "Second Company Development Battalion," 5.

79. The Board of Inquiry obviously used other means of assessment if the objectors were not religious. Those objecting on grounds other than religion usually faced a longer board evaluation and more questions about their political and economic ideologies.

80. Jacob C. Meyer, "Reflections of a Conscientious Objector in World War I," *Mennonite Quarterly Review* 41 (January 1967): 89.

81. David Kennedy, *Over Here: The First World War and American Society* (Oxford: Oxford University Press, 1980), 164.

82. Kellogg, *The Conscientious Objector*, 39.

83. Edith Cavell (1865-1915) was an English battlefield nurse whose execution by the Germans was well publicized in the United States; General Ferdinand Foch (1851-1929) was commander of French forces during the war; General John Pershing (1860-1948) commanded American forces.

84. Stone, "The Conscientious Objector," 260.

85. Kellogg, *The Conscientious Objector*, 41.

86. Mark May, "The Psychological Examination of Conscientious Objectors," *The American Journal of Psychology* 31 (April 1920): 48; Winthrop D. Lane, "Who are the Conscientious Objectors?" *New Republic* 14 April 1920: 217.

87. Kellogg, *The Conscientious Objector*, 127.

88. Homan, *American Mennonites and the Great War*, 137-38.

89. "On Farms in Iowa are Objects of Threats." *Oklahoma Leader* 26 September 1918. Microfilm copy in MLA.

90. Hostetler diary, 28 August 1918.

91. Gaeddert diary, 28 August 1918.

92. "Some Live Questions," *Gospel Herald* 1 November 1917: 561.

93. War Department Press Release. 26 February 1919. Microfilm copy in MLA.

94. See Kennedy, *Over Here: The First World War and American Society*, 164; and Homan, *American Mennonites and the Great War*, 145.

95. Order quoted in Kellogg, *The Conscientious Objector*, 21.

96. Order quoted in Thomas, *The Conscientious Objector*, 99.

97. Homan, "Military Justice for Mennonites," 367.

98. Homan, *American Mennonites and the Great War*, 144.

99. John Neufeld, "Diary of World War I," copy in MLA, 13

100. See John Neufeld, court transcript, copy in MLA.

101. Stephen M. Kohn, *Jailed for Peace: The History of American Draft Law Violators: 1658-1984* (Westport, Conn.: Greenwood Press, 1986), 34.

102. Leatherman, *Diary Kept by Noah Leatherman*, 38.

103. Ibid., 40.

104. Neufeld diary, 21.

105. Leatherman, *Diary Kept by Noah Leatherman*, 38.

106. Ibid.

107. Ibid., 69-70. This is not the only instance in which a Mennonite objector who died in camp was sent home wearing a military uniform he had earlier refused to don. The body of John Klaassen, who died of influenza at Leavenworth in October 1918, was shipped home in uniform. On the day his body arrived to his Oklahoma home, his father wrote this in his diary: "As soon as I got home with John's body I opened the coffin. There I found him—thin, pale, and dressed in an Army uniform! 'Oh, my son!' I cried in agony. 'Why have they done this to you? . . . If you would not wear this uniform in life, you shall not wear it in death!' Then, nearly overcome with grief, I told [his wife] to have the women change his clothes. Immediately the uniform was taken off and his clothes put on." Quoted in Rose M. Klaassen, "Mennonite Diary," *Liberty* (September/October 1985): 9-10.

108. Ibid., 41

109. Peterson and Fite, *Opponents of War*, 267.

110. "An Insult to the Uniform," *Kansas City Star* 23 January 1919, morning edition. Microfilm copy in MLA.

111. Resolution. Nebraska State Legislature. 5 February 1919. Microfilm copy in MLA.

112. Homan, *American Mennonites and the Great War*, 143.

113. Martin Gilbert, *The First World War: A Complete History* (New York: Holt, 1994), 541.

114. Juhnke, *Vision, Doctrine, War*, 241.

115. Ibid., 245.

116. Homan, *American Mennonites and the Great War*, 172-73.

Chapter 2

1. Wilfred Owen, "Dulce et Decorum Est," lines 25-28. Initially, Owen dedicated the poem to Jessie Pope, author of *Jessie Pope's War Poems* (1915) and of several prewar children's books; Owen removed the dedication "To Jessie Pope" and then "To a Certain Poetess" after the poem's second and third revisions. "Dulce et decorum est/Pro patria mori" translates to "It is sweet and meet to die for one's country. Sweet! Decorous!"

2. Horace, *Odes* 3.2.13

3. Rupert Brooke, "The Dead," sonnet 3, lines 5, 10, 11, 13.

4. Wilfred Owen, "The Ballad of Peace and War," unpublished manuscript. Quoted by Jon Stallworthy, "Rupert Brooke, 1887-1915," in Tim Cross, *The Lost Voices of World War I: An International Anthology of Writers, Poets and Playwrights* (London: Bloomsbury, 1988), 54.

5. Vera Brittain, *Testament of Youth* (New York: Macmillan, 1937), 155.

6. The story of Wilfred Owen's death seems especially tragic, given his great promise in English letters (though, of course, each death in the Great War was itself a tragedy). After convalescing for shell shock, Owen was sent back to the front on August 31, 1918. In the last months of the war, he was awarded the Military Cross for heroism. On November 4, one week to the day before the Armistice, Owen was killed. Jon Stallworthy wrote, "In Shrewsbury, the Armistice bells were ringing when his parents' front-door bell sounded its small chime, heralding the telegram they had dreaded for two years." See Stallworthy, "Wilfred Owen, 1893-1918," in Tim Cross, *The Lost Voices of World War I*, 77.

7. Owen, "Dulce et Decorum Est," line 26.

8. Ura Hostetler, "Diary of World War I," 26 May 1918, copy in Mennonite Library and Archives, North Newton, Kansas.

9. Gerlof Homan's seminal *American Mennonites and the Great War, 1914-1918*, published in 1994, did an especially good job of using the Mennonite conscientious objectors' diaries as primary sources in constructing his historical narrative of the Mennonite experience during the war.

10. John D. Roth and Ervin Beck, Preface, in *Migrant Muses: Mennonite/s Writing in the US*, ed. Roth and Beck (Goshen, Ind.: Mennonite Historical Society, 1998), v.

11. Felicity Nussbaum, "Towards Conceptualizing Diary," in *Studies in Autobiography*, ed. James Olney (London: Oxford University Press, 1988), 136.

12. Robert Sayre, "The Proper Study—Autobiographies in American Studies," *American Quarterly* 29 (1977): 247.

13. Samuel Hynes has averred that the canon is so exclusive that it ignores much of the literature written in other Great War theatres as well, including books written about combatant experiences in Mesopotamia, Persia, or Africa. According to Hynes, the only non-Western Front text to receive adequate critical attention is T. E. Lawrence's *Seven Pillars of Wisdom*, a romantic vision of the Arabs' war. See Hynes, *The Soldiers' Tale: Bearing Witness to Modern War* (New York: Viking Press, 1997), 74-76.

14. Ibid., 1-2.

15. Philip Gibbs, *Now It Can Be Told* (Garden City, N.Y.: Garden City Publishing Co., 1920), 8.

16. Robert Graves, interviewed by Leslie Smith, quoted in Paul Fussell, *The Great War and Modern Memory* (London: Oxford University Press, 1975), 170.

17. Far less attention has been paid to American combatant writers, for a variety of reasons. U.S. soldiers in the Great War were not as steeped in literary culture as their British counterparts; the brevity of the American's time in war also limited the possibility of developing a rich body of American Great War literary works. Additionally, many of Britain's Great War combatants later achieved acclaim as writers in their own right, including Robert Graves, Edmund Blunden, Siegfried Sassoon, and C. S. Lewis. American writers like e. e. cummings and Ernest Hemingway served as noncombatants during the war, and so are not often considered "trench poets."

18. See Sassoon, "The Rear-Guard," line 19; Owen, "Strange Meeting" and "Mental Cases," line 10; and Sassoon, "Blighters," line 3.

19. Brooke, "The Dead," line 3.

20. During the war, Sassoon published *The Old Huntsmen* (1917) and *Counter-Attack and Other Poems* (1918).

21. Tim Cross has anthologized many of the lesser known writers from the Great War in *The Lost Voices of World War I*. Cross's volume reprints the work of not only American and British wartime writers, but also writers from Germany, France, Armenia, Czechoslovakia, and Hungary, among other countries. While Cross includes interesting biographical material and commentary on each writer, his volume addresses only combatant literature from the war.

22. Fussell, *The Great War and Modern Memory*, 235.

23. Gibbs, *Now it Can Be Told*, 242.

24. Edmund Blunden, *Undertones of War* (1928; reprint, New York: Harvest, 1965), 39.

25. Paul Fussell, *The Great War and Modern Memory*, 75. Fussell argues that the penchant to dichotomize had its genesis in the trench warfare of World War I, and he provides compelling evidence. I remain somewhat skeptical, however, that binary thinking gained prominence in the First World War.

26. Ibid., 79.

27. Blunden, *Undertones of War*, 66.
28. Ibid., 68-69.
29. Ibid., 69. The Islands named a set of smaller trenches that lay ahead of the Cover Trench nearer to the German line. Blunden noted that the Islands each had "a small contingent of infantry . . . but Cover Trench was the real front line," a place where much of the battle time activity occurred.
30. Ibid., 70.
31. See the chapter "Oh What a Literary War" in Fussell's *The Great War and Modern Memory*.
32. Fussell has aptly argued that American combatant writers did not rely much, if at all, on literary allusion in constructing their wartime texts, in great part because Americans did not hold their national literary canon in the same esteem. Fussell writes: "In the absence of a line of important 'philosophic' poets running back to the fourteenth century, in a vacuum devoid of a Chaucer, a Spenser, a Shakespeare, a Milton, a Keats, a Wordsworth, a Tennyson, a Browning, an Arnold, and with no Malory or Bunyan either, American writing about the war tends to be spare and one-dimensional." Fussell, *The Great War and Modern Memory*, 158.
33. Sassoon, "On Passing the New Menin Gate," line 2, and Brooke, "The Dead," sonnet 4, line 3.
34. This recommendation was denied because the Allies were unable to capture Mametz Wood during the battle, and headquarters thus found the award of another Military Cross inappropriate, given the Allied failure. See Michele Fry, "Counter-Attack: The Biography of Siegfried Sassoon," 2, available online at < http://www.sassoonery.demon.co.uk/>.
35. Text taken from <http://www.sassoonery.demon.co.uk.>. Also appears in Sassoon, *Memoirs of an Infantry Officer*, 235.
36. In 1957, Sassoon joined the Roman Catholic Church. His 1967 obituary in *The Times* noted: "*The Path of Peace* (1960) was published in a finely printed and limited edition; some of these poems were written after his conversion and they demonstrate how complete and successful it had been. All his life had been deeply spiritual: and when he discovered a means of expressing a faith, fortunately for him it did not drive him from the world but brought him into it." From "Mr. Siegfried Sassoon: Poet, fox-hunter, soldier and pacifist," *The Times*, 4 September 1967.
37. Sassoon, "Statement Against the Continuation of War," reprinted at <http://www.sassoonery.demon.co.uk>.
38. Wilfred Owen to Susan Owen, 31 March 1918, *Collected Letters*, eds. Harold Owen and John Bell, (London: Oxford University Press, 1967), 544.
39. Ibid., 16 May 1917, 461.
40. Ibid.
41. Ibid., 14 October 1917, 498.
42. Hynes, *A Soldier's Tale*, 96.
43. Grace Ellery Channing, Introduction, in *War Letters of Edmond Genet*, ed. Grace Ellery Channing (New York: Scribners, 1918), xxii.
44. Ibid., xiii.
45. Edmond Genet to "Leah," 15 November 1916, *War Letters of Edmond*

Genet, 236.

46. Alan Seeger, "I Have a Rendezvous With Death," lines 1, 12, 21.

47. Seeger to his mother, 4 June 1916, *Letters and Diary of Alan Seeger* (New York: Scribners, 1917), 205.

48. Seeger to his mother, 17 October 1914, *Letters and Diary of Alan Seeger*, 7.

49. Seeger, Diary, 24 September 1915, *Letters and Diary of Alan Seeger*, 162.

50. Seeger to his mother, 18 June 1915, *Letters and Diary of Alan Seeger*, 119.

51. Hynes, *A Soldier's Tale*, 97

52. Fussell, *The Great War and Modern Memory*, 314. Despite Fussell's contention, it is important to note that D. H. Lawrence wrote extensively about the effects of the Great War on England's people; Virginia Woolf addressed the long-lasting casualties of war in *Mrs. Dalloway* and elsewhere; and Ezra Pound wrote about the war and its implications in his poetry, including his well-known "Hugh Selwyn Mauberly." These three authors are only representative of other "modern masters" who did not directly see the war yet wrote often and compellingly about it.

53. James Campbell, "Combat Gnosticism: The Ideology of First World War Poetry Criticism," *New Literary History* 30 (Spring 1999): 203-04.

54. Michele Fry, "Defining the Canon of English Poetry of the First World War," <http://www.sassoonery.demon.co.uk/ww1canon.htm>, 2.

55. Dominic Hibberd and John Onions, Introduction, in *Poetry of the First World War*, ed. Dominic Hibberd and John Onions (Hampshire, England: Macmillan, 1990), 11.

56. Frances S. Hallowes, *Women and War* (London: Headly Bros., 1914), 3.

57. Nosheen Khan, Introduction, in *Women's Poetry of the First World War*, ed. Nosheen Khan (Lexington,Ky.: University Press of Kentucky, 1988), 2.

58. Ibid., 3.

59. Margaret R. Higonnet, Introduction, in *Lines of Fire: Women Writers of World War I*, ed. Margaret R. Higonnet (New York: Penguin, 1999), xxiii.

60. Richard Eberhart, Introduction, in *War and the Poet: An Anthology of Poetry*, eds. Richard Eberhart and Selden Rodman (New York: Devin-Adair Co., 1945), xv.

Chapter 3

1. Ura Hostetler, "Diary of World War I," 28 August 1918. Copy at Mennonite Library and Archives (MLA), North Newton, Kan.

2. Lawrence Rosenwald, "Some Myths About Diaries," *Raritan: A Quarterly Review* 3 (Winter 1987): 111. Rosenwald contends that published literary works, which are often seen as more artful than diaries, are themselves guided by chance rather than by the author's own artistic design: "the length of the book, its subject, the treatment of its subject, are affected by publishers' desires, by the taste of the public, by the rate of pay. The language itself is given, not elected ... the typeface is what the printer has in stock; the line and page breaks, the configuration of a page generally, are the products of chance."

3. Hostetler diary, 7 July 1918.

4. Jacob C. Meyer, "Reflections of a Conscientious Objector," *Mennonite*

Quarterly Review 41 (January 1967): 79.

5. Gustav Gaeddert, "Diary of World War I," 12 March 1918. Microfilm copy in MLA.

6. Hostetler diary, 28 June 1918.

7. Examples of other Great War diaries by Mennonite conscientious objectors include Noah Leatherman, *Diary Kept by Noah H. Leatherman While in Camp During World War I* (Linden, Alberta: Aaron L. Toews, 1951); John Hege, "Camp Meade Diary," copy sent to author by Gerlof Homan; Benjamin Ebersole, "Diary of World War I," copy at Archives of the Mennonite Church (AMC), Goshen, Ind.

8. Gustav Gaeddert to H. P. Krehbiel, 1 October 1917, microfilm copy in MLA.

9. Hostetler diary, 7 July 1918.

10. Samuel Hynes, *The Soldiers' Tale: Bearing Witness to Modern War* (New York: Viking, 1997), xiv.

11. Ibid., 2.

12. Ibid., xiv.

13. May Sarton, *The House By the Sea* (New York: Norton, 1977), 79.

14. Ernest H. Miller, "Experiences of a C.O. in World War I." Menno Simons Library and Archives, Harrisonburg, Va., 12-13.

15. Hynes, *A Soldiers' Tale*, xiv.

16. James Olney, *Metaphors of Self: the Meaning of Autobiography* (Princeton, N.J.: Princeton University Press, 1972), 32.

17. William C. Spengemann and L. R. Lundquist, "Autobiography and the American Myth," *American Quarterly* 17 (1963): 502.

18. Felicity Nussbaum, "Towards Conceptualizing Diary," in *Studies in Autobiography*, ed. James Olney (New York: Oxford University Press, 1988), 137.

19. Jacob C. Meyer, Gustav Gaeddert, and John Neufeld each had articles of varying lengths published in Mennonite periodicals during and after the war. Included in the Jacob C. Meyer papers (Archives of the Mennonite Church) is an extensive draft of his family's genealogical history, as well as copious notes for other writing projects. Late in his life, Ura Hostetler wrote a history of the Pleasant Valley Mennonite Church.

20. Rosenwald, "Some Myths about Diaries," 103.

21. Ervin Beck, "The Signifying Menno: Archetypes for Authors and Critics," in *Migrant Muses: Mennonite/s Writing in the US*, ed. John Roth and Ervin Beck (Goshen, Ind.: Mennonite Historical Society, 1998), 59.

22. Robert Fothergill, "One Day at a Time: The Diary as Lifewriting," *A/B: Auto/Biography Studies* 10 (Spring 1995): 81-91

10 (Spring 1995), 87.

23. Beck, "The Signifying Menno," 59-60.

24. Ibid.

25. Jacob C. Meyer, "Diary of World War I," 1 August 1918; 4 August 1918; 7 August 1918. Copy in Jacob C. Meyer Papers, AMC.

26. Walter Guest Kellogg, *The Conscientious Objector* (New York: Boni and Liveright, 1919), 58.

27. Hostetler diary, 27 June 1918.
28. Ibid., 7 July 1918.
29. John Neufeld, "Diary of World War I," Copy in MLA, 26.
30. Dominic Hibberd and John Onions, *Poetry of the Great War: An Anthology* (New York: St. Martin's Press, 1986), 17.
31. William Evans, "The War," lines 9-11.
32. Ibid., line 14.
33. Hynes, "The Soldiers' Tale," 57.
34. Hibberd and Onions, *Poetry of the First World War*, 17.
35. John Oxenham, "The Vision Splendid," lines 4, 11, 12, 14-16.
36. Countess Anna de Noailles, "Our Dead" and "Verdun," lines 9-10; line 18.
37. Vera Brittain, *Testament of Youth* (New York: Macmillan, 1937), 264-65.
38. Ibid.
39. Eva Dobell, "Advent, 1916," line 13.
40. C. B. Schmidt, "Mennonites and the War," *Gospel Herald*, 8 November 1917, 589.
41. "The Martyrs' Spirit," *Gospel Herald*, 8 November 1917, 585.
42. J. G. Evert, "The Martyrs of Alcatraz," *Gospel Herald*, 2 October 1919, 490.
43. For examples, see Hostetler diary, entries for 30 June 1918 and 1 July 1918.
44. Hostetler diary, 3 July 1918.
45. Ibid., 7 July 1918.
46. Ibid.
47. Neufeld diary, 26.
48. Royden Loewen, *From the Inside Out: The Rural Worlds of Mennonite Diarists, 1863-1929* (Winnipeg: The University of Manitoba Press, 1999), 5.
49. Hostetler diary, 20 July 1918.
50. Meyer diary, 24 September 1918.
51. Guy Chapman, *A Passionate Prodigality: Fragments of Autobiography* (New York: Holt, 1933), 13.
52. Alan Seeger, *Letters and Diary* (New York: Scribners, 1917), 153.
53. Edmond Blunden, *Undertones of War*. (1928; New York: Harvest, 1965), 93, 100-101.
54. Hibberd and Onions, *Poetry of the First World War*, 25.
55. Siegfried Sassoon, "Banishment," lines 9-14.
56. Paul Fussell, *The Great War and Modern Memory* (London: Oxford University Press, 1975), 86.
57. Hostetler diary, 10 June 1918.
58. Fussell, *The Great War and Modern Memory*, 79.
59. Robert Sayre, "Rhetorical Defenses: The Autobiographies of WWI Conscientious Objectors," *A/B: Autobiography Studies* (Spring 1992): 70.
60. Gaeddert diary, 3 April 1918.
61. Ibid., 4 November 1917.
62. Hostetler diary, 27 June 1918.
63. Ibid., 5 July 1918.

308 • *Notes*

64. Ibid., 7 July 1918.
65. Osbert Sitwell, "Rhapsode," 31-36.
66. Samuel Hynes, *The Soldiers' Tale*, 30.
67. Wilfred Owen to Susan Owen, 2 October 1917, *Collected Letters*, eds. Harold Owen and John Bell (London: Oxford University Press, 1967), 498.

Chapter Four

1. Albert Gaeddert and Edna Gaeddert, *Story of Jacob D. and Katharina (Ratzlaff) Gaeddert Family* (N.p.:n.p., 1992).
2. Gustav Gaeddert, interview by John Waltner, 2 November 1967, Schowalter Oral History Collection on World War I Conscientious Objection, Mennonite Library and Archives (MLA), North Newton, Kan.
3. Gaeddert to H. P. Krehbiel, 21 November 1917, microfilm copy in MLA.
4. Gaeddert, "Diary of World War I," 22 November 1917, copy in MLA, microfilm 169. This microfilm also holds much of Krehbiel's correspondence with objectors during World War I, as well as other documents of interest about Mennonites and the Great War, including correspondences between Mennonite leaders and the government; newspaper clippings; and copies of church resolutions about objector issues.
5. Gaeddert to Krehbiel, 21 November 1917.
6. Gaeddert interview by Waltner, 2 November 1967.
7. Gaeddert to Krehbiel, 15 January 1918, microfilm copy in MLA.
8. Gaeddert diary, 5 February 1918.
9. Krehbiel to Gaeddert, 21 January 1918, microfilm copy in MLA.
10. Gaeddert interview by Waltner, 2 November 1967.
11. Gaeddert to H. P. Krehbiel, 25 March 1918, microfilm copy in MLA.
12. Ibid.
13. Gaeddert diary, 2 April 1918.
14. Gaeddert diary, 14 April 1918.
15. Gaeddert to Krehbiel, April 1918, microfilm copy in MLA.
16. Gaeddert to Krehbiel, 19 June 1918, microfilm copy in MLA.
17. Gaeddert's name was recorded on a list of 1-A objectors at Camp Funston, Kan. A copy of this list is filed, along with other records of the Adjutant General's Office, at MLA, mss. 72.
18. Gaeddert interview by Waltner, 2 November 1967.
19. Ibid.
20. Gaeddert to H. P. Krehbiel, 31 August 1918, microfilm copy in MLA.
21. Ibid.
22. Gaeddert to Krehbiel, 17 November 1918, microfilm copy in MLA.
23. Gaeddert interview by Waltner, 2 November 1967.
24. Krehbiel to Gaeddert, 12 January 1918.
25. Al Reimer, *Mennonite Literary Voices: Past and Present* (North Newton, Kan.: Bethel College Mennonite Press, 1993), 5-6.
26. Gaeddert to Krehbiel, 1 October 1917.
27. Henry Peter (H. P.) Krehbiel was a General Conference Mennonite from North Newton, Kan. During the Great War he was a member of the

Committee on Exemptions for both the Western District and General Conference; he traveled to Washington and to various detainment camps to assist objectors. According to historian James Juhnke, he was one of the most significant General Conference leaders during the Great War. See James Juhnke, *Vision, Doctrine, War: Mennonite Identity and Organization in America, 1890-1930* (Scottdale, Pa.: Herald Press, 1989), 212.

28. "We parted" appeared to be an addition to the diary, as it was written in the margin to the left of the September 19, 1917 entry. However, as Gaeddert was writing this entry some time after October 4, 1917 (when he presumably wrote many of the earlier entries), inscribing this passage in the margin may have been Gaeddert's attempt to have the September 19 entry finish on one line before he began working on his recall for the experiences of September 20.

29. Katharina (Ratzlaff) Gaeddert, Gustav Gaeddert's mother, and Marie Gaeddert, his older sister.

30. According to Noah Leatherman, another Mennonite objector conscripted at the same time, Gaeddert was the "chief spokesman" during this interview at company headquarters. Gaeddert maintained this leadership position among Camp Funston objectors throughout their detainment, a role he did not much address in his diary. See Noah Leatherman, *Diary Kept by Noah Leatherman While in Camp During World War I* (Linden, Alberta: Aaron L. Toews, 1951), 5.

31. Eight men were beaten for refusing officer demands to do sanitation work on Sundays. The other objectors in Gaeddert's detachment who were not beaten apparently acquiesced when ordered by their captain to board the garbage trucks and work. Those who ignored this order were marched to the edge of camp and knocked down by soldiers bearing guns, then beaten and marched back to their barracks.

32. Peter Herman (P.H.) Unruh was a General Conference Mennonite pastor of the Alexanderwohl Mennonite Church, Goessel, Kansas, and was a member of the Home Mission Committee of the Western District Conference. Peter H. (P.H.) Richert was a General Conference Mennonite and in 1917-1918, a pastor of the Tabor Mennonite Church in Goessel, Kansas. He was also a member of the Western District Conference Exemption Committee.

33. Abraham J. Dyck was associate pastor of Gaeddert's home congregation, Hoffnungsau Church, Inman, Kansas.

34. Younger brother John Gaeddert, who was drafted in 1918.

35. Several Mennonite objectors had refused to do any more sanitation work, and so were put in a guardhouse, given a diet of bread and water, forced to sleep on floor, and forbidden to speak with other objectors. See Leatherman, *Diary Kept By Noah Leatherman*, 8.

36. John W. (J.W.) Kliewer was the chair of the General Conference Mennonite mission board (1908-1935) and president of Bethel College (1911-20 and 1925-32).

37. Gaeddert was probably addressing the turmoil surrounding Camp Funston objectors that day: those who refused to do sanitation detail were ordered to stand by their barracks in the cold and snow during working hours.

Yellow placards affixed to their hats said "C.O. won't work," and they were forced to wear armbands noting their C.O. status. See Leatherman, *Diary of Noah Leatherman*, 8.

38. H. D. Penner was a professor at Bethel College and a member of the "Committee of Seven," a committee commissioned at a meeting held on April 11-12, 1917, and attended by delegates from the General Conference Western District, Krimmer Mennonite Brethren, Mennonite Brethren, Holdeman Mennonites, and Defenseless Mennonites. According to Gerlof Homan, the Committee of Seven was "charged with trying to preserve freedom from military service," and members were asked to "petition the authorities and to establish contact with other district conferences, Mennonite groups, and historic peace churches." See Homan, *American Mennonites and the Great War, 1914-1918* (Scottdale, Pa.: Herald Press, 1994), 45.

39. John Thiessen was a close friend of Gaeddert's from Bethel Academy. Thiessen was not drafted and attended Bethel College during the war.

40. Carl Schmidt of Moundridge, Kansas, was conscripted from September 1917 to January 1919. In October 1918, he was arrested for refusing to cut weeds and received a 25-year sentence to Fort Leavenworth.

41. One day earlier, Gaeddert wrote to Krehbiel and outlined his ambiguous feelings about accepting sanitation work. Because he believed the work was "harmless" and the military institution "destructive," he was unclear what action he and other objectors should take, and hoped that Krehbiel or the Exemption Committee could show the way. Gaeddert implored them to offer answers only after seeing clearly the objector's plights and "leav[ing] out of consideration all punishment that is such as may happen to come (I don't care about it) and knowing that a compromise between right and wrong is impossible." See Gaeddert to Krehbiel, 21 November 1917, microfilm copy in MLA.

42. Established in 1881, Christian Endeavor was the first youth ministry movement in the United States. At the time of the Great War (as now), it focused its mission in local churches, where youth were encouraged to express Christian charity in their local communities.

43. Sarah Lohrentz took over Gaeddert's classroom when he was conscripted; Lohrentz and Gaeddert would marry in 1921. Elsewhere in the diary, Gaeddert identified Lohrentz by her nickname, "Hans."

44. C. C. Ray was put in charge of conscientious objectors at Camp Funston on November 23, 1917. According to Sarah D. Shields, Ray "used imaginative measures in order to prevent widespread defection of soldiers to the conscientious objectors, and of the working objectors to those who would not cooperate. Those who would not work were ordered to stand outside while the others loaded the sanitation trucks." During an investigation of Ray's practices, instigated by the National Civil Liberties Union, Ray defended himself by saying such punishment was necessary and by arguing that he had never heard the executive order of October 10, 1917, demanding that officers treat pacifists with "tact and consideration." As a result of Ray's command and the investigation, a stockade was constructed at Camp Funston to house conscientious objectors who refused to work. See Sarah Shields, "The Treatment of

Conscientious Objectors During World War I," *Kansas History* (Winter 1981): 264.

45. In early December 1917, conscientious objectors were forced to file new claims from combatant duty. Gaeddert reported in a letter to Krehbiel that an order was posted on the company bulletin board stating "those who think that the Local Board has not given them a fair chance will be given another chance here in camp if they file their claim before Dec. 15." All previous exemptions had been cancelled by Judge Advocate General Enoch Crowder. Gaeddert assumed the new order was another way military officers could "take advantage" of objectors, but complied by filing new affidavits for exemption. See Gaeddert to Krehbiel, 6 December 1917, microfilm copy in MLA.

46. Apparently, on this occasion, religious services were not vengefully cancelled by Camp Funston's military officers. Instead, a general quarantine had been imposed on the camp; only eight men were allowed to meet in one place at any time. This specific quarantine was lifted around Christmas 1917.

47. Gaeddert wrote to Krehbiel on 27 December 1917 about his Christmas celebration at Camp Funston. He said: "Christmas presents crowded in by the 'wholesale' and everybody seemed to receive his share and more than that. Every body felt thankful for it also and yet it was not near what Xmas would have been at home. I hope this is the last Christmas that I need to spend in a camp. We had big doings here also, but they were Fourth of July celebrations, but not near a Xmas program." See Gaeddert to Krehbiel, 27 December 1917, microfilm copy in MLA. The Hutterite Jacob Waldner described the Camp Funston Christmas celebration more broadly, writing: "The soldiers, about 60,000 of them, gathered at a hillside and there had their kind of Christmas celebration with all sorts of frolicking. From our attic we observed what was going on. They shot balls into the air and they exploded.... Fiery beams went high up into the air and then stars fell out as if the last day of judgement had come ... One could also see the picture of the general projected on the hillside about 30 feet high. There you see how they bow down before such a picture like Nebuchadnezzar did. Yes, it was a very trying day for us to have to spend Christmas with these people under such commotion." See Jacob Waldner, "Diary of WWI C.O., a Hutterite," translated typescript, Archives of the Mennonite Church, 6.

48. Such lectures were a common event in Great War military camps. They were sponsored by the Commission on Training Camp Activities, whose task it was to mold soldiers' characters. Warning soldiers of sexually transmitted diseases was seen as one way to remove the scourge of immorality from training camps.

49. President Wilson's Fourteen Points were used as the basis for peace negotiations between Allied and Central Powers. He gave his Fourteen Points address to a joint session of Congress on January 8, 1918.

50. This word is indecipherable because of Gaeddert's uncharacteristicly obscured handwriting at this point.

51. During the meeting with Major Smith, Gaeddert was questioned about the treatment of Abraham Loewen. On December 26, Loewen had refused to

work at a warehouse when ordered; he was forced to stand in the cold and denied his evening meal. At the day's end, Loewen could not walk and needed assistance back to the barrack. See Leatherman, *Diary Kept by Noah Leatherman*, 15.

52. An ink splotch, approximately two inches in diameter, concealed two words in this entry.

53. Fritz was Sarah Lohrentz's sister, Anna Lohrentz. According to Raymond Regier, son of Anna Lohrentz, the names "Hans" and "Fritz" found origin in the Katzenjamer Kids, though Regier did not know who began using the nicknames for the Lohrentz sisters.

54. This sentence appeared in the top margin above the March 11, 1917, entry.

55. Peter C. (P. C.) Hiebert, professor at Tabor College, Hillsboro, Kansas, was a prominent leader among Mennonite Brethren.

56. Gaeddert's detachment was transferred to a detainment area about one mile from Camp Funston, on the banks of the Kaw River.

57. An arrow was drawn from the words "that's all" to the sentence beginning "That's all we are supposed to do . . ."

58. President Wilson's Executive Order defined noncombatant service as duty in the medical, quartermaster, or engineering corps.

59. A hand-drawn line appeared in the text between the end of the *Trench and Camp* piece and the conclusion of Gaeddert's entry for April 6, 1918.

60. Gaeddert did not here mean tried in the sense of a court-martial; rather, military officials tried to make thirty conscientious objectors take work. Only one of the thirty followed orders and performed the chores demanded of him. See Leatherman, *Diary Kept by Noah Leatherman*, 20.

61. This encounter with Judge Advocate Packer apparently troubled Gaeddert. In a letter to Krehbiel the following day, Gaeddert wrote about Packer's reading of Wilson's March 18 Executive Order. According to Gaeddert, Packer "had a peculiar way of interpreting it [the order], which did not harmonize with the interpretation give to us by our Lieut. Hickerson...What shall we think of this, shall we take it as a bluff or what about it? I wish I could get an interpretation of it which is authority and reliable. According to his remarks then we will see hard times yet." Later, Gaeddert reported to Krehbiel that "we have not been mistreated at all yet, that is, of what that Colonel Packer spoke of. Therefor it most likely was only a bluff which I really thot it was and still I could not see how a man of authority like he would speak words without it being carried out." See Gaeddert to Krehbiel, 12 April 1918, April 1918, microfilm copy in MLA.

62. At this point, objectors who filled out farm furlough applications were denied admission to the program. According to Gaeddert, the government's reasoning was that each man furloughed must "have received sufficient training so that when he is called back he can be sent to the fire directly, that is, he must have received the six months training of which we have had nothing." See Gaeddert to Krehbiel, April 1918, microfilm copy in MLA.

63. Krehbiel, a Republican, had served in the 1909 Kansas state legislature.

64. John Horsch, *Menno Simons: His Life, Labor, and Teachings* (Scottdale, Pa.: n.p., 1916).

65. Gaeddert no doubt had told his mother of his decision to apply for reconstruction work in France. In a letter to Krehbiel shortly thereafter outlining his desire to join the American Friends overseas, Gaeddert said, "My mother will take it somewhat hard, for that reason I would much rather stay here but I have told her and with it consoled her a little, that the danger zone is here in U.S. as well as over there, because of the mob spirit here, and that God can protect me there as well as here." See Gaeddert to Krehbiel, 19 June 1918, microfilm copy in MLA.

66. Probably the order issued by the War Department on June 1, 1918, establishing a Board of Inquiry. This ruling stated that the Board of Inquiry would determine the sincerity of objectors who would not accept noncombatant work and who were not facing courts-martial; the Board would then make recommendations for farm furloughs or for work in the American Friends Service Committee. According to Gaeddert, objectors in his camp believed the ruling "very considerate" and they felt they would now be allowed to "do our part." See Gaeddert to Krehbiel, 5 June 1918, microfilm copy in MLA.

67. Gaeddert had heard the objectors would be transferred to Fort Leavenworth, Kansas, to appear before the Board of Inquiry. Instead, they were transferred again to a detention camp at Funston, where they were put under new non-commissioned officers. These officers, Gaeddert wrote Krehbiel, developed different methods of provocation, though "always within the limits of reason taking everything in consideration." See Gaeddert to Krehbiel, 19 June 1918, microfilm copy in MLA.

68. Members of the Board of Inquiry included Major Richard C. Stoddard; Harlan F. Stone, Dean of Columbia Law School; Judge Julian W. Mack. Gaeddert left a space here, suggesting he could not recall the other man on the Board of Inquiry, Judge Julian W. Mack.

69. One of twelve classifications available to the Board of Inquiry; Class 4 Objectors were recommended to be sent to Fort Leavenworth, Kansas, for further examination. The different classifications are outlined in Walter Guest Kellogg, *The Conscientious Objector* (New York: Boni and Liveright, 1919), 30.

70. Noah Leatherman's published *Diary* recounted this experience in some detail. He explained that the entire camp was lined up in the drill grounds. Commanding officers read the charges against the three African-American soldiers (for raping a seventeen-year-old girl), as well as the court-martial sentence of execution. Leatherman wrote: "Many thousands of Negro soldiers were required to witness the execution but all were unarmed while the white soldiers and officers were armed with revolvers and rifles. Shortly before the time of execution the three men were brought out, heavily guarded and chained together. They were marched to the scaffold, placed in position and given several minutes during which time they appealed to God for mercy. Several of the Negro soldiers (relatives, we were told) went into hysterics and were taken away to preserve order. At the appointed time the trap was sprung causing instant death . . . . We were among the first to leave the ground. It was a very sad affair and seemed to have been the purpose of the

authorities to implant a deep fear of court martial as a rigid discipline for disobedience." The hanging seemed seared into the memories of objectors who witnessed it; both Leatherman and Ura Hostetler recalled the event years later when they were interviewed about their Great War experiences. See Noah Leatherman, *Diary Kept by Noah H. Leatherman*, 26.

71. The word here was rendered indecipherable because of Gaeddert's handwriting.

72. One of many Army chaplains brought in to convert the conscientious objectors, he apparently left the Sunday service in disgust. In a 1968 interview, Ura Hostetler remembered that the chaplain scolded the objectors, telling them, "you are a bunch of skunks!" See Ura Hostetler, interview by James Juhnke, 11 June 1968, Schowalter Oral History Collection on World War I Conscientious Objection, MLA.

73. The word here was rendered indecipherable because of Gaeddert's handwriting.

74. Those objectors accepted into the American Friends reconstruction program received training in Philadelphia before being dispatched overseas.

Chapter 5

1. Ura Hostetler, "Diary of World War I," 26 May 1918, copy in Mennonite Library and Archives (MLA), North Newton, Kan.
2. Ibid., 7 July 1918.
3. Harvey Hostetler, *Descendants of Barbara Hochstedler and Christian Stutzman* (Berlin, Ohio: Gospel Book Store, 1938), 25. Actual documents regarding this event are found in Richard K. MacMaster, et al., *Conscience in Crisis: Mennonites and Other Peace Churches in America, 1739-1789, Interpretation and Documents* (Scottdale, Pa.: Herald Press, 1979), 122-27.
4. Ura Hostetler, interview by James Juhnke, 11 June 1968, Schowalter Oral History Collection on World War I Conscientious Objection, MLA.
5. Ibid.
6. Ibid.
7. Ibid.
8. Ibid.
9. Hostetler diary, 13 June 1918.
10. Ibid., 27 June 1918.
11. Ibid., 3 July 1918.
12. Hostetler interview by Juhnke, 11 June 1968.
13. Hostetler diary, 20 July 1918.
14. Ibid., 16 August 1918.
15. Hostetler interview by Juhnke, 11 June 1968.
16. Ibid.
17. Ibid.
18. Ibid.
19. Ibid.
20. Hostetler diary, 27 June 1918.
21. Ibid., 26 May 1918.

22. Ibid., 27 June 1918.
23. Ibid., 7 July 1918.
24. Hostetler interview by Juhnke, 11 June 1968.
25. Ibid.
26. Hostetler diary, 22 July 1918.
27. Ibid., 22 August 1918.
28. A defining scriptural passage in the Mennonite doctrine of nonresistance: "But I say to you, Do not resist an evildoer. But if anyone strikes you on the right cheek, turn the other also; and if anyone wants to sue you and take your coat, give your cloak as well."
29. Hostetler probably intended John 18:36, as the Gospel of John has only 21 chapters. In John 18:36, Jesus says: "My kingdom is not from this world. If my kingdom were from this world, my followers would be fighting to keep me from being handed over to the Jews. But as it is, my kingdom is not from here."
30. Another core scriptural passage in the doctrine of nonresistance: "Do not repay anyone evil for evil, but take thought for what is noble in the sight of all. If it is possible, so far as it depends on you, live peaceably with all. Beloved, never avenge yourselves, but leave room for the wrath of God; for it is written, 'Vengeance is mine, I will repay, says the Lord.' No, 'if your enemies are hungry, feed them; if they are thirsty, give them something to drink; for by doing this you will heap burning coals on their heads.' Do not be overcome by evil, but overcome evil with good."
31. "For we were not overstepping our limits when we reached you; we were the first to come all the way to you with the good news of Christ."
32. The "H OM" probably stood for Durkenson's denomination, either Hutterite, Holdeman, or (Old) Mennonite. Whether he was a conscientious objector remains questionable, as there is no Eli Durkenson on military record lists of Camp Funston objectors.
33. Hostetler listed here various addresses while detained, the first two his location at Camp Funston, the last his mailing address at Camp Dodge.
34. According to Hostetler's daughter Thelma Kauffman, when he told the story about having his picture taken in puttees and boots, he said he wanted a copy of the picture because he thought it was funny—not because he wanted evidence of the mistreatment he received.
35. The word noted as unrecoverable has been rendered illegible because of Hostetler's obscured handwriting.
36. Probably John Hamilton, a friend of Hostetler's from Harper and a member of Hostetler's church. Hamilton had been conscripted three weeks before Hostetler. According to Hostetler, Hamilton's weaker constitution made him an easy victim of the soldiers' and officers' taunts. Hamilton was furloughed to Mason City, Iowa, and discharged before Christmas 1918. See Ura Hostetler, interview by James Juhnke, 11 June 1968, Schowalter Oral History Collection, MLA.
37. The missing word has been rendered illegible because of Hostetler's obscured handwriting.
38. The missing word has been rendered illegible because of Hostetler's

obscured handwriting.

39. An allusion to the parable of the ten virgins found in Matthew 25:1-13. The parable likens the kingdom of God to ten virgins who prepared for a bridegroom's arrival. Five had enough oil in their lamps, and five did not; the wise ones with enough oil were invited in to the wedding banquet, while the five foolish virgins desperately looked for more oil.

40. Jacob Waldner, in his translated diary, described the mistreatment of these nine Hutterites. Upon their arrival at Camp Funston, they were pushed to the ground, kicked, and mocked by soldiers who recognized them as objectors because of their clothes and beards. Several were taken to a bathhouse and put upside down under the faucet, so that they choked on the water. Then they were pushed out the window. "So godless they treated them that they threw some twice through the window," Waldner wrote. While the men were still wet from the showers, they were dragged through the camp's dirt streets. They were compelled to stay on the ground while soldiers pummeled them with a medicine ball. Finally, the Hutterites were taken by officers for their physical examination. "During the whole time," Waldner said, "they received many a kick and blow over their heads for not registering for work. The officers too maltreated them by poking their walking sticks into the men's stomachs that it sometimes took your breath away. But with the help of God our men were able to bear this." Before being sent to the conscientious objector detachment, the men were forced by officers to don yellow work clothes and had all their property taken from them. See Jacob Waldner, "Diary of a World War I C.O., A Hutterite," translated typescript at Archives of the Mennonite Church (AMC), Goshen, Ind.

41. Charles William Hollcroft who, according to Hostetler, was in the Navy when World War I broke out in 1914. After getting a dishonorable discharge, Hollcroft went to Kansas City, was converted to the Mennonite church, and became a conscientious objector. Hostetler was convinced the military would have re-enlisted Hollcroft and made him an officer. Hollcroft did not re-enlist as a combatant, and faced a more difficult hearing with the Board of Inquiry. After the war, he resided in Harper, Kansas. See Hostetler, interview by Juhnke, 11 June 1968, Showalter Oral History Collection, MLA.

42. In Luke 7:41-49, Jesus confronted Simon Peter, who was angry that a woman of ill repute had washed Jesus' feet with ointment. Jesus related the story of the two debtors, one who owed much money and one who owed little. Both debts were forgiven by the creditor. Jesus asked Simon which debtor would love the creditor more. Simon rightly answered that the one who was forgiven most would love the most.

43. From information related by Noah Leatherman and by Waldner, it seems Kintz was upset about more than the absence of three men's hats. Both men wrote that on June 30, 1918, several more Hutterites arrived at Camp Funston and were mistreated by soldiers at the camp, who beat the Hutterites on the face and back and tore their clothing. Several incurred noticeable bruises and cuts. At the same time, according to Leatherman, one of the objectors discovered a torn up letter from Kintz's wife to the captain, asking that he "not deal harshly with these men and be careful what he does." Leather-

man wrote: "Very much like Pilots wife at the time of Jesus. And we believe it had its fruit, as the Capt. seemed very much dissatisfied with the treatment the Hutterites had rec'd, and said he was going to Camp Funston to see about it." See Noah Leatherman, *Diary Kept by Noah Leatherman While In Camp During World War I* (Linden, Alberta: Aaron Toews, 1951), 13.

44. Objectors who received Class 4 status were recommended to be sent to Fort Leavenworth, Kansas, for further examination. There were three different designations for Class 2, all recommending that the objector be placed in noncombatant jobs. Those who were classified 2-A were deemed sincere conscientious objectors to combatant, but not to noncombatant, service; those who were classified 2-B were found to be sincere conscientious objectors who were willing to accept noncombatancy; those classified as 2-C were willing to accept service or were assigned to service in reconstruction hospitals. Those in Class 1-A were considered sincere conscientious objectors and were recommended for furloughs. See Walter Guest Kellogg, *The Conscientious Objector* (New York: Boni and Liveright, 1919), 30.

45. In his 1968 interview by James Juhnke, Hostetler had this to say about the experience: "There were three Negroes that had been sentenced. What we gather was that . . . some fellow out at Spurlock or there someplace told them [military authorities] that they had raped his girl. Anyway, they hung them. They had a scaffold set up during the night. Of course they didn't tell everybody what they were going to do, they just marched us out there to what looked like a forty-acre field. Around us they had them lined up, probably 40,000 people lined up and we were back a ways with the scaffold in the middle . . . so I was at a hanging."

46. In Hostetler's 1968 interview, he indicated that Jim Troyer was the man from Crystal, Kansas, with whom Hostetler spoke on the train to camp about taking noncombatant work. The man had said that he would probably take noncombatant service so that he could continue smoking cigarettes. Shortly after Hostetler arrived at Camp Dodge, he met the man from the train. According to Hostetler's report in 1968, "he [Troyer] said he was taking regular training but that he had put in an application for truck driving." This information agrees with the details in Hostetler's diary.

47. Benjamin Salmon was a Roman Catholic objector from Denver, Colorado; he objected to the war on humanitarian as well as religious grounds. An outspoken objector at Camp Funston, Salmon apparently argued for objectors' rights in camp, and challenged officers when they stepped outside the limits of governmental mandate. Salmon was eventually court-martialed and sentenced to Fort Leavenworth, where he spent two years.

48. An allusion to Matthew 9:37-38: "The harvest truly is plenteous, but the laborers are few; Pray ye therefore the Lord of the harvest, that he will send forth laborers into his harvest."

49. A possible allusion to 2 Timothy 2:3: "Thou therefore endure hardness, a good soldier of Jesus Christ" (KJV). Another possible source for this allusion is the hymn "Onward Christian Soldiers," which Hostetler later mentions.

50. The Hutterite Waldner described this experience in his World War I diary: "At 9 a.m. we walked two by two to the YMCA—We told the lieutenant

that this bothers our conscience, and he said that we may then leave the building. We discovered that they had a theater in there and showed pictures about venereal diseases. We did not think we should look at these pictures and left. That made the officers very angry. In the afternoon we had a long and heated discussion with the captain until we could convince him of the teachings in the Ten Commandments, which speak against making images or likenesses." See Waldner, "Diary of a World War I C.O., A Hutterite," AMC.

51. This interaction between the Hutterite Stahl (there were four Hutterites with that last name in Funston) and his officer was apparently a memorable one for Hostetler. In his 1968 interview, he recounted the "two man show" between Stahl and Bacheran after the Hutterites once again had refused to walk in formation: "One of the sergeants, he'd come back here [to the formation] and he got after this one boy, and promised that he'd give us a one man show, or two man show. He got after them [the Hutterites] for not walking in formation. Then he'd given [the Hutterites] a good bawling out. Stahl, he says, 'I'm not mad at you.' And that made the sergeant mad, I guess. He said, 'You're going to have to walk in line, he says, and if you don't, I'm going to have to get someone to make you.''

Chapter 6

1. See John Neufeld, "Forty Years of City Mission Work," *Missionary News and Notes* (July 1960): 1.
2. Ibid.
3. Quoted in Gerlof Homan, *American Mennonites and the Great War, 1914-1918* (Scottdale, Pa.: Herald Press, 1994), 120.
4. John Neufeld to H. P. Krehbiel, 3 March 1919, copy in Microfilm 169, Mennonite Library and Archives (MLA), North Newton, Kan..
5. Ibid.
6. John Neufeld, "Diary of World War I," copy in MLA, 6.
7. Court-martial record of John Neufeld, copy in MLA.
8. Ibid.
9. Neufeld, "Forty Years," 1.
10. Neufeld, "Diary," 16.
11. Ibid.
12. Neufeld, "Forty Years," 1.
13. Neufeld to Krehbiel, 3 March 1919.
14. Homan, *American Mennonites and the Great War*, 151.
15. Neufeld to Krehbiel, 3 March 1919.
16. Neufeld, "Diary," 21.
17. Neufeld to Krehbiel, 3 March 1919.
18. Neufeld, "Forty Years," 2.
19. Neufeld, "Diary," 26.
20. Neufeld, "Forty Years," 2.
21. Neufeld to Krehbiel, 8 February 1922, copy in Microfilm 169, MLA.
22. John Neufeld, "A Brief Story of the Grace Mennonite Church." Unpublished typescript, 1952, 4.

23. Neufeld, "Diary," 26.

24. "History of my" was scrawled in the upper margin of page one; however, Neufeld did not finish the sentence, only drawing a horizontal line after "my."

25. In the upper margin of page four, Neufeld wrote "One of these officers was Lieutenant Beeves of _____ but the others I did not know."

26. A rarity during the First World War, the objector Sheldon Smith was found "not guilty" at his court-martial, and was returned to his company at Camp Cody. According to Neufeld, however, Smith was twice beaten badly while at Cody: once for refusing to don a uniform, and another time in the prison stockade, when he refused to work around the camp. He was transferred to Camp Funston and released there in December 1918.

27. Page eight is missing from Neufeld's text, although it is not clear when or how it was extracted from the manuscript. Neufeld's daughter Esther Kressly inserted a page in the manuscript at this point, detailing the story of the physical abuse. Neufeld also related the experience of his abuse in a letter to H. P. Krehbiel dated 3 March 1919. He wrote: "After having laid the matter before God in prayer, many times, asking him for help, we refused to go with the company for drill. We stepped out of line, but were both grabbed by the neck and pushed to the drill ground. One corporal was put in special command of me to make me drill. As I did not obey the commands of right and left face as they were given, I was jerked around by the ears and also boxed around once or twice. Was also thrown to the ground and kicked at but not hurt. The men all around were swearing and cussing me." See Neufeld to Krehbiel, 3 March 1919, copy in Microfilm 169, MLA. Only much later, in his series of *Missionary News and Notes* essays, did Neufeld mention that part of their decision not to drill was based on the officers' commands to practice drill with arms.

28. Neufeld canceled a significant portion of the passage on this page; his markings were such that the original passage is now indecipherable. What exists in the text was written on top of the cancellation, from "commander in chief" to "we could not do it."

29. In particular, Neufeld was no doubt read Articles of War 64 and 65, which stipulated that "the willful disobedience of a lawful order or command" was punishable by trial and imprisonment. He was charged with violation of the 64th Article of War for refusing the "lawful command" to "Go and Drill as ordered by your officers."

30. In "Forty Years of City Mission Work," written in 1960, Neufeld described his "reception" thusly: "It was getting dark as we passed through the big iron gate at the Disciplinary Barracks at Fort Leavenworth. After some interviews with Colonel Hoisington and others we were led through more steel doors and finally to a basement cell corridor. Here we had to strip so as to make sure that we had no secret weapons on us; and finally were disposed of for the night in two separate cells in this basement jail." See John Neufeld, "Forty Years of City Mission Work," *Missionary News and Notes*, July 1960, 1.

31. Neufeld's heavy editing pen was at work here as well, again crossing out and revising significant portions of the page. His revisions, appearing in

this edition's text, were written in the upper margin of the page and above the cancellations; in this instance, at least, the canceled passages were readable, but were not deemed authorial.

32. At the end of the line "D.B. was the . . ." Neufeld drew a circle with an X inside. There is no indication of why he used the symbol or why it was included at this point in the text.

33. Aaron Loucks, an (Old) Mennonite, was general manager of the Mennonite Publishing House, Scottdale, Pa. During the war he chaired the (Old) Mennonite Military Problems Committee, working with the government on behalf of objectors and visiting men in camps. According to Gerlof Homan, Loucks journeyed great distances during the war to visit men in camps and to meet with military officials. A friend and colleague on the Military Problems Committee, Jonas Hartzler, noted that Loucks was beleaguered by the heft of his correspondence and the rigors of traveling, but still worked tirelessly for the objectors' cause. See Homan, *American Mennonites and the Great War, 1914-1918* (Scottdale, Pa.: Herald Press), 125. Daniel H. Bender was president of the (Old) Mennonites' Hesston College in Hesston, Kansas. He also visited and counseled objectors as part of the Amish Mennonite and (Old) Mennonite "Committee of Ten."

34. Neufeld drew a circle around the sentence "Several others had been there before I was in the D.B."

35. Reverend Jacob (J.D.) Mininger was a minister in the (Old) Mennonite Church and a Kansas City Mennonite missionary. Mininger became a familiar sight at Fort Leavenworth during the war, visiting objectors and holding worship services for them. Following the war, in March 1919, Mininger published "Religious C.O.'s Imprisoned at the U.S. Disciplinary Barracks, Ft. Leavenworth, Kansas," an extensive list of the objectors incarcerated at Leavenworth, their home addresses, denominations, the camps at which they were sentenced, the length of their sentences, and the date of their imprisonments and releases. Mininger's list remains a significant document for uncovering the identity of objectors imprisoned during the war.

Chapter 7

1. Meyer related this experience in "Reflections of a Conscientious Objector in World War I," *Mennonite Quarterly Review* 41 (January 1967): 89.

2. James Juhnke, *Vision, Doctrine, War: Mennonite Identity and Organization in America, 1890-1930* (Scottdale, Pa.: Herald Press, 1989), 39.

3. Theron Schlabach, *Peace, Faith, Nation: Mennonites and Amish in Nineteenth-Century America* (Scottdale, Pa.: Herald Press, 1988), 220.

4. James Lehman, *Creative Congregationalism: A History of the Oak Grove Mennonite Church in Wayne County, Ohio* (Smithville, Ohio: Oak Grove Mennonite Church, 1978), 128.

5. Jacob Conrad Meyer to Esther Steiner, 7 January 1918, J. C. Meyer Collection, Archives of the Mennonite Church (AMC), Goshen, Indiana.

6. Meyer to Steiner, 3 February 1918, J. C. Meyer Collection, AMC.

7. Meyer to Steiner, 17 March 1918, J. C. Meyer Collection, AMC.

8. Meyer to Steiner, 3 February 1918, J. C. Meyer Collection, AMC. Emphasis his.

9. Meyer to Steiner, 12 May 1918, J. C. Meyer Collection, AMC.

10. J. C. Meyer, "An Annotated Diary of a Conscientious Objector," J. C. Meyer Collection, AMC, 1.

11. Meyer to Steiner, 27 July 1918, J. C. Meyer Collection, AMC.

12. Meyer to Steiner, 1 August 1918, J. C. Meyer Collection, AMC.

13. Meyer, "An Annotated Diary of a Conscientious Objector," J. C. Meyer Collection, AMC, 10.

14. Ibid., 3.

15. Meyer to Steiner, 12 August 1918, J. C. Meyer Collection, AMC.

16. Lehman, *Creative Congregationalism*, 221.

17. Meyer to Steiner, 27 October 1918, J. C. Meyer Collection, AMC.

18. Meyer to Steiner, 20 October 1918, J. C. Meyer Collection, AMC.

19. J. C. Meyer, "Reflections of a Conscientious Objector in World War I," 90-91.

20. Meyer, "Diary of World War I," 26 October 1918, J. C. Meyer Collection, AMC.

21. Meyer to Steiner, 27 October 1918, J. C. Meyer Collection, AMC.

22. Meyer to Steiner, 3 November 1918, J. C. Meyer Collection, AMC.

23. J. C. Meyer, "Preliminary Developments for the Young People's Conference in France in 1919," *Mennonite Historical Bulletin* 1 (January 1968): 3.

24. Ibid.

25. Meyer to Steiner, 29 November 1918, J. C. Meyer Collection, AMC.

26. Meyer, "Preliminary Developments," 1.

27. Meyer to Steiner, 24 November 1918, J. C. Meyer Collection, AMC.

28. Jacob C. Meyer, "The Supreme Moment," *Gospel Herald*, 6 February 1919: 803.

29. Gerlof Homan, *American Mennonites and the Great War, 1914-1918* (Scottdale, Pa.: Herald Press, 1994), 176.

30. Melvin Gingerich, Introduction, "Reflections of a Conscientious Objector in World War I," 79.

31. James Juhnke, *Vision, Doctrine, War: Mennonite Identity and Organization in America, 1890-1930*, 250.

32. Meyer to Steiner, 19 August 1918, J. C. Meyer Collection, AMC.

33. Sterling was Meyer's hometown, located in Wayne County, Ohio, some sixty miles south of Cleveland.

34. John Gerig was the cousin of Meyer's father; his son was Meyer's roommate at Goshen College, and was at the time of Meyer's writing detained at Camp Sherman, Ohio. Jacob (J.S.) Gerig was bishop of the Oak Grove Amish Mennonite congregation, of which Meyer was a member.

35. Orrville is located in Wayne County, Ohio, a little more than five miles southeast of the present Oak Grove meetinghouse. Meyer later wrote about his "farewells" that "[m]y father and mother were considerably worried about me, for they seemed to feel that I was determined, stubborn, courageous, or what, and might get very severe treatment in the army. Father had been a conscript on two occasions in France about the time of the Franco-

Prussian War so he knew something of army life... I allowed myself not a single tear in all these farewells and smiled as I waved the last goodbye. This was deliberate and carefully planned lest my aged parents would be worried the more." In a letter to Esther Steiner he wrote, "I have concluded that the hardest part of the experience is that of the parents and those who remain at home." See Meyer, "Reflections of a Conscientious Objector," *Mennonite Quarterly Review* 41 (January 1967), 79-80; Meyer to Steiner, 27 July 1918, J. C. Meyer Collection, AMC.

36. Although Springer is a name somewhat common among Mennonites, there is no indication that Meyer's sergeant was a Mennonite. Meyer said of Sergeant Springer that, although he was a fifteen year veteran of the army, he could not pronounce "necessity" and "necessary" when reading to the objectors from the Manual of Arms. Thus, "after his first attempt he just pronounced the first syllable and then one of us would pronounce the word so he could go on." See Meyer, "Reflections of a Conscientious Objector," 80-81.

37. Psychological exams were given to all new conscripts, but were later criticized as culturally biased. Instead of testing the minds of soldiers, the questions reflected the social and cultural background of those who created the exam. Questions included "The Overland car is made in ——" and "Scrooge appears in ——." Meyer admitted that although he got an "A" on his test, he could not identify Mary Pickford, a famous actress of the time. One can easily imagine that those who had an eighth grade education or less, and who remained in isolated communities apart from popular culture, would fair poorly on such a test. See Edward M. Coffman, *The War to End All Wars: The American Military Experience in World War I* (New York: Oxford University Press, 1968), 61.

38. Because Meyer was helping register new arrivals but was not in uniform, he was repeatedly questioned about how he could work for the military without wearing a uniform. Some soldiers wondered if they could have a job like his; Meyer's reply was that they needed to talk with their captain. He admitted that he believed himself "something of a peace propagandist," as he had to explain his conscientious objection over and over to the new arrivals. See Meyer, "Reflections of a Conscientious Objector," 82.

39. Meyer had joined college-educated conscripts to take the trade exam. The other soldiers objected to Meyer's testing in civilian clothes, implying that Meyer might not be "interested in getting the Kaiser" because he refused to wear the military uniform.

40. Jacob Loucks Devers from York, Pennsylvania, was well aware of Mennonites and their beliefs, coming from a Mennonite background himself. Meyer felt it "providential" to have Devers as his commanding officer because of Dever's consideration and kindness to objectors.

41. S. J. Bunting was Samuel Bunting, director of the American Friends Service Committee in Philadelphia.

42. Apparently, this letter was from Secretary of War Newton Baker's assistant Frederick Keppel, writing at Baker's behest, and addressed personally to Meyer, who had written Baker prior to his conscription. Meyer pleaded for assistance in obtaining a visa so he could work in France. The letter from

Baker contained the latest executive order on conscientious objectors, dispatched June 30, 1918. According to Meyer, the letter from Baker proved helpful; Meyer was the only one who had the ruling, and officers borrowed it from him whenever necessary. He wrote, "[M]y impression is they had received the document but it was thought unimportant and got lost in the mountains of papers and orders that came to every commanding officer . . . my impression has grown that the officers developed respect for me because I was in touch with the highest officer in the army." See Meyer, "An Annotated Diary of a Conscientious Objector," J. C. Meyer Collection, AMC, 7.

43. Esther A. Steiner, who would marry Meyer in July 1923.

44. According to Meyer, "some of the Quakers and others refused to work because a guard with a fixed bayonet always accompanied us when we left the company street. Some of us as new arrivals went under guard and ere long the guard no longer accompanied us." See Meyer, "Annotated Diary of a Conscientious Objector," 7.

45. Elmer was Meyer's brother; Ben (B.C.) and David (D.F.) were brothers living in Wayland, Iowa; Clara was Meyer's sister, from Sterling, Ohio. The letter from Bunting informed Meyer that his passport had reached the American Friends Service Committee in Philadelphia.

46. Christian Conrad fell victim to an accidental death while detained as a conscientious objector at Camp Dodge, Iowa.

47. Meyer was called before his officers and asked if he knew anything of the letter or its writer; at the time, he did not. Apparently, an objector had smuggled a letter outside of camp and mailed it to Washington, D.C., without it having been censored. Meyer later believed a Quaker named Leonard Winslow had written from Camp Jackson to Washington demanding more rights for objectors, and that part of the offending letter was published in Rufus Jones's *A Service of Love in War Time* (1920). At any rate, the uncensored letter proved detrimental to the camp's objectors, who in Meyer's mind "lost some liberties because of its mailing." See Meyer, "Reflections of a Conscientious Objector," *Mennonite Quarterly Review* 41 (January 1967), 84.

48. The missing word here is indecipherable because of Meyer's obscured handwriting. Perhaps the word is *strict*, which would make sense given the context of the sentence.

49. Most likely a letter of consolation sent to the parents of Meyer's cousin, Christian Conrad. Two marginal notes, written in Meyer's distinct hand, explained that these people are "home community folks" and the "parents of" a cousin who was killed in an accident at Camp Dodge. This marginalia appears to have been written much later, perhaps when Meyer was annotating his diary for the *Mennonite Quarterly Review* article.

50. Russelites were followers of Charles Russell, known more formally as International Bible Students. In 1931, the Russelites took the name Jehovah's Witnesses.

51. Although men in Meyer's camp were anxious for a visit from the Mennonite leader Aaron Loucks, he apparently never came to Camp Jackson. Meyer later said that Mennonite young men who were conscripted had been promised visits from Mennonite leaders, but such never occurred at his

camps, a disappointment to him and his brethren. See Meyer, "Annotated Diary of a Conscientious Objector," 13.

52. In his "Annotated Diary," Meyer related that after the exam, an Amish man asked Meyer the answer to one of the questions: "What is the difference between a banana and an elephant?" The man was intelligent, but could not read or write English well, and so could not decipher the difference between the two; because of this, he and other objectors facing similar difficulties were labeled as unintelligent. See Meyer, "Annotated Diary of a Conscientious Objector," 14.

53. Roby L. Barnes, a Quaker objector from Fries, Virginia, was later court-martialed and sentenced to Fort Leavenworth for twelve years, but was released on January 27, 1919. Meyer termed him "our low IQ man." See Meyer, "Reflections of a Conscientious Objector," 91.

54. A regular conscript from Tuscarawas County, Ohio, Steele wandered into the objectors' Bible study, not realizing he had entered a segregated part of the camp or that his fellow worshipers were objectors. According to Meyer, "He seemed like an 'almost persuaded candidate.' At any rate, we did not think of casting him out of our kingdom. More ecumenicity!" See Meyer, "Reflections of a Conscientious Objector," 87.

55. Meyer was to contribute to the Goshen College "Class of 1916" letter, the first in his class to write from military camp; however, he did not know how best to do this when a censor might read it.

56. In his diary, Meyer wrote an entry for September 20, followed by an entry for September 19. In the margin next to the September 20 entry, Meyer wrote "see below"; a long line is drawn vertically next to the September 19 entry.

57. Simon Legain, a Quaker conscientious objector from Siloam, North Carolina, was sentenced on September 26, 1918, and according to a listing of objectors at Leavenworth, received five years. Meyer's diary, however, put Legain's sentence at ten years.

58. Paris, located north of Greenville, South Carolina, was then a small town that benefited greatly from its location near Camp Sevier.

59. Payson Miller and Russell Lantz, friends of Meyer's from Goshen College, were both court-martialed at Camp Zachary Taylor, Kentucky. Each received a ten-year sentence to Fort Leavenworth. Meyer had just received notice of their imprisonment.

60. This no doubt refers to John E. Hartzler's forced resignation as president of Goshen College. Hartzler was removed from Goshen College in part because of financial mismanagement, but also because his more liberal theology was not tolerated by some (Old) Mennonite leaders. His ouster was part of a growing conservative movement that would eventually clash with the Young People's Movement, of which Meyer was a part. See "Hartzler, John Ellsworth," *The Mennonite Encyclopedia*, v. 5 (Scottdale, Pa.: Herald Press, 1990).

61. Apparently, it was decided that sweeping grounds did little to prevent the rampant spread of influenza. Meyer believed sweeping the grounds was in fact detrimental to those who were ill with pulmonary infections, as

sweeping only stirred up dust and made the air more difficult to breathe.

62. John Nevin Sayre was Francis Bowes Sayre's brother. F. B. Sayre, the son-in-law of President Woodrow Wilson, had been in Meyer's class at Harvard.

63. Meyer later wrote that Kellogg "doubted whether I could ever get a good position in later life" because of being a conscientious objector. See Meyer, "Annotated Diary of a Conscientious Objector," 25.

64. Meyer believed officers wanted the objectors to place their payroll money in a company fund so that the officers could "get their hands on it." He was able to convince other Mennonite and Amish objectors to resist making a company fund. Still, the men worried about what they should do with their pay, as Meyer admitted in his diary. One Amish man was concerned that if he sent his paycheck to Secretary of War Newton Baker, Baker would return it. See Meyer, "Reflections of a Conscientious Objector," 90.

65. Meyer drew an arrow in the left margin from the words "At retreat" up to "furlough."

66. A copy of the letter from Loucks was also sent to Meyer, with a postscript saying Meyer could show the letter to other objectors, as Meyer's mail was not censored. However, Meyer later wrote, "I did no such thing for betraying confidence did not fit into my idea of conscientious objection." See Meyer, "Reflections of a Conscientious Objector," 91.

67. In the first few pages of diary three, Meyer listed the conscientious objectors of his detachment, cataloging them according to denomination and including as well their hometowns; this list has not been included in this edition's text of Meyer's diary.

68. Meyer drew a horizontal line from the left margin to the page's center between the entry from November 9 and that for November 10.

69. Meyer's Uncle Albert was a bachelor who lived with Meyer's parents and helped care for them. Meyer said he "seemed like a godsend for a penniless conscientious objector." See Meyer, "Reflections of a Conscientious Objector," 80. L.E.B. was a friend from Goshen, Lloyd E. Blauch, whose brother had been accidentally electrocuted.

70. Meyer affixed a short newspaper clipping to page 16. The article, distributed by International News Service, was headlined "Mennonites Wink at Religion to Help War." The article read, in part, "The Mennonites have finally found a way to wink at their creed and help the United States in the war . . . The money of Mennonites is deposited with the bankers who are 'wise to the game.' The bankers apply the deposits to the purchase of Liberty Bonds and then issue certificates of deposit to the members. At the expiration of ten years, depositors can claim bonds or their equivalent in money."

71. Bowser was probably one among a number of noncombatant Mennonites who came to see Meyer right after the armistice, worried about how they would be received by their home congregations following their discharges. Meyer thought they were right to be worried. One congregation had "disowned" a member who had accepted military services; other Mennonite noncombatants, Meyer wrote, received little support or direction from their home congregations, despite attempts by the noncombatants to "keep in

touch" with their ministers. See Meyer, "Reflections of A Conscientious Objector," 91.

72. Between pages 22 and 23, Meyer sandwiched a sheet of paper detailing his expenses in September 1919. The page appears to be a deposit certificate from the National Provincial Bank of England, though Meyer used it to list what he spent during his tour of the London area. When the page was placed in Meyer's Great War diary is unclear.

73. After discussions with Bowser, and after correspondence with several other young Mennonite men preparing to do postwar reconstruction, Meyer had concluded that the Mennonite Relief Commission was doing little, if any, important relief work. In a letter signed also by E. E. Miller, J. J. Fisher, and D. S. Gerig, Meyer proposed the development of "a form of an independent Mennonite relief work." Wrote Meyer, "the Mennonite church [should] develop and utilize the talent of its young men and women . . . in some form of positive service. Under no circumstances should the latter by excluded." See Meyer, "Reflections of a Conscientious Objector," 92.

74. On this occasion, Meyer accidentally spoke German to an officer—a mistake that could easily have raised the ire of the military man. Still, the ease with which Meyer conversed and wrote in English suggests that this was his primary language, though his parents still spoke primarily German. According to James Lehman, Meyer's father had attempted to learn English when he first settled in America, but because of difficulty with English pronunciation, students at his language school laughed at him; Jacob G. Meyer quit his formal education in English after one week. Jacob C. Meyer spoke English fluently; his German education came mostly from instruction in the Oak Grove Mennonite Church. See Lehman, *Creative Congregationalism: A History of the Oak Grove Mennonite Church in Wayne County, Ohio* (Smithville, Ohio: Oak Grove Mennonite Church, 1978), 56, 98.

75. Those conscientious objectors who evaded the draft and did not report to camp when conscripted were classified differently than religious objectors and from those who had political but not religious objections to warfare.

76. As noted earlier in the diary, an order from Washington stipulated that men who were farther than 350 miles from home would be channeled through camps closer to their home communities to alleviate the government's burden of travel costs; thus, Ohio objectors at Camp Sevier were sent first to Camp Zachary Taylor, Kentucky, then discharged.

77. Meyer left a space of about one inch after writing "Clair &," as if he were trying to remember a name. He apparently hoped he would recall the name later.

78. Because Monroe Schlabach had been ill and in the hospital when the Board of Inquiry was in camp, he did not receive a hearing. Until such could occur, Schlabach would not be discharged. He finally received a discharge in early 1919.

79. The final entries were written on the back cover of diary book three, and on some loose sheets of paper.

80. Meyer later wrote that "during much of this time the cold, weary soldiers—several hundred of them—who came with us vented their wrath on

us. There was some danger of mob action." See Meyer, "An Annotated Diary of a Conscientious Objector," 28.

81. Meyer believed that the constant questioning by the soldiers at Camp Zachary Taylor provided an opening for the conscientious objectors to explain their stance. The objectors' willingness to prepare food also changed attitudes. The soldiers, Meyer wrote, were "unwilling to work" because the "war was over." As a result, "not enough food was prepared." The objectors stepped in to help the overburdened mess sergeant and cooked more than enough food for the soldiers. After this, their relationship to the regular conscripts changed. See Meyer, "An Annotated Diary of a Conscientious Objector," 29.

82. Meyer hoped to attend the Relief and Mission Conference at Elida; the conference was postponed in attempt to stem the tide of influenza. See Meyer, *Reflections of a Conscientious Objector*, 94.

Bibliography

Abrams, Ray H. *Preachers Present Arms*. New York: Round Table Press, 1933.

Beaver, Daniel R. *Newton D. Baker and the American War Effort, 1917-1919*. Lincoln, Neb.: University of Nebraska Press, 1966.

Blauch, Levi. "The Lesson of the War in Europe." *Gospel Herald*, 22 April 1915, 58.

Blunden, Edmund. *Undertones of War*. 1928. Reprint. New York: Harvest, 1965.

Brittain, Vera. *Testament of Youth*. New York: Macmillan, 1937.

Brooke, Rupert. *The Collected Poems of Rupert Brooke*. 1915. Reprint. New York: Dodd, Mead, 1928.

Brunk, George R. "War." *Gospel Herald*, 19 April 1917, 42.

Bush, Perry. *Two Kingdoms, Two Loyalties: Mennonite Pacifism in Modern America*. Baltimore: John Hopkins University Press, 1998.

Campbell, James. "Combat Gnosticism: The Ideology of First World War Poetry Criticism." *New Literary History* 30 (Spring 1999): 203-15.

Cardinal, Roger. "Unlocking the Diary." In *Comparative Criticism: An Annual Journal*, edited by E. S. Shaffer. Cambridge: Cambridge University Press, 1990.

Chambers, John Whiteclay. "Conscientious Objectors and the American State from Colonial Times to the Present." In *The New Conscientious Objection: From Sacred to Secular Resistance*, ed. John Whiteclay Chambers and Charles C. Mosleos. Oxford: Oxford University Press, 1993.

Chapman, Guy. *A Passionate Prodigality: Fragments of Autobiography*. New York: Holt, 1933.

Cross, Tim. *The Lost Voices of World War: An International Anthology of Writers, Poets, and Playwrights*. London: Bloomsbury, 1988.

Dewey, L. A. to Aaron Loucks. 29 September 1917. Reprinted in *Gospel Herald*, 11 October 1917, 523.

Eberhart, Richard and Selden Rodman, eds. and comps. *War and the Poet: An Anthology of Poetry*. New York: Devin-Adair Co., 1945.

Ellmann, Richard, and Robert O'Clair, eds. and comps. *The Norton Anthology of Modern Poetry*. New York: Norton, 1988.

Ettinger, Albert M. *A Doughboy with the Fighting 69th: A Remembrance of World War One*. New York: Simon and Schuster, 1992.

Evert, J. G. "The Martyrs of Alcatraz." *Gospel Herald*. 2 October 1919: 490.

Executive Order. 20 March 1918. Microfilm copy in Mennonite Library and Archives (MLA), North Newton, Kan..

Fothergill, Robert. "One Day At A Time: The Diary as Lifewriting." *A/B: Auto/Biography Studies* 10 (Spring 1995): 81-91.

Fry, Michele. "Defining the Canon of English Poetry of the First World War." <http://www.sassoonery.demon.co.uk>.

Fussell, Paul. *The Great War and Modern Memory*. London: Oxford University Press, 1975.

Gaeddert, Albert and Edna. *Story of Jacob D. and Katharina (Ratzlaff) Gaeddert Family*. Unpublished, 1992.

Gaeddert, Gustav. Diary. Unpublished, n.d. Microfilm copy in MLA.

———. Correspondence with H. P. Krehbiel. Microfilm copy in MLA.

———. Interview by John Waltner, 2 November 1967. Tape recording, MLA.

Genet, Edmond. *War Letters of Edmond Genet*. Ed. Grace Ellery Channing. New York: Scribners, 1918.

Gibbs, Philip. *Now it Can be Told*. Garden City, N.Y.: Garden City Publishing, 1920.

Gilbert, Martin. *The First World War: A Complete History*. New York: Holt, 1994.

Hallowes, Frances S. *Women and War*. London: Headly Bros., 1914.

Hart, A. B., and Herbert R. Fergleger. *Theodore Roosevelt Cyclopedia*. New York: n.p., 1941.

Hartzler, J. S. *Mennonites in the World War or Nonresistance Under Test*. Scottdale, Pa.: Herald Press, 1921.

Hege, John. "Camp Meade Diary." Unpublished, n.d.

Hibberd, Dominic, and John Onions, eds. and comps. *Poetry of the First World War*. Hampshire, England: Macmillan, 1990.

Higonnet, Margaret R., ed. *Lines of Fire: Women Writers of World War I*. New York: Penguin, 1999.

Higham, John. *Strangers in the Land: Patterns of American Nativism, 1860-1925*. New York: Atheneum, 1963.

Homan, Gerlof D. *American Mennonites and the Great War, 1914-1918*. Scottdale, Pa.: Herald Press, 1994.

——— "Mennonites and Military Justice in World War I." *Mennonite Quarterly Review* 65 (July 1992): 365-75.

Hostetler, Harvey. *Descendants of Barbara Hochstedler and Christian Stutzman.* Berlin, Ohio: Gospel Book Store, 1938.

Hostetler, Ura H. "Diary of World War I." Unpublished, n.d.

———. Interview by James Juhnke. 11 June 1968. Tape recording, MLA.

Huxman, Susan Schultz. "In the World, But Not of It: Mennonite Rhetoric in World War I as an Enactment of Paradox." Ph.D. dissertation, University of Kansas, 1987.

Hynes, Samuel. *The Soldiers' Tale: Bearing Witness to Modern War.* New York: Penguin, 1997

Johnson, Donald. *The Challenge to American Freedoms: World War I and the Rise of the American Civil Liberties Union.* Louisville, Ky.: University of Kentucky Press, 1963.

Juhnke, James. *A People of Two Kingdoms: The Political Acculturation of the Kansas Mennonites.* Newton, Kan.: Faith and Life Press, 1975.

———. *Vision, Doctrine, War: Mennonite Identity and Organization in America, 1890-1930.* Scottdale, Pa.: Herald Press, 1989.

Kauffman, Thelma. Telephone conversation with author, 20 June 1999.

———. *Hostetler Family History.* n.p., n.d.

———. Letter to the author. 20 June 1999.

Kellogg, Walter Guest. *The Conscientious Objector.* New York: Boni and Liveright, 1919.

Kennedy, David M. *Over Here: The First World War and American Society.* Oxford: Oxford University Press, 1980.

Khan, Nosheen. *Women's Poetry of the First World War.* Lexington, Ky.: University Press of Kentucky, 1988.

Klaassen, Rose M. "Mennonite Diary." *Liberty,* September/October 1985, 9-10.

Knock, Thomas. *To End All Wars: Woodrow Wilson and the Quest for a New World Order.* Princeton, N. J.: Princeton University Press, 1992.

Kohn, Stephen M. *Jailed for Peace: The History of American Draft Law Violators: 1658-1984.* Westport, Conn.: Greenwood Press, 1986.

Krehbiel, H. P., Correspondence with Gustav Gaeddert. Microfilm 169, MLA.

Landis, Cliff. "A Soldier for Christ." Unpublished essay, 1973. Archives of the Mennonite Church (AMC), Goshen, Ind.

Lane, Winthrop D. "Who are the Conscientious Objectors?" *New Republic,* 14 April 1920, 215-17.

Lehman, James O. *Creative Congregationalism: A History of the Oak Grove Mennonite Church in Wayne County, Ohio.* Smithville, Ohio: Oak Grove Mennonite Church, 1978.

Leatherman, Noah. *Diary Kept By Noah Leathernman While in Camp During World War I*. Linden, Alberta: Aaron L. Toews, 1951.

Leisy, E. E. "The Martial Adventures of a Conscientious Objector." Typewritten, n.d. MLA.

Loewen, Royden. *From the Inside Out: The Rural Worlds of Mennonite Diarists*. Winnipeg, Manitoba: University of Manitoba Press, 1999.

"The Martyr Spirit." Editorial. *Gospel Herald*, 8 November 1917, 585.

May, Mark. "The Psychological Examination of Conscientious Objectors." *The American Journal of Psychology* 31(April 1920): 152-65.

"Mennonites on Military Service: A Statement of Our Position on Military Service as Adopted by The Mennonite General Conference, August 29, 1917." Reprinted in *Gospel Herald*, 6 September 1917, 420.

Meyer, J. C. "An Annotated Diary of a Conscientious Objector," Unpublished, 1966. AMC.

———. Correspondence with Esther Steiner. J. C. Meyer collection, AMC.

———. "Diary of World War I," Unpublished, n.d. J. C. Meyer Collection, AMC.

———. Letter. *Gospel Herald*, 07 November 1918, 585.

———. "Preliminary Developments for the Young People's Conference in France in 1919." *Mennonite Historical Bulletin* 1 (January 1968): 1-4.

———. "Reflections of a Conscientious Objector in World War I." *The Mennonite Quarterly Review* 41 (January 1967): 79-96.

Miller, Ernest. "Experiences of a C.O. in World War I." Unpublished, n.d. Menno Simons Library and Archives, Harrisonburg, Va.

Morrison, J. L. *Josephus Daniels: The Small-d Democrat*. Chapel Hill, N.C: University of North Carolina Press, 1966.

Mumaw, Adam H. "My Experience as Conscientious Objector in World War I." Unpublished, n.d. Menno Simons Library and Archives, Harrisonburg, Va.

———. "Second Company Development Battalion." Unpublished, n.d. MSLA.

Neufeld, John. Court-martial transcript. Copy in MLA.

———. "A Brief Story of the Grace Mennonite Church." Unpublished, 1952. Illinois Mennonite Historical and Genealogical Society, Metamora, Ill.

———. "Diary of World War I." Unpublished, n.d. MLA.

———. "Forty Years of City Mission Work." *Missionary News and Notes* 11 (July 1960): 1-2.

———. Correspondence with H. P. Krehbiel. Microfilm copy in MLA.

Nussbaum, Felicity. "Towards Conceptualizing Diary." In *Studies in Autobiography*, ed. James Olney. New York: Oxford University Press, 1988.

Olney, James. *Metaphors of Self: the Meaning of Autobiography*. Princeton, N.J.: Princeton University Press, 1972.

"Our Attitude." Editorial. *Gospel Herald*, 12 April 1917, 25.

Owen, Wilfred. *The Collected Poems of Wilfred Owen*. 1920. Reprint. London: Chatto and Windus, 1963.

_____. *Collected Letters*. Ed. Harold Owen and John Bell. London: Oxford University Press, 1967.

Palmer, Frederick. *Newton D. Baker: America at War*. New York: Dodd, Mead, 1931.

Peterson, H. C. and Gilbert C. Fite. *Opponents of War: 1917-1918*. 1957. Reprinted Westport, Conn.: Greenwood Press, 1986.

"The Real Issue." Editorial. *Gospel Herald*, 11 October 1917, 513.

Resolution. Nebraska State Legislature. 5 February 1919. Microfilm copy in MLA.

Rosenwald, Laurence. "Some Myths About Diaries." *Raritan: A Quarterly Review* 3 (Winter 1987): 97-112.

Roth, John D., and Ervin Beck, eds. *Migrant Muses: Mennonite/s Writing in the US*. Goshen, Ind.: Mennonite Historical Society, 1998.

Sarton, May. *The House by the Sea*. New York: Norton, 1977.

Sassoon, Siegfried. *Collected Poems, 1908-1928*. Boston: Faber and Faber, 1986.

———. *Counter-Attack and Other Poems*. New York: E.P. Dutton, 1918

———. *Memoirs of an Infantry Officer*. 1930. Reprint. New York: Macmillan, 1957.

———. *The Old Huntsman*. London: W. Heinemann, 1917.

Sayre, Robert. "The Proper Study—Autobiographies in American Studies." *American Quarterly* 29 (1977): 241-62.

_____. "Rhetorical Defenses: The Autobiographies of WWI Conscientious Objectors." *A/B: Autobiography Studies* (Spring 1992): 62-81.

Schlabach, Theron. *Peace, Faith, Nation: Mennonites and Amish in Nineteenth-Century America*. Scottdale, Pa.: Herald Press, 1988.

Schmidt, C.B. "Mennonites and the War." *Gospel Herald*, 8 November 1917, 589.

Seeger, Alan. *Letters and Diary of Alan Seeger*. New York: Scribners, 1917.

_____. *Poems*. New York: Scribners, 1916.

Shank, Clarence S. *A Mennonite Boy's World War I Experience*. Marion, Pa.: n.p., 1963.

Shields, Sarah D. "The Treatment of Conscientious Objectors During World War I." *Kansas History* (Winter 1981): 255-69.

"Some Live Questions." Editorial. *Gospel Herald*, 1 November 1917, 561.

Spengemann, William C. and L.R. Lundquist. "Autobiography and the American Myth." *American Quarterly* 17 (1963): 501-19.

Sprunger, Keith, James C. Juhnke, and John Waltner, eds. *Voices Against War: A Guide to the Schowalter Oral History Collection on World War I Conscientious Objection*. North Newton, Kan.: 1981.

Stoltzfus, Grant M. *Mennonites of the Ohio and Eastern Conference From the Colonial Period in Pennsylvania to 1968*. Scottdale, Pa.: Herald Press, 1969.

Stone, Harlan F. "The Conscientious Objector." *Columbia University Quarterly* 21 (October 1919): 253-72.

Swartzendruber, Emanual. "Nonresistance Under Test." Unpublished, n.d. AMC.

"Things We Have Seen and Heard—and Think." Editorial. *Gospel Herald*, 4 October 1917, 489-90, 501.

Thomas, Norman. *The Conscientious Objector*. New York: B.W. Huebsch, 1925.

Waldner, Jacob. "An Account by Jacob Waldner: Diary of a Conscientious Objector in World War I." Ed. Theron F. Schlabach; trans. by Ilse Reist and Elizabeth Bender. *Mennonite Quarterly Review* 48 (January 1974): 73-111.

War Department Press Release. 26 February 1919. Microfilm copy in MLA.

Western District Conference Resolution. 25 October 1917. Microfilm copy in MLA.

Wilson, Woodrow. *The Papers of Woodrow Wilson*. 59 vols. Ed. Arthur S. Link, et al. Princeton, N.J.: Princeton University Press, 1966-1994.

The Index

A

Adventists, 48
Alcatraz, 74
American Friends Service Committee, 64-65, 68, 128, 146, 173, 227-231, 236, 238, 254, 266, 274, 277, 280, 284, 291
Amish, 43, 178, 179, 226
Amish Mennonites, 31, 223, 226
Ammann, Jakob, 31
Anabaptism, 52, 80, 126-127
Articles of War, 58, 71
Asquith, Cynthia, 117

B

Baker, Newton, 38-40, 44-47, 64-65, 76, 146, 148, 211, 229, 248-249
"Ballad of War and Peace, The," 84
Barnes, Roby, 250-251, 273
Beaves, J. S., 207, 217
Beck, Ervin, 86, 118-119, 126
Bender, Daniel H., 219
Bethel Academy, 30, 143
Bethel College, 143, 148
Bethel Mennonite Church, 30, 204
Blauch, Levi, 26
"Blighters," 89, 132
Blunden, Edmund, 88-93, 101, 130
   "Steel Helmets and All," 92
   Undertones of War, 91, 92
Board of Inquiry, 65-69, 146, 174, 182, 195, 224, 231-233, 264, 266, 269, 285
Bowser, Eggart, 277-280
Brittain, Vera, 84, 125
   Testament of Youth, 84
Brooke, Rupert, 84-85, 93
   "Dead, The," 84
Brunk, George R., 25-26
   "War," 25-26
Bunting, Samuel, 229, 244, 246, 260, 274

Bush, Perry, 33-34

C

Camp Cody, New Mexico, 203, 205, 210, 215-217
Camp Dodge, Iowa, 146-147, 178, 182-183, 174-175, 195-201, 219
Camp Funston, Kansas, 41-45, 50, 53-55, 62, 127, 141, 153-174, 177, 181-182, 190-194, 205
Camp Greenleaf, Georgia, 54
Camp Jackson, South Carolina, 61-63, 229-233, 242-258
Camp Lee, Virginia, 41
Camp Lewis, Washington, 40, 74
Camp Meade, Maryland, 40, 46, 248
Camp Sevier, South Carolina, 53, 61, 223, 233-234, 256-287
Camp Sherman, Ohio, 54
Camp Travis, Texas, 40
Camp Zachary Taylor, Kentucky, 45, 54, 60, 62, 234, 284-285-291
Campbell, James, 101
Camps, general description of, 42
   departure for and travel to, 40-41, 141, 146, 152-153, 177-180, 182, 190, 195, `204-206, 215, 217, 229-230, 242
Caveness, Hugh L., 231
Channing, Grace Ellery, 99
Chapman, Guy, 90, 130
   A Passionate Prodigality, 90
Chicago Technical College, 212
Christdelphians, 48, 255
Christian Exponent, The, 238
Church and state, 29-32, 34
Civil liberties. *See* conscientious objectors, abuse of; conscientious objectors, courts-martial of; conscientious objectors, imprisonment of

335

Civil religion, 33-34, 122
Civilian Public Service, 80, 115, 184, 185
Clergy, American, attitudes of, 33, 123, 183, 227-228
Clermont-en-Argonne, 237
Cody, Camp. See Camp Cody
Combat gnosticism, 101-104
Conrad, Christian, 242
Conscientious objectors. *See also* camps; combatants; draft; drill; Exemption committee, General Conference Mennonite Church; Exemption Committee, Western District Conference; War Problems Committee (Old) Mennonite Church; noncombatancy; nonresistance; pacifism; Selective Service Act
   abuse of, 49, 125-126, 181, 190, 206, 210, 216-217
      physical, 43-47, 53-54, 190, 193, 204-207, 216
      psychological, 43, 47-48, 53-54, 204-207
   courts-martial of, 55, 58, 70-72, 204-209, 217, 249, 256, 273
   deaths of, 74-75, 78
   detachments of, 48-49, 60-63, 128-129, 134, 141-145, 154-175, 181, 193-201, 230-231, 245-291
      discharge of, 69-70, 76, 183-184, 235
      draft boards and, 37-39, 184
      drilling of, 43, 71-72, 195, 206-208, 210, 215-216
   farm furloughs and, 64-70, 106, 145-147, 166, 169, 175, 178, 182, 183, 200-201, 208, 248, 254-257, 264, 266, 272
      hospital work and, 175, 205
      imprisonment of, 70-77, 204, 209-211, 216-220
      intelligence of, 67-68, 208-209, 223-224
      military pay of, 64, 69-70, 249, 269, 271-272, 277-278, 282
      military uniforms, wearing of, 43-45, 59, 181, 190, 206, 216, 286, 289
   noncombatancy. *See* noncombatancy, pastoral counseling for, 61
   profile of, 27-32, 41, 178
   public opinion and, 32-35, 42-43, 48-50, 76-79, 104, 203, 213-214
   reconstruction work by, 175, 233, 235, 269, 271, 281
   segregation of, 39, 45-48, 58
   units of. *See* conscientious objectors, detachments of
   Wilson, Woodrow, view of, 26, 37
   work in camps, 40, 43, 49-60, 119-120, 140-145, 149-151, 153-162, 165, 167-170, 172, 180-182, 190, 196-200, 205-208, 215-216, 228, 231, 234, 243—244, 246-247, 250-252, 258-260, 263-281, 283-290
   work in prison, 73, 180, 209-211, 218-219
   World War II, 184
Conscription, 34, 35-37, 40, 42-45, 80
Corps of Engineers, 58
Counter-Attack and Other Poems, 88
Courts-martial. *See* Conscientious objectors, courts-martial of
cummings, e. e., 100-101

D

Daniels, Josephus, 27
"Dead, The," 84
Democracy, 32, 76
Devers, Jacob Loucks, 243-244, 246
Dobell, Eva, 125
Dodge, Camp. *See* Camp Dodge
Doughboy with the Fighting 69th, 98
Draft, 35-39
   boards, 37-39, 184
   exemption, 34, 35, 37-38
Drill, 43, 71-72, 195, 206-208, 210, 215-216
"Dulce et Decorum Est," 83, 93

Dunkers, 48
Dyck, Abraham J., 153

E
Eberhart, Richard, 103
Engineering Corps. *See* Corps of Engineers
Espionage Act, *See* Espionage and Sedition Acts
Espionage and Sedition Acts, 59, 111, 117, 235-236, 239
Ettinger, Albert, 98-99
   Doughboy with the Fighting 69th, 98
Evans, William, 122
Evert, Jacob G., 75,127
   "Martyrs of Alcatraz, The," 75, 127
Exemption Committee, General Conference Mennonite Church, 56-59, 142
Exemption Committee, Western District of General Conference Mennonite Church, 56-58

F
Farm Furlough Act, 64
Farm furloughs, 64-70, 106, 145-147, 166, 169, 175, 178, 182, 183, 200-201, 208, 248, 254-257, 264, 266, 272
Fort Leavenworth, Kansas, 72-74, 182, 203-204, 209-210, 217-220
Fothergill, Robert, 118
Fry, Michele, 101-102
Funston, Camp. *See* Camp Funston
Fussell, Paul, 90-93, 101-102, 132-133
   The Great War and Modern Memory, 90-92, 101

G
Gaeddert, Albert, 141
Gaeddert, Diedriech, 143
Gaeddert, Gustav, and
   American Friends Service Committee, 146, 173
   Board of Inquiry, 146, 174
   Camp Dodge, 174-175
   Camp Funston, 153-174
   conscientious objector detachment, 134, 141-145, 154-175
   death, 151
   education, 30, 143-144, 148
   farm furlough, 69, 145-147, 166, 169, 175
   final return home, 148
   General Conference Mennonite Church, 29-31, 56, 143-144, 151
   H. P. Krehbiel, 55-56, 112, 134, 141-151, 153-154, 161, 170, 173, 219
   Iowa State Hospital, 69, 147, 175
   John Thiessen, 145, 155, 172-173, 161, 163
   Mennonite Central Committee, 149
   parents, 30, 141, 153, 155, 158, 160-161, 163, 169-171
   Red Cross, 148-149
   relationship with officers, 141, 153, 156, 159, 154-166, 170-175
   rhetorical style, 150
   Sarah Lohrentz (Hans), 145, 148, 155-159, 161-164, 168-174
   travel to Camp Dodge, 146, 174
   travel to Camp Funston, 141, 152-153
   visits home, 145, 153-158, 160-161, 163, 169-171
   work in camp, 55-56, 119, 140-145, 149-151,154-162, 165-170, 172
   World War II, 148-149
Gaeddert, Jacob, 143
Gaeddert, John, 154, 171, 158
Gaeddert, Katharina (Ratzlaff), 143, 153
Gaeddert, Marie, 141, 153, 156-157, 172
Gannett, William Channing, 227
General Conference Mennonite Church, 29-31, 39, 56, 143-144, 151, 204

338 • Index

Genet, Edmond, 98-100
  War Letters of Edmond Genet, 98-99
Gerig, D. S., 273-274, 277-280, 285, 287
Gerig, Jacob S., 226, 242, 260, 271-272, 289
Gerig, John, 242
German-Americans, 30, 78-79
Germany, 26-27
Gibbs, Philip, 88, 90
  Now it Can Be Told, 88
Goertz, David, 141
Goshen College, 224, 226, 238
Yellow Creek, Indiana Mennonite Meeting, 58
Gospel Herald, 25, 52, 53, 69, 75, 126, 237
Graves, Robert, 88, 89, 95, 101
Greenleaf, Camp. *See* Camp Greenleaf

H

Hallowes, Frances, 102
Hamilton, John, 190-192, 198, 201, 315
Hartzler, Jonas S., 59, 219, 263
Harvard University, 223-224, 227-228
Hege, John, 41
Heidebrecht, Paul, 141
Hemmingway, Ernest, 100-101
Hess, Maurice A., 73
Hiebert, Peter C. (P. C.), 164, 171
Higham, John, 32
Higonnet, Margaret, 87, 103
Hochstetler, Jacob, 178
Hofer, David J., 74
Hofer, Joseph J., 74
Hofer, Michael, 74
Hoffnungsfeld Church, 30, 143
Hoffnungsau Preparatory/Bible School, 30, 143
Holdeman Mennonites, 297
Hollcroft, Charles William, 121, 129, 193, 197-201
Homan, Gerlof, 39, 50-51, 57, 59, 81, 205, 210, 238

Hostetler, Della (Balmer), 177-183, 187, 190-193, 196-201
Hostetler, Gladys, 180
Hostetler, Henry, 179
Hostetler, Lester, 184
Hostetler, Salome (Slabach), 179
Hostetler, Ura, and
  Board of Inquiry, 182, 195
  boyhood, 29
  Camp Dodge, 178, 182, 195-201
  Camp Funston, 45, 62, 177, 190-194
  cantonment stockade, 181, 192
  conscientious objector detachment, 129, 181, 193-201
  death, 187
  Della (Balmer) Hostetler, 177-283, 187, 190-193, 196-201
  education, 29, 179
  farm furlough, 69, 106, 178, 182-183, 200-201
  Harper County, Kansas, 177-180, 187
  Mason City, Iowa, 183, 201
  military language, 106-107, 178, 186-187
  (Old) Mennonite Church, 28-29, 178-179
  parents, 29, 179, 191
  Pleasant Valley Mennonite Church, 179, 184, 187
  relationship to officers, 45, 181, 185, 190-196, 199
  relationship to other conscientious objectors, 181-183, 193-199, 201
  relationship to soldiers, 45, 133, 178, 180-181, 185, 190, 192
  release, 183-184
  travel to Camp Dodge, 182, 195
  travel to Camp Funston, 177-180, 190
  wedding, 179-180
  work in camp, 180-182, 190, 196-200
  World War II, 184
Hutterites, 43, 74-75, 193-200

Hynes, Samuel, 88, 97, 101, 113-115, 124, 135

I
"I Have a Rendezvous with Death," 99-100
Imprisonment, 58, 70-77, 204, 209-211
Inter-Mennonite activity, 36, 58, 80-81
Iowa State Hospital, 69, 147, 175

J
Jackson, Camp. *See* Camp Jackson
Jehovah's Witnesses. *See* Russellites.
Juhnke, James C., 37, 40, 64, 79- 80, 226, 240

K
Kansas City Times, 76
Kauffman, Thelma, 187, 189
Kellogg, Walter C., 51, 65-68, 121, 224, 233, 269
Kennedy, David, 66
Keppel, Frederick P., 64, 231
Khan, Nosheen, 102-103
   Women's Poetry of the First World War, 102
Kilbourne, C. E., 50, 134
Kliewer, John W. (J. W.), 143, 154, 161, 163, 173
Kohn, Stephen, 72
Krehbiel, Henry P. (H. P.), 55-56, 112, 134, 141-151-154, 161, 170, 173, 206, 209-212, 219
Krimmer Mennonite Brethren, 39

L
Lantz, Russell, 262
Larkin, Philip, 77
   "MCMXIV," 77
Lawrence, D. H., 101
Leatherman, Noah, 41, 55, 73, 117
Leavenworth, Fort. *See* Fort Leavenworth
Lee, Camp. *See* Camp Lee
Legain, Simon, 256

Lehman, James, 226
Leisy, E. E., 41
Letters and Diary of Alan Seeger, 99
Lewis, Camp. *See* Camp Lewis
Literature of the First World War
   romantic, 83-85, 89, 98-100. *See also* Brooke, Ettinger, Genet, Seeger
   trench writers. *See* Blunden, Chapman, Gibbs, Graves, Owen, Pope, Rosenberg, Sassoon, Thomas
Loewen, Royden, 128
Lohrentz, Anna (Fritz), 161, 312
Lohrentz, Sarah (Hans), 145, 148, 155-164, 168-174
Loucks, Aaron, 59, 219, 248, 272
Lund, Frank, 207
Lundquist, L. R., 116

M
Mack, Julian W., 65, 174, 266
Martyr archetype, 126-128
Martyrdom, 74-75, 124-126
"Martyrs of Alcatraz, The," 75, 127
Martyrs Mirror, 118, 126
"MCMXIV," 177
Meade, Camp. *See* Camp Meade
Medical Corps, 58
Memoirs of an Infantry Officer, 94
Chicago Mennonite Bible Mission, 212-213
Mennonite Brethren Church, 39
Mennonite Central Committee, 81, 115, 149, 185, 238
Mennonite Central Peace Committee, 80
Mennonite Quarterly Review, 111, 239, 240
Mennonite Relief Committee, 278-280
Mennonite Young People's Movement, 79, 225, 236-238
"Mental Cases," 89, 123
Meyer, Albert, 274, 284
Meyer, Ben C., 246, 267, 282, 285
Meyer, Clara, 246, 250, 254, 256, 262

Meyer, David F., 246, 265, 270
Meyer, Elmer, 228, 234-235, 246, 250, 256, 261-262, 272, 276, 282-288, 291
Meyer, Esther (Steiner), 227-233, 236-238, 245-246, 249-252, 256, 261-262, 264-269, 271-274, 278-288
Meyer, Jacob C., and
    American Friends Service Committee, 128, 227-228, 231, 236, 238, 244, 254, 266
    Amish Mennonites, 31, 223, 226
    army initiation, 230, 242
    Board of Inquiry, 66-67, 224, 231-233, 246, 264, 266, 269
    Camp Jackson, 61-63, 229-233, 242-258
    Camp Sevier, 53, 61, 223, 233-234, 256-287
    Camp Taylor, 234, 284-285, 287-291
    church membership, 226
    Clermont-en-Argonne, 237
    conscientious objector detachment, 230-231, 245-291
    creation of camp school, 63, 232, 267-269
    death, 240
    discharge, 235, 290-291
    education, 223-224, 226-228, 238
    Esther Steiner, 227-233, 236-238, 245-246, 249-252, 256, 261-269, 271-274, 278-288
    farewell in home community, 229, 242
    furloughs, 248, 254-257
    life in Boston, 227-228
    marriage, 238
    Mennonite Young People's Movement, 79, 225, 236-238
    Oak Grove Amish Mennonite Church, 226, 240
    parents, 226, 229, 235
    passes outside camp, 61, 231, 246-259, 261-276, 279-280, 286
    psychological testing, 230, 243, 270
    reconstruction, 233, 235
    "Reflections of a Conscientious Objector in World War I," 239
    registration, 227
    relationship to officers, 53, 225, 230-231, 234, 243, 246-247, 250, 259-260, 265-268, 279, 282-284, 288
    teaching career, 238
    travel to Camp Jackson, 229-230, 242
    travel to France, 235
    Wayne Co., Ohio, boyhood, 225-226
    work in camp, 53, 119-120, 228, 231, 234, 243-247, 250-252, 258-260, 263-290
Meyer, Jacob G., 226
Meyer, Mary (Conrad), 226
Military Problems Committee. *See* War Problems Committee
Miller, Daniel, 205
Miller, E. E., 256, 280, 283
Miller, Ernest H., 115
Miller, Payson, 262
Mininger, J. D., 75, 210, 219
Missionary News and Notes, 213-214
Mob action, 33, 45
Moine, Clair, 229, 244, 251-256, 264-267, 270, 273, 280, 284
Mumaw, Adam, 45, 54, 60-62, 66, 289-290

N

Nationalism, 26, 32. *See also* patriotism
Nativism, 32. *See also* patriotism
Neufeld, Abraham, 204
Neufeld, Abraham F., 72, 205-209, 215, 219
Neufeld, John T., and
    Abraham F. Neufeld, 205-209, 215, 219
    abuse in camp, 204-207, 215
    arrest, 207, 216

career as Mennonite minister, 212-213
Catherine Weins, 212
Chicago Mennonite Bible Mission, 212-213
court-martial, 72, 204, 207-209, 217
death, 213
education, 212
Fort Leavenworth, 204, 209-210, 217-220
General Conference Mennonite Church, 29, 31, 204
H. P. Krehbiel, 206, 209-212, 219
illness in prison, 211, 219
Inman, Kansas, 204, 211
J. D. Mininger, 210, 219-220
missionary work, 30, 204
parents, 204, 211, 219
prison sentence, 72, 204, 209, 217
registration, 215
relationship to officers, 43, 206, 207, 215-217
release, 211, 219-220
travel to Camp Cody, New Mexico, 204-206, 215
travel to Fort Leavenworth, 203, 209, 217
work in camp, 215
work in prison, 73, 209-211, 218-219
New York Herald, 42
Nin, Anais, 109
Noailles, Countess Anna de, 125
Noncombatancy, 34, 37-39, 58-59, 180
Noncombatant duty. *See* conscientious objectors, work in camps
Nonconformity. *See* conscientious objectors; religious attitudes
Nonresistance, 28, 32-34, 50, 67, 80
North Newton, Kansas, Mennonite meeting, 36
Now It Can Be Told, 88

Nussbaum, Felicity, 86-87, 116
Oak Grove Amish Mennonite Church, 226, 240
Oklahoma Leader, 68
(Old) Mennonite Church, 28-29, 31, 39, 56-59, 178-179
Old Order Amish, 31, 248
Olney, James, 116
"On Passing the New Menin Gate," 93
Onions, John, 122, 124, 130
Owen, Wilfred, 83-85, 88-89, 93, 96-99, 101, 123, 136
    "Ballad of War and Peace, The," 84
    "Dulce et Decorum Est," 83, 93
    "Mental Cases," 89, 123
    Poems of Wilfred Owen, 89
    "Strange Meetings," 89
Oxenham, John, 124
    "The Vision Splendid," 124

P

Pacifism, 28, 185-186, 227
Passionate Prodigality, A, 90
Patriotism, 32-35, 38, 43, 76
Peace literature, Mennonite, 80, 85-87, 97, 102-137
Peace Problems Committee, (Old) Mennonite Church. *See* War Problems Committee, (Old) Mennonite Church
Penner, H. D., 154, 156
Pepys, Samuel, 109
Philpott, S. B., 207, 216-217
Pleasant Valley Mennonite Church, 179, 184, 187
Poems of Wilfred Owen, 89
Pope, Jessie, 93
    Jessie Pope's War Poems, 93
Pound, Ezra, 101
Progressive Mennonites, 30, 31, 226

Q

Quakers, 48, 134, 227, 231, 236
Quartermaster General Corps, 58

R

Ray, C. C., 156-157
Red Cross, 36, 39, 42, 148-149
Registration, 36-38, 227
Reimer, Albert, 150
  Mennonite Literary Voices, 150
Relief, 149, 235
"Rhapsode," 135
Richert, Peter H. (P. H.) 153, 160, 162-165, 171
Roosevelt, Franklin D., 184
Roosevelt, Theodore, 42, 228
Rosenberg, Isaac, 88
Rosenwald, Lawrence, 108-109, 117
  "Some Myths about Diaries," 108-109
Roth, John, 86
Russellites, 48, 247-249, 255

S

Salmon, Benjamin, 195
Sarton, May, 114
Sassoon, Siegfried, 88-90, 93-99, 101, 130-132
  "Blighters," 89, 132
  Counter-Attack and Other Poems, 88
  Memoirs of an Infantry Officer, 94
  "On Passing the New Menin Gate," 93
  Soldier's Declaration, A, 95
Sayre, Francis Bowes, 267
Sayre, Robert, 86-87, 133
Schlabach, Monroe, 263-266, 269, 285, 287
Schlabach, Theron, 29, 31, 226
Schmidt, Carl, 155, 174
Sedition Act. *See* Espionage and Sedition Acts
Seeger, Alan, 99-100, 117, 130
  "I Have a Rendezvous with Death," 99-100
  Letters and Diaries Diary of Alan Seeger, 99
Selective Service Act, 1917, 35-37
Sevier, Camp. *See* Camp Sevier
Shank, Clarence, 41
Sherman, Camp. *See* Camp Sherman
Shields, Sarah, 43-44
Sitwell, Osbert, 135
  "Rhapsode," 135
Smith, Sheldon, 215, 217
Socialists, 48
Society of Friends. *See* Quakers
Soldier's Declaration, A, 95
Spanish Influenza, 233, 235
Spengemann, William, 116
"Steel Helmets and All," 92
Steer, James, 232, 256-257, 263, 267-278, 283-289, 291
Stoddard, Richard C., 65, 174, 246-249
Stone, Harlan F., 65-68, 174
"Strange Meetings," 89
Swartzendruber, Emanuel, 54

T

Taylor, Camp. *See* Camp Zachary Taylor
Testament of Youth, 84
Thiessen, John, 145, 155, 161, 163, 172-173
Thomas, Edward, 88
Thomas, Norman, 48
Toews, Heinrich, 204
Trench and Camp, 150
Troyer, Jim, 195
Tschetter, Peter, 54
Two Kingdoms, Theology of, 33-34, 79, 132

U

Undertones of War, 91, 92
Uniforms, military. *See* conscientious objectors, military uniforms, wearing of.
Unruh, Peter H (P. H.), 153, 156, 160, 166

V

Verdun, France, 235
"Vision Splendid, The," 124

W

Waldner, Jacob, 42-43, 47, 54
"War," 25-26
War Department, 36, 40, 51, 70, 73, 76, 80, 207. *See also* Baker, Newton D.; Keppel, Frederick P.
War Letters of Edmond Genet, 98-99
War Problems Committee, (Old) Mennonite Church, 56-59
Waring, Robert, 207
Weins, A. F., 212
Western District of the General Conference Mennonite Church, 56-57
Western Front, 35, 83
Wilson, Woodrow, 25-27, 35-37, 50, 58, 75, 145
Winslow, Leonard, 247
Wipf, Jacob J., 74
Witmer, John, 54
Wood, Ben, 208-209
Wood, Leonard, 42, 51, 54
Woolf, Virginia, 101
World War II, 80, 148, 149, 184, 185

Y

Yellow Creek, Indiana Mennonite Meeting, 58
Young Men's Christian Association (YMCA), 42, 62, 145, 180, 190-192, 195, 232, 243-245, 249, 251, 254, 256-260, 262
Young People's Conference, 235, 238

Z

Zachary Taylor, Camp. *See* Camp Zachary Taylor

Acknowledgments

The stories of Mennonite objectors' Great War lives could not have been told without the generosity of their families, many of whom donated the men's diaries and other Great War effects to Mennonite archives and libraries for public perusal. I am grateful, then, for the opportunity to study at the Mennonite Church USA Archives—North Newton, Kansas and at the Mennonite Church USA Archives—Goshen, Indiana, as well as for the material provided me by the Menno Simons Library and Archives in Harrisonburg, Virginia.

I appreciate the willingness of both professional and avocational historians to help with this volume. Dr. Gerlof Homan's *American Mennonites and the Great War, 1914-1918* provided both the initial impetus for this project and a wonderful bibliography to guide my own search; perhaps more significantly, Dr. Homan personally gave me several leads in my search for diaries. Thelma Kauffman, Calvin Zehr, Albert Meyer, Elvina Martens, and Ray Regier sent me World War I artifacts from their own families and corresponded with me about their ancestors' experiences during the war. Their dedication to their families' contribution to Mennonite history was inspiring; I was equally inspired by their willingness to share their families' histories with me, a stranger, and by extension with a larger, more anonymous reading audience.

My thanks also go to the Mennonite Historical Society, which provided research funds for my project. Theron Schlabach, former editor of the Studies in Mennonite and Anabaptist History Series, gave much-needed advice on this book's earliest draft; Steven Nolt, the current editor of the SAMH Series, continually and kindly offered criticism and reassurance as my manuscript took form. In the project's later stages, I profited from the editorial assistance of Michael A. King, publisher at Pandora Press U.S. (now becoming Cascadia Publishing House), and editor David Graybill. I offer both of them my appreciation.

The manuscript found its shape to some degree because of my institution's own support, in the way of a one course load reduction in the spring of 2001 and through work study help, and so I am thankful for the labors of Mindy Joy Thompson and Rose Passione, work study students extraordinaire. Louise Newswanger, librarian at George Fox University and fellow Mennonite-amongst-Quakers, was an invaluable and trustworthy resource who took unnecessary interest in my project.

Although I am tempted to thank every educator who ever encouraged my writing and researching interests (including my fifth grade teacher at Hillsboro Middle School in Kansas), I will limit my acknowledgements to a number of professors at Oklahoma State University who first instilled in me a love for autobiographical narrative and for the writing of the Great War, and who taught me the rigors of textual scholarship. My thanks, then, to William Decker and Elizabeth Grubgeld, autobiographical scholars and friends who sincerely listened to my initial wanderings and wonderings about this book. I am especially indebted to Jeffrey Walker, who tried to educate me about everything there is to know regarding textual editing but who taught me unfathomably more about what is important to the scholar's life: family and friends and humor and joy, rather than emendations and interlineations and substantive errors.

Finally I am grateful for all those family and friends who sustain me. My husband, Ron Mock, has consistently encouraged me in all my endeavors and makes me think reasonably when I would rather not do so. And I have been blessed with wonderful siblings and incredible parents. Ed and Esther Springer raised me to appreciate my Mennonite heritage and to seek peace, in my own life and in the lives of others. My parents' instruction has allowed me to listen more confidently to the witness of peace lived by Mennonite conscientious objectors nearly one century ago.

—*Melanie Springer Mock*
Newberg, Oregon

The Author

Melanie Springer Mock is an Assistant Professor of Writing and Literature at George Fox University, an Evangelical Friends school in Newberg, Oregon. At George Fox University, Mock teaches courses in writing, autobiography, and literary research.

She attended George Fox University (then College) as an undergraduate, earning a Writing and Literature degree in 1990. In 1994, Mock received her MA degree in English at the University of Missouri-St. Louis; in 2000, she received her PhD in English from Oklahoma State University in Stillwater, and was awarded the College of Arts and Sciences Graduate Research Excellence Award.

She found her interest in Great War writing and in autobiography while studying at Oklahoma State University. *Writing Peace: The Unheard Voices of Great War Mennonite Objectors* is a result of Mock's dissertation research on the Great War, autobiography, and the Mennonite response to war. A lifelong pacifist and Mennonite, Mock sees this research as a confluence of both scholarly and personal interests.

Mock was born in Bloomington, Illinois, in 1968. Her husband, Ron, is an Associate Professor at George Fox University, teaching peace studies, conflict resolution, and law. Both Ron and Melanie attend Newberg Friends Church. Mock has two stepchildren, Melissa and Ryan. The Mocks have also adopted Benjamin Quan from Vietnam.

www.ingramcontent.com/pod-product-compliance
Lightning Source LLC
Chambersburg PA
CBHW071236160426
43196CB00009B/1088